JOAN ROBINSON
AND THE AMERICANS

JOAN ROBINSON AND THE AMERICANS

Marjorie S. Shepherd Turner

M. E. Sharpe, Inc.
Armonk, New York · London, England

Library of Congress Cataloging-in-Publication Data

Turner, Marjorie Shepherd, 1921–   .
   Joan Robinson and the Americans / by Marjorie S. Turner.
     p.   cm.
   Bibliography: p.
   Includes index.
   ISBN 0-87332-533-8
   1. Robinson, Joan, 1903–   . 2. Economists—Great Britain—
Biography. I. Title.
HB103.R63T87   1989
330.1′092′4—dc19   88-30858
                                          CIP

Printed in the United States of America

To Aaron and Neil

JR

CONTENTS

JR

PREFACE

Without the help of the many persons mentioned in this preface, I could never have written this book. And I must add that it was no fault of Joan Robinson's that I did. As she wrote to me (June 25, 1977), "I don't think that I am at all a suitable subject for a biography as the outward flow of my life has been quite conventional and uninteresting. As for my intellectual development I think it is very hard to understand for someone who has been brought up in modern American economics. . . . The idea of the 'achievement' of gaining a professorship at Cambridge is somehow quite a wrong way of looking at it."

However, she offered some help (July 25, 1981): "I think the best plan would be for you to send me your drafts or any queries you want to raise and I will reply to them as they come." I did that, and received a one-line reply (October 17, 1981): "It is your business to do this research, not mine." She was right, as she so often was, but I did need help. After her death, I found her family willing to allow me to see her papers in King's College Archives. English and American colleagues permitted formal interviews, and in many cases lent me copies of correspondence they had had with her. This was especially important, since Robinson had destroyed most of her copies of letters. Sir Austin Robinson said gravely, "Joan was a great destroyer."

Joan Robinson died in 1983 in her eightieth year. Because an official biography is to be written by G. C. Harcourt, I felt free to write on a topic where I could bring some American insights to Joan Robinson's work without delving into the details of her personal life. She had told me that she did not want to write any more about her own works than she had already (June 6, 1981). Certainly in her published works she did often refer to her intellectual development. Yet, as an American, I was aware that very few of my countrymen had a grasp of the complexity of her contributions, of how many subjects she had written on, of the variety of her interests. So that while she had said what she wanted to say and said it better than another could, there was a need to put some focus on the whole of her fifty years of intense involvement with economics. If my work can stimulate readers to pick up some of her books again or for the first time, they will be doubly rewarded, both as readers and as philanthropists. For characteristically,

Joan Robinson willed that the proceeds from the sale of her books should go to finance the graduate education of students from the developing nations.

In 1984 I was granted interviews in Cambridge, England with Lord Kahn, Lord Kaldor, Sir Austin Robinson, Phyllis Maurice, Ruth Cohen, Lady Margaret Wilson, Frida Knight, Frank and Dorothy Hahn, Geoffrey C. Harcourt, and Sukhamoy Chakravarty. The next year I interviewed in Cambridge, Massachusetts John Kenneth Galbraith, Paul A. Samuelson, Robert M. Solow, Stephen Marglin, and Juliet Schor. I found the post Keynesians Paul Davidson and Alfred S. Eichner at Rutgers University in New Brunswick, New Jersey, and Sylvia Hewlett in New York City. Robert Clower and Axel Leijonhufvud let me interview them in their offices at the University of California at Los Angeles. I talked to Clifton Grubbs, Michael Weinstein, and Paul Sweezy over the phone. When Sol Adler visited the United States from his home in China, Paul Sweezy put me in touch with him, again by phone. Michael Straight answered my plea for information which had appeared in *The Nation* magazine. For pictures, I am grateful to Frida Knight; the Preservation Department of Butler Library at Columbia University; the public relations departments of the University of Utah, MIT, and Williams College; Joe Wrinn and the Harvard News Office at Harvard University; Monique Spalding; Juliet Schor; Peter Lofts Photography of Cambridge, England; and Michael Nagy Photography of Cambridge, Massachusetts.

Several economists gave helpful advice on the manuscript: G. C. Harcourt, Dorothy Hahn, and Pervez Tahir in England; Warren Samuels, Graydon Anderson, J. William Leasure, E. F. Patterson, Frederick B. Jennings, and David S. Brookshire in the United States. Errors and slips remaining are my sole responsibility.

Because I wanted to give the reader a flavor of the exchanges which Joan Robinson had with various Americans, the loan of personal papers by Robert Solow, Paul Davidson, Alfred Eichner, Juliet Schor, Robert Clower, Axel Leijonhufvud, and Monique Spalding (for E. H. Chamberlin's papers) was invaluable.

For the use of papers in archival collections, I particularly appreciate the indulgence of Michael Halls of King's College Archives, who made the mandatory copying by pencil of the contents of Robinson's papers seem easy. I also consulted with profit the University of Texas (Austin) Archives, Harvard University Archives, and the New England Depository. I relied on four libraries, depending on my own location—those of Cambridge University, San Diego State University, the University of Oregon, and Oregon State University at Corvallis. Anne Fox at Corvallis was most helpful in correcting the References.

For editorial assistance I called on Merle B. Turner, Joan Lucas Prince, Dorothy Hahn, Warren Samuels, J. William Leasure, Graydon Anderson, and Margaret Cooney Leary in the initial stages of the manuscript, and Frederick B. Jennings much later. Editor Jacqueline Steiner guided me with both wisdom and firmness in making the manuscript into a book.

The following persons and publishers granted permission for the use of materials collected from interviews, letters, and from published works: Sol Adler, Kenneth J. Arrow, Gwendolen Ayres, M. C. Bradbrook, Robert Clower, Ruth Cohen, Paul Davidson, Alfred S. Eichner, John Kenneth Galbraith, Sylvia Hewlett, Barbara Jeffrey, Lord Kahn, Clarissa Kaldor, Axel Leijonhufvud, Daliah Lerner, Stefan Machlup, Phyllis Maurice, Walt W. Rostow, Professor Sir Austin Robinson, Paul A. Samuelson, Juliet Schor, Aubrey Silberston, Robert M. Solow, Monique Spalding, Michael Straight, Paul Sweezy, Michael Weinstein, Sheila Weintraub, *American Economic Review,* American Sociological Association, Basic Books, Inc., Cambridge University Press, *Canadian Journal of Economics and Political Science, Econometrica,* Basil Blackwell, *Economica,* Harvard University Archives, Harvard University *Gazette,* Harvester, Houghton Mifflin Company, *Journal of Economic Issues, Journal of Economic Literature, Journal of Post Keynesian Economics,* Augustus M. Kelley, Macmillan, McGraw-Hill, the MIT Press, *Monthly Review,* New York University Press, the *New York Review of Books,* The Nobel Foundation, Oxford University Press, A. D. Peters & Co. Ltd., *The Public Interest,* Routledge, Kegan Paul Ltd., Rowman & Littlefield, *Science, Science & Society,* University of Chicago Press, University of Pennsylvania Press, and Unwin Hyman Ltd. The story of Robinson and the Americans was better told with the help of the statements I was generously allowed to quote from these many sources. I have made my best effort to report these statements faithfully in context and to make it possible for others to find and use the books in which they have appeared.

There is more to be said of Joan Robinson and her work. I hope my book will provide a useful beginning.

Marjorie Shepherd Turner
Professor Emeritus of Economics
San Diego State University

JOAN ROBINSON
AND THE AMERICANS

JR

INTRODUCTION

Economics is not made in a test tube. The history of political economy is punctuated by outstanding and passionate figures, many of them English—Reverend Thomas R. Malthus pleading for population restraint among the working classes; stockbroker David Ricardo fighting the protectionist Corn Laws and ushering in an era of free trade; John Maynard Keynes battling the British Treasury and the orthodox members of the economics profession in an effort to raise levels of employment in capitalist economies.

Joan Robinson belongs on this list of outstanding and passionate English economists. For more than fifty years of the twentieth century, her living influence was felt wherever economics was taught or discussed. This book is a study of her relationships with American economists, her efforts to influence mainstream economics, and her contributions to Keynesian economics. Among the cast of characters are some of the most important American economists of this century, such as Paul Samuelson and John Kenneth Galbraith. Her professional friends and adversaries also included economists from a wide perspective of political economics—Marxists, institutionalists, and post Keynesians, as well as orthodox economists.

Joan Robinson was a complex person of great vitality who, at her death in 1983, left an important legacy in the annals of economic thought. Although her relationship with Americans and American economics was only a small part of her life, a study of those associations reveals her personality, her brilliance, her popularity, and her frustration with orthodox economics. And the contrast of her teaching to American mainstream pedagogy provides a revealing chapter in the history of economics in English-speaking countries.

Robinson learned her economics at Cambridge University in the early 1920s when Alfred Marshall's *Principles* dominated the teaching there. At Cambridge, economics was considered to be one of the moral sciences and was treated as a study of the causes of material welfare, a part of the long tradition established by Adam Smith's *Wealth of Nations*. Keynes stirred undergraduates by lecturing on the problems faced in his work at the Treasury and the impact on world economies of the Treaty of Versailles. The overriding tradition at Cambridge was scientific empiricism. Even so, the economics taught was primarily economic theory, employing deductive methods but always with an eye on the "real world." Cambridge economists disdained the use of mathematical deductive methods which were then popular among some of the continental economists.

The marginalist revolution had come and gone without materially affecting the definition of economics for Cambridge. Joan Robinson was exposed to a pure brand of Marshallian economics as interpreted by A. C. Pigou. Leon Walras' general equilibrium analysis was neither taught nor discussed.

Economics in North America was less unified than at Cambridge. While Marshall's theory was dominant, the European marginalists were also a strong influence. General equilibrium analysis was often tacked onto Marshallian partial equilibrium analysis without apology. There were other currents as well. The American institutionalists, influenced by Thorstein Veblen and the German "battle of methods" (*Methodenstreit*), had come to prefer the inductive method of research over the deductive method of theorizing. Consequently, many American departments were split between theorists who preferred to use Austrian deductive methods (without the mathematics) and applied economists who sought to use induction.

Lionel Robbins of the London School of Economics published an essay in 1932 which became influential in redefining what the study of economics was to encompass. He argued that marginalist economics required a new and precise definition which would leave politics aside and thus be different from the old classical study of political economy.[1] Rather than inquiring into the causes of material welfare, Robbins believed, economists should concentrate on a central problem—the multiplicity of ends or desires and the scarcity of means. He was prepared to neglect historical and political aspects of questions in favor of using deductive methods of analysis. His essay, published just as Joan Robinson began her career, was in fact an attack on Cambridge economics where British empiricism was still admired. One of Robbins' targets was "probability theory," a subject to which Keynes had given deep thought.[2] Robbins also attacked the American institutionalist economists who pursued realistic, statistical studies in preference to deduction. He used American W. C. Mitchell's *Business Cycles* to illustrate "the futility of these grandiose projects . . . [where] not one single 'law' deserving of the name, not one quantitative generalization of permanent validity has emerged from their efforts."[3]

There had always been rivalry among Oxford, Cambridge, and the London School of Economics. Robbins was instrumental in bringing Friedrich von Hayek to the London School to lead the English down the Austrian paths of purely deductive theory. Much of the profession willingly followed, but not those at Cambridge. Joan Robinson adhered firmly to her early education, which saw economics in a broader context. The narrower definition of economics put forward by Robbins was based on an exclusive reliance on deductive analysis and on a view that laissez-faire was inevitably the preferred policy. Such a challenge was of the utmost importance. Logical positivism fostered a belief that only the narrowest of definitions could qualify economics as a science. Understandably, one of the reasons for attempting a "mechanics" of economics, as some Austrians did, was to assert that economics was a science. On the other hand, Cambridge economists, imbued with the philosophy of scientific empiricism, never doubted that they were "doing science."

These definitional, methodological, and policy differences have never been resolved within the profession, and they are at issue in Joan Robinson's interaction with Americans. Many of the "causes of material welfare" are clearly outside the definition of the "allocation of scarce means." Keynes, who never lost his connection with the real world, had no interest in limiting himself to a study of the "allocation of scarce means." Nor did Joan Robinson. In her first book, *The Economics of Imperfect Competition*, published at the depth of the 1930s depression, Robinson constructed a theory which could explain why, contrary to Marshallian theoretical predictions, industrial plants were operating below capacity. During that same period, the Circus[4] of critics and encouragers who surrounded Keynes were pushing him toward a theory which could explain how so much unemployment could exist when traditional theory said it could not. In her *Accumulation of Capital*, Robinson was seeking growth paths applicable to real economies. These theories went beyond the "allocation of scarce means."

In North America, the story was a different one. After World War II, a mainstream of thought emerged, and though not Austrian, the narrower definition of the economic problem was applied, and the use of deduction was championed. The institutionalist influence, which demanded both inductive methods and an evolutionary or "post-Darwinian" definition of economics, declined. Marxists simply couldn't get jobs in universities.

The new American mainstream economics was not itself narrow in conception. Theories from many sources were amalgamated into a "neoclassical synthesis," where Keynesian and Walrasian economics were taught as macroeconomics and traditional supply and demand (marginal) analysis as microeconomics. An equally important aspect of this mainstream was the adoption of mathematical tools in theorizing. Statistics had once been the preserve of the institutionalists. Now a branch of econometrics welded mathematics to the mainstream theory and its deductive proclivity.

Quarrels over methodology underlie many of the differences between mainstream and Robinsonian economics. Robinson did not believe that one could investigate political and policy questions with traditional assumptions of perfect competition. Were you then to drop such questions from economics? She said no, to do so would be an "abdication." The Cantabrigian tradition holds that method is subject to revision as problems require, that toolmaking is the major concern of a theoretical economist. Joan Robinson spent her life pursuing these ideals. She attempted to show how to do economics using neither general equilibrium nor assumptions of perfect competition. To the orthodox economist, this may have appeared "destructive" of the preferred method. To her it was an offer of liberation from an irrelevant procedure.

Once mathematics became a popular tool in economics (mainly after World War II), the schism between Robinsonian and orthodox methods became even more pronounced. But Robinson stuck to the literary means of communication. Her remarkable style sets her apart from mathematicians, though she shares with them an essential reliance on logic.

With determination, Robinson questioned the orthodox yearning for a science which excludes all politics and morals and which reduces the word "value" to a metaphysical principle. The Robinsonian approach to economics is distinguishable from the mainstream in several ways: her definition of economics (the classical "causes of material welfare"); her source of problems for analysis (real world problems, especially where theoretical predictions depart from what is observable in the economy); her techniques for analyzing the problems (to be invented as needed but most certainly not limited to either a priori or deductive methods); her method of presentation (literary rather than mathematical). She thought the role of politics and class conflict should not be ignored. Finally, she was convinced that history and uncertainty should be in the analysis itself and that problems such as the arms race should not be excluded.

Hilary Putnam, a philosopher of science, offers an image of what such a bequest can mean to a science:

> My picture of our situation is not the famous Neurath picture of science as the enterprise of reconstructing a boat while the boat floats on the open ocean, but it is a modification of it. I would change Neurath's picture in two ways. First, I would put ethics, philosophy, in fact the whole culture in the boat, and not just 'science', for I believe all the parts of the culture are inter-dependent. And second, my image is not of a single boat but of a *fleet* of boats. The people in each boat are trying to reconstruct their own boat without modifying it so much at any one time that the boat sinks, as in the Neurath image. In addition, people are passing supplies and tools from one boat to another and shouting advice and encouragement (or discouragement) to each other. Finally, people sometimes decide they do not like the boat they are in and move to a different boat altogether. (And sometimes, a boat sinks or is abandoned.) It is all a bit chaotic; but since it is a fleet, no one is ever totally out of signalling distance from all the other boats.[5]

Joan Robinson bequeathed such a boat, with tools, supplies, and crew aboard. She sailed with it to the end of her days, and left us the craft and crew.

Putnam has advice for us: "We are not trapped in individual solipsistic hells (or need not be) but invited to engage in a truly human dialogue; one which combines collectivity with individual responsibility." Robinson could not have put it better. Her life was spent trying to communicate with other economists, including those she regarded as influential in the American mainstream of economic theory.

In Joan Robinson's continuing dialogue with Americans, the reader can see fifty years of the evolution of economics. In the 1930s her mission was to let the wider world know what was developing at Cambridge in value theory and the theory of employment. In the 1940s Robinson first experienced rebuttal when she advised economists that she had read Marx and so should they. In the 1950s, in reaction to her complaints about traditional capital theory, the decibels rose. Robinson, in turn, realized that there were "bastard Keynesians" abroad. The battle was on. On her visits to North America in 1961 and thereafter, she found other currents in American thought—institutionalism, post Keynesianism—and graduate students in a state of rebellion. In the last years of her life, Robinson's task was to raise the alarm about the "Second Crisis in Economic Theory."[6]

This intellectual biography of Joan Robinson examines her triumphs and her frustrations as an economist from an American perspective, and underlines her leading role in fifty years of economic thinking.

JR

CHAPTER ONE

Joan Maurice at Cambridge

Joan Robinson the economist is inseparable from the complex person that she was. A strong woman, who as a teacher could make her men students cry themselves to sleep in despair, who as a colleague could cause some of the world's leading economists to tremble with rage, she was never a feminist. An admirer and critic of Marx, she was never a Marxist. She approved of the communist social experiments, particularly those in China and North Korea, but was not a communist. She expressed deep sympathy for the working class, but she was sometimes a critic of the Labour Party. She was a tender mother and grandmother, and a devoted and popular teacher. She never yielded a point until she could see it plainly. Joan Robinson's family background, her education in economics at Cambridge, and the changing times through which she lived were important factors in molding her views and personality.

Family background

Joan Violet Maurice was born in 1903 in Surrey into an upper-middle-class family. Her father was well-launched into a promising career as an army officer. Joan was one of four girls in a family of five children.

In England, before the many changes brought about by World War II, it was difficult for intelligent and ambitious boys, and even more so for girls, to go very far unless they were born into fairly wealthy, upper-class families who sent them to private schools to be educated. Schooling in state schools ended at age fourteen, except for the few outstanding students who qualified to go on to a Grammar School. University educations were almost entirely for the privileged classes. For Joan Maurice, as a member of an ancient and distinguished family, opportunity was her birthright.

Joan's family had many ties to Cambridge University. Her maternal great-great-grandfather Spencer Perceval (1762–1812) and paternal great-grandfather Frederick Denison Maurice (1805–1872), attended Trinity College, one of the more famous of the many colleges attached to Cambridge. Spencer Perceval was the second son of the second earl of Egmont, and distinguished himself in politics by becoming Prime Minister, only to be assassinated by a bankrupt madman while in office. As Prime Minister he had tenaciously carried on the war against Napoleonic France. F. D. Maurice was one of the "invigorators" of the celebrated Apostles society, and his bust still looks down from its post in the Cambridge University Library.[1]

During her girlhood, Joan's maternal grandfather Frederick Howard Marsh was professor of surgery and Master of Downing College, Cambridge. Her father, Major General Sir Frederick Barton Maurice, was given an honorary doctorate of laws by Cambridge the same year that Joan received her titular degree. Her uncle, Sir Edward Marsh, for whom she had deep affection, was a Cambridge man as well. He was both a supporter of the arts and a collector of paintings and sculpture in the 1920s. Under his influence, Joan Robinson also became a collector of art objects.

There had been well-educated, achieving women in her family, although Joan was the first to go to the university. Her grandmother, Jane Perceval Marsh, a nurse, had founded the Alexandra Hospital for Children with Hip Disease in London. Great-great-aunt Mary Maurice (sister of F. D. Maurice) established a school for governesses at Southampton.

Joan Maurice's bonds to teaching were equally strong. Both her father and her paternal grandfather, Major-General Sir John Frederick Maurice, taught in the Staff College at Sandhurst. In one of the first efforts to establish higher education for women (1848), F. D. Maurice helped found Queen's College in London. He also helped to organize a Workingmen's College (1853) of which he became Principal, and encouraged the founding of Girton College at Cambridge where Joan later matriculated.

Among family scholars and authors were Joan's grandfather, Major General Sir John Frederick Maurice, whom the *New York Times* called "one of the ablest writers in the British Army." Her uncle, Sir Edward Marsh, edited for both Winston Churchill and Somerset Maugham.[2]

After his military career ended, Joan's father turned his attention to writing, both as a journalist and a military historian. His historical studies and biographies were "noted for their clarity and conciseness."[3] As for F. D. Maurice, a bibliography of his works published by Macmillan (which much later published Joan Robinson's *Imperfect Competition*) mentions a novel, sermons, and philosophical works, some fruits of his career as a writer for fifty years. In such a family it is not surprising that Joan Maurice came to enjoy poetry at a young age. As a schoolgirl she went up to Hyde Park Corner once a week. There she stood under a lamppost and read poetry to anyone who wanted to listen. She had a regular group who came to share with her.[4]

Strong personalities and values can be fostered by the self-awareness which comes from family stories and experiences. Within this great family, forthrightness was expected. F. D. Maurice had engaged in fundamental controversies over religious questions. And in 1918, a controversy erupted that was much closer to Joan—the Maurice debate in Parliament. Joan was fourteen years old, a student at St. Paul's School for Girls, when her father, Major General Sir Frederick Maurice, wrote an unprecedented letter to the London *Times* accusing Prime Minister Lloyd George's government of deceiving Parliament and the country about the strength of the British army on the western front. While on the imperial general staff, Maurice and his superior, Sir William Robertson, had warned the cabinet that the Germans would attack in the West. The cabinet had ignored their recommendations for reinforcements. When, in March, the Germans broke through the British lines and drove them almost to the Channel ports, the government was charged in Parliament with having contributed to these disasters. Lloyd George defended himself successfully in April, but on May 7, General Maurice's letter "gave the direct lie to this and other statements made by the government."[5]

Maurice's biographer John Kennedy argues:

> Whether he was right or wrong in what he did there can be no difference of opinion regarding his supreme moral courage and sense of duty. His action was instigated by a sincere belief confirmed by a visit to France that the morale of the troops was in danger of being undermined by attempts to shift responsibility for the March disaster on to the shoulders of the military leaders and by the conviction that a plot was being hatched to remove Haig [Field Marshal Lord Douglas Haig]. To the end of his life Maurice believed that he had saved Haig, whose only reaction at the time was a characteristic disapproval of conduct which he regarded as mistaken and improper.[6]

The Maurice debate was covered daily in the London *Times*. Before Maurice's letter appeared in the press, he wrote to his daughter Nancy, then seventeen, telling her that he fully realized what the consequences might be for himself and his family. He closed by saying, "I am persuaded that I am doing what is right and once that is so, nothing else matters to a man."[7]

These events came in Joan Robinson's formative years, and ever after she felt a great injustice had been done. It is very likely that this had a profound effect on the development of her view that one must act on conscience.[8]

Her family background, permeated with innovative accomplishments and acts of courage, helps explain Joan Robinson's independence of mind. It was written of her great-grandfather F. D. Maurice that he had "an even excessively scrupulous sense of honor, and throughout his life was devoted exclusively to setting forth what he held to be the truth. He was at times moved to vehement indignation, and could be very sharp in controversy; some natural irritability joined with his keen sense of the importance of certain truths, and with the consciousness that, from whatever cause, his meaning was very liable to be misconceived."[9]

How like him his great-granddaughter Joan Robinson was!

Titular degrees for women

Joan Violet Maurice had a seriousness of purpose early on which made her eligible for the outstanding St. Paul's School for Girls in London and subsequently for the Gilchrist Scholarship to Girton College, Cambridge. Her younger sister Phyllis remembers vividly Joan's persistence at her study table in their shared room. In the large family of Maurices, it was determined that the sharing of rooms between daughters of greatly different ages would promote amicable relations among the four girls.[10]

Girton College was the first of the women's colleges to be attached to either of the Great Universities (as Cambridge and Oxford are known in England). Founded in 1869, Girton was followed by Newnham College, Oxford, in 1873. Women students were first admitted to the Tripos, the honors examinations leading to Class I and Class II degrees, in 1881. The right to earn a titular degree was conceded in 1921, the year of Joan Maurice's matriculation. However, the right actually to earn a Cambridge University degree with full university privileges was withheld from women at Cambridge until 1948, when Joan Robinson had been on the faculty for some fourteen years. At Oxford after 1920, women could earn university degrees. Austin Robinson does not think this particularly bothered his wife.*[11]

Men had the option of both the honors and the "ordinary degree," the latter provided by men's colleges for those who were perhaps more interested in cricket and socializing than in a particular field of study. Such students might take all of their work within their own college and never attend a university lecture. Women could go only for honors. Girton was "founded on the clear principle of aiming at the highest education" and playgirls were not encouraged. For a girl to attend university was unusual even among the upper classes. She had to be not only bright and ambitious but determined. "Honors degrees" required an intense interest in a single subject, and careers for women were limited. Even though a girl was very bright, her family might discourage her from seeking a university education for fear that she would be branded as a bluestocking and unsuitable for a good marriage. Many of the women graduates continued into careers in teaching.

Mary Paley Marshall, the wife and former student of Alfred Marshall, had been a student at Newnham College at Cambridge and continued to be intellectually active through her long life. According to Austin Robinson, Alfred Marshall's treatment of his wife was one of the few things which aroused Joan Robinson's feminism. She would storm in private against Marshall's attitudes. Mary Marshall had been a lecturer in economics at Newnham College, and Austin Robinson says it was known that Mary had helped Alfred with his early book, *The Economics of Industry* (1879). Joan Robinson thought Alfred Marshall treated his wife as a housekeeper and secretary rather than as an intellectual equal. Perhaps Mary Marshall did also. After the publication of *The Economics*

---

*See Appendix Note 1.1 English economists and women's rights.

of Imperfect Competition, she wrote to Joan Robinson, "Thank you for helping to lift off the reproach cast on the Economic Woman."[12] Robinson, on the other hand, always seems to have thought of her own reputation as being that of an economist, not a woman-economist.

Young ladies at Girton College

In 1922, Girton College had fifty-two acres of grounds—one for every under-graduate. The college was more than two miles from the university campus, placed so as to be "not too inaccessible yet not too near the men." Buses plied back and forth and cyclists covered the ground even more quickly. Some said the place had a "hoydenish blush." Undergraduates were free to be out and about until the college gates closed at 11:15 p.m.[13] The original founder, Emily Davies, a friend of Joan Maurice's paternal great-grandfather, felt that Girton should be some miles from the University. Originally it was situated at Hitchin, a full twenty-six miles away.

Girton's architecture is forbidding. C.S. Lewis called the "vast edifice in the three main courts 'The Castle of Otranto'."[14] Others described Girton as "most uncomfortable to inhabit . . . designed with its claustrophobic corridors by successive members of the Waterhouse family."[15] Some of the college rooms were traditionally associated with St. Paul's and other famous public schools, but I was told that Joan Maurice did not have one of these.[16] There is no evidence that she was particularly fond of the place. In later years, though she was a fellow both at Newnham and Girton, she was more inclined to have her meals at Newnham.[17]

E.M.R. Russell-Smith, a contemporary of Joan Maurice's, remembered that women students at Cambridge felt accepted and were treated courteously in university lectures, which were coeducational. She wrote, "Anti-feminism with which earlier generations had had to contend had disappeared completely. My contemporaries were for the most part hardly aware that it had ever existed."[18] This view seems to have been shared by Joan Maurice.

While women could join most of the university societies, they were not permitted to join the Union Society, which was the center of undergraduate political debates. Nor were they invited to become members of the Political Economy Club founded by Keynes. A few organizations were for women alone. The Women's Research Club was one, but Joan Maurice was not a member. With Dorothea Morison (afterwards Mrs. R. B. Braithwaite) she once presented a satirical paper to the Marshall Society—their rendition of an economist's version of "Beauty and the Beast," which is now considered Joan Robinson's earliest professional work.

Perhaps the vestiges of nonacceptance of women (other than Keynes' club) did not affect Joan Maurice. In England, separate men's and women's clubs had a long tradition. She would not have cared that the famous Sir Arthur Quiller-Couch would not allow women in his evening classes on Aristotle's *Poetics*. She was probably aware that A. C. Pigou had required Barbara Wootton to deliver scripts to the porter's lodge at King's College rather than to his rooms, as was customary for male students.[19] Women could sit in the Gallery and listen to the debates of the Union Society, although they could not take part. Joan may have heard Maurice Dobb there in their shared years. *Granta* recorded that it was mainly Dobb who helped defuse, among university circles, the "unreasoning hatred of the Labour Party" in those early post-World War I years.[20]

Life at Girton was that of a young lady as well as a serious student. Gladys Crane, who worked as "gyp" or maidservant at Girton for fifty years, wrote that in the 1920s there was a full staff of between forty and fifty, twenty-six of whom were housemaids, all to serve the fifty-two young women who lived in the "vast edifice."[21] Traditionally women undergraduates did not wear academic gowns, but street dresses and hats. By the mid-twenties, "dresses were loosely tubular, with a belt somewhere round the hips." One contemporary reflected that it helped to be flat-chested.[22]

Sylvia Hewlett, while doing graduate work at Cambridge in the 1970s, interviewed Joan Robinson. Hewlett knew her well, and believes that as a young woman Joan Maurice saw herself as being unattractive. "It's something which I believe," Hewlett said, "because she told me and Maurice Dobb told me he didn't like her legs; but then *The Cambridge Journal* published that lovely picture of her in its memorial issue, and I realized that it was probably all in their minds. Probably she dressed badly; probably she was a bluestocking."[23]

It was at Girton that Joan Robinson met one of the first Americans to be of any importance to her, Marjorie Tappan, who had a doctorate in economics from Columbia University in New York, and who later became Mrs. Tappan-Hollond. She held the position of Director of Studies at Girton and later Lecturer in Economics for the university. Austin Robinson said that Keynes was grateful to Tappan-Hollond on more than one occasion for sharing her intimate knowledge of the American banking system. Yet she was "always somewhat diffident and retiring, too precise and scholarly to be an exciting, popular lecturer, not an aggressive propounder of new and exciting generalities."[24]

Tappan-Hollond was also a conservative with little sympathy for Joan Robinson's views or style. Married to Henry Arthur Hollond of Trinity College, she had a long career in the department of economics and in university social circles. She is remembered by those who knew her for her long cigarette holder, which she used before many women smoked. Ruth Cohen, known to economists for her "curiosum," remembers also that Tappan-Hollond invariably kept her students waiting when they came for supervision.[25] Though she was on the economics faculty for nearly as many years as Joan Robinson, Tappan-Hollond was never promoted beyond lecturer. In Cambridge circles, it is not considered an accident that Robinson was never made a Fellow of Girton until Tappan-Hollond was no longer an influence there. But in the early years, she was important to Joan Robinson and some warm and friendly correspondence survives to prove it.

"It's all in Marshall"

In comparison with schools in the United States, economics as a university subject was relatively late to develop at Cambridge. Until 1903, papers in Political Economy, if taken at all, were part of the Moral Sciences or History Tripos. Alfred Marshall long fought for the separate curriculum for economics. It was finally established in 1903, the same year that John Maynard Keynes came to the university to study mathematics. Marshall had studied mathematics also, but he urged Keynes to take the Economics Tripos in 1905. Instead, Keynes abandoned economics to concentrate on the Civil Service exam. As Robert Skidelsky points out, Keynes never took an economics degree: "In fact, his total professional training came to little more than 8 weeks. All the rest was learnt on the job," beginning with his association with the India Office. Keynes had written his friend Lytton Strachey: "Marshall is continually pestering me to turn professional Economist and writes flattering remarks on my papers to help on the good cause. Do you think there is anything in it? I doubt it."[26]

Leaving the India Office in 1908, Keynes joined the university department of economics as a lecturer. He had been disappointed earlier in the year when he had failed to be elected a Fellow of King's, so that the affiliation with the department was in a way a second-best solution.[27] That same year Pigou, who had read history but also had studied mathematics on his own, succeeded Marshall as Professor. Soon Dennis Robertson, who had studied for the classics, joined the department. Both Pigou and Robertson had won prizes in poetry. So it was intelligence and general cultivation rather than what Americans might call professional training, which were the important elements in the making of a Cambridge economist in those early years. The younger lecturers in the department in turn had studied at Cambridge under Marshall and Pigou. (Tappan-Hollond was an exception.) It was a small world and continued to be so until the arrival of Piero Sraffa in the mid-twenties.*

The aura of Alfred Marshall hung over the department of economics. Though Marshall had retired from teaching, his work continued. He published his *Money, Credit and Commerce* in 1923 after he was eighty years old. Moreover, his *Principles of Economics* was still accepted as the greatest economic treatise of his generation.[28] Pigou carried on "the oral tradition of Marshall's economics . . . giving Marshall's ideas a clarity and architecture they had lacked in Marshall's own lecturing."

This, then, was the intellectual world of economics into which Joan Maurice stepped, fresh from studying history at St. Paul's. "It's all in Marshall," Pigou would say, as he gave generations of students their training in the disciplines and techniques of economic reasoning. "Clarity of analysis and a willingness to follow an argument through to the end were the essence of his own exposition and of what he [Pigou] demanded in others."[29]

Pigou had a powerful influence on all students reading economics, including

---

*See Appendix Note 1.2 Cambridge department of economics in 1921.

Joan Maurice. "Pigou was a tall, powerfully built, athletic player of all ball-games—the former head of the school at Harrow who thought poorly of a small boy called Winston Churchill—the keen climber, with his cottage among the mountains in Cumberland where he led his friends up the climbs" (including Joan Robinson in later years). In Joan Maurice's student days Pigou was in his prime, "an excellent lecturer—very clear, very systematic, but at the same time very rooted in the Marshall tradition," and "remote and aloof from us all."[30] Austin Robinson as a Research Fellow was reading papers for Pigou when Joan Maurice was Pigou's student. He found her papers quite exceptionally good.[31]

While Pigou dominated the theoretical teaching in economics, it was Keynes who lectured on the economic issues of the day. After World War I, Keynes never returned to full-load teaching. He delivered "seldom more than eight, remarkably inspiring, lectures in any one year, concerned with problems at which he was himself working." Austin Robinson, who had a close relationship with Keynes, said that Keynes insisted on "making us search out the assumptions which underlay our argument." Students were inspired by Keynes' work on these contemporary problems and were avid readers of *The Revision of the Treaty* (1922), *A Tract on Monetary Reform* (1923), and *The Economic Consequences of the Peace* (1919).[32]

Other lecturers were also important to Joan Maurice in her subsequent career. Among them were Gerald Shove and Claude Guillebaud, both of whom helped her with her first book. Austin Robinson, who remembers Shove in later years as one of the most interesting and effective Cambridge lecturers, thought that in 1921–22, Shove's lectures were "inordinately dull." Shove was painfully shy at the time, a person who had "endured all the miseries of being a pacifist in a world that was war-mad." His central interest became the rethinking of Marshallian value theory, and it was in this that he became important to Joan Robinson. Guillebaud, a nephew of Marshall's, was " too modest, too self-effacing and because this was the sort of person he was, he was a diffident and ineffectual lecturer." On the other hand, Guillebaud was "one of the best tutors of Cambridge" and was very helpful to Joan in her first book.[33]

Dennis Robertson played a different role in Joan Robinson's development. Robertson was "a master of the precise and exact use of words but also of the cautious, critical, analytical scholarship that belonged to Eton and Trinity," and Austin Robinson thought Robertson was, in important ways, "the best scholar of all of us." Keynes was known to have immense respect for Robertson. Joan Robinson's relationship with Robertson in later years was marred by controversy. Their disagreement was over the question of how and when Keynes' theory of employment should be taught. However, such divisions had not occurred when Joan Maurice was an undergraduate.

The proper picture for those years was of study in a Marshallian department where the teaching faculty were linked by class, kinship, friendship, and intellectual ties, where students in their turn became tutors and lecturers in the traditions of their own teachers. A small, tight social and intellectual world, Cambridge was the proverbial "ivory tower." This is how Joan Robinson remembered it: "When I came up to Cambridge, in 1922, and started reading economics, Marshall's *Principles* was the Bible, and we knew little beyond it. Jevons, Cournot, even Ricardo, were figures in the footnotes. We heard of 'Pareto's Law', but nothing of the general equilibrium system. Sweden was represented by Cassel, America by Irving Fisher. Austria and Germany were scarcely known. Marshall was economics." Another time, she said of her first year, "I did not have much idea of what it [economics] was about. I had some vague hope that it would help me to understand poverty and how it could be cured. And I hoped that it would offer more scope for rational argument than history (my school subject)."[34]

So there it was. Joan Maurice was one of fifty-two young ladies, not allowed to wear a university gown but wearing a hat and dress instead, busing or bicycling between Girton College and the university, probably waiting now and then to be supervised by Marjorie Tappan, attending Pigou's lectures on Marshallian economics, and Keynes' exciting ones on economic issues. Given the oral tradition of Cambridge, you would not dare to rely entirely on your supervisor. It was important for an honors student to know what the lectures were about.*

Prizes and seconds, undergraduate years

The progress and achievements of a Cambridge university student are catalogued and printed regularly in the Cambridge University *Reporter*. It was recorded in June 1923 that Joan Violet Maurice was the only person to place Class I in the Intercollegiate Examination in Economics. There is no further record of her progress until June 1924 when, along with thirty-five men and three other women, she stood for the Tripos Part I in economics.[35]

There were no firsts. Two women, Joan Maurice and L. C. M. Ouwerkerk of Newnham, and four men placed in Division I, Class II. Six men and two women placed in Division II, Class II. The rest, all men, were given Class IIIs (the ordinary degree). After the intercollegiate examination of the year before, this must have been disappointing. It was not that a woman had never won Class I Honors. Barbara Wootton had earned a Class I in 1919 in her Part II of the Tripos and had been mentioned for Special Distinction.

Was there a personal element in the grading of examinations? Joan Maurice was already showing some disdain for Marshallian economics—to wit, the previously mentioned retelling of the story of Beauty and the Beast in economic (Marshallian) jargon, read before the Marshall Society. Were undergraduate women to be allowed such levity?

Joan Maurice took the Economics Tripos Part II in 1925. This time there were two Class I degrees, both awarded to men. Three women, Joan Maurice, L. C. M. Ouwerkerk, and S. M. S. Archer, placed in Division I of Class II.

*See Appendix Note 1.3 Cambridge courses for students reading economics.

G. C. Harcourt quotes Robinson as saying this was "a great disappointment."[36]

Joan Maurice's dismay was probably short-lived. Austin Robinson was a dashing young man and she was soon married to him and off to India where he was to tutor the Maharajah of Gwailor. They left in 1926 and returned in 1929. Once she had returned, she never again left Cambridge for so long a time.

The Robinsons in India

In India, Austin was very much occupied with his tutorial work. With servants to take care of daily needs, the new bride was free to pursue other interests. Joan had no job in India, but Austin said they

> . . . did naturally enough get involved in things. It so happened that there was an argument going on between the Indian States, the parts of India which were still governed by Maharajahs and people like that and the [British] Government of India over the rights of the Government to tax their imports and that sort of thing. One of our special friends was Colonel Haksar, the foreign member of the minority administration of the Gwailor state, and he at the same time was acting as secretary and organizer of a big group from a whole number of Indian States who were engaged in arguing these issues. An official committee came out from London to discuss this matter with the Indian States and thereafter the further discussions were carried on in London. Joan became involved with the foreign secretary and others in the presentation of the Indian case for the Indian States, and subsequently went back to London to help the foreign secretary present the case.

Meanwhile, Austin worked on the memoranda in his spare moments, but was very busy with the tutoring of the Maharajah.[37]

After this residency, Joan Robinson always had great affection for India. She never wrote anything to reveal whether living there had influenced her views on economics. She was there only in the capacity of wife of the Tutor to the Maharajah. She had already shown an interest in the have-nots, having done work while a school girl at one of the Settlement Houses in London. India provided her first glimpse of the economically underdeveloped world. She would never in her long life turn her back on the problems of the poor as being beneath her interest as an economist.

JR

CHAPTER TWO

The Years of High Theory

When Joan and Austin Robinson sailed to India in 1926, they had left the tight little world of a Marshallian hegemony. When they returned in 1929, they stepped into the "years of high theory," in which Joan Robinson was to play a significant role in the revolution of value theory and the development of Keynes' General Theory.[1] In the Robinsons' absence, both value theory and monetary theory were challenged.

As Richard F. Kahn put it, the Cambridge Faculty of Economics had been for some years "in a state of quiescence." But it was aroused by Piero Sraffa's criticism of the Marshallian system. Sraffa wrote, first in Italian and then for the *Economic Journal*, that "the foundations were replaced without the building standing above receiving a single jolt from it all, and it was the great ability of Marshall which allowed the transformation to pass unnoticed."[2] Sraffa's articles marked the beginning of the revolution in value theory, to which Joan's first book, *The Economics of Imperfect Competition*, was to contribute. This is the accepted Cambridge view.

Monetary theory was challenged by Keynes' *Treatise on Money,* published in October 1930, and was the subject of his fall lectures which Richard Kahn and the Robinsons attended. Within months of publication, Keynes began rethinking the issue of money. In this case the pressure for rethinking was partly external, for the Great Depression was deepening. Keynes found that his policy recommendations to the Treasury were not necessarily supported by his *Treatise.* Kahn created the multiplier for Keynes' line of argument at Treasury. Out of these exchanges grew the "Circus" of friendly critics which began meeting in January 1931 and met formally until May. Kahn, the Robinsons, Sraffa, and James Meade (visiting from Oxford) were the major participants.*

Austin Robinson had returned to join the economics faculty as lecturer. The department of economics was a part of the university, while each college offered

---

*See Chapter 5.

its own program. As a fellow of Sidney Sussex College, he would supervise (as tutoring is called at Cambridge) for his college and lecture for the university.

Joan Robinson paid her five-pound fee and gained her master's degree. She would begin her family and her career in economics simultaneously during this exciting period. One way to break into a university career was to earn a Class I degree, and she had not done that. Another was to be invited to be a fellow at one's old college. This did not happen. Still another was simply to make oneself available for supervisions and lecturing and to begin writing scholarly works. This combination was to be her route to becoming recognized as a professional economist.*[3]

Supervising at 3 Trumpington

When the Robinsons returned to Cambridge, Marjorie Tappan-Hollond, eight years older than Joan (exactly that, since they shared the same birthday, October 31), was in a position to recommend supervisors to the women's colleges. In addition to her position as a Fellow at Girton and Director of Studies and Lecturer in Economics at Girton College, Tappan-Hollond was also a lecturer both at Newnham College and for the university. She sent Joan Robinson a few students from Newnham,[4] and Robinson would hold tutorial sessions with them at her residence upstairs at 3 Trumpington Road, quite near the university. Austin Robinson would have been lecturing and teaching in his college or in university rooms. (Fellows are provided rooms in their colleges.)

When Joan Robinson was pregnant with her first child, she carried on as usual. One of her early Newnham pupils (now Lady Margaret Wilson) remembers speculating whether they would be able to finish the term before the baby arrived. During this period Robinson began the disciplined work routine for which she became famous (if not loved) within the department: she would write from nine o'clock until noon each weekday. There was a servant to fix the meals and take care of the household chores, and after her two daughters were born, there was a nurse for them. Even in later years, Joan Robinson was known for never so much as opening a can. This was appropriate for a woman of her class and had nothing to do with feminism.

In 1931, Joan Robinson's name appeared on the university lecture list for the first time. Austin Robinson remembers that the way the department determined whether people had any teaching skills was to ask them to do a short series of lectures, even before they were given any official status. Not until three years later did Joan Robinson have an official university job—Faculty Assistant Lecturer in Economics and Politics on probationary status.[5]

She was by then thirty-one years old, and a mother and published author as well. Three important articles had already appeared in leading journals and her *Economics of Imperfect Competition*, which received international recognition, had been published in 1933, all before she was made an assistant lecturer. For any

*See Appendix Note 2.1 Becoming a professional.

who might believe that she fell easily into a career because of her connections at Cambridge, this sequence is important.

In an interview, I asked Austin Robinson whether it was difficult for her to get an assistant lectureship. Was it a highly competitive situation?

> No, we were more inbred in those days. We were most apt in Cambridge to appoint someone inside Cambridge, and the normal way of doing things was to allow someone to give a series of lectures and see if they were any good, see if they had a gift of teaching. They might then be made an assistant lecturer. Remember our rather twofold method of teaching: the university post and doing college teaching. And she'd been doing college teaching for a long, long time before she was given an assistant lectureship.

I inquired whether the publication of *Imperfect Competition* was a help.

> Yes, it was certainly so that the book helped. I think she climbed the ladder more slowly at that stage, because she was a wife, rather than somebody with a college fellowship who was doing college teaching. I'm sorry, I'm getting into all the entanglements. You see, if you were made a fellow of a college, it was your job to teach the people in your college, but there were not as many university posts as there were colleges and so one would teach in more than one college, teaching in the sense of sitting in an armchair and listening to an essay and one used more people than had university posts to do the college teaching; she came in on it that way.

Did she resist becoming a college fellow?

> I don't think she wanted to get involved in a great deal of heavy commitment to doing college teaching. It might be in those days anything up to twelve hours a week, tutorials as well as lecturing. She always liked to be able to choose whether she would or would not teach a particular person.

Was Harry Johnson right in saying that she tried to cream for the best students? "That's one way of putting it."[6] Joan Robinson seems to have been well satisfied with the progress of her career.

Economics is a Serious Subject

Joan Robinson's first publication was a pamphlet with a pedagogical twist, *Economics is a Serious Subject*, published by the Students' Bookstore at Cambridge in 1932. In it she stated her belief that economists could agree if they would use the same assumptions. Keynes wrote her concerning the pamphlet, "The enclosed strikes me as much too serious for a popular pamphlet. Why not try it on 'The Political Quarterly,' saying to the Editor that you sent it to him at my suggestion?"[7]

As ever her irreverent self, Robinson attached an anonymous dedication to some of the copies (for instance, Sraffa's), facetiously characterizing the members of the economics department. Of "M-T-H" she wrote, "To the economist who thinks that the shield is white." Of "JMK" she said, "To the optimist who showed that optimism can be justified."[8] This dedication does not appear in the published version, but it illustrates her independence of mind and confidence in herself, for some of the references might have displeased colleagues who were in powerful positions.*

Economics is a Serious Subject reached the United States by a circuitous route. Joseph Schumpeter, who always had his ear to the ground when it came to Cambridge, heard from Richard Kahn that Robinson had "prepared a sort of memorandum on the teaching of economics." Schumpeter requested a copy, saying, "I have to confess that in my old age I am getting interested much more than I used to be in the problems of the teaching of our science."[9] After reading the pamphlet, Schumpeter wrote, "In fundamentals we fully agree—in fact it is a stock phrase of mine that the economist should aim to be the physiologist rather than the doctor of the economic organism, and that his practical contribution should consist in sharing in the training of the 'doctors'. . . . I also agree that we should cease treating our students as if they were feeble-minded."[10] And the pamphlet got around. Paul Samuelson saw it while an undergraduate at the University of Chicago.[11]

Joan Robinson never reprinted *Economics is a Serious Subject.* The reason she gave was that she had written it in the midst of those years of high theory when she had believed that "economics was emerging from the long sleep of laisser-faire doctrines, 'marginal products' and equilibrium." She "soon ceased to believe in its main argument—that if economists could avoid certain bad habits and arrive at a consistent set of assumptions, however abstract, they could approach reality step by step merely by making more complicated models."[12]

Joan Robinson's spirited optimism glows in this first publication. Important American economists were interested, in the early 1930s, in any publication at Cambridge, however brief.

An American as colleague: Marjorie Tappan-Hollond

Marjorie Tappan-Hollond was the first American with whom Joan Robinson had any important professional dealings. Their educational backgrounds were quite different. Tappan had attended Bryn Mawr in Pennsylvania as an undergraduate, pursuing what Americans call a "liberal education," meaning a broad selection of courses from many different fields. Two years later (1917) she earned a doctorate in economics from Columbia University. Joan Maurice, after St. Paul's, had read economics for three years. Formal education in subjects other

---

*See Appendix Note 2.2 Dedication of *Economics is a Serious Subject.*

than those for the Economics Tripos exams was not required. Moreover, their styles of living differed. (Tappan-Hollond was quite elegant.) And their politics and alliances within the department clashed.

The Cambridge economics department was now somewhat changed. Piero Sraffa and Richard F. Kahn had joined the department, and the fundamental reexamination of value theory was in progress. The Circus surrounding Keynes had begun meeting in 1931, undertaking a reexamination of the role of money in light of the current depression problems. Joan Robinson, in the thick of these discussions, wanted to teach what she was learning. She was off and running with revolutionary fervor and either proceeded to teach the new principles to first-year students or proposed to do so.

Tappan-Hollond, as Director of Studies, objected to Joan Robinson's subjects and her style. She wrote Robinson that the board (presumably of one or other of the women's colleges), "with longer teaching experience than yours or mine," concluded that principles were best deferred until the second year. Robinson had written that she thought it better to stick to the butcher, the baker, and the candlestick maker and Tappan-Hollond agreed. However, she specifically objected to Robinson's trying to teach recent developments in theory: "Isn't it a little soon to be certain that they represent a 'self consistent system based on common sense' when the evidence of controversy is thick upon the ground and the chief protagonist in the monetary field (say) is constantly rebutting his own views and making new excursions?"

Tappan-Hollond continued:

> I don't personally like a gospel view of economics, whether the gospel be new or old and Robbins comes to my mind as an awful example of the result of despising what has gone before and taking upon oneself the role of Messiah. In teaching, I feel that one has to distinguish the stronger from the weaker students, helping the former to think their own way through most questions and sticking in the case of the latter to less debatable ground. It is certainly a very real difficulty to determine what is of educational value in teaching economics to weaker students but it seems to me to be glossing the difficulty to speak of "feeding spoonfuls of the stuff in the books" to them as the alternative to launching them upon controversial refinements of analysis.

Tappan-Hollond added a soothing ending: "As for you personally, if I did not believe in you, I should not have urged your taking charge."[13]

This exchange must have referred to the teaching of the developments discussed in the Circus. Tappan-Hollond was not a member and shared neither the excitement of discovery nor the conversion which was taking place there. She warned Joan Robinson,

> I seem to remember in my own case a period when I was working with Karl Pearson when I found myself in the throes of intellectual discovery which stirred

me tremendously emotionally both as regards the subject matter involved and the persons associated with it. . . . But it is dangerous I think to let oneself go for fear of creating windmills in one's imagination and repeating the history of Don Quixote.

Tappan-Hollond said she did not see very much difference between herself and Joan Robinson or other Cambridge economists. She accepted the Cambridge view that "the subject matter of economics is neither more nor less than its technique," as distinguished from the Austrians who teach economic problems "by showing that a number of equations could be set up corresponding to the number of unknown variables in question and hence a theoretically determinate solution attained."

At Columbia, where German historicism and American institutionalism had influence, Tappan-Hollond had apparently been taught the "physiology point of view"—to "insist that the factors are like those say with which the biologist deals and the technique must be appropriate." Tappan-Hollond's remark, "I don't incidentally want you to run away with the idea that I think Keynes muddle-headed. . . ." underscores the real differences in the thinking of the two women and their departmental alliances. Tappan-Hollond added, "Some of us may find Dennis's [Robertson's] approach and some Keynes's approach" clearer, but "we're all using Marshall and Pigou, pointing out where we find difficulties and vagueness and recognizing advances towards clarity as they arise." Tappan-Hollond then returned to her point: "I have very great respect for you intellectually. Why shouldn't I believe in your making a *rolling* good teacher if you don't let yourself get unduly carried away in dealing with weaker students by your own ability to go far and fast."[14]

From this correspondence we know that Robinson was already teaching a new economics in 1932, four years before the publication of *The General Theory,* and that departmental politics was already affected. Joan Robinson was engaged in writing her *Economics of Imperfect Competition,* but her excitement seemed to center on the theory of employment. Tappan-Hollond inquired, "Do the more recent developments of Cambridge economics require flag-waving or battle cries or those who are responsible for them to be assigned the role of gladiators?" As the established director of studies, Tappan-Hollond asked her younger colleague for "more light and less heat."[15]

JR

CHAPTER THREE

The Making of
Imperfect Competition

Ideas have distinct and memorable origins in Cambridge lore. One day in early 1930, Richard Kahn was having lunch with the Robinsons. Austin Robinson discussed his student Charles Gifford's work on "what we subsequently called a marginal revenue curve," and this discussion led to the writing of *The Economics of Imperfect Competition.* [1]

What had worried Cantabrigians most about value theory was that Marshall, in elaborating the economies of scale wherein firms grow larger and larger, had failed to give up the idea of perfect competition. A world of perfect competition meant that price would always just cover cost because of that competition. A demand curve where price equals marginal revenue is termed "perfectly elastic." On the traditional diagram, such a horizontal curve indicates that the producer can sell all of his product without affecting the price, a condition associated with "perfect competition." However, if there were increasingly large firms, perfect competition would be impossible. Pigou had proposed that there was no problem, since price equals marginal cost. But the new concept of marginal revenue indicated that this might not be so. Since marginal cost (mc) is the cost of producing an additional unit and marginal revenue (mr) is the revenue associated with selling that additional unit, then any firm maximizing profit would sell just the number of units where mc=mr. The downward sloping revenue curves associated with larger firms would mean that the firm could sell those units at which it maximizes profits at a price (average revenue) which exceeds both marginal and average cost, yielding a monopoly profit. Thus Robinson could prove that such firms could maximize returns even while operating at a restricted output. This in turn helped to explain why firms were operating with restricted outputs during the depression, rather than closing down as a perfectly competitive firm might be forced to do. Robinson could also demonstrate what she called the monopoly exploitation of labor.

Using the new concept of marginal revenue, Robinson introduced "imperfect competition." This luncheon discussion was a fitting origin for a major Cambridge theoretical contribution, and within the context of the oral tradition the book which emerged, though clearly Joan Robinson's, was Cambridge's too.

Many years later she wrote, "When I returned to Cambridge in 1929, they were still arguing about the representative firm . . . but meanwhile Piero Sraffa had turned up, rescued by Keynes from Mussolini. He was calmly committing the sacrilege of pointing out inconsistencies in Marshall, and, moreover, introducing us to other contemporary schools of thought (but they were no better)." In this retrospective, she says that *Imperfect Competition*, "though inspired by a hint from Sraffa, was mainly influenced by Professor Pigou." Thus her mature view was that her book was Marshallian.[2]

Joan Robinson commented several times on the origins and development of her theory. In the foreword to the first edition she thanked Richard Kahn first of all for his "constant assistance," adding: "In general I have endeavored to build on the foundations laid by Marshall and by Professor Pigou. This is a debt which all economists owe, and which may be taken for granted. I have for the most part referred to their works only where I believe that I have detected them in errors of detail."[3] She mentioned numerous other sources of independent discovery of the marginal revenue concept. Almost in passing, she wrote, "Professor Chamberlin's *Theory of Monopolistic Competition* provides a plentiful crop of coincidences, but it appeared too late for me to notice them in detail."[4] This offhand reference was to cause Edward H. Chamberlin of Harvard much pain.

In later years Joan Robinson reminded her readers that in 1930–31, it was "absurd" to argue theoretically that plants would be either working full-time or be closed down, when in fact most plants, because of the slump, were working part-time. She added, "With the aid of Richard Kahn, who had been studying actual pricing policy in the British cotton industry, I used the newly invented concept of 'marginal revenue' to show how short-period profits are positive even at under-capacity working."[5]

The oral tradition at Cambridge

The oral tradition of the senior commons room at Cambridge fostered a veritable ferment of ideas. Colleagues then relied on one another for criticism and correction. For example, when Dennis Robertson published his *Banking Policy and the Price Level* in 1926, he wrote there, "I have had so many discussions with Mr. J. M. Keynes on the subject matter of Chapters V and VI, and have re-written them so drastically at his suggestion, that I think neither of us now knows how much of the ideas therein contained is his and how much is mine."[6]

Keynes, in turn, wrote to Joan Robinson about his reliance on Kahn: "I am going through a stiff week's supervision from R.F.K. on my M.S. He is a marvellous critic and suggester and improver—there never was anyone in the history of the world to whom it was so helpful to submit one's stuff."[7] Hence, it is not surprising to find Joan Robinson writing in 1978 of herself and Kahn, "With this apparatus (marginal revenue) we produced a complete restatement of the Pigovian system with various amendments. . . ."[8]

What matters is not that some of the work and some of the ideas were attributable to others, but the fact that Cambridge had then a working technique which contrasted strongly with continental or American methods of scholarship. The difficult part for an American is to discern who did what at Cambridge. Paul Samuelson confided, "There are people, I guess I won't quote any names, who just do not believe that Joan could have done some of the geometry and algebra of *Imperfect Competition* without Richard Kahn." I suggested that she conceded Kahn's role in the second edition. Samuelson replied,

> Right. I would say that they had an uncanny interrelationship which I never could fathom. It made me entertain the hypothesis that a few people had—that Richard Kahn wrote a lot of Keynes' *General Theory.* I think the upshot is that that's not the case, as I compare notes of Austin Robinson and other people who knew him as a very important influence on Keynes. But Kahn's selflessness defies description. So I could be prepared to believe that if you could get inside the black box anything could be true.[9]

Joseph Schumpeter wrote of Joan Robinson's tributes to Gerald Shove and Richard Kahn in this way:

> Both are scholars of a type that Cambridge produces much more readily than do other centers of scientific economics or rather of science in general. They throw their ideas into a common pool. By critical and positive suggestion they help other people's ideas into definite existence. And they exert anonymous influence—influence as leaders—far beyond anything that can be definitely credited to them from their publications.[10]

Perhaps Shove was not quite as selfless as Kahn. When Joan Robinson had only begun her book, Kahn discussed it with Shove. Shove wrote to her:

> From conversations with Kahn, I gather that, though the theorems in your book about monopoly are new and original, a good [part?] of the fundamental apparatus or line of approach (e.g. the treatment of "costs" or "rents" . . .) is review . . . from suggestions which I have put forward at various times in teaching, lectures, etc. I am delighted that any of my ideas or methods of exposition should bear fruit in this way, but may I say that I think some acknowledgment should be made of their source? I am sure that you will agree with me; but past experience has taught me that it is best to make one's feelings on these matters quite plain from the first,—so I hope you will forgive me for writing.[11]

Apparently Robinson replied immediately, for Shove answered, "Thank you very much for your generous letter. It makes me ashamed of having written. I really felt sure all along that you intended to acknowledge anything you might owe to me. Please forgive me."

However, Shove was also a little worried about an overlap between their lectures. (Robinson was lecturing for the first time in 1931.) He wrote her, "About lectures. I certainly do not want to interfere with your plans. I remember too well what one feels like when giving one's first course. I have, it is true, been feeling a little uneasy about the possible overlap between us. . . ."[12]

Robinson and Shove settled these matters through discussions with Kahn and several letters. At one point Shove said of "exploitation": "I have never gone deeply into the subject."[13] But all was not settled, after all. On June 17, 1932, Shove wrote to her: "It is very kind of you to offer to postpone publication but *please* don't. I shall probably never publish and anyhow I should hate to keep you back." And again June 24, 1932: "As to publishing: I don't suppose I ever shall but I like to keep on working at my stuff."

Joan Robinson did not lecture again until Michaelmas term 1933.[14] Shove wrote the spring before (May 24, 1933), "I am very glad that you are going to lecture again next year. In order that there may be no misunderstanding between us this time, it will perhaps be well that I should tell you straight over how I had proposed to arrange my course in theory. If there is any serious overlap with what you are planning, will you let me know?" In July 1933, Shove was "just getting to the 'Economics of Imperfect Markets' seriously and with eager anticipation." In August he wrote this note to her: "Did I make clear to you at lunch the other day how much I admire 'Imperfect Competition'?"

Joan Robinson's letters from Pigou were of a different sort and were sometimes undated. He raised a question that Americans would raise in the future. He wanted proofs: "Unless this can be found the thing is not mathematically watertight. . . . However, last night in bed I found a way of proving this in general for all . . . cases. So I *do* now think your thing is all right. But I still think you ought to put in a *proof* . . . because it is certainly not obvious."[15]

Other surviving letters suggest that Pigou advised Robinson to shorten her presentation by using more calculus and less geometry. Long after the book was out, Pigou wrote her in a lighter vein: "I have just found in my proofs a greatly improved title for your book—The economics of *Improper* Competition!"[16]

For Joan Robinson's career, this first book was very important. Pigou informed her, "I think it's a very firm effort containing any amount of stuff and should give you a very strong claim to the next lectureship that we have going. . . . Of course there are some things I don't much like."[17] And in May 1933 it was clear that she would lecture the next year.

Imperfect Competition in précis

Robinson wrote *Imperfect Competition* in a spirit of toolmaking, devoting Book I to "The Technique." She employed geometry "to demonstrate that the analysis of the output and price of a single commodity can be conducted by a technique based upon the study of individual decisions." Thus it is a book based on behavioral considerations. One of the concepts used is "perfect competition," which prevails when the demand for the output of each producer is perfectly elastic. Under perfect competition, the producer can sell all of his products at a market-given price—that is, the price will be unaffected by his selling his entire output. The meaning of the assumption of perfect competition is important because it underlies traditional economic analysis, particularly general equilibrium analysis, and all arguments that labor receives the value of its marginal product. Perfect competition entails markets where the number of sellers is large, so that the output of any one seller constitutes a negligible proportion of the total output and furthermore, buyers are indifferent to any choice between sellers.

In an imperfect market, these conditions are not met. Since most real-world markets are imperfect, Robinson was trying to construct a theory somewhat closer to reality. She did this by comparing monopoly equilibrium, competitive equilibrium, and the output and price discrimination possible in imperfect markets. In Books VII and VIII she applied monopoly and pure competition models to the demand for labor as a factor of production. She concluded in Book IX that there was both monopolistic and monopsonistic (buyer as a single firm) exploitation of labor—all demonstrable because the demand curves in imperfect competition are not perfectly elastic. Thus Robinson was doing several things at once—providing a new analysis of price and income determination, using the new concept of marginal revenue, and following through to the implications which such new analysis requires.

The reception of this work further clarifies these issues, or in some ways obfuscates them, for not everyone was ready for either the analysis or the implications. The American reception was split along lines of those who preferred the traditional theory and those, like American institutionalists, who had long been critical of it.*

Impact of *Imperfect Competition*

Shackle has said that Joan Robinson's main part in what he calls the "years of high theory" was the "veritable destruction" of traditional value theory.[18] The dilemma which Sraffa had addressed had lain untouched, wrote Shackle, from Cournot to Marshall, and from Marshall to Sraffa. "Why at that moment in the 1920s, did a half-dozen or more people suddenly start to work on it . . . ?"[19]

---

*See Appendix Note 3.1 Reviews of *The Economics of Imperfect Competition*.

There had been many critics of "perfect competition," notably Thorstein Veblen, but there had been no serious effort in the twentieth century to provide a substitute economic theory, that is, one based on an assumption other than perfect competition.

What is meant by Shackle's conclusion that Robinson had "destroyed" traditional value theory? To the economist, value theory represents first, the explanation of how prices are set in a market and second, how that procedure affects the public interest and welfare and in particular the distribution of income in the economy. Received value theory of Joan Robinson's day was founded on assumptions of perfect competition and thus had in fact ignored Cournot (and others) who had discussed monopoly and duopoly earlier.[20]

In *Imperfect Competition*, Robinson had, at least for Shackle, destroyed the old theory by challenging the major assumption of traditional theory and applying the new analysis to the distribution of income. One of her most significant conclusions was that the existence of imperfect competition provided a means of "monopolistic exploitation of labor" and that therefore the welfare implications attributed to a purely competitive society could not be extended to a society of imperfect competition (that is, one where producers could influence the price of their product).

The appearance of such a theory was timely during the depression, for the old theory had implied not only that labor was fairly treated, receiving its due in the form of marginal product, but that there was no need to worry about either prices or production levels (that is, the level of employment) in the competitive society. The traditional theory had fostered complacency and had supported a philosophy of laissez-faire in dealing with economic issues. Joan Robinson's theory represented an attack on both the complacency and the policies of laissez-faire. This was an important, earthshaking change in English economics, as Shackle claimed.

In the United States, the new theory was welcomed at once by the institutional school, which had been trying to bury the "economic man" and "pure competition" at least since the appearance of Thorstein Veblen's *Theory of Business Enterprise* in 1904. More traditional American economists acclaimed the new tools of analysis Joan Robinson was providing as well, seeing them as filling in the gaps of traditional theory, but not necessarily destroying the old theory. Robinson's mature view, in 1967, of what she had done in *Imperfect Competition* was that she had "succeeded in proving within the framework of the orthodox theory, that it is not true that wages are normally equal to the value of the marginal product."[21] This statement supports the view of Canadian Harvey Gram and Anglo-American Vivian Walsh that the questions raised by Joan Robinson were motivated by an interest in the political aspects of market versus nonmarket solutions of economic problems, though presented in the guise of formal theory.[22]

The other respect in which *Imperfect Competition* departed from books on economics of the 1930s was that Joan Robinson, while using some Marshallian techniques, had provided "a model, a set of precise assumptions which allowed the play of logic and mathematics." In Shackle's view, this was an important step in the methodology of economics. Shackle thought that the traditional Marshallian theory had the drawback that "clear and definite questions cannot be asked about a vague, richly detailed, fluid and living world," and that Robinson's model made a better analytical tool. Indeed, Shackle argued that Joan Robinson had invented the theory of the firm "without quite acknowledging it."[23]

Schumpeter gave Robinson credit for adding the concept of "monopsony" (a single buyer) to the vocabulary of the economist, and also for providing a logical, as distinguished from a sociological (Marxian), concept of "exploitation."[24] (Exploitation was due not to classes but to market structure.)

Robinson's first book thus provided new tools of analysis which allowed many economists to see that there was no escape from the logical condition of "exploitation of labor" if firms were monopolistic or monopsonistic.*

Joan Robinson's intention of challenging marginal productivity theory was missed by many in the profession. Perhaps some did not read the footnotes. Her most direct reference to the importance of the assumption of perfect competition to the marginal productivity theory of wages was in a footnote, buried on page 301. Referring to the dispute between Marshall and Sidney and Beatrice Webb about the marginal productivity theory of wages, she wrote that it seemed to have arisen because the Webbs "failed to realize the implications of the assumptions of perfect competition while Marshall failed to recognize the extreme unreality of those assumptions."[25]

How the book was received

In one of the outstanding coincidences in economic theory, *The Economics of Imperfect Competition* was published within a few months of *The Theory of Monopolistic Competition*, written by Edward H. Chamberlin of Harvard. (This will be discussed at some length in Chapter 4.)

The Great Depression of the early 1930s conditioned economists to be open-minded toward new theory. As early as 1929, unemployment had been such a problem in England that it was given credit for making the Labour Party the largest party in Parliament.[26] The United States had to wait for the 1932 election to bring in Franklin D. Roosevelt. That winter fifteen million persons were unemployed in the United States with many more millions working only part-time.[27] Clearly these were not times to defend complacency and laissez-faire. The ovation given these two young economists, Robinson and Chamberlin, cannot be separated from those times.

The reviews of *Imperfect Competition* praised the theory but occasionally damned the geometric method employed by Robinson. Schumpeter found "genu-

---

*See especially Books VII, VIII, and IX of *The Economics of Imperfect Competition*.

ine originality.'' The most prophetic remark came from Corwin Edwards of New York University, who wondered whether these new approaches to value theory "might be substituted for or might enfold the competitive analysis.''[28] Robinson and Chamberlin differed on this score. Robinson thought of her book as a substitute for traditional theory; Chamberlin saw his as a modification, an extension.

As for method, Schumpeter noted that *Imperfect Competition*

> . . . is Marshallian to the core. Everything about it is Marshallian: the approach, the fundamental ''conceptual scheme,'' the manner of reasoning, the starting-points as well as the goals, even the general social vision (although somewhat ''modernized'') which floats about it. The author steps out of the Cambridge circle only as far as the marginal revenue curve makes it necessary to do so by virtue of the fact that it was simultaneously discovered by a number of economists outside of Cambridge. But on no other occasion.[29]

At the time, Robinson may have doubted the justice of this view, though in later years she accepted it. Her way of saying, yes it was Marshallian, was finally to give most of the credit to Pigou.[30]

Schumpeter admired the wide-ranging implications of Joan Robinson's *Imperfect Competition*: ''A book of such range and power always leaves our minds with a question. Having been carried so far by this Virgil, where shall we go now?''[31] His suggestions were prophetic for Robinson's career, though not for the direction of the profession. He thought economists should work on the ''element of time,'' the ''element of money,'' and that ''we probably all agree that our equilibrium analysis is really a tool of analysis of chronic disequilibria.'' Finally, he admitted that ''in some lines of advance the time has probably come to get rid of the apparatus of supply and demand.''[32]

Imperfect Competition was used as a text in the United States. Schumpeter wrote to Kahn about his experience with it. He had ''discussed it in class at length. It is a remarkable achievement, and has put all of us, both as teachers and as regards our own work, under obligation to the author, to whom kindly convey my congratulations.''[33] Paul Douglas wrote Robinson from the University of Chicago:

> Your introduction of the marginal revenue curve gives us a most powerful weapon in the analysis of monopoly price and as you well bring out alters greatly the discussion of the problem of distribution. If I were re-writing my book on *The Theory of Wages* I would certainly include another chapter discussing the effect of monopoly and of imperfect competition upon the shares of factors. And it would, of course, be very largely based upon your work.[34]

There were some detractors. Fritz Machlup thought that the concept of ''elasticity of substitution'' had become conspicuous for its ''unintelligibility'': ''To say this is not at all to belittle the pioneering work of the 'tool-makers', J. R. Hicks (in *Theory of Wages)* and Joan Robinson (in *Imperfect Competition).*"[35] Machlup was answered by both Milton Friedman, who defended Robinson's and Hicks' use of the concept through a mathematical proof, and by Joan Robinson herself. She replied in a comment: "It must appear ungracious for one of the unintelligible authors whom Dr. Machlup has popularized to reply with a counter-charge of obscurity. But the kind of explanation which he has undertaken cannot avoid the danger that the sacrifice of precision to simplicity may cause as many difficulties for the ordinary reader as it removes."[36] Three years later, Robinson heard from Machlup when he was at Cornell University. He said he had spent twenty-two class meetings of two hours each on *Imperfect Competition* and thought the "final chapters more hasty, particularly 276–8 where the reader doesn't know whether it was productivity of capital or of labor which she means."[37] By the time she received this letter, Robinson had completed two newer books on the theory of employment.

Summary and some explanation

The sequence of events, then, is that the luncheon where Austin Robinson "retailed" to Richard Kahn and Joan Robinson the work of his student occurred early in 1930. After dubbing it the marginal revenue curve that day, "Joan and he were quickly away on the lines that led up to *The Economics of Imperfect Competition* and the English contribution to all that rethinking."[38] Almost simultaneously, a book on "monopolistic competition" was published in the United States. How different was the Cambridge origin of *Imperfect Competition* as compared with the lonely, individual trek of Chamberlin who conceived of his basic idea perhaps as early as 1921 and published his book, *The Theory of Monopolistic Competition*, only a few months ahead of Robinson's *Imperfect Competition.*

Other contrasts are in order. In America, a person interested in having an academic career would have sought a doctorate, taking the time to learn two foreign languages well enough to pass a written examination. Though the Ph.D. had been established in 1919 at Cambridge University, economists did not seek it. They simply began working with the help of colleagues.

In 1929, Pigou's Sidney Ball Lecture had defined for Joan Robinson what her role as an economist was to be. In his address, he distinguished between the "tool-makers" and the "tool-users." So, in her first book, she "presented to the analytical economist . . . a box of tools."[39] As Schumpeter approvingly remarked, "Economic theory is not a stock of political recipes but, to use Mrs. Joan Robinson's felicitous phrase, a box of analytic tools."[40]

A look into the future: two Joan Robinsons

The Marshallian method of analysis employed in developing *Imperfect Competition* was one Robinson later rejected. In this sense there were two Joan Robinsons. One was "Marshallian to the core," as Schumpeter and also Kaldor observed. This Joan Robinson was consistent in her thinking between *Economics is a Serious Subject* and *The Economics of Imperfect Competition.*

But a second Joan Robinson was soon to emerge. And this Robinson was eventually to criticize the method employed by the first, saying that in *Imperfect Competition* she had started the argument "from a purely *a priori* set of assumptions—the assumptions that Pigou had distilled from Marshall— and then . . . [introduced] a minor improvement in them, instead of making a radical critique of the relationship between the traditional assumptions and the actual economy that they pretended to describe."[41] The Marshallian and similar methods have remained in good standing with orthodox or traditional economists, and so has the first Joan Robinson. The second Robinson spent a great deal of energy trying to eradicate the method and assumptions she had once embraced.

Other critics of traditional theory—the American institutionalists and more recently, radical economists—have attacked the unreality of assumptions underlying traditional economics, without necessarily providing alternative models or assumptions. One must use assumptions to build models or theories. Certainly Robinson never attempted to do without them. Consequently her rejection of "*a priori* assumptions" was not meant to indicate that she intended to use none. Not everyone has understood this. For example, T. W. Hutchison argued that in her text *An Introduction to Modern Economics* (co-authored with John Eatwell in 1973), Robinson employed the same method of unrealistic assumptions she had used in *Imperfect Competition.*[42]

The real point is that Robinson did *not* use the assumption of perfect competition. Even in *Imperfect Competition,* she did not rely on perfect competition other than as a basis of comparison. I cannot find that she has used it in any other way since. Rather, she strove for greater realism through avoiding the assumption of perfect competition, showing that we can indeed build models without that assumption. In this she was in step with some other Cantabrigians, particularly Nicholas Kaldor. In fact, this is the major methodological difference between her approach to capital in the early 1950s and that of the American school which she called the "neo-neo-classicals." It remains a defining characteristic of the post Keynesian school that assumptions of perfect competition, and the laissez-faire implications of these assumptions, are to be foresworn.

Robinson was always sensitive to the issue of the realism of assumptions. How could she not be when this was one of the widely discussed issues among the philosophers of science at Cambridge, namely, R. B. Braithwaite of King's and his circle, many of whom she must have known personally? In reference to

Chamberlin's theory of monopolistic competition, she freely admitted, "in some respects, Chamberlin's assumptions were more realistic than mine."

And she knew that assumptions might be the crux of differences. She felt Chamberlin's "one-sided controversy" with her "was a bad case of confronting the conclusions of two arguments without examining their assumptions. Where he and I set up the same questions (errors and omissions excepted) we found the same answers."[43]

Finally, Shackle, in identifying Robinson's contributions through *Imperfect Competition* to the methodology of economics, observed that Joan Robinson had exchanged Marshall's fluid world for a model, a set of precise assumptions which allowed the play of logic and mathematics.[44]

The revolution that never was

Joan Robinson believed she had undermined the whole argument by economists that workers in a capitalist society receive a fair wage. In the historical context, economists, particularly the Austrian school, had reacted strongly to Marx's nineteenth-century challenge to the fairness of the capitalist system. Eugen von Böhm-Bawerk had constructed a capital theory which purported to answer Marx's accusations. Böhm-Bawerk argued that the source of value was not to be found in labor, but rather in the productivity of capital. In the United States, J. B. Clark theorized that under purely competitive conditions, the worker's marginal product (i.e., that value which he added to productive value at the margin) was equal to his wage.[45]

What Robinson had done was to show, using traditional tools, that under conditions which were imperfectly competitive, wages would not equal their marginal product. And since no one could argue that conditions of perfect competition obtained, certainly not in manufacturing where there were obvious economies of scale, then "in Pigou's own terms, it is not true that wages are equal to the value of the marginal product of labor."[46]

Revolutionary changes in theory, method, and implications ordinarily raise a storm of controversy. Shackle thought that the value-theory revolution never produced violent opposition of views because it was really a struggle "against the tremendous grip of received doctrine, the established image of the economic world." In fact, said Shackle, even Robinson and Chamberlin "papered-over the gaping rents they had hewn in the old fabric."[47]

Robinson laid part of the blame on Chamberlin who, she said, "refused to admit that his argument damaged the image of the market producing the optimum allocation of given resources between alternative uses."[48] On the other hand, it was Chamberlin, not she, who spent a lifetime trying to get monopolistic competition accepted as the central view of economic theory. Robinson withdrew, dismissing *Imperfect Competition* as "Pre-Keynesian" and "based on a fudge— confusing comparisons of possible alternative equilibrium positions with the analysis of a process taking place through time,'' a method she grew to loathe.[49]

She also accepted the criticism that her assumption that each firm was selling a single commodity was misleading. What she regretted most was that some of these "weaknesses" of her book became "frozen into orthodox teaching," while her demonstration that consumers' sovereignty cannot be established had had so little impact on teaching.[50] Thus the end result was that, rather than destroying the inherited wage theory, monopolistic and imperfect competition were simply added to it, making it appear to successive generations of economists that all cases (perfectly competitive to monopolistic) were covered by the theory. Corwin D. Edwards' hunch that monopolistic and imperfect competition might just be enfolded into the traditional theory was borne out.[51]

Joan Robinson had a child the year after her book appeared. (Ann was born May 25, 1934.) With book, baby, and some lecturing in hand, she was granted a teaching position in the university. Claude Guillebaud wrote to congratulate her on the birth of her daughter and sent notice of the informal meetings of lecturers and teachers of economics which were to take place on alternate Thursdays in full term.[52] This famous woman was now a university probationary lecturer, the beginning rank, in the department of economics at Cambridge University.

JR

CHAPTER FOUR

American Economics and the Chamberlin Controversy

Economics was a major field of study in American universities in the early 1920s. There were more students, more courses, more faculty, more controversy, more applied economics, even in the Ivy League schools than in England. Compared to Cambridge, the study of economics in the United States was, like the country, bigger and more various. Nevertheless, English economic theory dominated American teaching of theory, and there was a universal reverence for Cambridge University. The doctorate was the common professional entrée to American university teaching as early as 1900, though it was virtually unknown even in the 1920s at Cambridge. Before World War I, many Americans sought further study in Germany, so that the continental influence was strong.

American economics was already characterized by schisms in method and approach. While Cambridge, Oxford, and Manchester Universities differed from each other as among Marshall and Edgeworth and Jevons, American universities differed as among these several influences: English economics (Edgeworth and Marshall being seen as similar); Austrian, particularly Menger marginalism; German historical influences, particularly those of Sombart and Schmoller; indigenous institutional influences from Veblen, Ely, and Commons; and finally, Marx. The major methodological schism in the United States was a carry-over from the continental argument over the importance of history and observation (induction) relative to the preferred English-Austrian method of a priori reasoning. (Of course, Cambridge method differed in turn from the Austrian.)

In addition, American philosophical pragmatism supported the idea that policy-making (application of theory to problems) was as important as theorizing. Business schools, first developed in Germany, were already a part of the American university scene on the graduate level. The study of accounting was common among American students even in liberal arts programs of economics. Statistical theory and its application were regarded in the United States not only as an integral part of the study of economics, but perhaps the important part. W. C. Mitchell's *Business Cycles* was considered a landmark.

Cambridge University had courses in statistics, history, and applied problems in the 1920s, but in the United States these studies seemed to be more on a par in status with theory than they were in England. For many American economists, pure theory played only a minor role in education and practice.

These characteristics of economics in North America conditioned the reception by American economists of Joan Robinson's work, and in turn may have inhibited her understanding of the eclecticism of her American colleagues.

Edward H. Chamberlin reacts

From Eliot House, Cambridge, Massachusetts, Edward H. Chamberlin wrote to Joan Robinson on October 3, 1933, "If I had not succeeded in slipping out of Cambridge last June several weeks before I really should have, your book would probably have made the rounds of Italy and France with me this summer and your note of June 16 would have been acknowledged with only a reasonable delay." He had not read her book yet, but commented jovially, "I'm not sure yet what assumptions are appropriate to our peculiar case of academic duopoly, but they must be found and it's up to us."[1]

This mood did not last.

In her foreword to *Imperfect Competition,* Robinson made a brief acknowledgment of Chamberlin's *Theory of Monopolistic Competition*, which convinced him that she had known more about his work than she admitted. Chamberlin had been pursuing the subject for nearly ten years and could not have been aware that, given the Cambridge oral tradition, a work on the same subject as his could have flowed from a luncheon conversation about a graduate student's work.

There is some evidence that Chamberlin may have believed Robinson helped herself to certain of his paragraphs or ideas. His suspicions did not go away. Thirty-four years after the initial publication of *Monopolistic Competition*, Chamberlin decided "to spell out more fully the 'intellectual history' of the book." He took pains to point out that his book was substantially complete in his doctoral thesis, accepted in 1927, a full six years before the book's publication. "Some account of the thesis as distinct from the book is of interest because the former was not merely a manuscript put away in a drawer, but a bound volume in Harvard University Library, freely available to all, including visiting scholars, etc. Library records show that it was in fact extensively consulted during the period 1927–1933, as well as later and down to the present time."[2]

That record is still readily available in the New England Depository. Persons who want to read Harvard theses, then and now, must sign and date their perusal. Of the twelve signatures which preceded the appearance of Robinson's book, none was that of a foreign scholar who was in any way close to Robinson.[3]

Allyn Young, the thesis adviser, did in fact go to England, but he was in

London rather than in Cambridge. He died there when only fifty-three in 1929, within a year of his arrival.[4] Since Joan Robinson returned to England from India that year, it is unlikely that she ever knew Young.

Robinson's intellectual pursuits during these years are well documented. She returned to England from India in 1929; began her work on imperfect competition with the help of Richard Kahn in early 1930; and fell in with the work of the Circus after the publication of Keynes' *Treatise* (it was published on her twenty-seventh birthday, October 31, 1930). The Circus met formally January to May 1931. Robinson completed what she called her "nightmare" (an early draft of *Imperfect Competition)* about April 25, 1932. Her foreword is dated October 1932. Her book was sent to Chamberlin in June 1933.

The real curiosity is how she might have mentioned a book published in 1933 in a foreword dated 1932. When Chamberlin sent his mother the new book, he dated his accompanying note to her February 18, 1933. The answer must be that Robinson added the acknowledgment some time in 1933 while going through proofs of her book, after seeing a copy of *Monopolistic Competition. Imperfect Competition* appeared in print in the spring of 1933, so that she could have done so. There would have been no purpose in her failing to give any credit due to Chamberlin. She felt herself to be, in Cambridge, at the center of the crisis in value theory. Robinson had plenty of help on her *Imperfect Competition*, but it came from Cambridge colleagues rather than foreign scholarship. Youthful arrogance she may have been guilty of, but cheating was never her style.[5]

A case of multiple discovery?

The Chamberlin-Robinson publication coincidence is one of the six examples customarily cited of multiple discovery in economics.[6] Don Patinkin, however, is skeptical of the theory of multiple discovery, and thinks Chamberlin "quite rightly emphasized that his theory of monopolistic competition differed from Joan Robinson's theory of imperfect competition."[7]

For Harvard, the question is partly one of the timing of the discovery. The Harvard view, according to an obituary of Chamberlin signed by several leading Harvard scholars, has been that

> . . . there is no doubt that the central ideas of both contributions were in the air and a number of economists had been nibbling round the edges. But Chamberlin's claim to priority by no means rests on the few months by which his volume had preceded that of Mrs. Robinson. His contribution in all its essentials was already to be found in his doctoral dissertation submitted in 1927. Moreover, one important part of this dissertation had been published in an article in the *Quarterly Journal of Economics,* 1929, entitled "Duopoly: Value where Sellers are Few." And, entirely apart from the question of priority, there is now general agreement that Chamberlin presented by far the more complete and elegant

exposition of the relation of competitive and monopolistic elements in market theory.[8]

Since Robinson did not discuss duopoly in her book, this published work of Chamberlin's was probably unknown to her at the time, which may have seemed incredible to a person of Chamberlin's careful scholarship.[9]

On the question of multiple discovery, the Cambridge, England stance was one of boredom. What seemed important at Cambridge was the issue of overall contributions. It was generally agreed there that Chamberlin had rather a one-track mind. Lord Kahn has emphasized that Joan Robinson very soon went over to other things. Kahn thought "she was rather annoyed that she had wasted so much time on imperfect competition." Chamberlin, on the other hand, was "a one-subject man."[10]

In response to the Cambridge view that Chamberlin's focus was narrow, the Harvard evaluation remains that "there are eminent scholars whose fame rests mainly on one major contribution and whose lives are devoted to elaborating and perfecting this contribution. . . . Chamberlin clearly belongs" in this group. At Cambridge University this would seem to be a charitable way of putting it. However, Harvard colleagues conceded that Chamberlin was interested neither in empirical work nor in the policy implications of his work; that rather than taking any interest in new developments in economic theory, Chamberlin was unhappy when the attention of leading economists shifted toward the macroeconomics of Keynes.

Herein lies the greatest difference between Chamberlin and Robinson. She experienced a Keynesian "conversion" while still writing her "nightmare." Chamberlin reacted to new theory differently: "When, after the appearance of Keynes' *General Theory*, the attention of leading economists shifted away from micro economics to the macro economic problems associated with the determination of national income and its variations, he refused to run with the pack and concentrated his efforts on the further development of his own theories." Still, Harvard colleagues did not consider Chamberlin a man only of narrow focus, but instead "a broadly cultivated person," whose interest in music, painting, the theater, and literature sometimes "competed actively with his professional and scholarly concerns."[11]

Chamberlin's thesis won him the David A. Wells Prize of 1927-28 and a permanent position at Harvard. But nothing, none of his many honors, really assuaged his bitterness at the coupling of his book with Robinson's. Perhaps if there had been a Nobel Prize then—but one surmises that it would have been unsatisfactory to share that as well.

Thus what is fascinating is not the issue of multiple discovery (after all, economists as different as Cournot and Marx had discussed monopoly), but that in the same year two economists so different in training, background, interest, and politics should publish theses on the same subject.

What's in a name?

From the beginning, the question of what to call the new theory was at issue. Allyn Young had suggested that Chamberlin call his thesis the "theory of imperfect competition," but Chamberlin rejected that title, since what he meant to do was to amalgamate competitive and monopolistic elements. However, few people in the profession, Don Patinkin being one of the exceptions, cared for this distinction.

Chamberlin was dogged in his insistence on "monopolistic competition" as the proper name. The original title in the preliminary announcement for the American Economic Association Round Table in 1936 was "The Economics of Imperfect Competition." Chamberlin wrote to Alvin Johnson, who was arranging the conference, "I am anxious that the announced subject of the round table include the words 'monopolistic competition'. Why not this: 'Monopolistic and Imperfect Competition', instead of the 'Economics of Imperfect Competition' . . . ?"[12]

Johnson accepted his suggestion. In a handwritten summary, Chamberlin wrote of his presentation at the conference: "In my paper I had meant to contrast monopolistic competition with the 'imperfect competition' of Mrs. Robinson, and it is interesting to note that she emphatically denies any connection between the concept as she uses it and 'freedom of entry'."[13]

Again in 1952, when the International Economic Association (IEA) was arranging a conference on monopoly and its regulation, Chamberlin insisted that the title should be "Monopoly, Competition and Their Regulation." He wrote to Austin Robinson, who was acting for the IEA, "Haberler tells me that you thought it better not to use 'Monopolistic Competition' in the title of the Talloires volume."[14]

Throughout his life, Chamberlin insisted that a real difference in their theories lay in the name. In one effort, Chamberlin used several pages of the *Quarterly Journal of Economics* to explain the differences between monopolistic and imperfect competition.[15] Nicholas Kaldor, in response, gave what became the English view of imperfect versus monopolistic competition: Robinson and Chamberlin were talking about the same things. Kaldor wrote,

> A careful perusal of the ten pages devoted to this question fails to bring out any evidence in support of the contention that the two theories relate not to the same subject, but to different subjects. What Professor Chamberlin really contends, is that there is a difference in "approach," in economic "Weltanschauung," between Mrs. Robinson and himself; but the reader could hardly fail to carry away the impression that here, at any rate, Professor Chamberlin has fallen a victim to the general tendency among producers in an imperfectly competitive market—a tendency he so convincingly describes—and is trying to differentiate his product too far . . . . Now I do not think that this difference in fundamental conception really exists.[16]

In 1984, this was still Lord Kahn's opinion. "They were," he said, "talking about the same things."[17] In 1953 in "Imperfect Competition Revisited," Robinson wrote, "I should like to take this opportunity of saying that I have never been able to grasp the nature of the distinction between *imperfect* and *monopolistic* competition to which Professor Chamberlin attaches so much importance."[18] Most opinion has followed from hers. On the other hand, she willingly admitted that some of Chamberlin's subjects were unique to him:

> I did not attempt to tackle duopoly and oligopoly and, concentrating on price as the vehicle for competition, I said very little about non-price competition, such as artificial product-differentiation, advertising and sales promotion, which in fact accounts for the greatest part of the wastefulness of imperfect markets. (The twin to my book, Chamberlin's *Monopolistic Competition*, opened up these subjects. . . .)[19]

The case of *Monopolistic Competition* and *Imperfect Competition*, then, is one of nonidentical twins, so that it is acceptable that there should be two names.

Origins of the theories

Another sore spot with Chamberlin was the fact that many in the profession accepted as gospel the Robinson foreword on the origin of the problem in value theory: that is, that Sraffa's exposure of the contradictions in the Marshallian theory of value initiated the search for new theory. In tracing the early development of his own theory, Chamberlin particularly objected to an article by Peter Newman[20] which argued that "Marshall's theory of value . . . was attacked vigorously and effectively soon after his death," and that "a new doctrine—the theory of imperfect competition—(rose) from the ashes." Chamberlin also objected to Robinson's statement that "the experience of slump conditions in the inter-war period, which gave rise to Mr. Keynes's theory of employment" also led to a "new type of analysis" which is "imperfect competition." The fact is, wrote Chamberlin, that his theory "was written at the height of 'Coolidge prosperity', and is without reference to any particular period of business, either good or bad."[21]

Nor did Chamberlin like the fact that Professor W. H. Hutt "stated in 1934, in effect, that since my [Chamberlin's] own work had the disadvantage of being produced on the other side of the Atlantic, whereas Mrs. Robinson's was produced at the very source itself of this discussion, he would regard her analysis as the more 'authoritative' and confine his attention to it."[22]

Since the theories were initiated at different times, historical convergence does not adequately explain the near simultaneity of the publications. Rather the two theories, from essentially different traditions, were generated and written in different ways, and thus were different ways of looking at the same subject.

Other differences

Chamberlin continued to elaborate monopolistic competition, so that comparisons between the original editions of Chamberlin-Robinson theses fall flat. He kept issuing new, beefed-up editions until there were eight in all. Robinson, on the other hand, having lost interest in imperfect competition, limited her effort on the subject to a few articles. She did not issue a second edition of her book until 1969, and this was mainly a reprinting.

Upon receiving one of Chamberlin's new editions (probably the fifth edition, 1946) she wrote to him:

> Dear Professor Chamberlin, Many thanks for sending your new edition. I haven't thought about these questions for some time. I expect if I read my own book through it would seem frightfully primitive. I took over the Marshallian conceptions of enterprise as a factor of production and of long-period equilibrium much too uncritically, and if I had to do it now I should start from quite a different angle. Yours sincerely, Joan Robinson.[23]

Do these theories challenge the status quo or not? Politics was an interest not only of Robinson's, but also of Chamberlin's, though their political beliefs differed radically. Those differences were made obvious when Chamberlin became a member of the Mont Pelerin Society, founded in 1947 by a group led by Friedrich von Hayek and Milton Friedman. Chamberlin's membership is curious, in that the society was founded because the group discerned "a decline of belief in private property and the *competitive market.*"[24]

Joan Robinson observed, "Chamberlin appeared to be more concerned to defend the market system than to expose its drawbacks."[25] Chamberlin did defend capitalism, for instance, in one of his last publications before his years of illness. In the *Atlantic Monthly,* June 1959, he posed the question, "Can Union Power Be Curbed?" and answered in the affirmative: "Unions have achieved their present position largely through public indulgence, and if the public becomes less indulgent, union power can be curbed. What is needed is a general awakening to the real nature of the problem."[26] This was the kind of work that members of the Mont Pelerin Society thought valuable in stemming what they identified as an "ideological movement" which endangered the "central values of civilization."[27]

Robinson perceived Chamberlin as unwilling to follow his theory to its logical conclusions. Her argument was this: she had begun with Sraffa's objection to the lack of logic in orthodox (Marshallian) economic theory while Chamberlin's objection was to its lack of realism. Thus she felt they had both opened up a general indictment of the operations of the economic system itself. Joan Robinson insisted that after World War II, the climate of opinion had changed, and for the worse: "For obvious reasons (especially in the United States) fashion favors the defense of capitalism rather than criticisms of it. . . ."[28] In the early days she had been "delighted to find that I had proved (within the accepted assumptions) that it was not true to say that wages equal the marginal productivity of labor, while Chamberlin wanted to maintain that advertisement, salesmanship and monopolistic product differentiation in no way impaired the principle of consumer's sovereignty and the beneficial effect of the free play of market forces." While Chamberlin's assumptions were in some respects more realistic, "he did not want to draw realistic conclusions from them."[29]

In 1974, some years after his death, she repeated this accusation: Professor Chamberlin "was reluctant . . . to draw the conclusion that the market system cannot perform the function of an ideal allocation of resources when it is being manipulated by salesmanship."[30]

One of the differences between the original versions of the two books had been that Chamberlin had no interest then in the problem of distribution: "...the welfare problem was no part of my original objective at all, and concern with it was at the vanishing point in both thesis and book."[31] In his second edition, however, he added the subtitle, "A Reorientation of the Theory of Value." And in later editions, for example the fifth (1946) and thereafter, he recognized that his monopolistic competition (like her imperfect competition) meant that wages would not be equal to the marginal products of the workers.[32] It was not so much Chamberlin as the profession which paid no attention to this and continued to cling to the old value theory.

Personal relations and exchanges

Chamberlin and Robinson never knew one another well. Joan Robinson first met Chamberlin at the International Economic Association conference in 1953, long after she had put aside imperfect competition as an interest. Austin Robinson has said, "I seem to remember that she took Chamberlin for a walk and they learned to live in amicable detachment."[33] Chamberlin told his family that Robinson had worn "red pajamas" at the conference.[34] By the time she made her first visit to the United States in 1961, Chamberlin had already suffered a stroke.

Immediately after publication of the two books, Robinson praised Chamberlin's separation of the "notion of perfect competition and the notion of free entry into an industry," while objecting to his terminology.[35] Chamberlin preferred his approach which, he argued, allowed him to discuss oligopoly. He objected particularly to an article in the *Economic Journal* in which K. W. Rothschild accused Chamberlin of having neglected oligopoly, when it had been Robinson who did so.[36] In her turn, Robinson pointed out that his reliance on the numbers of buyers to establish perfect competition was a blind alley: for example, one buyer would produce similar results on sales.[37] Thus went the exchanges of the early postpublication years.

By 1953, when Chamberlin's *Monopolistic Competition* was in the sixth edition, Robinson was writing that her own work, *The Economics of Imperfect Competition,* "was a scholastic book." Some economists may find it baffling that she was generally more critical of her own book than of his.[38] Privately, she wrote to Chamberlin:

Dear Ed, Many thanks for your letter. I do not think we can ever really settle this question because we have different ideas about what an argument can be about. My idea is that one should formulate questions to which the answers bring out differences, but I do not find any such questions between us— the purely analytical field, though plenty in the moral and political implications of the analysis. I am not at all interested in learned questions about who said what.

(1) I freely admit that I did not deal with oligopoly, and that my definition of an individual demand curve that purports to eliminate it was an error. I can't say fairer than that? (2) I agree that oligopoly in fact is very important. (3) I do not think we should disagree about the analysis of any problem set out on clearly defined assumptions. (4) I do not think we should disagree, except for lack of clear evidence which leaves room for guess work, about what sets of assumptions are realistic. (5) Disagreement about what questions are interesting to discuss are bound to exist. You seem much more interested than I am in the questions that arise on static assumptions (See the Preface to my "Collected Papers") and so you are more interested in my book than I am. Sorry not to be able to give more satisfaction. Yours, Joan Robinson.[39]

Meeting of the minds: the international conference

In 1953, the International Economic Association called a conference on the subject of monopoly and its regulation. (This is the conference where Austin Robinson and Chamberlin differed on how it was to be named.) Of the thirty-three participants, Chamberlin was one of eight from the United States. The United Kingdom delegation included four, two of them being the Robinsons. The conference papers and debates mark some of the striking differences between Joan Robinson's and Chamberlin's economics. Robinson threw down the gauntlet with a paper entitled, "The Impossibility of Competition," and thereby challenged nearly everyone else at the conference. Her ideas were much discussed in debate, though not agreed to by many. She confessed that "in choosing such a 'shocking' title for her paper, she had hoped to provoke discussion on whether competition was, after all, a feasible substitute for monopoly." In the discussion following the presentation of papers, Joan Robinson concluded, "I went too far. You were too shocked to respond."[40]

In her paper, however, she claimed, "Nowadays everyone is willing to admit that the traditional theory of value based on the assumption of perfect competition is highly unrealistic and that competition in practice is very imperfect. I wish to carry the argument a step further and to maintain that there are logical contradictions in the basic conception of competition as an equilibrium state of affairs."[41]

As was to become obvious over the years, Joan Robinson made an incorrect assumption about what the economics profession understood. Economists were still utilizing perfect competition and equilibrium states in their work. Her plea to replace the static equilibrium theory by a dynamic approach "more relevant to modern conditions" fell on deaf ears. What she heard in reply were "voices in defense of equilibrium theory and the static analysis." In dismay, she remarked, "I make no apology for having written my book twenty years ago, but I find it shocking that people still read it."[42] Chamberlin, on the other hand, harked back to his book with some determination. Regarding the "new definitions of monopoly" which had appeared in efforts to measure monopoly and competition, he wanted "to make clear from the beginning that I do not accept any of them." He didn't mind being "the only one who has kept without a particle of change the old traditional definition of monopoly as control over supply."[43]

Chamberlin still wanted to measure the degree of monopoly and competition, but he wanted to do so with his original definitions. He wanted it known once more, even if the English "did not seem to understand it," that he had something different from Robinson: "I conclude that monopoly and competition are *not* blended in *Imperfect Competition*, and that the fact that they *are* blended in *Monopolistic Competition* was missed by Mr. Kaldor."[44]

In every one of the debates, either Joan Robinson participated or someone else focused on her ideas. She was one of two women at the conference (the other being Jane Aubert-Krier of France), and one of four participants who did not carry the title of professor.[45] Yet it is fair to say that she was clearly the most stimulating as well as the most argumentative participant. Chamberlin was no match for her at such a meeting. His style was to continue the debate in his subsequent editions.*

End of the affair

Chamberlin had a stroke in 1959 and a more devastating one in 1961. His colleagues viewed his attitude toward his decline with uncommon admiration:

> His pride and courage kept him on his feet and active long after most men would have given up in defeat. He fought off increasing paralysis and continued to teach for another four years. Although his mind was clear to the end, his last years were spent in bed unable to move or to communicate. During this long and torturing period he was nursed, supported, and encouraged by the deep and tireless devotion of his wife Lucienne and his daughter Monique. Chamberlin was singularly fortunate in his family and his friends. He was a social being of a

---

*See Appendix Note 4.2 Successive editions of *Monopolistic Competition*.

most engaging sort, a man who esteemed excellence above all else, a courageous gentleman and a scholar.[46]

Chamberlin died July 16, 1967.

The second edition of Robinson's *Imperfect Competition* (1969) did not appear until two years after Chamberlin's death. Her last extant letter to him had been written ten years before he died: "Dear Ed, Many thanks for having your new volume sent to me. [Apparently he had sent her his sixth edition, which included a new analysis of the cost curve.] I had not seen the last piece before. Can we now settle down to a retrospective peaceful co-existence on the basis that we made different assumptions? But I think it is rather hard that you will not allow me to retract my own errors."[47]

In her preface to the second edition of *Imperfect Competition*, she once more decried the static approach of her book and admitted "other serious limitations on my argument." In saying that Chamberlin had opened up the subject of duopoly, she thus conceded to him a kind of win that was rare for her to grant. Robinson was quite ready to admit where she had made an error, but she did not often concede that another, particularly an American, had been correct.

When she was seventy-six and Chamberlin was long dead, Robinson remembered the bitterness of it all: "My twin, Professor Chamberlin, spent many years protesting that his 'monopolistic competition' was quite different from my 'imperfect competition'. (It used to be said at Harvard at one time that any student could be sure of getting a good degree by abusing Mrs. Robinson.)"[48]

Perhaps this statement is useful only in showing that even at the end of her life, and after many visits to American campuses, Robinson remained unfamiliar with the American system of education.[49]

Whatever happened to imperfect competition?

With a new macroeconomic or Keynesian revolution hard upon the heels of the revolution in value theory, the question often arises as to what Keynes made of imperfect competition. Lorie Tarshis asked Austin Robinson at the University of Western Ontario Conference in the late 1970s "whether Keynes took an active part in the other revolution . . . the one that had to do with the theory of value." Austin Robinson replied,

> I think a quick answer to that is almost none. He saw the manuscript of Joan's *Imperfect Competition* and told Macmillan that, though it might not at first glance look an exciting book to them, they certainly ought to publish it—a surprising but welcome decision. He may have read it with care; he may not have. He was editor of the *Economic Journal* of course, and published the 1930 "symposium" on "Increasing Returns and the Representative Firm"—the

Robertson-Sraffa-Shove exchanges. He was encouraging, he was interested, but he wasn't a partaker in that particular operation.[50]

Joan Robinson wrote,

Keynes himself was not interested in the theory of relative prices. Gerald Shove used to say that Maynard had never spent the twenty minutes necessary to understand the theory of value. On these topics he was content to leave orthodoxy alone. He carried a good deal of Marshallian luggage with him and never thoroughly unpacked it to throw out the clothes he could not wear.[51]

She also wrote (1969): "Keynes was not much interested in the theory of imperfect competition, though he had given my book on that subject a vague blessing."[52]

Kaldor said that Joan often told him, "she tried to interest Keynes in imperfect competition for many years, and its relevance to the problem of the insufficiency of effective demand—but she never succeeded."[53] Nor did Keynes make use of the economics of imperfect competition in his theory of employment. In *The General Theory*, Keynes objected to the idea that the "utility of the wage when a given volume of labor is employed is equal to the marginal disutility of that amount of employment." He did not object to the other traditional belief that the wage was equal to the marginal product of the laborer.[54] Because of Keynes' neglect or disinterest, imperfect competition simply played no part in the Keynesian revolution. According to Robinson, it was left to Michal Kalecki to bring imperfect markets into the macroeconomic picture.[55]

Kaldor noted,

Later Kalecki succeeded [in interesting Keynes] as shown in the article which Keynes published in the March/1939 issue of the *Economic Journal*, where Keynes spoke about "our prevailing *quasi*-competitive system." This is the nearest that he [Keynes] came to dealing with a situation in which average costs were falling and marginal costs were well below average costs and so were at variance with the general rule which he enunciated all through the *General Theory*, that prices are equal to marginal costs, that the wages are equal to the marginal product of labor, and that, as a universal rule, there is an inverse relationship between employment and real wages.[56]

This belated concession by Keynes of the "quasi-competitive" nature of markets in turn had no impact. The initial neglect of imperfect competition by Keynes is important in the history of American economics, for it was Keynes', not Kalecki's ideas that came to the United States.

In 1968, the year after Chamberlin's death, Lester Telser wrote a review of a commemorative volume dedicated to the late scholar. In his review entitled,

"Monopolistic Competition: Any Impact Yet?" Telser noted that throughout his life, Chamberlin had "struggled to gain acceptance for his theory of monopolistic competition as a general theory of value. Happily Chamberlin lived long enough to see the fruits of his efforts in this *Festschrift*. On the surface, this volume makes it appear that his hard struggle met success at last. However, the plain fact is that the theory of monopolistic competition has had little impact on economics. . . . The fault lies in the theory and not in the profession."

Telser's views are in the Chicago tradition: "The theory of competition enjoys a renaissance that owes nothing to the theory of monopolistic competition and much to the core and the equilibrium point, concepts whose full implications are still being developed and which promise healthy progeny from the marriage of game theory to classical economics."[57]

In discussing Chicago economics, Melvin W. Reder made a similar point. Chicago economics relies on "Tight Prior Equilibrium" or TP, said Reder, which "is rooted in the hypothesis that decision makers so allocate the resources under their control that there is no alternative allocation such that any one decision maker could have his expected utility increased without a reduction occurring in the expected utility of at least one other decision maker."[58] And he adds, "Especially repugnant to TP is the suggestion that price and marginal cost (or marginal product and input price) may vary independently of one another, or of quantity bought and sold. . . ."[59]

The preference for TP helps explain why Chicago traditionalists would never incorporate either imperfect competition or monopolistic competition into their thinking. In this, they were following Milton Friedman's rejection of any meddling with perfect competition. One of Friedman's objections was in the matter of assumptions. Holding that realism in assumptions was an inappropriate goal, Friedman said the development of monopolistic and imperfect competition was "explicitly motivated and its wide acceptance and approval largely explained, by the belief that the assumptions of 'perfect competition' or 'perfect monopoly' said to underlie neoclassical economic theory are a false image of reality."[60] Friedman felt that the theory of imperfect or monopolistic competition failed to qualify as a more general theory, that it offered no tools of analysis (only enriching the vocabulary), and that it was "incompetent to contribute to the analysis of a host of important problems."[61] This became the Chicago view.

Paul Samuelson does not agree with Telser that Chicago was the world:

> American Keynesians like me believed that imperfections of competition and deviations from strict constant returns to scale are an important part of the Keynesian under-employment equilibrium story. We knew that the Fortune 500 corporations were there to stay and we also knew that Chamberlin-Robinson diagrams didn't explain why the system was so Pareto-nonoptimal in 1933 and so much more nearly Pareto-optimal in 1929 or 1952. Keynes-cum-Chamberlin-

and-Means would have been better than Keynes alone, but we pragmatists were grateful for what we had.[62]

Reder also points out that economists outside Chicago relied on "diffuse prior equilibrium," which considered a competitive general equilibrium model as only one of many possible models.[63] But Spiro Latsis, like Telser, calls the attempted extensions via imperfect competition and monopolistic competition a failure. He insists that the dominant research program in the theory of the firm remains "situational determinism," that is, "highly constrained reaction." He viewed Chamberlin's controversies with Chicago as "mere family quarrels."[64]

Chamberlin did, at least, battle with Chicago for his theory. One must conclude that part of Robinson's lack of interest in her own theory of imperfect competition was that it did not become a part of Keynes' General Theory, which she embraced.

The attention that Chamberlin and Robinson attracted was brilliant but brief. The Keynesian revolution riveted attention elsewhere. World War II intervened. Robinson's concerns (though not Chamberlin's) turned toward Keynes. Still, the two of them did wreck the old value theory, and economists have yet to pick up the pieces.

JR

CHAPTER FIVE

Keynesian Conversion in Both Cambridges

Joan Robinson became an initiate and apostle simultaneously with the emergence of Keynesian thought. She was thoroughly of a Keynesian mind at least by 1933, three years before the appearance of Keynes' *General Theory of Employment Interest and Money.* This was the result of an evolution rather than an instantaneous change in her thinking. The process involved her as a leader in the Circus and as confidante of Keynes in his battles with critics of his *Treatise on Money.*[1] She also wrote two articles which provided insights into the then-current developments. Again, it is pertinent that these events took place during economically depressed times.

The Circus was first an informal and then a formal discussion group which met to discuss Keynes' *Treatise on Money* after its publication in October 1930. Austin Robinson related, "[W]e were busily reading it and digesting it. . . . Inevitably some of us—Richard Kahn, Joan Robinson, Piero Sraffa, James Meade, and myself—found ourselves arguing together about it. What came to be called the 'Circus' first emerged by accident rather than design."[2]

The initial informal talks took place in Kahn's rooms at King's. Soon the meetings were expanded to seminar size, though participation remained by invitation. (Austin Robinson, Kahn, and Sraffa interviewed undergraduates who expressed a wish to be invited.) The more formal meetings occurred between January and May 1931. Keynes took no part in the seminar. After each meeting, however, Kahn would report orally to Keynes the subject matter and lines of argument.

James Meade gave his impression:

> From the point of view of a humble mortal like myself Keynes seemed to play the role of God in a morality play; he dominated the play but rarely appeared himself on the stage. Kahn was the Messenger Angel who brought messages and prob-

lems from Keynes to the "Circus" and who went back to Heaven with the result of our deliberations.[3]

Joan Robinson was also in close contact with Keynes. He regularly consulted her about his exchanges with other economists, particularly concerning his running battle with Hayek over the *Treatise*. Her first article on the unfolding theory was the "Parable of Saving and Investment," written in the summer of 1931, after the formal meetings of the Circus. In this article, she addressed criticisms by Hayek of Keynes' analysis. Hayek argued that it was theoretically impossible for savings and investment to be unequal. Keynes had claimed in the *Treatise* that there was no automatic mechanism in the economic system to keep the two rates equal, "provided that the effective quantity of money is unchanged." Robinson used a parable of gold and green peas to defend Keynes' argument.[4] However, she also criticized Keynes' use of an assumption of constant output in the face of changing levels of saving, investment, and prices.

She wrote to Keynes before submitting the article to *Economica* (where some exchanges between Keynes and Hayek had taken place): "My dear Maynard, I hope you will like my green peas. If you have any suggestions perhaps you could send this back with notes. If not send me a post card saying O.K. and I will send another copy which I have by me to *Economica*. . . ."[5] Keynes replied: "My dear Joan, This is excellent. . . . I think that the green peas and gold parable may help people a good deal."

Keynes made some suggestions, and countered her criticism of him with:

> I think you are a little hard on me as regards the assumption of constant output. . . . My own general reaction to criticisms always is that of course my treatment is obscure and sometimes inaccurate, and always incomplete, since I was tackling completely unfamiliar ground. . . . But the real point is not whether all this is so, as of course it is, but whether this sort of way of thinking and arguing about the subject is right. And that is what I am grateful to you for defending and expounding.[6]

After the success of the green peas, and many further discussions with Keynes and members of the Circus, Robinson wrote a second article, "The Theory of Money and the Analysis of Output." This article is credited with presenting the new theory of employment "as far as it had got in 1933."[7] Robinson attacked crude forms of the quantity theory of money and tautologies which begged the question of unemployment. She both praised Keynes for showing that one could attack the problems by thinking in terms of the demand for output as a whole, and blamed him for failing to see where his analysis led. She also cited examples of Keynes' "failure to realize the nature of the revolution that he was carrying through." She insisted that the "Theory of Money" be relieved of its "too-heavy task" and that instead the analysis of output proceed.[8]

She called for an economist who would tackle the problem of how changes in the price level affect the amount of employment and the wealth of the community.[9]

Due to editorial or publishing delays at *Economica* where the first article had been accepted, both articles appeared in 1933, one in February and the other in October, though the first had been written nearly two years earlier. Many years later, this circumstance was to create an interesting incident which involved two Americans. After Keynes' death in 1946, Paul Samuelson remarked in a footnote to an obituary:

> I should like at this point to pass a clue on to the future historian of economic thought. What was happening in Cambridge in the months between Mrs. Robinson's patient elucidation of an aspect of the *Treatise* entitled "A Parable on Savings and Investment" . . . and her publication of "The Theory of Money and the Value of Output" . . . ? Could it be that Mrs. Robinson was let in on a little secret in between?[10]

Joan Robinson believed it was Samuelson's hint that led Lawrence Klein to date the birth of *The General Theory* between February and October 1933. She wrote, "I tell this tale as an awful warning to historians." Since the first article was part of the working through of the *Treatise*, it is not surprising that by 1950 Robinson found it "somewhat tedious" and declined to collect it.[11]

The second article, written three years before Keynes' *General Theory* was published, remains the basis for her claim that the Circus did at times get ahead of Keynes in stating the "point of his revolution."[12] Samuelson later changed his mind about these two articles. He said,

> Joan Robinson's 1933 article on "The Theory of Money and Output" (which I now look at in a different way, both as a creative force in its own right, but also as simply a reflecting signaling device)—whatever the date when this article was actually written, I thought of it in my 1946 obituary of Keynes, as showing that they had by then arrived at the theory of output. It now looks as if what was arrived at was a realization that therein lies the variable for which you must find the equation, and the actual formulation of a theory of output was a little bit later. I'm assuming she was in close touch throughout with Keynes.[13]

So much was happening so quickly that the historical process can never be reconstructed. For the participants in the revolution, these were exciting days. Joan Robinson wrote of these times, "In the days following the meetings of the Circus there was a clear distinction between those who had seen the point and those who had not. Austin Robinson said that we went about asking: Brother, are you saved?"[14]

Part of the excitement was that the young economists saw that a non-Marxian solution to the problems evidenced by the depression was evolving. Lorie Tarshis, a Canadian, who was a student at Cambridge in the early thirties and later had a long career at Stanford University, found that one of the distinguishing characteristics of his fellow students of economics at Cambridge in that period was that they "seemed to have a much greater difficulty in accepting [Marx's] *Capital* than did students in other fields." Even before *The General Theory* had been published, Tarshis was confident that Keynes "could show us how to run a capitalist economy that was not subject to crisis."[15] Robinson has argued that "the 'Keynesian Revolution' in Western academic economics is rightly so called. For without Keynes' wide sweep, his brilliant polemic, and above all, his position within the orthodox citadel in which he was brought up, the walls of obscurantism would have taken much longer to breach."[16]

The word of what was happening at Cambridge spread to London, where Abba Lerner was a student of Hayek's at the London School of Economics. An extension of the argument between Keynes and Hayek was debated by their students and younger colleagues. The argument was not only over theory but over policy as well. Lerner suggested that the younger generation on each side should get together and settle the debate amongst themselves. They arranged a weekend meeting at an inn halfway between London and Cambridge. The Robinsons, Meade, and Kahn represented Cambridge and Lerner brought several contemporaries, including Sol Adler, Ralph Arakie, and Aaron Emanuel.[17]

The object was to argue each point out on its merits. These meetings were spirited affairs. Lerner wrote Joan Robinson after one of these weekends that their support of Hayek "must give the impression of a subordination of reason to faith. . . . The weekend was certainly a success for us inasmuch as we were brought into close contact with a doctrine which we had certainly not given the attention it deserved, but we feel you did not 'get your money's worth'. We did not get at the roots of our differences."[18] He wrote again in November: "Miss Webb showed me your letter. . . . It is high time we got to grips with our differences. . . . I do not think that your diagnosis of the trouble—that we have the propensity to think you 'nuts'—is correct. . . . There is rather, at least on our side, a fear of appearing foolish by asking too elementary questions which are really not fundamental ones." He inquired about the Cambridge meaning of "income" and "saving" and "investment goods."[19]

There are several more letters asking questions and discussing concepts. Then, beginning in October 1934, Lerner spent a term at Cambridge, during which he and Joan Robinson had prolonged arguments.[20] Afterwards, Lerner "became for some time an only too fanatical supporter of Keynes," according to Robinson.[21] In November 1936, Robinson wrote in the footnote of a letter to Keynes, "Don't you think Lerner is a credit to me? I have got Heffers to sell offprints of his article which will be useful for our young men."[22]

English conversion, American pragmatism

Conversion to Keynesianism was probably exceptional outside of Cambridge University. Two anecdotal examples suggest reasons: Vivian Walsh, who was educated as an economist in England, was "struck by an important distinction between the reactions of young Americans as they encounter economics for the first time and the reactions I [Walsh] learned to expect from European, Indian and African students," particularly in discussions of the social implications of economic theory. In the English situation, Pigou's *Economics of Welfare* had a powerful social message. Not all economists agreed with Pigou. "The point, however, is that they all *spoke out:* they lived in an atmosphere in which they could speak their minds without fear on major issues and habitually did so." In that era, "To be reading economics at a university was to be an intellectual— possibly a radical intellectual—and did not at all suggest the image of a student at an American business school."[23]

Traditionally the American scene has differed from that in Cambridge, England. Samuelson has remarked that Thomas Kuhn "doesn't prove that we think about only one paradigm at a time. This is an oversharp distinction. Scientists are opportunistic: on Monday, Wednesday and Friday, I [Samuelson] can be a Say's Law person working with a Ramsey-Solow model with no problem of effective demand, while on Tuesday and Thursday I can work with another paradigm."[24] Such an eclectic attitude may be pragmatic. Certainly it excludes the kind of conversion to Keynesian thought that took place at Cambridge University.

On the other hand, North Americans who were at Cambridge University, like Canadians Lorie Tarshis and Robert Bryce, did come under the spell of the revolutionary times. This was true also of Michael Straight, an American undergraduate. Straight, at Trinity College from 1935 to 1937, has told of the excitement of the time. Like other Cantabrigians, he saw the Keynesian influence as all-pervasive:

> In Cambridge and throughout the free world, economic doctrine was dominated by the overpowering intellect of John Maynard Keynes. The largest lecture hall in Cambridge was crowded when Keynes, in a series of talks, set forth the principles of his General Theory. It was as if we were listening to Charles Darwin or Isaac Newton. The audience sat in hushed silence as Keynes spoke. Then, in small circles, he was passionately defended and furiously attacked.[25]

Keynes delivered three or four lectures on the General Theory during that period. Straight recalls that

> . . . they were attended by a very large audience, and they led at once to excited and at times acrimonious discussions. Joan and Kahn were the two young Keynesians who were in effect his apostles. Kahn was a dry lecturer; Joan in

contrast was brilliant. . . . She lectured to a large group of students. I remember that on one occasion she said to me, "I would look up from my notes and see you frowning at me. And I would think: Good God, I must have made some blunder!"

. . . She was of course being too generous. I frowned when I concentrated, trying to keep up with her. . . . Joan did not teach Marshall save to note where he was archaic and obsolete (i.e.: in assuming perfect competition). The way in which I marked up her *Economics of Imperfect Competition* suggests pretty emphatically that it was a text book. It follows that she would have been lecturing on matters related to the book, even in 1936. She was by far the most exciting and brilliant lecturer as far as economics students were concerned—leaving Keynes aside that is, since he did not lecture to students save to present in that one series the essence of the General Theory.[26]

Straight was supervised in Trinity first by Maurice Dobb and then by Dennis Robertson. As one of the three students who received First Class Honors, he was admitted to the Political Economy Club. He wrote,

I had a very close relationship with Dennis Robertson. Nonetheless, Keynes's General Theory was the most important and exciting intellectual development of the time; comparable perhaps to Darwin's Origin of Species. I was wholly caught up in the Keynesian movement, and, for that reason, asked permission to be assigned to Joan Robinson who was willing to be my supervisor. Robertson was, I believe, quite hurt by my request but it was granted."[27]

Straight said the "shift to Mrs. Robinson took some time." He had first to "force" his way to the "front rank of the two hundred students who were enrolled in the Economics Tripos."

At Cambridge the communist influence was separate from the Keynesian. Straight's first tutor, Maurice Dobb, was a leading member of the British Communist Party. Straight remembers him as "persuasive . . . when he turned to politics; as an economist, he had little influence."[28] Though Straight became a Keynesian, he also, partly under the influence of friends of his in the Apostles society, became a member of the communist movement. Years later the English read in their morning papers of the "middle-aged American belonging to a rich and famous family" who told the FBI of Anthony Blunt's association with Soviet Intelligence.[29]

How Keynes' ideas came to the United States

John Kenneth Galbraith has said, "Harvard was the principal avenue by which Keynes's ideas passed to the United States."[30] This parochial view is close to the truth. Two Canadians, Lorie Tarshis and Robert Bryce, were instrumental in bodily carrying Keynesian theory to Harvard. Both had left Canada in 1932 to read economics at Trinity and St. John's Colleges, Cambridge. They attended all of Keynes' lectures during this period of the development of the General Theory, and were members of Keynes' Political Economy Club. Bryce said,

> I need not say that I was impressed with Keynes; far better critics than I have described his able and complex mind. . . . I was most impressed by his institutional knowledge, and to this day I am still criticizing various professors, not only economists . . . because of a lack of knowledge of the institutional framework and processes of which they're talking. . . . Well, I was not just convinced, I was converted.[31]

As early as December 31, 1933, Keynes had written a letter to the *New York Times*, saying, "I lay overwhelming emphasis on the increase of national purchasing power resulting from government expenditure which is financed by loans." He also visited President Franklin D. Roosevelt during the summer of 1934 to press his case. Galbraith thought that "each, during the meeting, developed some doubts about the general good sense of the other."[32]

It is important to make a distinction between the *policies* which are loosely associated with the Keynesian revolution, and the *theory* of Keynes. Keynesian theory was macroeconomic in the sense that it approached the economy as a whole—total output, gross national product, and so on. Though Keynes suggested policies of deficit spending for the depression period, real Cambridge Keynesians never thought that policy was for all times. What Joan Robinson and others did was to apply the Keynesian tools to problems which included, but were not limited to, unemployment. Robinson's book, *Essays in the Theory of Employment* (1937), would provide such applications. In the United States what took hold was the *policy* aspects of Keynes and of course some of the *tools* without their being embedded in his *theory.* This has meant that American Keynesians have differed from Cambridge Keynesians, not so much in policies, but in both the use of Keynesian tools and in their understanding of Keynesian theory.

The intellectual situation at Harvard in 1933–34 was one where the traditional theory taught seemed irrelevant to the problems of the depression. Business cycle theory existed, but it was based on the assumption that cycles were self-curing in the long run. Walter Salant summarized: "In short, the classical compartment was long-run and the business cycle introduced dynamics, but there was no concept of any long-run equilibrium of output." Salant recalled that the situation was typified by the publication in 1934 of *The Economics of the Recovery Program*, written by seven members of the Harvard economics department. Samuelson said of this book, "I think the Boston *Transcript* called it in a headline, 'Harvard's second team strikes out'. Schumpeter was the only full professor among them; almost all the others were then only assistant professors or instructors." Salant believed this book was by "people as up to date, presumably, in theory as you would have found at the time." Yet, while there were chapters like "Helping the Farmer" or "Helping Labor," there was no chapter on fiscal policy and monetary policy. "Monetary policy is discussed in the chapter called 'Higher Prices' but fiscal policy receives only scattered attention."[33]

During the spring of 1935, Bryce, still at Cambridge, went down to the London School of Economics one or two days a week "as a missionary." He attended Hayek's seminar on monetary theory: "This was the nearest concentration of heathen available from Cambridge and I was encouraged to go and tell them about it, about what the true faith was." The next year, when he went to Harvard for six months, he used these same notes "to start the indoctrination of Harvard, before the *General Theory* appeared. I hesitate to say that it gave them a running start on the *General Theory,* but at least I had softened things up a little by the time the book came out."[34] Bryce found his listeners at Harvard quite receptive. So Canadian missionaries brought the new theory to Harvard.

In 1936–37, after Keynes' work had been published, Tarshis was also in the Harvard area, having accepted a job at Tufts University. He was trying to work out some extensions of the General Theory and thought it might help to sit in on some of the Harvard seminars:

> Harvard was so empty in 1936-37 of people who properly understood Keynes— apart from Bob Bryce—that going it alone was almost mandatory. I got more out of my students in that first year than from Harvard's best. In the second year matters improved: Emile Després and Bill Salant came back for a year, I got to know Dick Gilbert, by then Paul Sweezy had moved from Hayek to Keynes, and theory and policy could be discussed without our getting bogged down in, "Well how can *I* [Investment] be equal to *S* [Saving] if I save and put the money under the mattress?" I should have mentioned Alvin Hansen too, whose seminar I attended.[35]

Alvin Hansen was at the height of his career when he gave his presidential address to the American Economic Association in 1938 on a topic which came to be called his "stagnation thesis." In it he supported Keynes' view of the impact of population change on national income.[36] Harvard had hired Hansen away from the University of Minnesota, leaving Minnesota without a Keynesian. Graydon Anderson went there to study under Hansen and found himself studying traditional economics instead. Galbraith remembered Hansen as "about fifty, an effective teacher and popular colleague. But, most of all, he was a man for whom economic ideas had no standing apart from their use."[37] Only two years earlier, Hansen had written a rather cool review of *The General Theory*.[38]

However, Hansen changed his mind, and began persuading his students and younger colleagues that they should not only understand the ideas but should "win understanding in others and then go on to get action." Without intending to, he became a "leader of a crusade."[39] William J. Barber claims that Hansen was "one of the few Americans of prominence in the older group to make such a shift."[40]

Galbraith explained how Harvard in turn influenced Washington in the late 1930s: "Hansen's seminar in the new Graduate School of Public Administration was regularly visited by the Washington policy-makers. Often the students overflowed into the hall. One felt that it was the most important thing currently happening in the country and this could have been the case. The officials took Hansen's ideas, and perhaps even more, his sense of conviction, back to Washington." There was also a strong migration of younger economists from Harvard to Washington.

Within a year, wrote Galbraith, Paul Samuelson was recognized as "the acknowledged leader of the younger Keynesian community. . . . Here was a remedy for the despair that could be seen just beyond the Yard. It did not overthrow the system but saved it. To the nonrevolutionary, it seemed too good to be true. . . . The old economics was still taught by day. But in the evening and almost every evening from 1936 on, almost everyone in the Harvard community discussed Keynes."[41]

This did not occur at other American universities. For example, when Kenneth Arrow studied at Columbia in 1940-41, he remembered that "Keynes was not mentioned (for that matter the *General Theory* was not mentioned even in the course on business cycles, though there were some glancing references to the *Treatise on Money*)."[42]

However, those at Harvard who were caught up by the new theory thought of it as a revolution but not an unchallenged one. Certain powerful people at Harvard remained unconvinced. Samuelson says flatly that Schumpeter was "jealous of Keynes and he was very jealous of the fact that all his best students went tearing after this fellow." Then Samuelson added a self-revealing comment: "Schumpeter misunderstood the mind of a graduate student who doesn't really care a rip about policy but all he wants is an elegant model."[43]

As we have seen, Chamberlin ignored these developments altogether, while Haberler preferred his work in business cycles. In such an atmosphere, Harvard Keynesians were not "converts." They had not shared in the process of the development of the ideas as Joan Robinson had; rather they had been handed the new theory on a silver platter. Like all inheritors of wealth, they had to be different from the persons who accumulated the wealth. Within a decade, Joan Robinson would begin to call them "bastard Keynesians."

In retrospect, many prominent American bureaucrats who applied policies that were identified with Keynes, and who were often called Keynesians, were neither converts nor theoretical Keynesians. (In this they were like Pigou in the 1930s, who agreed with Keynes' policies, but not with his theories.) Hansen told Salant in 1971 that neither Marriner Eccles nor Harold Ickes nor Harold Moulton were Keynesian, though all had favored public spending during the depression; that "people who in the old days supported public works as offsets to 'lapses' from full employment were not Keynesians.'' Salant said Hansen's point was, ''it takes a theory to kill a theory.'' Keynes had provided ''a theoretical refutation of the established theory to make acceptable a policy that flies in its face.''[44] Keynesianism in America, then, was not a revolution so much as a convenience, as far as policy-makers were concerned. Is it possible that Keynesian models became fashionable in some quarters merely because they could be made elegant?

Chicago says no

Keynes' ideas did at least receive an enthusiastic hearing at Harvard. At the University of Chicago, this was not so. Milton Friedman became curious about the very different impact which the Keynesian revolution had on Abba Lerner as compared to himself. Both were students at the time of the change in ideas. Friedman thought the difference was due to Lerner's being at the London School of Economics, ''where the dominant view was that the depression was an inevitable result of the prior boom . . . that the only sound policy was to let the depression run its course. . . .''

Thus for Lerner, ''when by contrast with this dismal picture, the news came seeping out of Cambridge [England] about Keynes's interpretation of the depression and of the right policy to cure it, it must have come like a flash of light on a dark night.''

However, added Friedman,

> . . . the intellectual climate at Chicago had been wholly different. My teachers regarded the depression as largely the product of misguided governmental policy—or at least as greatly intensified by such policies. They blamed the monetary and fiscal authorities for permitting banks to fail and the quantity of deposits to decline. Far from preaching the need to let deflation and bankruptcy run their course, they issued repeated pronunciamentos calling for governmental action to stem the deflation.''[45]

In one action, a telegram was sent to President Herbert Hoover, January 1932, recommending continued deficit spending to finance public works. It was signed by twenty-five representatives of the University of Chicago. These included Paul Douglas, Harry Gideonse, Frank Knight, H. C. Simons, and Jacob Viner. Frank Knight wrote to Senator Robert F. Wagner, ''As far as I know economists are completely agreed that the Government should spend as much and tax as little as possible, at a time such as this.''[46] Friedman wrote, ''There was nothing in these views to repel a student; or to make Keynes attractive. On the contrary, so far as policy was concerned, Keynes had nothing to offer those of us who had sat at the feet of Simons, Mints, Knight, and Viner.''[47]

The comparative excitement over Keynes thus varied from school to school in the United States. What preceded and what followed Keynes was eclecticism.

Keynes' tools, but not his views, became a part of traditional economics. His policies had always had a following. The difference was that Keynes was unwilling to recommend policies for which there was no theory, so he had to invent one. Some Swedish economists thought he might just have asked them.

What is the Keynesian revolution which never occurred on this side of the Atlantic? In Joan Robinson's view, Keynes had done three things, which constituted his revolution: (1) Keynes had "brought back something of the hardheadedness of the Classics" in seeing the "capitalist system as a system, a going concern, a phase in historical development"; (2) Keynes had "brought back the moral problem that *laisser-faire* theory had abolished"; and (3) Keynes "had brought back *time* into economic theory . . . which took economics a great stride forward, away from theology and towards science."

From the American point of view, what Keynes had done was to provide a theory of aggregate output and a new set of concepts to economists of all persuasions. His theories strengthened the hands of institutionalists who were already convinced that intervention in the economy was necessary to its very functioning, and who were oriented toward historical and evolutionary approaches. To the new breed of economists, led by Samuelson, Keynes' models offered new avenues for the exploration of economics using mathematical tools. This latter result was no doubt contrary to his intent for, as Joan Robinson remarked, "Keynes was very skeptical of econometrics."[48]

The theory of employment

As a convert, Joan Robinson turned increasingly toward proselytizing the theory of employment. In addition to her several articles, she published two books. The first was addressed to her colleagues; the second to her students whom she fondly called "our young men." Both appeared before there was widespread understanding of Keynes' General Theory in North America. Her first book on the new topic was a group of *Essays in the Theory of Employment*.[49] These essays applied the General Theory to the mobility of labor and other questions not considered by Keynes. They were not studies of data related to these problems but of the theoretical issues involved. Keynes advised her during the writing of these essays. At one point, he wrote, "I beg you not to publish. For your argument as it stands is most certainly nonsense." She rewrote that chapter and then Keynes found that the "general effect is splendid, full of originality and interest." She replied, "I am more grateful than it would be decent to say for all the trouble you have taken, and I am most delighted to have your approval in general for the book."

Joan Robinson's adversarial spirit was prominent in the *Essays*. Keynes urged "a slight modification of what you say about Hicks. . . . Your fierceness may quite possibly land you in trouble in some quarters, but I like these chapters and would not dissuade you from publishing them as they are." She replied, "I hope I shan't be landed in any libel actions."[50]

Robinson's thrusts were not stylistic tricks but signaled an intention to force reactions. Plain talk became a recurring theme in her career. Austin Robinson gave the Cambridge view of the Circus group when he said, "Let me emphasize again that it is only by argument, by conflict if you like, that economics makes progress. It is painful, but it is inevitable, and never to be deprecated."[51]

Before the reviews were in on the *Essays*, Joan wrote to Keynes: "Do you remember I asked you about doing a told-it-to-the-children book? I knocked up this for immediate use with our own pupils, and now I am rather inclining to the idea of polishing it up and publishing it." Keynes did not give his immediate blessing. He replied ambivalently on March 25, 1937. On April 20, however, he wrote, "I do not really feel the least objection in the world to your preparing something on the line you have, that is to say, practically following my *General Theory.* Indeed I expect you are right that it would be found extremely useful."[52] And Robinson went ahead, producing in her *Introduction to the Theory of Employment* a much used "pony" for understanding the new General Theory.[53]

Both of Robinson's new books were published the year her second daughter was born. (Barbara was born October 9, 1937.) The books were widely reviewed. Among economists, Keynesians inevitably praised them; traditional economists found fault. Roy Harrod, a Keynesian, praised the *Essays* as "another volume of great distinction in economic studies."[54] R. G. Hawtrey, a traditional economist, complained "it is a matter of regret that Mrs. Robinson is tempted to apply her great powers of economic analysis and reasoning to matters so remote from real life."[55] Henry Smith of Oxford particularly admired the statement in Robinson's *Introduction* that the controversies and the political issues are bound up together.[56]

Robinson's former pupil Michael Straight wrote a review for the then left-wing magazine, *The New Republic*, warning that social reformers should understand the Keynesian theory. "If used in the right way, General Theory may be made the economic theory of social reform . . . but unless the theory behind the reform movement is understood by its supporters, the movement may not survive the continual opposition of vested interests; and the theory itself may come to serve precisely the opposite interests from those for whom it was written."[57]

Through the publication of these two volumes, Robinson established her reputation and image in the United States as a Keynesian.* But it was to be an evolving image, for like Keynes, she soon found new interests. Robinson was no more intent on defending past work for the sake of standing firm than Keynes was. To her Marshallian tools she had added the Keynesian tools, but she was not ready to make either a dogma.

World War II, which began for England in 1939, brought an abrupt end to the "Years of High Theory."

---

*See Appendix Note 5.1 Other reviews of *Essays* and *Introduction to the Theory of Employment*.

JR

CHAPTER SIX

How Economics Changed in England and America

Even before World War II began, there were important new currents in economic analysis besides the value and Keynesian revolutions. The world depression and the political upheavals it brought had set in motion a widespread migration of economists moving from Eastern and continental Europe to England and the United States.

Kalecki comes to Cambridge

Soon after the publication of *The General Theory* there appeared on the Cambridge scene someone who had, without traveling the same intellectual path, arrived at similar conclusions to Keynes'. This was the Polish economist Michal Kalecki, whom Joan Robinson called "a strange visitor who was not only already familiar with our brand-new theories, but had even invented some of our private jokes." Kalecki had published his own theory of employment in Polish in 1933, and Joan Robinson came to insist that he therefore had the claim to priority of publication. But, as she noted, Kalecki had started his thinking not with orthodox economics, but with Marx, "the only economics he had studied."[1] Austin Robinson said that Kalecki "could talk English of a sort, and he shouted at the top of his voice." Robinson admitted that he "used quietly to vanish from the room in which Kalecki and Joan were arguing. Each trying to shout down the other became absolutely deafening."[2]

Kalecki had left Poland on a Rockefeller scholarship and it became increasingly apparent that he should not return, given the political situation there. In spite of some efforts on the part of Joan Robinson and Sraffa to gain a position for Kalecki, he was not invited to remain permanently at Cambridge. Nevertheless, his was a permanent influence.[3]

Joan Robinson reads Marx

As Michael Straight and Lorie Tarshis made clear, Marxism was *au courant* among undergraduates in Cambridge during the 1930s, not only because of the depression, but also in solidarity with the democratic forces in Spain which were aligned with communists and anarchists against the new fascist powers during the Spanish Civil War. Keynes' teaching offered an alternative economic program to Marxism and most students of economics at Cambridge were Keynesian converts rather than Marxists. In answer to a direct question as to whether there was any Marxism in the Circus, Austin Robinson replied, "I don't think so, not at that stage. Piero Sraffa, of course, was the best Marxian scholar among us. Joan in 1931 had not yet begun her interest in Marx. I don't think there is a Marxian influence into this at that stage."[4] However, there was Marxist thinking about. Joan Robinson wrote a review of John Strachey's *The Nature of Capitalist Crisis* for the *Economic Journal*.[5] At that time, she seemed to feel uneasy about what she was saying. Keynes, as editor of the *Economic Journal*, had written urging her to send him her review, since "[it] is already very late." Keynes reassured her, saying that "the point about Marx and Ricardo is, I assume, common knowledge."[6]

Joan Robinson was thirty-two years old when she wrote this review. Her sympathies were Keynesian. She saw Strachey's work as that of "a sincere and intelligent amateur," who had analyzed the views of economists ranging from Major (C. H.) Douglas and J. A. Hobson to Friedrich von Hayek. Strachey found all of them wanting, writing, "To what strange paradoxes has our argument led us!" for in order to increase expenditure on investment during a slump, it is necessary to reduce consumption!

At the time of the review, the General Theory was well advanced, though not yet in print. Robinson did not refer to it. She noted instead that Strachey should have insisted that any analysis which asked us to reduce consumption was faulty. Instead, "The moral he draws is quite different: . . . the capitalist system is inevitably doomed."

Robinson attacked Marx, expressing disappointment that Strachey had stopped short of "admitting that the labor theory of value is a piece of formalism." She put Marx with orthodox theorists who, like Ricardo, thought there was a tendency for the rate of profit to fall. "Mr. Strachey's remedy is to overthrow the capitalist system, not to abandon the assumptions." What she would have had him do was to question Say's Law: "We cannot be recommended to overthrow a system merely because its economists have talked nonsense about it," she concluded.[7]

The review of Strachey's book is important in the development of her thinking. Strachey apparently criticized her for judging Marx without having read *Capital*. According to Lord Kahn, this exchange led Joan Robinson to read Marx: "She was interested in Marx, but that is the reason why."[8]

Immigrant economists and American economics

Both English and American teaching have been powerfully affected by scholars who in peripatetic careers carry ideas with them to new places and settings. Sraffa's arrival in England in the 1920s had already deeply influenced the thinking about value theory. Hayek had taken Austrian economics to the London School of Economics. American economics was similarly influenced by notable refugees and immigrants, many of them fleeing from anti-Semitism in the 1930s.[9] Higher education in the United States benefited from the immigration of economists of great talent and established reputation. These included Joseph A. Schumpeter, Jacob Marschak, Oskar Lange (who also visited Cambridge), Tjalling Koopmans, Abraham Wald, Abba Lerner (who had left the London School of Economics for the United States), Gottfried Haberler, and Wassily Leontief. There were others, but each of these was important to Joan Robinson as a colleague who influenced American mainstream teaching, bending it away from what she considered the proper course—Keynesianism and nonmathematical method.

In part because of the continental influence of these immigrants, postwar American economics absorbed the European (Walrasian) equilibrium theory and econometrics in addition to Keynesian economics, all in varying degrees of lumpiness. Those among these immigrants who were not mathematical theorists or econometricians were often anti-Keynesian (Schumpeter and Haberler).*

A split in methodology

G. L. S. Shackle claimed that the split in methodology between mathematical and linguistic economics began in the 1930s. The division was between

> . . . the mathematicians who wrote down in formal algebra the conditions to be fulfilled and found the solution by formal manipulations . . . and the conceptualists who saw before them on the intellectual workbench a number of component parts, some still serviceable, some perhaps requiring to be reshaped, some obsolete; and who then tried to conceive a workable composition made from such parts, a machine as much like the old one as possible, improved in just the indispensable respects but not radically transformed.[10]

Joan Robinson remained with the conceptualists to the end of her life. One of her notable aphorisms was that not knowing mathematics, she had to think. She was in fact, however, following the method of Marshall and Keynes, who did know mathematics, but did not trust it.† In the United States conceptualists,

---

*See Appendix Note 6.1 Immigrants bring continental economics to the United States.
†See Appendix Note 6.2 Mathematical theory at Cambridge before World War II.

particularly the institutionalists, lost influence to mathematical economists. Samuelson dates the "withering away" of the institutionalist influence from the 1930s or 1940s.[11]

Axel Leijonhufvud raised a question of whether, for the immigrants, the choice between conceptualism and mathematics did not have some ideological motivation. Having interviewed a number of the immigrants, Leijonhufvud concluded that there was a clear indication "in some cases" of this impetus.

> They had been brought up in and they had seen value-laden social science, and they wanted to put the science on a basis that made it immune to that kind of ideology. It was also related to a desire to imitate the successful physical sciences. When you look at the Cowles Commission [which was near Chicago], Marschak played an important role, and Friedman and Arrow and others were researchers there, so there is some influence of the immigrants on this generation.[12]

Methodological differences lay dormant during World War II, but after the war the American influence with a preference for mathematical methodology in economics ascended to new heights, in step with the United States' political influence. At first Joan Robinson was unaware of and unaffected by this shift of power. Toward the end of her life, she remained the last of the important conceptualists, since Cambridge University in the postwar years no more resisted the clarion call of mathematics than did MIT of Cambridge, Massachusetts.

World War II: England and Cambridge

The tight little world that Robinson inhabited at Cambridge was brutally interrupted by World War II. Americans generally forget that Europe had been in turmoil at least since 1936, when the Spanish Civil War began. In March 1938, Germany annexed Austria; in September, the Munich pact sacrificed much of Czechoslovakia to Germany. When, in April 1939, Great Britain and France abandoned their policy of appeasement, it was easy to see that dark days were ahead. The fact that Robinson had been granted a full lectureship in 1938 was probably not as satisfying as it might have been in more peaceful times. The Italian-German military alliance of May and the Soviet-German nonaggression pact of August cleared the way for the German invasion of Poland September 1, 1939, and the British, French, and Commonwealth countries (except Ireland) declared war on Germany. (The United States was not to enter the war as an ally for two long years.) Within eleven months of the declaration of war, France signed an armistice with Germany (June 22, 1940), and Great Britain was left to bear the brunt of the Battle of Britain which began in the air in August and lasted until October 1940.

No institution, no individual was unaffected. Probably the stress of it all was the cause of Joan Robinson's missing a term of teaching in 1939. Her parents came to live in Cambridge when the college where General Maurice taught was evacuated from London.[13]

The London School of Economics (LSE) was also evacuated to Cambridge, bringing with it Nicholas Kaldor and Friedrich von Hayek. Thus, for a time, both Robinson and Hayek taught on the same campus, though for different universities.

Austin Robinson had played a role in this move of the LSE. The London School was to have been evacuated to North Wales, but as Austin Robinson was walking one day down King's Parade across from King's Chapel, he encountered Carr-Saunders, the principal of LSE. Robinson took him to lunch at Sidney Sussex. The principal and the Cambridge University treasurer, who was also a fellow of Sussex, "worked out across the lunch table how the London School of Economics might come to Cambridge." Austin Robinson claimed no influence in this move except as catalyst. "Over lunch we agreed that we could pool all lectures for the duration of the war, because I had already got a job I had to go off to, and a lot of people at the London School of Economics had jobs they had to go to in wartime and by pooling resources, we could release at once half the staff of the two institutions."[14]

Of the regular Cambridge faculty, Pigou, Dobb, and Joan Robinson were still in residence. Both Lionel Robbins and Hayek were on the lecture list in 1939, the year that Kaldor lectured at Cambridge for the first time. Wartime visitors included Werner Stark and P. N. Rosenstein-Rodan.[15] Although Pigou retired as professor in 1944, he continued to teach. Robertson, who had moved to the LSE in 1938, returned to Cambridge as professor upon Pigou's retirement. Keynes was offered this professorship, but refused and strongly recommended Robertson.[16]

Joan Robinson began reading Marx in 1940 "as a distraction from the news."[17] "I began to read *Capital,* just as one reads any book, to see what was in it; I found a great deal that neither its followers nor its opponents had prepared me to expect."[18] Her *Essay on Marxian Economics* was published in September 1941, at the height of the war, in spite of paper shortages.

The Soviet Union was now an ally. On June 22, 1941, Germany had invaded the Soviet Union and was moving rapidly through that country. The United States entered the war in December 1941. Robinson's book was not reviewed in the United States until 1944. During this period, besides writing her *Essay on Marxian Economics,* she also contributed a few articles, pamphlets, and reviews.[19] She reviewed Schumpeter's *Capitalism, Socialism and Democracy,* published in 1942, which predicted that capitalism could not survive in the long run. Schumpeter hated socialism, the supposed successor of capitalism, but he thought he could see the handwriting on the wall. At the time his book appeared, fascism was considered an aberrant form of capitalism. I. G. Farben was operating full swing, in some cases employing concentration camp labor—cheaper labor than other modern capitalists had dreamed of having. That same year the heroic stand of the Soviets at Stalingrad resulted in the surrender (February 2, 1943) of the German Sixth Army and a turning point in the war.

In reading Schumpeter's book, Robinson found herself "swept along by the freshness, the dash, the impetuosity of Professor Schumpeter's stream of argument." But she asked, "Does present-day experience really lead us to expect that capitalism is destined to a quiet and pious death?"[20] She remained unconvinced.

During the war, the remaining Circus members drew together for Sunday walks. These rather strenuous undertakings (often of ten miles) included Joan Robinson and Kahn and usually Sraffa, Kaldor, and Austin Robinson, if he were visiting for the weekend from his wartime post in London. In 1945, Ruth Cohen, who had spent two years at Stanford and several at Oxford, joined the economics department as assistant lecturer and the Sunday walks as well. As for students, there were few "straightforward Cambridge students, but there were a large number of cadets."[21] Among these cadets was Harry G. Johnson from Canada, who was a student in the academic year 1945–46.

Cambridge University after World War II

Life at Cambridge was never to be quite the same again. Keynes died in 1946, having negotiated brilliantly at Bretton Woods in spite of failing health. Austin Robinson returned to Cambridge, finding there "all sorts of schools of thought that developed in the war years which were in conflict [with each other] and all wanting to take over Cambridge economics." As for himself, he was determined to make Cambridge economics much more quantitative than it had ever been before. To accomplish this, he helped to initiate the department of applied economics. "At the same time mathematicians were scrounging to make economics more mathematical and the Marxists were all panting to make Cambridge economics more Marxist."[22] Thus the postwar Cambridge economics department would become more like American departments—less unified in methodology and purpose.

John Veazey wrote a vivid account of studying economics at Cambridge in 1948. The division between the Keynesian and non-Keynesian faculty was "highly personalized." Dennis Robertson was the non-Keynesian leader, "bald, elegant, feline." Joan Robinson led the Keynesians in "battle dress of dyed navy blue, brilliant and ferocious." Since Robertson's return in 1944 as professor, the teaching had been polarized, with the first year covering the traditional Marshallian studies and the second year consisting of lectures in the "immensely exciting Keynesian economics."

Veazey arranged to be taught by Robinson, but his college tutor, "who denounced her as a Communist, refused to pay her." Veazey would read her his essays, which she would dismiss "with contempt in supervisions that lasted two hours or more." He would walk back to his rooms through the dark and sometimes cry himself to sleep. He vowed that he had never since thought so hard as in trying to write those essays. During this period, Paul Samuelson visited Cambridge. Veazey recalled one meeting of the Marshall Society, where "Robinson had a fearful row with Paul Samuelson, and for reasons unclear, annihilated him."[23]

Controversy had not always been welcome at Cambridge. In Keynes' undergraduate years, the prevailing view had been that conflict of opinion should be avoided, as "unsatisfactory and distasteful."[24] But the impact of the revolution in value theory, the activities of the Circus, and the Keynesian revolution made controversy inevitable. Keynes was clearly the provocateur of this newer style, but as Veazey suggested, Joan Robinson was a general in the fray. As long as she lived, the controversial style continued, for she early adopted Keynes' mature view that "controversy may assist progress and be healthy in spite of being disagreeable."[25]

Canadian protégé gone astray: Harry G. Johnson

Into this divided postwar Cambridge came a Canadian-American with whom Robinson was to have a long association. Harry G. Johnson arrived at Cambridge University in 1945 in a Canadian corporal's uniform. As with the American Michael Straight, Johnson's first supervisor was Maurice Dobb.[26]

Aubrey Silberston, who became a friend of Johnson's, said that it was Joan Robinson who, being in close touch with students, "met Harry and recognized his quality. She asked Dennis Robertson . . . to waive the usual rules and accept Harry as a member of the Political Economy Club."[27] Johnson himself, not always generous toward Robinson, merely recalled that "student membership was by invitation, automatic for Part I Firsts and almost so for II.1's, that is, for A or top B students."[28] "I was eventually invited to join this club," he said.[29]

Johnson wore his corporal's uniform for the rest of the year, bearing, along with the 150 American GIs, "the brunt of the discrimination against North Americans . . . which the British love to inflict on ordinary Americans."[30] "Canadian-style," Johnson attended most of the lectures. Dennis Robertson's lectures were brilliant, "but you had to know at least enough economics for a Ph.D. before you could understand them."[31]

> The only exciting lecturer was Joan Robinson; and this, again, was a bit of a surprise. We had had female lecturers at Toronto who appeared nicely dressed and perfumed and wearing skirts and other kinds of recognizable sex symbols. But we all assembled for Joan Robinson's lecture—and in strode a mousy-looking woman, wearing a sort of blouse-and-vest combination on top and a pair of slacks down below, and sandals. She proceeded to put an elbow on the lectern, peered out at us, and started out in a rather flat monotone. "Well, it's very difficult these days to lecture on economic theory because now we have both

socialist countries and capitalist countries.'' Everyone thought, "Gosh, what a wonderful new idea!"[32]

After this year at Cambridge, Johnson returned to the University of Toronto as an instructor, earning a master's degree there in 1947 and an M.A. at Harvard in 1948.[33]

He must have made quite a favorable impression at Cambridge as an undergraduate, for while at Harvard, he heard from Dennis Robertson inquiring whether he was interested in returning to Cambridge to teach. Johnson found Robertson's handwritten letters "infernally difficult to read," but he must have been somewhat flattered to be asked to return. In 1949, Johnson began lecturing there and was made a Fellow of King's College.

Johnson wrote with acerbity of those years at Cambridge. He rather objected to being made to call Kahn "Richard" and to becoming involved several times in controversies with Joan Robinson. His view of her efforts to have mental exchanges with him was: "She would send me a handwritten note in the morning, and I would scribble my answer by noonday; and then I would get a note back in the evening saying, 'Where you made your mistake is as follows. . . .' I could keep that up for two days; but I soon wearied of the game. Why was I the only one who made hopeless mistakes in pure theory?"[34] Robinson saved one of his replies, a friendly enough answer to her inquiry on one of her papers closing with, "as I don't disagree with you, I don't think a discussion is really necessary. Yours, Harry."[35]

Johnson remained at Cambridge from 1949 to 1956. In his retrospective account, he failed to mention that he shared the lecture series conducted by Richard Kahn and Joan Robinson, and thus there was a reason for collaboration and for airing of differences.[36] Both Kahn and Robinson "took a lot of time with Harry." Lord Kahn, when asked whether he could account for Johnson's bitterness toward Robinson said, "He bit the hand that fed him."[37]

Some of Johnson's antipathy toward Joan Robinson seems merely sexist. He claimed that Robinson "—I would say not necessarily consciously—certainly used the attitudes of the opposite sex toward her as an excuse for behavior which often would not have been acceptable from a male economist, I mean in terms of distorting arguments and abusing the privileges of academic discourse."[38]

Apparently it was also during this period at Cambridge when Johnson established his prodigious drinking and writing patterns. In his lifetime, he produced over 500 academic papers, 150 book reviews, thirty-five books and pamphlets, and hundreds of newspaper articles.[39]

After he had been at Cambridge for two years, Johnson took Silberston aside and opened his filing cabinet: "Look at that," he said, "nineteen articles in the last year!" Silberston, though a close friend, stopped calling on Johnson. He recalled that Johnson "would open his door, look loweringly at you, say curtly 'I'm busy!', and close the door in your face." On the other hand, Silberston insisted that Harry Johnson was a loyal friend "and would go out of his way to help you."

Both Johnson and Silberston were attendees of the secret seminar organized after the war. The seminar was held weekly during the term in Kahn's rooms in King's College. The membership was selective. The criteria for membership were, according to Silberston, "a mixture of political and personal consider- ations, including one's degree of commitment to Keynesianism . . . it was an understood thing that Kahn and Joan Robinson were in charge of it." Silberston thought that in the early 1950s the seminar was at its height, and "we had some wonderful evenings."[40] Johnson's view was that the purpose of the seminar "was (on the one hand) to direct the strategy and tactics of left-wing academic political maneuvers in the Faculty, and (on the other hand) to marshal all the intellects in support of Joan Robinson's version of Keynesianism."

The degree of Johnson's commitment to Kahn's and Robinson's understood version of Keynesianism is difficult to establish. Perhaps all along Robertson had sensed that Johnson would be an ally of the Robertsonian views. Perhaps it was difficult for Joan Robinson to imagine that an intelligent person might not agree with her.

In the meetings of the secret seminar to which he was probably invited as one of the supposed "believers," Johnson recalled mainly discussions of loanable funds versus liquidity preference. Silberston remembered a broader list of topics. Particularly, Johnson remembered that the secret seminar "increasingly became a forum for the advance testing of the technical analysis of Joan Robinson's *Accumulation of Capital*."[41]

There was no chairman. Usually one of the members read a paper and that paper would be discussed. Silberston said that "one of the features of the seminar were the frequent interventions at all times of Joan and Nicky [Kaldor]. It descended into near-chaos at times."[42]

For Johnson,

. . . the fact was that the "secret seminar" became more and more an occasion for Joan Robinson to present her new thoughts and writings on her criticisms of "orthodox" capital and growth theory and the constituents of the analysis that ultimately became *The Accumulation of Capital*—with the adoption of a title borrowed from Rosa Luxemburg and the use of Hebrew letters to stress the departure from traditional analysis and the adventure into new analytical fron- tiers that the book sought to achieve.

Johnson understood the "in" jokes, but apparently did not relish them. He added,

The presentation of the work of others became less frequent, and regarded more and more as an interruption of the main task of assisting Joan Robinson to complete her revolutionary work on the theory of capitalist growth. I understand that after I left the seminar deteriorated still more, with increasingly intense arguments between Joan Robinson and Nicholas Kaldor over their rival theories of capitalist growth.[43]

The secret seminar seems to have symbolized for Johnson the intellectual forces that drove him from Cambridge. He left there for Manchester in 1956. In 1973 he recalled his reasons for going:

> It was about that time—the 1950s—that I began to appreciate the difference between scientific and ideological motivations for theoretical work. I began to realize more and more that Cambridge people in my judgment were perverting economics in order to defend intellectual and emotional positions taken in the 1930s. In particular, for them Keynesian economics was not a theoretical advance to be built on for scientific progress and improved social policy. It was only a tool for furthering left-wing politics at the level of intellectual debate.[44]

Silberston, admitting that there was ''a political element in the economics of people like Joan,'' found equally strong political elements in others outside Cambridge. He believed that ''Joan Robinson has always striven after the truth as sincerely as anyone else in the profession, and with a good deal more passion and conviction than most.'' Though Silberston was not particularly close to Johnson at the time of the latter's leaving, he had not ''sensed a profound disaffection with Cambridge economics on his part while he was there. . . . [Johnson] seemed to share their general view of the subject.'' Apparently Johnson fooled Robinson and Kahn as well.

Silberston believed that at Manchester Johnson came under the influence of Ely Devons with his ''Manchester school'' free competition views, and that Johnson ''really turned against Cambridge economics and economists. Indeed, it was a feature of Harry's career after Cambridge that he seemed to lose few opportunities of belittling its personalities, its system and its contributions to economic theory.''[45]

Johnson had a distinguished career after leaving Cambridge, but he burned the candle at both ends. He did not complete the requirements for his doctorate at Harvard until 1958, when he collected a list of his published papers into the book, *International Trade and Economic Growth.* He then returned to the United States as professor of economics at the University of Chicago. Two years later Johnson became editor of the *Journal of Political Economy,* and from 1966 to 1974 he combined his professorship at Chicago with a commuting professorship at the London School of Economics. He died in 1977 at the age of fifty-three, a life span about equal to Joan Robinson's career as an economist.

Looking at their published articles, one is struck by the similarity of Johnson's and Robinson's reliance on geometric illustrations and proofs. Johnson also shared with Robinson another trait—his "zeal for exploring the policy implications of analytical concepts." Also like Joan Robinson, Johnson attacked friend and foe with the same verve. In his famous paper, "The Keynesian Revolution and the Monetarist Counter-Revolution," he "ridiculed" the monetarists and predicted their "imminent decline." What separated Johnson from the Cambridge group which had first recognized his merits was what Mark Blaug calls his "general suspicion of vulgar Keynesianism, interventionism, and collectivism in all its varieties."[46]

Johnson admired Robinson's *Economics of Imperfect Competition*, which he had always considered exceptionally fine. In his course in the theory of income distribution at the University of Chicago, *Imperfect Competition* was included as a required text in the theory of rent section. But when his course covered the theory of economic growth, Robinson was not even among the recommended, much less required texts.[47]

Some of his affection from the early days must have survived, however, for Joan Robinson was invited to address Johnson's students when she visited Chicago.* Silberston thought this an instance of Johnson's never underestimating the great ability of Robinson (as well as the others at Cambridge).[48]

In 1961, soon after going to Chicago, Johnson addressed the American Economic Association on "The General Theory after Twenty-five Years."[49] In this address, which was certainly not wholly critical of Cantabrigians, he gave credit to Joan Robinson, Richard Kahn, "and others" who had extended the theory of liquidity preference to comprise choices among a multiplicity of assets. He did not here attack the "Marxo-Keynesians," as he did on other occasions.

Nevertheless, his address provoked Robinson. She remarked in a review of his book *Money, Trade and Economic Growth*, "Unluckily, he was just the wrong age to make such an appraisal." She argued that a younger man "would have felt obliged to do some research to find out the orthodox theory that Keynes was attacking; an older man would himself have once been submitted to it." She was patronizing: "Professor Johnson, who grew up amid the controversies around the *General Theory*, thinks that he knows what it was all about, but actually he does not discuss the changes which Keynes' theory made in economic thought; he is confronting it with its own bastard progeny."[50]

Johnson, in whom both Robinson and Kahn had invested a great deal of effort and attention, spurned his teachers, their views and sympathies, and the place, Cambridge itself. But clearly he learned much from them. And Joan Robinson learned from his work that there was bastard Keynesianism in the United States.

Postwar American economics

As the mantle of chauvinism was slipping from English to American shoulders, economics as a study in the States was developing a distinct "mainstream." This

---

*See Chapter 14.

mainstream accentuated mathematical theory and deductive reasoning.

The takeover of the mathematical economists from conceptualists (who included both institutionalists and traditional theorists like Chamberlin) is symbolized by the publication of Paul Samuelson's *Foundations of Economic Analysis*, written before the war (1937). Samuelson was awarded the David A. Wells Prize at Harvard (1941), and the book was finally published after the war in 1947.[51]

Another landmark, published in 1941 but begun in the 1930s, was Wassily Leontief's *The Structure of American Economy 1919-1929: An Empirical Application of Equilibrium Analysis*.[52] In this work, Leontief utilized a matrix to solve the input-output problem. Shackle asserted that Leontief's book and its method represented "a great landmark in logical-quantitative economics, 'econometrics'."[53]

The changeover to mathematical theory could not be immediate. On the title page of *Foundations*, Samuelson quoted J. Willard Gibbs' statement: "Mathematics is a Language." A language requires time to learn, particularly when the teachers in place do not know it. (In 1947 Leontief was the only mathematical economist at Harvard, and many schools had none.) By the time *Foundations* was reissued in 1964, however, Samuelson could announce with pleasure, "a new generation is growing up with that minimum training in mathematics which opens the door not only to the language of science but also to new realms of aesthetic delight."[54] This aesthetic delight was, of course, just the characteristic that Marshall and Keynes distrusted.

Even at the outset, there were detractors of the new mathematical route. Kenneth Boulding, in a review of the first edition of *Foundations*, had warned readers that he felt "a certain sense of rapidly diminishing marginal productivity in the application of mathematics to economics. . . . It may well be that the slovenly literary borderland between economics and sociology will be the most fruitful building ground during the years to come and that mathematical economics will remain too flawless in its perfection to be very fruitful."[55]

Samuelson quoted this warning in his reissue because he felt that in the time between the two printings, "mathematical economics ceased to be the preoccupation of an *avant garde* and became part of the main stream of creative scholarship."*

Samuelson added: "Far from closing out the prewar tradition of Jevons, Edgeworth, Walras, Wicksell, Marshall, Pigou, Frisch, Hotelling, Hicks and Allen, Tinbergen and Leontief, the *Foundations of Economic Analysis* can now be seen as part of the dawn we associate with the postwar names of K. J. Arrow, R. M. Solow, J. Tobin, M. Allais, H. Wold, L. Hurwicz, M. Morishima, F. Hahn, and numerous other economists all over the world."

Samuelson fairly chortled. Without claiming there was nothing to be done by nonmathematical scholars, "still it is true that, whether in Washington, Rotter-

---

*See Appendix Note 6.3 Samuelson on mathematics in economics.

dam, or Moscow, we today live in a golden age for analytical economics: duality, turnpike theorems, stability of dynamic equilibrium—was there ever a time of more fruitful progress in conquering such new frontiers of knowledge?''[56] This was Samuelson's mood of pride during the early sixties, when Joan Robinson was trying to engage him in arguments about the possibility of multiple equilibrium solutions, and perhaps represented the zenith of the influence of the MIT Keynesians on the American mainstream, as well as a benchmark of the success of the mathematicians in pushing for their methodology.

A more recent insight into the characteristics of the American mainstream is a letter written by Leontief which appeared in *Science,* July 1982. There Leontief charged that economists, unlike their colleagues in the natural and historical sciences, had ''developed a nearly irresistible predilection for deductive reasoning.'' Leontief documented the fact that more than half (and a growing proportion) of articles in the *American Economic Review* between 1972 and 1981 had been devoted to ''mathematical models without any data.'' In lamenting the decline in the number of articles of a more empirical, policy-oriented, or problem-solving character, Leontief suggested how this decline in interest in real problems on the part of the profession had come about and how it perpetuated itself: ''That state is likely to be maintained as long as tenured members of leading economics departments continue to exercise tight control over the training, promotion, and research activities of their younger faculty members and, by means of peer review, of the senior members as well.''[57]

Even so, other worlds of nonmathematical economics and some interest in inductive methods persisted, particularly in applied fields. The most famous theoretical alternative to the mainstream of mathematical Keynesianism (which was oriented toward intervention) was the Chicago tradition and its monetarism (oriented toward laissez-faire).

Robinson and the quantity theory of money

Joan Robinson never had much exchange with the American monetarists. Since the early days of the Circus she had written periodically on the role of money, particularly the rate of interest. The quantity theory of money was, however, anathema to her.[58] She had considered that theory bankrupt from the early 1920s when Keynes ''had thoroughly exposed its hollowness'' in his *Tract on Monetary Reform.* Still, when she was an undergraduate, she remembered that the ''Quantity Theory was dominant,'' in spite of Keynes.[59]

In her famous early essay, ''The Theory of Money and the Analysis of Output,'' Robinson compared the Cambridge quantity equation with the American Irving Fisher equation. She noted that it was in protest against the naïve view of the theory of money that Mr. Kahn set out the Quantity Equation for hairpins: ''Let P be the proportion of women with long hair, and T the total number of women. Let V be the daily loss of hairpins by each woman with long hair, and M

the daily output of hairpins. Then . . . $MV=PT$." Her objection was a philosophical one—that the equations were all "tautologies without causal significance."[60] As early as 1933, then, Robinson was arguing that the quantity theory of money needed to be moved out of the way insofar as teaching was concerned.

But she did not let it go at that. When she discussed Roy Harrod's trade cycle in 1936, she noted with approval that Harrod had further exposed the "Quantity Theory truism," elaborating "suggestions made by Mr. Keynes."[61] In regard to the post-World War I German inflation, she agreed that the quantity of money was important, "not because it caused inflation, but because it allowed it to continue."[62] Thus Robinson was quite unprepared for what seemed to her "the extraordinary vogue [in the 1960s] of an argument so unplausible as the Quantity Theory of Money." She blamed this resurgence on the refusal to admit that "the level of prices is determined by the level of money-wage rates."[63]

In her 1972 presidential address to Section F of the British Association for the Advancement of Science, she announced her belief that

> . . . the extraordinary revival of the quantity theory of money in recent years (in an even more hollow form than of old) must be accounted for by the longing to have some kind of theory that provides something to tether the value of money to, some defense against the horrid thought that under laisser-faire the private-enterprise system does not tend towards equilibrium in any way at all.[64]

In her one reference to Milton Friedman in her *Collected Economic Papers,* she accused him of confusing the "changes in the stock of money deliberately brought about by the authorities and the effects of changes in the flow of government expenditure."[65]

Robinson argued that Keynes had broken down the old dichotomy between monetary and "real" forces which can be relied on to reestablish equilibrium when a monetary system or its managers misbehave. But this "old dichotomy still haunts modern theory. It has been revived in a curious form by the Chicago school." The Chicago view amounts to a belief that "money is the only thing that matters."[66] She added, "There is an unearthly, mystical element in Friedman's thought. The mere existence of a stock of money somehow promotes expenditure. But insofar as he offers an intelligible theory, it is made up of elements borrowed from Keynes."[67]

Milton Friedman visited Cambridge for a year soon after the war. He was not invited to the secret seminars. Lord Kahn said of this,

> I don't think we did invite him. I think we felt he was out of his element. There was such a wide gap between his economics and our economics that it was impossible to bridge it. I enjoyed talking to him but at that time I felt he regarded economic discussion as sort of a game. It was only after he went to India that we

began to take him seriously, going from one country to another and actually destroying them. I forget what inflation rate Chile now has. . . .[68]

Other postwar developments

Three other developments were important to Joan Robinson's intellectual growth and to the world of economics. The first was the institution of the Marshall Lectureships which brought outstanding foreign lecturers to Cambridge.*

The second development affected the whole profession. Both in England and North America, the number of economists increased dramatically. As Phyllis Deane observed for England: "The wartime trickle of newly trained economists expanded into a flood as soon as the universities returned to normal." This was due in part to the high prestige gained by economists in government service during the war.

The third, a consequence of the war and postwar efforts to manage economies, was the "unprecedented and irreversible flow of statistical data, data designed to measure the levels, structure and growth in the nation's economic activity in relation to a Keynesian macroeconomic framework."[69]

The resulting dispersion of activity among so many persons and over mountains of data was to change economics forevermore. New associations and journals came into being to serve the new specializations, methods, or even the life views of the many economists. Perhaps it was in answer to this diversity that American economics developed what is called a theoretical mainstream. Joan Robinson, no longer a powerful influence on this mainstream, remained a power nonetheless. Her role in postwar economics became once again the one she had played in the Circus, that of challenging the orthodoxy.

---

*See Appendix Note 6.4 American visitors to Cambridge and Marshall lecturers.

JR

CHAPTER SEVEN

Joan Robinson and the Marxists

Until 1942, Joan Robinson's reputation in North America was that of a brilliant theorist (*Imperfect Competition*, 1933) who had a thorough understanding of the new Keynesian economics (*Introduction to* and *Essays in the Theory of Employment,* 1937). Robinson's renown placed her in a position of leadership of both traditional and contemporary economic theory.

The changing image of Joan Robinson

With the publication of *An Essay on Marxian Economics* (1942), the image of Joan Robinson in the minds of Americans began to change.[1] The Cambridge program in economics ignored Marx. In the United States, the acquaintance of a graduate student with Marx depended on where he was studying. At Berkeley, for example, Galbraith did study Marx under Leo Rogin, but even there, Thorstein Veblen was considered the more powerful theorist.

Schumpeter was one of the few resident economists in America who had a thorough academic background in Marx, for Marx was taught in Europe. However, Schumpeter's view was that Marx's pure economics had become obsolete by the early 1920s. Schumpeter spoke in horrified tones of those who "actually try to revitalize Marx's pure economics, thus joining forces with the surviving neo-Marxists." He considered Joan Robinson and Paul Sweezy "outstanding examples" of this heresy. He could understand Oskar Lange's acceptance of "much or all of Marx's economic sociology"; he could understand anyone who might wish to pay respect to Marx's historical greatness, or even those who might try to "Keynesify Marx or to Marxify Keynes." But he did not count Robinson among those who tried to Keynesify Marx; instead, her essay was "something of a psychological riddle."

Schumpeter could even recognize that Marx might appeal to English and

American students as "something new and fresh, something that differs from the current stuff and widens his horizon." But to revitalize Marx's pure economics when this had "become obsolete" was to Schumpeter a step backward. He could not understand "economists of high standing" who had "turned Marxists." He argued that "the evolution of a genuinely scientific economics" required economists, even those who are socialists, to realize that "it is a mistake to believe that something is to be gained for socialism by fighting for the Marxist or against the marginal utility theory of value."[2] And this is undoubtedly what he taught Paul Samuelson, who in turn taught the many.

Thus Robinson soiled her image in Cambridge, Massachusetts with the publication of her *Essay on Marxian Economics*. This had an effect on the reception of all of her subsequent work and, some believe, on her eligibility for a Nobel Prize. American institutionalists, on the wane after the war, were perhaps puzzled by this departure of hers, this interest in a predecessor of Veblen. Orthodox theorists, who had seen imperfect competition neatly added to perfect competition models in some sort of additive theory of knowledge, could ignore her plea that they should read Marx. Keynesians, interested in neither imperfect competition nor Marxism, were busy working out the meaning and application of the General Theory. Marxists—and there were still a few in the early fifties—had to deal, as did Schumpeter, with the phenomenon of an economist of high standing commending Marx for his understanding of effective demand while attacking his labor theory of value.

An Essay on Marxian Economics

In her introduction, Robinson came immediately to the point. The fundamental differences between Marxian and traditional economics were two: first, orthodox economists assumed the capitalist system to be a part of "the eternal order of Nature," while Marx thought it "a passing phase"; second, orthodox economists saw a harmony of interests in the community, while Marx conceived of economic life in terms of a conflict of interest. Thus orthodox economists became apologists for the status quo, while, equally unfortunately, Marxists saw Marx as "an inspired prophet."[3] After setting up her understanding of Marx's definitions, Robinson tackled his labor theory of value which, she concluded, failed to provide a theory of prices, though it was useful in showing the development of the capitalist system.[4]

Robinson was interested in Marx's "long period theory of employment" but found it no better than orthodox theory in providing any law governing the distribution of income.[5] She felt Marx's explanation of the alleged tendency of profits to fall over time "explains nothing at all."[6] She admired his efforts to understand the role of "effective demand" but again, found Marx failing "to realize how much the orthodox theory stands and falls with Say's Law." Because of this failure, Marx became "confused."[7] As a Keynesian, Robinson had been struck by Marx's emphasis on effective demand. However, she thought Marx was wrong to accept the orthodox teaching of the falling rate of profit. Most emphatically, she said, "no point of substance in Marx's argument depends upon the labor theory of value." Her contempt for the labor theory of value is what separated her from the Marxists:

> Voltaire remarked that it is possible to kill a flock of sheep by witchcraft if you give them plenty of arsenic at the same time. The sheep, in this figure, may well stand for the complacent apologists of capitalism; Marx's penetrating insight and bitter hatred of oppression supply the arsenic, while the labor theory of value provides the incantations. [8]

As Lord Kahn remarked, "she realized there was something seriously wrong with the labor theory of value. This is something that she learned from Marx, and she thought that the civilized economists ought to read Marx and very few do." [9] The rest of her *Essay on Marxian Economics* compared Marx's ideas with the orthodox and Keynesian theories, presenting criticisms of both Marx and orthodox economists.

The fallout of writing on Marx

No careful reader of her essay could possibly conclude that Joan Robinson had become a Marxist. Yet because of this essay and her continuing interest in some aspects of Marx's economics, she was now to be subject to name-calling, even by those who otherwise had enjoyed her company, her books, and the intellectual stimulation her work provided. The foremost of the name-callers was to be Harry G. Johnson, who ought to have known better. Johnson would call her one of the Marxo-Keynesians, for example. [10]

Johnson carried over his attitude toward Robinson's politics when he wrote about the capital controversy: "Thus Joan Robinson writes the most arid of technical capital theory in the belief that, contrary to all the empirical evidence, capitalism cannot possibly work, because she can to her own satisfaction make a nonsense of the concept of the production function and of distribution by marginal productivity." [11] However, her writing of this essay on Marx opened up other possibilities for Robinson. She was asked, for example, to write the introduction to the English edition of Rosa Luxemburg's *Accumulation of Capital*. [12] This gave her an opportunity to object to the fact that both Marxists and academic economists had neglected Luxemburg's theory of the dynamic development of capitalism, which, after reading it for the first time, she greatly admired.

Robinson criticized Luxemburg on many points, including style: "The argument streams along bearing a welter of historical examples in its flood, and ideas emerge and disappear again bewilderingly." [13] Robinson admired the title enough to use it in her own book four years later. Luxemburg's views on colonial investment particularly impressed Robinson. Essentially, Luxemburg's thesis was that such investment may be a powerful influence in fending off stagnation in the capitalist sector of the colonial power. Robinson referred to this idea in her own *Accumulation.*[14]

Nevertheless her *Essay on Marxian Economics* was written from the vantage point of a Keynesian convert, one acquainted with the development of Kalecki's Keynesian-type theory arrived at from Kalecki's study of Marx. In the second edition of the essay, Robinson reported that Sraffa teased her, saying that she had treated Marx "as a little-known forerunner of Kalecki."[15] Robinson was impressed with certain similarities, such as the resemblance between Marx's "absolute over-production of capital" and Kalecki's "analysis of the top of a boom." Still, she thought the resemblance was superficial and that Kalecki was right in asserting that the level of effective demand regulates the total profits, while Marx thought profits were limited because of other factors.[16] Furthermore, she was not ready to accept Marx's notions of distributional effects on the income of workers. She feared that the Marxian view, like the orthodox, implied that unemployment was caused by rises in real wages.[17]

From the very first, Joan Robinson approached Marx with critical curiosity. Sraffa's jibe is a good indication of her distance from Marx in her thinking.

Reception of *An Essay on Marxian Economics*

The English and North American reviews of Robinson's new book stressed her Keynesianism, her criticism of Marx and of orthodox economics. Only her English colleague, Gerald Shove, introduced the idea of her personal politics.

In some ways, the fairest review of her *Essay on Marxian Economics* in the United States was the very first one, which was not published in an economic journal but in *The New Republic.* Harold Mager, lawyer and economist, titled his review "Marx Without Incense." He concluded that "the comrades would be hard put to make out a case against Mrs. Robinson as a Marx Baiter. She attacks orthodoxy in economics with at least as much gusto and with much more penetration and insight than have the Marxists."[18]

The English, or rather Cantabrigian, reception of the essay was represented by Shove's review in the *Economic Journal.* In the *Essay* he also found both "a critique of Marx and an attack on the doctrines of the 'orthodox economists'." Agreeing that it was high time that trained economists "set themselves to sift the truth from the error" in Marx, Shove found her well qualified for the task: "Politically her sympathies are with Marx, and she is fully abreast of the latest developments in economic analysis."[19] Shove was not satisfied with her criticism of the orthodox economists. Of his fourteen-page review, ten pages were an airing of his objections to her "onslaught on the 'orthodox' economists."[20] He stoutly defended Marshall and others, and flatly concluded that Robinson had "allowed her moral sentiments to run away with her."[21]

Shove also questioned her attributing to Marx "modern ideas about the nature and significance of 'effective demand'." Nor was he pleased with her "glazing over" the "infamous" alleged contradiction between theory of value in Volume I, and the theory of prices in Volume III of *Capital*. But on the whole, Shove thought her commentary on Marx succeeded "as few commentaries . . . do, in being sympathetic without becoming uncritical."[22]

One American review was written by a Marxist, Leo Rogin of Berkeley. He concluded that while her essay was sympathetic and very able, it would not change the pattern of neglect of Marx. Rogin believed academic economists would continue to neglect what Marx had initiated, namely, "an exhaustive investigation of the category of capital and the pathology of capitalism."[23] Rogin also objected to Robinson's line of argument. He predicted that she "cannot be, consistently, both a Keynesian in the scope of her criticism of capitalism and of its theoretical defenders, and a Marxian in the choice of her strategic factor." He explained that the strategic factor for both Marx and Robinson is "the institution of private property in the means of production." It is this institution "in the last resort" and not the maldistribution of income which "is the cause of crises for both of them."

Rogin thought that as a Keynesian, Robinson was inevitably subject to "blind-spots." He accused Keynes in particular of relying on a "dubious assumption of constant technology in the short run" and offering only "an impressionistic treatment to long-run accumulation." Marx had concerned himself with secular long-run accumulation, but Keynesians had not. Mostly, Rogin was disappointed that Robinson had not tried to refine and develop the implications of Marx's model for the "maldistribution of income," which both Marx and Robinson had recognized as "the central inescapable contradiction of capitalism."[24]

Rogin, writing in 1944, seems to have been pointing in the direction in which Robinson's own thought would lead her—toward a concern with long-run accumulation and its linkage with income distribution. Like Shove, Rogin felt that she had neglected important parts of Marx's argument. Rogin wished Robinson had not stopped her analysis short of the chapter in *Capital* Volume III on "Internal Contradictions," where she would have encountered Marx's highly abstract theoretical model of a society "composed only of industrial capitalists and wage workers."

This advice is particularly interesting in view of the kinds of Marxian models which emerged in the 1950s and 1960s, the so-called two-sector Marxian models. Rogin put his finger on a reality: in the early forties, Joan Robinson was still predominantly a Keynesian. Only after working her way through problems of "accumulation" in the 1950s did she find herself more influenced by Kalecki (and thus Marx) than by Keynes (and thus Marshall). Those who, like Shove, seemed to suspect some political motivation for an interest in Marx and those who, like Schumpeter, saw some disgrace in any effort to understand or use Marx's pure economics, would have been greatly disturbed at subsequent events.

For Robinson's *Essay on Marxian Economics* was merely the early sign of a revival of concern with the problems which classical economists, including Marx, had set for themselves, and of a return of interest in Marx himself.

Changing views of Marxism and political economy

In the United States, most postwar departments of economics retreated from political economy in favor of what came to be called "scientific" or "positive" economics. This may have been partly due to the influence of the immigrant economists. Graduate students now studied mathematics rather than Veblen and Marx, even in the western outposts of higher education like Berkeley. Furthermore, the controversies in American academe in the late forties were more often about Keynesian economics than about Marx. For example, when Lorie Tarshis's Keynesian elementary text was published by Houghton Mifflin in 1946, one virulently right-wing anti-New Dealer, Merwin K. Hart, took the trouble to send letters of warning to every trustee of every university in the country.[25]

During the 1950s, the Cold War and the McCarthy Senate hearings further dampened interest in political economy. Suspected Marxists were fired or never hired. Outspoken Marxists virtually disappeared from academic departments of economics. Economists who had attended the Bretton Woods Meetings cowered. Some college presidents invited the FBI and CIA to screen their faculties and report back. Robinson was told that people who went to Washington, D.C. bookstores and asked for *An Essay on Marxian Economics* had their names taken.[26]

Over the years, Robinson's interest in Marx evolved and matured, as evidenced in her collected papers. However, she was steadfast in several views: (1) that the labor theory of value was useless as an analytical tool; (2) that nevertheless Marx should be studied and admired; (3) that Marxists themselves were usually ideologues. But she also saw Marx increasingly as a major classical economist who, though influenced by Ricardo, was unique in asking the right questions, questions that all economists should be asking.

Her "Essays 1953," which were first published by the Students' Bookshop at Cambridge, touched on Marx but also offered some straightforward revelations of her own political position. She considered herself a "left-wing Keynesian," by which she meant that unemployment "is not just an accident—it has a function." This took her beyond Keynesianism into political economy. On the other hand, she threw this gauntlet down before the Marxists: "I understand Marx far and away better than you do. . . . What I mean is that I have Marx in my bones and you have him in your mouth."[27]

Robinson seemed to feel it her duty to point out mistakes in Marx, for example, his allegedly confusing the stock of embodied labor with the annual flow of value given up by embodied labor. But she also perceived similarities in Marx, Marshall, Ricardo, and Keynes, to her great amusement. Robinson wrote her

1953 essays "in a hilarious mood after reading Piero Sraffa's Introduction to Ricardo's *Principles,* which caused me to see the concept of the rate of profit on capital is essentially the same in Ricardo, Marx, Marshall and Keynes." She also argued that Marshall's and Keynes' "quasi-rent" and Marx's "surplus" were much like Ricardo's "rent," and that all had political elements. However, by the time she collected the essays in 1973, Robinson had changed her mind about this: "It was a mistake to identify the nature of surplus in Marx with Ricardo's rent. Marx did not think profits were a bad thing. He thought that exploitation was a necessary part of the process by which capitalism will destroy itself." Robinson persisted in her general view that Marx should be neither shunned and ignored nor worshipped and adored. As she remarked in 1973: "This pamphlet [*An Essay on Marxian Economics*] caused a great deal of offense, both to Marxists and to Walrasians."[28]

As for ideas and ideology, Robinson considered it

> . . . the greatest possible folly to choose the doctrines that we want to accept by their political content. It is folly to reject a piece of analysis because we do not agree with the political judgment of the economist who puts it forward. Unfortunately, this approach to economics is very prevalent. The orthodox school has been largely stultified by refusing to learn from Marx. Because they do not like his politics they attend to his economics only to point out some errors in it, hoping that by refuting him on some points they will make his political doctrines harmless.

In 1955 she accused orthodox economists of neglecting the most valuable parts of Marx's theory. Among the valuable parts she placed "the schema for expanding reproduction," which was "rediscovered and made the basis for the treatment of Keynes' problem by Kalecki and reinvented by Harrod and Domar as the basis for the theory of long-run development." If Marxian economics had been taken seriously, she argued, "it would have saved us all a great deal of time."[29]

In 1969, Robinson understood Marx primarily as a Ricardian (but not a minor one) who had taken Ricardo's ideas and had given them "a political twist that made them disagreeable and dangerous."[30] "In particular, Marx did not 'construct' a theory of prices based on labor value. He took it over from Ricardo as an established, orthodox doctrine and it seemed to him obvious."[31] And Marx made the point that "to understand political motivation we must look to material interests."[32]

In 1977 she clarified this view. Marx had founded his analysis upon the English classics, but he imported into it an element that they lacked: "the view of capitalism as a particular economic system that had grown up in particular historical circumstances and would evolve according to its own inherent characteristics." Now in her seventies, Robinson was seeing western Marxists as "intending to promote" a renaissance of political economy. Robinson did not find the Marxists doing a good job of this. She still found Marxism "impoverished by refusal to refine and develop the analytical apparatus that Marx bequeathed."[33]

From her own words one cannot deduce that Joan Robinson was ever a Marxist. Yet G. C. Harcourt has at times referred to her as a "neo-Marxist" in the sense that "Joan Robinson and Piero Sraffa made some of Marx's views respectable."[34]

The record is clear. Robinson never shrank from seeing herself as a bourgeois rather than a Marxist economist; she never flagged in her determination to criticize orthodox economic theory; she was equally eager to criticize Marxists when she thought them wrong; her contempt for "believers" as distinguished from "scientists" extended in all ideological directions. Her contributions to the American *Monthly Review* underline these consistent stands.

Monthly Review articles (1950–1983)

Joan Robinson wrote fourteen pieces which were published in the *Monthly Review*, an intellectual magazine treating political and economic issues from a Marxist point of view. Leo Huberman and Paul Sweezy, the editors, invited her to contribute. Robinson commented freely on her travels to communist countries and on her opinion of the American-Soviet Cold War. Through these articles, she reached many readers who learned to trust her honesty and fearlessness. Prominent Marxists or socialists shared this forum with Robinson, often in symposia. The object was to present points of view to magazine readers that otherwise were unavailable in the United States. For example, the *Monthly Review* editors periodically contacted Michal Kalecki in the early 1950s to learn about economic issues in the world economy. Kalecki was, at that time, one of the authors of the United Nations World Economic Report.[35]

Sweezy had known Robinson since his student days in 1932–33 at the London School of Economics, where he, like Lerner, studied under Hayek. The resumed contacts were friendly but professional in nature. Huberman became very fond of Robinson, according to Sweezy, and would make a "big point of taking care of her when she was in New York."[36] Most of Robinson's contributions to the *Monthly Review* were in the form of reprints of articles which were less technical and more political than her theoretical articles for economic journals. She was identified for the readers as "one of the leading economic theorists in the English-speaking world today," which she surely was.[37]

Her articles over the thirty-two years of their appearance revealed Joan Robinson's evolving opinions on topics ranging from rearmament to the realities in the socialist countries she was to visit: the Soviet Union, North Korea, China, and Cuba. Her reputation for being anti-American was occasionally documented, for she believed that the 1950s Cold War and American rearmament were threats to world peace. In addressing Americans, she would often observe that all Keynesianism had meant to the United States was that American prosperity could be built on rearmament. Since she was never a political activist, her left-wing reputation rested in large part on her opinions expressed in these articles. Over time, her judgments on a number of subjects were modified. The outstanding example of such a change of mind is the case of the Cultural Revolution in China.

Joan Robinson visited China six times. During these sojourns, she traveled extensively both by river and overland in much the same way that tourists do today. Her first visit was in 1953, when she was vice-president of the British Council for the Promotion of International Trade with China. She made another visit in 1957 and was accompanied on this one by Sol Adler, an American friend who had studied economics in England. The two of them were very impressed with the leadership of the cooperatives they visited in 1957, for the co-op manager seemed to have all of the economic details at his fingertips. Robinson liked to attend the Chinese opera in the evening. During the day she would go to visit cooperatives (in 1957) or communes (after 1963), a factory, a museum, or one of the many universities. On a journey in the late 1960s during the Cultural Revolution, she found the trip very unrewarding until she reached Shanghai, where she could get a full report on the economic situation there. She often gave lectures, mostly on theoretical points, at one of the many universities. Mainly, her Chinese visits were concentrated on economic discovery.

Over the years, Robinson made many Chinese friends. The Chinese are great handshakers, said Adler. Robinson offered a more diffident, almost Edwardian handshake. In 1962 Adler became a resident of China and continued to see her when she made her visits. Adler remembers her as having something of the English bulldog in her temperament. His impressions of Robinson were, "She was basically a patriotic Englishwoman and yet also clearly an internationalist. She was neither a Marxist nor a communist, nor did she pretend to be either. Among her Chinese friends she was known for doing her own thinking, though she might consult them. She tended to think that the Chinese had a greater sense of reality than the Soviets." When she ran out of books, she would borrow from Adler. He found her tastes and character roughly that of the Bloomsbury group: she had their broadmindedness and love of painting and of classical literature. Adler added,

> Among other things, she was unquestionably a highbrow and she had the same tolerance of eccentricity and deep loyalty to friends. One other characteristic which is generally associated with the Bloomsbury group, although it is often—in my opinion wrongly—supposed to be British, was great reticence in the expression of emotions. This reticence was often mistaken for lack of feeling, both in her in particular and in the Bloomsbury group generally. Certainly in Joan's case this was wide of the mark since, if one knew her fairly well, one soon realized she had deep emotions.

On her last visit to China in 1978, she told Adler and other friends, "The romance has gone out of China for me." In one of her last letters to Adler she reminded him that she thought the labor theory of value was wrong because it did not allow for technical knowledge.[38]

The *Monthly Review* offered Robinson a forum for her views as a bourgeois economist. She lashed out right and left, antagonizing Marxists as well as any American jingoist or orthodox economist who might perchance read one of her articles. The following chronological summary tells this story.

Preparation for war: 1951[39]

Her first article, a reprint of an interview in the undergraduate magazine *Cambridge Today*, appeared in October 1951. Five years after World War II, she had been asked to comment as an economist on the current preparation for war. She replied, "The great question which overshadows everything is whether Russia is planning aggression, for, if not, our whole policy is nonsensical."

She had noted a strong tendency, "especially in American propaganda," to confuse military and ideological aggression. Already she could see that "the great boom in America built up on rearmament has gone too far for comfort . . . and yet the prospect of a peaceful *détente* and a sudden cessation of rearmament expenditure is a menace to their economy. . . . The line of least resistance is to keep on with it. That is what seems to me the biggest menace in the present situation." She never changed her mind about this.

Visit to Moscow: 1952

In April 1952, Robinson was a delegate to the Moscow Economic Conference. Most of her impressions were personal observations, including one that the Americans ought to watch their manners: "It is said that the British lost the Indian Empire because they were so rude. I think the Americans should be told that they are in a fair way to lose their allies." She began the sketch of her impressions with a quotation from a conversation overheard in the lobby: "First British Delegate (earnestly): I am sure you agree with me on the importance of telling the exact truth about all we have seen here. Second Ditto (disconcerted): That's all very well, but I don't want to have people at home saying that I am a Communist." Robinson told it as she saw it: "No tarts to be seen. No kissing in public . . . ." Robinson's general conviction was:

> Of course, on such a point there is no hard evidence to offer, but I soak through every pore the conviction that the Soviets have not the smallest desire to save our souls, either by word or sword. If they could once be really assured that we will leave them alone, they would be only too happy to leave us to go to the devil in our own way. If our local Communists think otherwise, they are the more deceived.[40]

The kinds of lopsided accusations of Marxism leveled at Robinson by anti-Marxists can be illustrated in connection with this rather innocuous pamphlet. T. W. Hutchison, a former student of hers, in whose books Robinson plays a prominent though derogated role, claimed that she made this "pilgrimage to Moscow in quest of Marxian hope." Hutchison wrote, "Mrs. Robinson was able to find the 'hope', originally 'released' by Marx, amply implemented and fulfilled in Stalin's Moscow."[41]

Having earlier in his book set up Robinson as an "enthusiastic" Marxian,[42] Hutchison alleged that Robinson was within ten years of her visit "comparing 'Stalinist' with 'McCarthyist' persecution."[43] Neither Robinson's enthusiasm for nor her criticisms of the Soviet Union pleased Hutchison.

Visit to China: 1953

In July of 1953 Robinson traveled to what the *Monthly Review* called the New China with a delegation of businessmen. She found laudable improvements: "Marx-Leninism is denying the complex of ideas and attitudes which they call 'feudal'," for example, selling children to pay the rent. She also observed, "what have long been commonplaces to us are new revelations to China, and Marx-Leninism gets the credit since it was the medium through which the revelation came." Marx-Leninism also, to her approval, denied "the sophistries of classical economics by which the doctrine of comparative advantages was used to justify the foisting of a permanent colonial status on the primary-producing countries, and has revealed to China that she can become a great industrial nation." She concluded, "China seems to me to provide the final proof that communism is not a stage beyond capitalism but a substitute for it."[44] This was, at least to some, an anti-Marxist statement.

Robinson admitted difficulties in trying to generalize about individuals, partly because of her dependence on interpreters. However, she finally found someone with whom she shared mutual friends, "and we got straight down to real talk." She observed that two-thirds of the inmates of a prison she visited were "counter-revolutionaries" and the rest were in for "ordinary crimes such as theft, traffic, manslaughter, or (among the women) beating their daughters-in-law."[45]

She wrote about her sightseeing and how the people looked. In her last letter, she explained the program for land reform: "You must not think of dukes, nor yet of village squires. Here ten or twelve acres was a large estate and the landlord was not much better educated than the peasant. A large part of the income that the landlords squeezed out of the country came from usury and from cuts out of taxes that they were responsible for collecting." She could appreciate the difficulty of land reform in such a setting, and concluded that "the great test of the whole affair" is whether the transition to collective farming can be made smoothly. "A once-and-for-all distribution of land is no permanent solution. . . . Land reform was intended to be a break with the feudal past and the foundation for a socialist future, not a new system in itself.'' She found that not everyone was happy with the results, but

> . . . Taking it by and large, the substitution of 15 percent taxes for 50 percent rents, the provision of cheap loans, the organization of marketing through the co-ops, the provision of health services and of relief in floods and famines, the taming of the rivers, the elimination of bandits, and the substitution of the disciplined, helpful and chaste Liberation Army for a soldiery hardly distinguishable from bandits—all these make up a substantial list of benefits to the countryside.

Robinson was alarmed over the then current Chinese attitude toward birth control: ''Birth control is too much associated with a pessimistic, defeatist, anti-Marxist view of life'' and so ''no one will hear of Malthus.'' She concluded that in China ''it is of no use to argue with the economists.'' She knew that her report would be discounted in the West: ''I suppose I must prepare to meet skeptical smiles at home. It is more inconvenient to be disbelieved when you are lying, but it is more annoying when you are not.''[46]

Robinson was to return to China again and again and to write two pamphlets on that country.[47] Her efforts to understand the rationale and success and failure of the changes taking place in China is best described in Harcourt's terms as containing a ''leaven of advocacy, a conscious effort to try to offset what she believes to have been unsympathetic critiques of Chinese politics emanating from orthodox circles.'' Her enthusiasm for China, not surprisingly, drew fire from friends and foes alike. Friend Harcourt added that her qualities as a theoretician explain ''why her political analyses and judgments are sometimes simplistic and distorted, by-products of a good theoretician's ability to abstract and simplify.''[48]

Has capitalism changed? 1961

Robinson was invited to participate in a symposium on the question, ''Has capitalism changed?'' which was edited by Shigeto Tsuru and published by the *Monthly Review.* Other contributors included John Kenneth Galbraith, Paul Sweezy, Paul Baran, and Maurice Dobb. Her feeling was that neither the Keynesian nor the Marxian prognosis of the future of capitalism was being fulfilled ''and we are left without any particular theory as to what will happen next.''

She felt it was fairly clear that ''private enterprise has ceased to be the form of organization best suited to take advantage of modern technology.'' While England had ''learned to realize that we are no longer running the world . . . public opinion in America seems to be taking up the attitude of the wrong mother in the judgment of Solomon—rather blow the world up than allow someone else to lead it.'' Until that mood passed in the United States, she found nothing else worth discussing. After that, ''there seems no very clear indication to make it obvious that capitalism will not have a long future as the second best economic system in the world."[49] This remark is interesting for two reasons. One was the "second best" category to which she relegated capitalism without naming the best; the other is that she still maintained (contra Harry Johnson's accusations) that capitalism was durable.

Is Marxism a religion or a science? 1962

The next year, she tackled the Marxists with equal enthusiasm in her much quoted essay, "Marxism: Religion or Science?" Her theme burned deeply into the consciousness of some Marxists: "Ideology demands acceptance. Science demands doubt." She still wanted the Marxists to give up their habits of belief, while she wanted all economists to consider the fact that for a discussion of questions "nowadays found to be interesting—growth and stagnation, technical progress and the demand for labor, the balance of sectors in an expanding economy—Marxian theory provides a starting point where academic teaching was totally blank."[50]

Visits to North Korea and Cuba: 1964–65

Robinson preferred North Korean socialism to Cuban socialism. In 1964, she visited North Korea, writing a glowing report of what she called the "Korean Miracle," based in part on a North Korean Statistical Bureau report. She admired "the intense concentration of the Koreans on national pride" as markedly more effective than the "sunny, expansive Cuban style." (She had visited Cuba in 1961.) She predicted, "As the North continues to develop and the South to degenerate, sooner or later the curtain of lies must surely begin to tear." North Korean Prime Minister Kim Il Sung was "a messiah rather than a dictator." Robinson challenged "professed liberals" who might find all this abhorrent: "Their duty is plain: let them explain clearly to the people in the South what is happening in the North and leave them to choose which they prefer."[51]

Robinson made her second visit to Cuba in 1965. She still found that "foresight, exactitude, and steady slogging do not come easily to them. Moreover they feel that it is their task to prove to Latin America that socialism can be gay." However, she found Cuba was done with its "romantic period of Cuban Revolution" and that "unromantic economics is now the order of the day." She felt there was some confusion in the ongoing Cuban debate "between incentives to achieve success and criteria of what success consists of."[52] She argued against the use of monetary incentives both for political and economic reasons. She found a lot of zigzagging in Cuba but did not condemn this. If nothing else, she observed, President Lyndon Johnson would guarantee the popularity of Fidel Castro. On the whole, her picture of Cuba was less glowing than that of North Korea or China.

Revisionism or predictable development? 1967

In 1967 Joan Robinson, among others, was asked to comment on the changes in economic organization being introduced in the Soviet economies [USSR] and "People's Democracies of Eastern Europe . . . which the Chinese castigate as revisionism and the West hails as a return to the profit motive." The reforms seemed, instead, "a predictable stage in the industrialization of a formerly backward country." They were due in part to the success of the productive system rather than to any failures. Her incipient anti-Americanism is voiced: "The socialist world is stepping into the region of affluence—where will they want to go? The dismal prospect of overtaking America is all that they have been offered so far." Analyzing the problems of employment, efficiency, and income distribution in the "Peoples Democracies," she asked, "Will the outcome be a reproduction of managerial capitalism, with merely a little more public spirit, greater equality of opportunity, and less waste of trained manpower in futile occupations? That would no doubt be a great improvement on any industrial system yet known, but is this the socialism for which so much blood was shed?"[53] Clearly Robinson was disappointed in this probable outcome.

Setting the record straight: 1971 and 1976

In 1971, near the end of the debates on capital theory, Robinson objected that Marxists "generally dismiss the whole thing [the capital controversy] as a deception without bothering to understand it." She exhorted the "radical economists who have established a new movement in American universities" to be well versed in Sraffa and Kalecki and take on the "mainstream."[54]

In 1976, Robinson reviewed the eyewitness account of the Cultural Revolution in China written by an English couple, John and Elsie Collier. This time she had questions, not answers: "Was unleashing the Cultural Revolution a colossal gamble? Was the gamble too rash? Indeed, the fact that it led up to the Lin Piao affair makes one shudder. But as recent events show, the two-line struggle will never end."[55] She wrote this two years before she told Adler that the romance had gone out of China for her.

In a review of Ronald Meek's *Studies in the Labor Theory of Value*, Robinson moved to set the record straight on some other issues. For one, it had been Meek's leg she was pulling in "An Open Letter from a Keynesian to a Marxist."[56] Meek was "a rigid dogmatist" at the time of writing his book and had treated her then as a hostile critic of Marxists. For another, she had not intended her *Essay on Marxian Economics* (1942) as a criticism of Marx. Robinson insisted, "I wrote it to alert my bourgeois colleagues to the existence of penetrating and important ideas in *Capital* that they ought not to continue to neglect, but since I was a bourgeois myself," she was accused of trying to reconstruct orthodox equilibrium theory. She now considered her essay as "the first round of the 'Cambridge criticism'."

Otherwise, her main objection to Meek was his attempt "to squeeze out" of Sraffa's model "an historical process." Instead, Sraffa's contribution to Marxism "is mainly negative, to dispose of the rubbish." She called once more on the Marxists "to break out of the husk of dogmatism and set about building the political economy of today in the space that he [Sraffa] has cleared."[57]

By North Korea she stands: 1977

In 1977, Robinson reviewed Ellen Brun's and Jacques Hersh's *Socialist Korea: A Case Study in the Strategy of Economic Development*. She felt that Korea divided came close to providing a controlled experiment for social scientists "to observe how the same forces of production develop in different relations of production." She had no doubts about the strength of the two societies: "Obviously, sooner or later the country must be reunited by absorbing the South into socialism." She observed that "there is now talk of removing U.S. troops, but the KCIA [Korean CIA] will remain to preserve 'order'. The American multinationals could remove themselves without much loss, but Japanese capital is now deeply involved. What new international maneuvers must the Korean people await before unity and independence at last?"[58]

Chinese versus Soviet ways: 1979

In her review of a translation of Mao Tse-tung's *A Critique of Soviet Economics*, she remained more sympathetic to the Chinese than toward the Soviets. But Robinson was not a worshipper of any person. On the question of ownership of the means of production, she found Mao's "open-mindedness . . . limited by dogma" in his preference for ownership "by the whole people." She noted this would entail control of production by bureaucracy in preference to ownership by collective units such as cooperatives.[59]

Last word on China: 1979

In 1979, when she was seventy-five, Joan Robinson participated in a symposium on "China Since Mao." She now averred,

> The content and style of Chinese internal propaganda is very misleading when read from a Western point of view. . . . I think we all had a lot of wind in our heads; it was hard to believe that, in a socialist country, policy could have been the sport of personal ambition, and it was deflating to be told that the Cultural Revolution is over and that the new aim of policy is modernization. We know only too well what it is like to be modern. But it is foolish to judge policy merely

from slogans. There is now more freedom and frankness of discussion, both amongst Chinese and between Chinese and foreigners, than over the last twenty-five years, but there is still a hangover from the past in official propaganda which remains heavily monolithic—101 percent one way or the other—and therefore unenlightening.

She remained a friend of China, attempting to understand what they were trying to do, but she freely admitted that "the history of the decade, 1966–76, has been a profound shock. How could it happen that, under cover of Mao Tse-tung Thought, a medieval drama of ambition and treachery could play itself out?" Charles Bettelheim had resigned from the French Friendship Society in disgust. Robinson's view of the Chinese reforms so despised by Bettelheim was that "the leadership has embarked upon a hitherto unprecedented course of combining an ambitious plan for accumulation and growth with open discussion and freedom of thought."[60] Robinson thus repeatedly showed herself to be more a friend of China and socialist experiments than of dogmatic Marxist thought.

Last word of all: 1983

The month Joan Robinson died, her friends at the *Monthly Review* published the text of a talk she had given in 1980 in Toronto: "The Economics of Destruction."

> What is the point of sitting here discussing useless things? We are again in a slump and governments are incapable of applying policies that might reverse the present recession—they instead listen to bad economists who tell them that inflation is the root, rather than the symptom, of a sick economy. What we have are programs that aggravate the economic crisis while the means of destruction are multiplied. Economics should begin to address the important issue of our impending doom.[61]

Thus ended her publications in the *Monthly Review.* There she had allowed herself to express her admiration of socialist experiment without sheltering Marxist ideology. And there her anti-Americanism showed. But what showed most was her openmindedness, her willingness to take a stand and to change her mind, to admit shock and dismay when that seemed appropriate. For thirty-two years she was known to the small American audience which reads the *Monthly Review*, most of whom probably agreed with her opposition to American sabre-rattling.[62]

Robinson's articles in the *Monthly Review* show her to be the "friendly enemy" of Marxist dogma, as one Marxist alleged. More to the point, her role as the bourgeois economist whom she believed herself to be shines through. From her own upper-class, privileged position at Cambridge, she could see class struggle and conflicts of interest as a permanent feature of human society without becoming a Marxist.

Name-calling from right and left*

Robinson's interest in Marx drew fire from both the right and the left. Schumpeter introduced the term "Marxo-Keynesian" in an article in the *Journal of Political Economy* in 1949,[63] and while he did not mention Joan Robinson by name, the implication was there. Later, Harry Johnson did call her a Marxo-Keynesian, as we have seen. Others must have also. As for response from Marxists, the best example is the careful analysis made by Roman Rosdolsky and published in German in 1953, which committed an entire chapter to showing that her analysis was "in error."[64]

In addition to the *Monthly Review* articles, Robinson had some professional exchange with American Marxists during the 1950s. In *Science & Society* she debated Joseph M. Gillman of New York both on the labor theory of value and the falling rate of profit, holding to the views she had expressed in her *Essay on Marxian Economics*.[65]

Her theme was familiar: "Commenting from this side of the Atlantic, it seems very sad that the small heroic band of Marxists surviving in America should have to occupy themselves, in this theological style, with trying to find new meanings for old formulae instead of attending to real problems." Nevertheless, her disenchantment with what she considered Marxist dogma did not shake her own faith in a case for socialism: "A very good case for socialism can be made out on the ground that under capitalism waste (particularly the enormous wastes of the cold war) does *not* cause the rate of profit to fall."[66] Nor did she care for "a fellow bourgeois economist's" argument that Soviet planners might have done better had they looked at our textbooks.[67]

Once Marxism had revived in the United States in the 1960s, Robinson began to draw criticism from the left. James F. Becker of New York University saw her as a "friendly enemy" of Marxism, particularly in her "curious misinterpretation" that Marxism had "developed into a faith rather than a science." Becker conceded that in her generation "this view of Marxism as secular religion was widespread and to some extent justified."[68] In 1980, Arun Bose had a new epithet: a "modern post-Keynesian ideological sheep in make-believe Marxist ideological wolves' clothing." And Frank Roosevelt accused Robinson of "commodity fetishism," of failing to grasp what the struggle for socialism is all about, and for a "total lack of understanding of Marx' concept of value."[69]

To say that Robinson was attacked from both right and left does not imply that she was in some "middle," nor even that she did not provoke such response. She was just what she claimed to be, a bourgeois economist who thought orthodox economics was attacking the wrong problems with faulty tools, that Marxists were more interested in religion than science, and that much time could be saved if traditional economists would consider what Marx had suggested were the right problems. And she promoted these views wherever she went.

*See Appendix Note 7.1 A variety of critics.

JR

CHAPTER EIGHT

Generalizing the General Theory

After World War II, Cambridge economics remained distinct from the major fashions which swept over American economics. Via new textbooks, the new economics first drowned the institutionalists, then emerged as a mainstream of Walrasian-Keynesian theory bristling with econometric studies and austere mathematical models. Later, American economics was permeated with the arguments of the monetarists who revived the quantity theory of money. More recently, Americans toy with the arguments of the new classical economists that markets do clear, regardless of circumstances.

Cambridge traditions stood firmly against such incursions. The Cambridge University department of economics remained, and still is, a department of theory. (There is a separate department for applied economics.) The oral tradition and the method of teaching through lectures and supervisions continued. Students still developed their own skills by writing essays and suffering criticism. The two Triposes were the only examinations in the student's undergraduate career. For one thing, Joan Robinson and Richard Kahn were still at Cambridge to say what Keynes had meant. The Cambridge tradition was one of *evolution* of economic theory in response to problems in both construction of theory and a theory's relation to the real world. When world consciousness dictated that countries which had participated in the war and had become members of United Nations should henceforth participate in world economic development, Cambridge responded with efforts to make economic theory suitably dynamic. Robinson and Cambridge built on Keynes but carried theory into the new problem areas.[1]

Robinson called these new efforts "generalizing the General Theory." Immediately after the war, she moved steadfastly forward in this task. Later she confided that at the time she had taken for granted that "the habitual modes of thought and expression from which Keynes had a long struggle to escape" had been left behind.[2] She hailed the atmosphere at Cambridge as one of "a great proliferation of dynamic theorizing," as distinguished from the old days of "Marshallian hegemony."[3]

Economics was the major focus, not just of her career, but of her leisured moments as well. In 1948, Robinson, Sraffa, and Kahn visited Italy, staying on the Passo Sella in the Dolomites, bent on doing some rock climbing. There was too much snow to climb, so they studied and discussed the page proofs of Roy Harrod's new book, *Towards a Dynamic Economics*, which Kahn had brought along. Kahn says, "So far as Cambridge is concerned this was the origin of the economics of growth."[4]

Robinson called this the beginning of the shifting of the "center of interest" to the "classical problems of over-all growth of the economy."[5] She also gave credit to Harrod for being the first to point out "the need to introduce liquidity preference into the 'classical' scheme."[6] For some time the collective thinking around Cambridge had been shifting to the long-run considerations that Keynes' General Theory had excluded. Among Robinson's *Essays in the Theory of Employment* was one entitled "The Long-Period Influences" (circa 1935). Harrod, in his review of her essays, had thought this article the "pièce de résistance" of the volume. But in the 1930s, the long period meant the period "in which, with the existing population, tastes, etc. all opportunities for investment at a given rate of interest have been taken and saving has consequently sunk to zero."[7]

Then Joan Robinson had read Karl Marx and Rosa Luxemburg, who prepared her to see the economic long period in terms of something more like historical time, that is, irreversible. Robinson wanted to draw others into the search for new theory. In 1952, when she wrote "The Generalization of the General Theory," she thought of it merely as "an agenda for discussion, rather than a completed piece of analysis."[8]

In 1946 Robinson and Nicholas Kaldor had a continuing debate following the publication of Erwin Rothbarth's posthumous article, "Causes of Superior Efficiency of USA Industry compared with British Industry."[9] Robinson and Kaldor were close friends as well as colleagues, and the discussion led her to consult Kaldor on what she might profitably read in the area of capital theory. Kaldor has said that at that time Robinson was unacquainted with the literature on capital—Böhm-Bawerk, for instance—and Kaldor suggested readings, including his article, "The Recent Controversy on the Theory of Capital." Then the two would discuss these in detail. Kaldor confided, "I must say I taught Joan quite a little capital theory, because the knowledge of capital theory at Cambridge was zero. It really was, you see, because Marshall never knew anything about it." Kaldor felt that he "aroused in Joan an interest in capital theory. She found it fascinating and worked out this book on the accumulation of capital." He did not claim that her *Accumulation* was based on his or anyone else's work, "because she sort of integrated Marx and various other people as she was working."[10]

Continuing this new interest in capital and growth, Robinson reviewed Harrod's *Towards a Dynamic Economics* in 1949. "No one will disagree with Mr. Harrod that modern economic theory lacks, and badly needs, a system of analysis dealing with a dynamic society," she concluded.[11] Kaldor said it was during this period that Robinson became convinced that "the role of capital accumulation is essential to the working of a capitalist economy."

Both English and American reviewers of *The Rate of Interest and Other Essays* understood Robinson's intention to extend the General Theory into dynamics. R. M. Goodwin, who knew the Cambridge score, noted that Harrod had set off a chain reaction when he brought together the multiplier and the accelerator of Keynesian economics.[12] Arthur Smithies of Harvard thought Robinson should have entitled the volume "The Generalization of the General Theory," since "her main effort is to break through the short-run Marshallian confines of the *General Theory.*" (She did this when the book was reprinted in 1979.) Smithies applauded Harrod and Robinson and also J. R. Hicks "for recentering attention on economic growth." But he thought Robinson painted "an agnostic picture of capitalistic instability." Smithies' mention of Hicks is significant. In 1939, Oxford's Hicks had published *Value and Capital*, a work which provided the English leadership for a neoclassical synthesis (that is, a synthesis between the new Keynesian tools and the traditional or orthodox economics) which was taken up enthusiastically in the United States. Cambridge Keynesians had ignored these developments, which led, in the United States, to what Joan Robinson would call "bastard Keynesianism." Smithies concluded that in spite of these many efforts, the General Theory had not been generalized successfully.[13] At that time, Joan Robinson would have agreed.

Secret seminars

With so many promising ideas floating around, Robinson, Kahn, and Kaldor saw a need for a forum similar to the Circus which had aided Keynes. They organized the secret seminar. Kaldor said, "It was part of a joke, calling it a secret seminar. It really was that we met in houses [while Kahn was away] and only invited senior members, so we didn't invite all the faculty, only the ones we liked. It wasn't a secret."[14] Distinguished American visitors to Cambridge were often invited— Samuelson, for example, although not Friedman.[15] Samuelson believes that he was at the seminar when Robinson first began thinking along the lines of her book, *Accumulation of Capital*.[16]

The secret seminar in the early 1950s thus became the forum for the work in growth and accumulation that Kaldor and Robinson were developing. The "classic" description of the secret seminar attributed to Samuelson is "Nicky [Kaldor] talking 75 percent of the time and Joan talking 75 percent of the time."[17] During this period the seminar was "at its height." One of the members would read a paper and then the paper was discussed after refreshments provided by Kahn. Harry Johnson, bored with it all, said that the discussions were devoted to loanable funds versus liquidity preference arguments.[18]

In any case, Joan Robinson worked out many of her ideas on the accumulation of capital in this forum. The period was also a tense one for her. Once more, in 1952, she took a term off from lecturing.

The Accumulation of Capital

In an ambitious and daring book, *The Accumulation of Capital* (1956), Joan Robinson directly challenged orthodoxy by offering alternative formalistic models which attempted to deal with both logical and historical (irreversible) time. She used her customary tools—language but not calculus—and she introduced some new symbolic phrases—"golden ages," "platinum ages," "bastard ages"—which had been important in differentiating ideas in the seminar discussions. Each "age" postulated a relationship between the desired rate of accumulation and the possible rate, also postulating resources and other variable conditions, for purposes of comparison. This was to be her magnum opus.

The text of *Accumulation of Capital* followed the pattern which was so admired in *Imperfect Competition*. First there was a systematic presentation of economic concepts (classes of income, meaning of wealth, etc.), and then the presentation of models. Her first model was "a simple model" with many strong assumptions. Robinson then examined the accumulation of capital under different technical conditions. Books III-VIII analyzed varying models in a short period and applied them to financial issues, to the rentier class, to land and labor, to relative prices, and to international trade. Forty pages of explanatory notes and fourteen pages of diagrammatic illustrations were followed by a mathematical note by R. F. Kahn and D. G. Champernowne on the value of invested capital.

Once more Robinson had written a book of pure theory in literary form. The economic systems of the models were named *alpha, beta,* and *gamma.* The alternative processes of growth were nicknamed "golden ages," and so on. Every important economic issue was touched on; the theory was universal in that it was applicable to both industrialized and underdeveloped economies. If the book had a major fault, it was that of requiring too much of the reader. Robinson came to realize this. Six years later, she published her *Essays in the Theory of Economic Growth* as "an introduction rather than as a supplement" to *Accumulation.* "That book was found excessively difficult," she said.[19]

The Accumulation of Capital aroused worldwide attention. The English reviewer, T. Barna, understood what Robinson was after: "[W]hat are the conditions for the achievement of a cumulative long-term growth of wealth and what is the outcome for the relation between wages and profits?" She had answered this through building abstract models. Barna felt that Robinson had written "a full-scale text-book on what is probably the most important post-war subject by making use of an efficient dynamic theory."[20]

Lawrence Klein, at that time at the Institute of Statistics at Oxford, also wrote a laudatory review for the international audience of *Econometrica*. He felt much of the analysis, however, "to be a verbal, graphical exposition in two dimensions or in simple two-industry models of long familiar results in the theory of linear programming." Klein thought it too bad that Robinson's "intellectual outlook" had not allowed her to go beyond her "select range of references" into the "powerful fields of linear programming, input-output analysis, mathematical general equilibrium systems, and theory of balanced growth," but conceded that "Mrs. Robinson, of course, does a remarkably good job with her own tools." Klein asserted that the basic philosophy of her analysis of the capitalist process is that entrepreneurial decisions rule the economy. He felt that more emphasis should have been given to the consumer for "a real understanding of modern capitalism (and socialism!)."[21]

Joan Robinson responded to Klein's review in a letter to the editor, saying that he had raised a point of general interest: "Can the level of wages and profits and the rate of profit on capital be deduced from a production function?"[22] Robinson continued,

> For a hundred years economists have been trying to fiddle the assumptions to evade this issue. Surely by now we can look it in the face? This is not mere priggishness. The ambiguity in the meaning of "capital" points to a fatal weakness in the conception of a production function. If capital is specified in terms of value we have to know the propensities to consume and the rate of investment (which may be zero—for all this is just as true of a stationary state as of any other) in order to know the level of real wages and the current rate of profit. On the other hand, if the stock of capital is specified in physical terms, so that we know the capacity output of each sector of the economy, there is nothing to show that the stock of capital is in equilibrium with the rate of profit.[23]

Robinson offered alternatives which sounded suspiciously like those she objected to, such as postulating "that the economy always has been in equilibrium, with correct expectations." The problem was not easily solved in a letter to the editor. Her *Accumulation* was thereafter seen as part of the capital controversy, and perhaps suffered neglect because of it.

The Canadian reviewer B. S. Keirstead was much cooler toward *Accumulation* than either Barna or Klein. Keirstead wrote a double review of L. M. Lachmann's *Capital and Its Structure* and Robinson's *Accumulation*. He preferred the former. He was put off by her "mechanistic models" and assumptions of "passive reactions of workers and entrepreneurs." Essentially he was objecting to Keynesianism when he complained, "preoccupation with stability has characterized British economic thinking for a generation."[24]

Abba Lerner's review in the *American Economic Review*, though written by an old acquaintance, bordered on the insulting. Lerner belittled Robinson's "attempt to direct the attention of the economists from the theory of value . . . to the causes of wealth of nations."[25] He began by quoting Solow's barb in the course of the capital controversy. Solow had said, "She seems to have written her article the way an oyster makes pearls—out of sheer irritation."[26] Then Lerner altered the statement, saying the book was a pearl "whose most conspicuous product is irritation."

Practically everything about *Accumulation* irritated Lerner: "the proclivity to produce aphorisms, wisecracks, 'contradictions,' 'paradoxes' and 'anomalies' which look rather Marxist," and more important, "the method employed of using abstractions which seem so far beyond the call of necessity." He also found her methodology "a convenient stage for disobliging remarks about capitalism."

His most biting remarks were those recommending the book as an "excellent experience for such graduate students as are not terrified by the extreme abstractions of the models and are not too intimidated by the intricacy of the arguments."[27] "The most useful parts of the book are the errors and the ingenious confusions the search for which can give such first-class exercise in economics to graduate students (and to professors) who could do with a tough workout and who can stand the tough cuteness of Mrs. Robinson's style."[28] Lerner rejected the subject as emphatically as the effort. "Reading this book does not alter one's previous feeling that there is not really very much that economics can tell us about the accumulation of capital."

Periodically he lashed out at something he considered done "in true Marxian fashion." Yet he hedged his bet, saying that it was "an important book" for it "brings into focus and develops the kind of thinking on the subject of economic development that is going on in Oxford and Cambridge." Lerner had once been a part of the English scene, but now he was more American in his views. He did not see this line of development as "too helpful."[29] As it turned out, Lerner had a good ear for the groundswells of American economic thought. Interest in growth theory was soon dropped in the United States.

Essays in the Theory of Economic Growth

In 1962, Robinson published her "easier" *Essays in the Theory of Economic Growth*. In the preface, she expressed the hope that she could "get economic analysis off the mud of static equilibrium theory." She promised, "Once it is afloat enticing voyages beckon in many directions." *Accumulation* had 440 pages, while the essays required only 137, but as she stated, the essays provided an introduction to the larger book. She presented the models without their detailed application, and emphasized her argument that the conception of equilibrium was unhelpful in economic analysis. "In time," she argued, "there is no motionless rest. Time marches on."[30]

The reviews of the essays followed the earlier pattern—favorable in England, critical in North America. To G. D. N. Worswick of Oxford Robinson's was a "great enterprise." He had only one complaint, but even this was expressed with some wonder:

> In the ascent of Mt. Growth Mrs. Robinson scorns the mathematical paraphernalia carried by most rival expeditions. Over the lower slopes she whisks us along at an exhilarating pace, while the others are still having trouble with porters getting all their assumptions and equations up to base camp. Out on the North Face of Technical Progress, however, the climbing is very arduous and this reviewer would have given much for a mathematical piton or two to hang on to."[31]

Worswick felt that nonmathematical students would remain in her debt.

In Canada, H. A. John Green linked the essays with other "recent contributions" to the theory of economic growth. He saw the essays as a part of the boiling capital controversy. Green referred to "remarks she has made in recent years" which made clear that her questions about the measurement of capital were "attacks on symptoms of the neo-classical disease, not on the disease itself. . . . The disease consists of a lack of concern for the assumptions that are being made about the beliefs and objectives of economic agents." Green feared that as a result of her efforts to challenge orthodoxy, "Mrs. Robinson's tide set us adrift on a trackless ocean." But Green did like her admonition "to set out explicit hypotheses concerning the motives and expectations of entrepreneurs." He wrote, "I find the emasculated role assigned to the entrepreneur by neo-classical theory impossible to accept."[32]

Once more the *American Economic Review* provided a forum for a scathing attack, this time by D. Hamberg of the University of Buffalo. Hamberg wondered if republishing one's journal articles in book form wasn't "immensely profitable" when "immodestly selected for republication by the authors themselves." Hamberg and his editors must have been unacquainted with the value the *Essays* might have had for a student preparing for the Tripos. He must also have been unaware that a person using the Cambridge University Library is not allowed to use a copy machine to copy an article there, nor to take the volume elsewhere. The English are very strict on copyright rules.

Hamberg's review then concentrated on the "Model of Capital Accumulation," which had not been published before. He concluded, "Mrs. Robinson's growth model lies between the Kaldor and Harrod models, with the neoclassical production-function model lying to the far extreme of the Harrod model." None of the differences mattered much to Hamberg. "So, given our limited knowledge of real-world technical and behavioral relations, what is the significance of the differences? Or maybe Mr. Harrod is right after all. Who knows?"[33] It seems he barely restrained himself from asking, "Who cares?"

Such ill-mannered American reviews signal the primacy of the neoclassical synthesis and the mathematical form achieved in North American economics during the 1950s. In general, American economists no longer looked up to Cambridge. Each person considered himself (and Joan Robinson was the only woman in this game at the time) quite capable of building a growth model, using assumptions which seemed mathematically convenient. Thus began a period which—to borrow from Robert Solow's description of his efforts to communicate with economists of the New Classical School—was essentially one of noncommunication among economists of different persuasions.

Solow added,

> There are two reasons for that, I guess. One reason is that we really start from very different assumptions about the economy, so it is very hard to communicate seriously. Frank Ramsey, a philosopher, once said that many conversations strike him as analogous to the following conversation: "I went to Grantchester today." "That is funny, I didn't." After you have said that, there is not much else to say. If we had time, we could sit down and try to start with the crude assumptions and ask each other about them. It may be that we come to recognize that we have different sources of evidence. . . . The other reason is that in any conversation between, say, Lucas or Sargent and me, there is an element of game playing. There is a tendency to grab a debating point whenever you see it. [34]

These remarks also serve to suggest why the capital controversy was, as Harry Johnson remarked, mainly between MIT and Cambridge University. The two Cambridges were still peopled by economists who did at least try to talk to one another. But the reasons for American theoretical economists' dropping their interest in economic growth is more clouded.

Whatever happened to economic growth theory?*

Where Robinson led the profession, it was not to follow. This can be explained partly by what happened to the popularity of growth theory. Classical economists like Adam Smith had founded the field as a search for the "nature and causes of the wealth of nations." However, the orthodox economics that Joan Robinson reacted against had abandoned this quest in favor of a narrower focus on the problem of the allocation of existing resources. Robinson's *Accumulation* was a return to the earlier definition of economics. The postwar interest in growth theory among economists was soon split into three currents: (1) a concern with the very real problems of developing economies; (2) the Cambridge effort to make Keynesian analysis dynamic through the abandonment of assumptions of perfect competition and equilibrium; and (3) the mainstream effort to make traditional theory dynamic while still retaining the assumptions of full employment, perfect competition, and competitive equilibrium. [35] This split in theory

---

*See Appendix Note 8.1 An account of growth theory.

profoundly influenced the reception of Robinson's *Accumulation*, since nearly everyone interested in growth in the United States followed a different path from hers.

Perhaps even more important was the fact that mainstream economists, once a few neoclassical growth models had been built, lost interest in the subject of economic growth. Because of this, Robinson's *magnum opus* was far too soon just a book on the shelf in the United States.

The new Cambridge tradition*

But Cambridge University did not lose interest in the difficult theory required to examine economic growth. For one thing, Cambridge was more internationally, even colonially oriented than most American universities were in the 1950s and 1960s. Harrod and Robinson had already begun the work of a new Cambridge tradition which further differentiated their work from the mainstream of American economics.

This trend was reinforced through the publication of two works by Piero Sraffa: his introduction to his edition of Ricardo's works (1953); and *Production of Commodities by Means of Commodities* (1960), subtitled, *Prelude to a Critique of Economic Theory.* Sraffa's view of Ricardo profoundly influenced Robinson in her conduct of the capital controversy. Cambridge had never shrunk from intellectual confrontations with the rest of the profession and would not do so now. Robinson was in her late fifties during this emergence of the new Cambridge theory, in which she played a large part. Her role in battling the American "neo-neoclassicals" took the form of the capital controversy, which is the subject of the next two chapters.

---

*See Appendix Note 8.2 Sraffa harks back to Ricardo, and Appendix Note 8.3 The new Cambridge tradition and the Anglo-Italian School 1949–1975.

JR

CHAPTER NINE

Standoff between
the Two Cambridges

Efforts to generalize the General Theory led not only to Joan Robinson's largest book, *The Accumulation of Capital*, but also to a new controversy in capital theory. The nineteenth-century controversy over capital had centered on the differences between the works of Karl Marx and Eugen von Böhm-Bawerk of Austria. Marx argued that when the fruits of production were distributed, workers were exploited in that they received less than they contributed in value. Böhm-Bawerk and J. B. Clark, in the United States, answered that workers received exactly the value of their contribution, that is, the value of their marginal product (as it came to be called).[1]

The newest controversy began in the 1950s. Harcourt named it the Cambridge controversy because economists at Cambridge University and at The Massachusetts Institute of Technology (MIT) were the leading figures. What followed was a huge debate on many issues which stimulated work by economists from many countries. To some extent, though, Joan Robinson dramatized her exchanges with Americans at MIT as if these questions could only be decided through negotiation between the two citadels. From 1956 to the late 1970s, she focused her verbal attacks mainly on that famous pair, Paul Samuelson and Robert Solow, both of MIT.

The debate, however, was not a separate issue in Robinson's work but a part of her efforts to develop an alternative to what she called neoclassical economics. The reason she focused on Solow and Samuelson was that she identified them as leaders in mainstream economics teaching in America. And she decided that this mainstream was not Keynesian but ''neoclassical.''

In her long review in 1949 of Harrod's *Towards a Dynamic Economics*, Robinson had hailed Harrod's effort to extend the Keynesian revolution into a long-run dynamic theory. She saw the need for a ''long-run dynamic theory to supplement the short-period analysis of the General Theory and to swallow up, as a special case, the long-run static theory in which the present generation of academic economists was educated."[2]

Not until the 1950s did Robinson realize that the neoclassical synthesis taught in the United States, the amalgam of Walrasian theory and Keynesian tools, had relegated Keynes' theory of employment to the inferior status of a special case. At the same time, she had become convinced that economics should be the study of political economy in the spirit of the classical economists, including Ricardo and Marx. Therefore, she considered it a fault that Harrod had neglected both the measures to increase useful investment and the issue of the distribution of income. Had Harrod taken up these questions, he would have brought "politics into the economic argument." She argued that "his resolution to avoid these questions is itself a political decision."[3] Joan Robinson believed that the accumulation of capital and the distribution of income are inevitably related in the real world and must be so related in any theoretical model. The measure of the capital which is being accumulated is the key to this relationship. In other words, if economists were going to discuss growth, then there was no way to avoid discussing the distribution of income and thus politics.

When Robinson began examining the question of growth, she was struck by the fact that the meaning of capital in economic analysis was, to say the least, fuzzy. She initially compared models of Karl Marx, Gustav Cassel, Roy Harrod, and E. D. Domar, in "A Model of an Expanding Economy," noting that "none of our authors gives a very perspicuous account of how capital is measured."[4]

I think the capital controversy began with this article. Harcourt, however, cited the real beginning of the capital theory controversy as Robinson's 1953 article, "The Production Function and the Theory of Capital," probably because this was the article that Robert Solow answered.[5] In it she complained again of the ambiguity concerning the unit in which capital was measured in the neoclassical aggregate production function.[6] But her complaints went deeper than that. Right from the beginning it was her belief that "the ambiguity of the conception of a quantity of capital is connected with a profound methodological error, which makes the major part of neo-classical doctrine spurious."[7]

Neoclassical doctrine was her true target in the capital controversy, as it had been from the time of her first book, *The Economics of Imperfect Competition*. But this time, there was a response to the question she was raising. Looking back more than twenty years later (1975), she characterized the early response in the controversy as "incomprehension . . . ridicule and indignation."

> I can understand this now better than I did at the time. In Cambridge, the meaning of the capital to labor ratio in a long-period sense was a well-known unsettled question that Dennis Robertson has left in an admittedly unsatisfactory state. Elsewhere, as I since found, there was a convention of agreeing to believe that it was no problem. My article (written in a somewhat light-hearted style) was innocently remarking that the Emperor had no clothes.[8]

But at least there was a response. By the early 1970s, Harcourt could list a bibliography of 237 items relevant to the current capital controversy.

Over the years, the argument escalated to the higher reaches of mathematics, without resolving the differences. Harcourt challenged the profession to compare those early articles (1950s) with the later ones (early 1970s). The reader who claims to understand the later articles must be "an intuitive genius, a liar or a graduate of M.I.T.," wrote Harcourt.[9] He did not find the controversy altogether good-humored. Even Solow, says Harcourt, "in a rare display of bad temper, opened his 1962 paper with: 'I have long since abandoned the illusion that participants in this debate actually communicate with one another, so I omit the standard polemical introduction and get down to business at once'."[10]

Harcourt detected ideological elements as well:

It is my strong impression that if one were to be told whether an economist was fundamentally sympathetic or hostile to basic capitalist institutions, especially private property and the related rights to income streams . . . one could predict with some degree of accuracy both his general approach in economic theory and which side he would be on in the present controversies.[11]

By 1970, Robinson was disillusioned. In a review of C. E. Ferguson's *The Neoclassical Theory of Production and Distribution*, she concluded:

No doubt Professor Ferguson's restatement of "capital" theory will be used to train new generations of students to erect elegant-seeming arguments in terms which they cannot define and will confirm econometricians in the search for answers to unaskable questions. Criticism can have no effect. As he himself says, it is a matter of faith.[12]

Since neither side "won" in the controversy, the question remains whether the whole exchange was pointless. I think not, for the arguments did focus the attention on the necessity of reexamining received doctrine, and on the conflicting and thus alternative approaches to methodology. American mainstream economists have generally tried to avoid such quagmires of philosophical issues and to get on with their empirical work.

Robinson's quarrel with neoclassical economics

The capital controversy was not altogether a new dispute as far as Joan Robinson was concerned. She had long quarreled with what she now called neoclassical economics.[13] One possible image of her is as a toolmaker in her garden shed, working to devise ways of ridding the garden of that detested hardy perennial, neoclassicism. For her, the Keynesian revolution had been the unmasking of this weed for what it was, and the generalization of the General Theory was intended to take its place. What did she see when she looked at neoclassicism?

First, she viewed orthodox economic theory, by which she meant "equilibrium economics," as irrelevant to economic problems. Thus, in her view, neoclassical theory had "abdicated" from economic problems. Robinson did not argue that all problems were ignored, but that some of the most important, such as distribution of income, were untreatable with neoclassical theory. Because of these alleged deficiencies, Robinson held that neoclassical theory was a poor source of governmental economic policy. In support of her view she quoted Kaldor, who pointed out that Nobel Laureate Debreu conceded that "the theory is 'logically entirely disconnected from its interpretation'."[14]

Second, Robinson associated the dominance of the neoclassical theory with the marginalist revolution, circa 1870, when economics dropped the study of the wealth of nations and its accumulation, and concentrated instead on the allocation of resources to satisfy human wants. By this she meant that through the adoption of a new definition of economics along with the new marginalist tools, the neoclassicals had dropped the real-world problems which had interested the classical economists.* For English-speaking economists, Lionel Robbins had codified this view in his early essay.†

Third, Robinson associated the neoclassical doctrine with the neglect of income distribution. In marginal analysis, given equilibrium, distribution was *already determined* within the system of production itself, said Robinson. Thus distribution was a question excluded by definition. Robinson considered "capital" in production functions important because, according to neoclassical theory, capital was entitled to a return simply because it existed.[15] Thus her question arose: How is such capital measured? And this question ushered in the new capital controversy.

Finally, Robinson believed that the neoclassical theory was "consciously or unconsciously, a reaction against Marx."[16] Marx had said workers were exploited; neoclassicals had replied no, by definition they were not. Robinson was not the first to claim that this was a self-serving defense of the status quo. Clark had encountered similar reactions to his distribution theory.‡

What Robinson was really objecting to was not so much the neglect of income distribution theory but a particular view of distribution—the marginal productivity theory. While Samuelson found this line of reasoning shocking,§ it was consistent with her early work on imperfect competition which had been admired.

Robinson also complained of neoclassical methodology. Neither Marshallian nor Walrasian equilibrium theory pleased her. She objected to Marshall's "waiting" as a justification for a return on property, saying it was merely a rationalization. The Walrasian equilibrium of simultaneous determination of production

*See Appendix Note 9.1 How marginalism came to America.
†See Introduction.
‡See Appendix Note 9.2 American response to Clark's defense of the status quo.
§See Chapter 10.

and income streams begged the whole question of income distribution, said Robinson. Her adversaries in the capital controversy were not interested in this philosophical point unless she could provide an alternative. (Actually Cambridge did develop an alternative theory of income distribution.)

American practice has been to teach (at least in the textbooks) what Robinson styled as the "vulgarized American version of neo-classical thought that was put out by J. B. Clark."[17] Perhaps some, like Ferguson, believe in it. Others teach it to fill the gap, or rather as Dobb taught Marshall faithfully, considering it his duty. Thus, in attacking mainstream teaching, Robinson was touching a point about which many American economists remain uneasy. They may not accept the received distribution theory, but duty is done. Many American economists of the 1930s (probably mostly institutionalists) were disappointed when Keynes failed to challenge the "classical" assumption that "the wage is equal to the marginal product of labor." It is, after all, this assumption which supported the neoclassical synthesis and allowed Americans to teach Walrasian and Keynesian theory together. The introduction of general equilibrium theories of Walras only supported an already existing structure, one carefully, and from Robinson's point of view unfortunately, preserved by Keynes.[18]

In sum, Joan Robinson's quarrel with neoclassicism was directed at equilibrium analysis, which she attacked on grounds of relevance, realism, and method. All of these perceptions of hers had developed over the long period of her professional practice. It is as though she were struggling to free *herself* from "the mud of static equilibrium." At first she saw no problem in comparing static equilibrium positions and making these appear to represent a process going on through time: "The assumption of full static equilibrium is made merely for convenience, and the classical model can be adapted to deal with a world in which capital accumulation is going on."[19] In her preface to the second edition of *The Economics of Imperfect Competition* she blamed herself for a "shameless fudge" in making it appear that a firm could in effect learn its demand curve from comparing static equilibrium positions over time.[20]

By 1953, in her "Production Function and Theory of Capital," Robinson had decided that

> . . . the ambiguity of the conception of a quantity of capital is connected with a profound methodological error, which makes the major part of neo-classical doctrine spurious. The neo-classical economist thinks of a position of equilibrium as a position towards which an economy is tending to move as time goes by. But it is impossible for a system to *get into* a position of equilibrium, for the very nature of equilibrium is that the system is already in it, and has been in it for a certain length of time.[21]

She felt that Walras had guarded himself from this criticism by assuming that the equilibrium position is "discovered" before any trade takes place.[22]

The methodological error she perceived was a confusion of space and time. Space allowed one to move from position A to position B and back again. Time allowed only unidirectional movement. Consequently she saw neoclassical equilibrium theory as an attempt to obfuscate the role of time in economic analysis, to remove economics from history and from reality.[23] Her most explicit statement of this idea is contained in "A Lecture Delivered at Oxford by a Cambridge Economist," which she groups with "Essays 1953."[24] Here is more evidence that this methodological argument was foremost in her mind from the very beginning of the capital controversy.

Robinson saw general equilibrium, then, as a block to appropriate analysis, for it had assumed away the economic problems. She objected to economists who admired equilibrium analysis for its "logical elegance and completeness" even though they knew it was "useless": "Human life does not exist outside history and no one has correct foresight of his own future behavior, let alone of the behavior of all the other individuals which will impinge upon his. I do not think that it is right to praise the logical elegance of a system which becomes self-contradictory when it is applied to the question that it was designed to answer."[25]

On the other hand, Robinson reserved the right to compare positions of equilibrium "each with its own past and its own expectations about the future." She complained that American economist "Dr. Findlay" (Ronald Findlay) failed to recognize the difference between such a comparison of existing positions and "the analysis of a process going on through time, with expectations changing."[26] To the end of her life she believed that "mainstream teaching" had "been inculcating defective methodology," especially in the United States:

> The exposition both of general equilibrium and of long-run accumulation seems generally to be conducted by drawing a two-dimensional diagram on a blackboard and then introducing historical events into it. A change cannot be depicted on the plane surface of the blackboard. Changes occur in time, and as soon as a point moves off the blackboard into the third dimension of time, it is no longer bound by the relationships shown in the diagram.[27]

Robinson was particularly critical of Samuelson who, as a mathematician,

> . . . knows that a functional relationship is timeless and makes no reference to history or to the direction of change. . . . However, Professor Samuelson continues to use his construction to describe a *process* of accumulation that *raises* wages, *alters* technology, and *changes* a stock of inputs made, say, of wood into one made of iron and then into copper. . . . To Kornai, Harcourt, and myself, this methodology is unacceptable, but Professor Samuelson assures us that it is quite all right."[28]

The final development in Robinson's opposition to neoclassical and equilibrium analysis was her realization that post-Keynesianism had a definite meaning:

". . . it applies to an economic theory or method of analysis which takes account of the difference between the future and the past." According to Robinson, Keynes had replied to his critics in 1937 that the basic difference between his theory and those he was opposing "lay in his recognition of the fact that, at any moment of time, the future is unknown," in other words, that a position of equilibrium is "never realized." She admitted some problems in terminology when a state of expectations was described as a position of equilibrium. Still, she castigated John Hicks for arguing that "Keynes's analysis was only half *in time* and half in equilibrium."[29]

The most important characteristic of Joan Robinson's attack on neoclassical theory was that it displayed her determination to dispose of a method/theory/model which, she held, separated economics from real problems, from relevance, and from history. Stated this way, it appears to be the same argument that American institutionalists had been stressing since Veblen's time. However, as Sukhamoy Chakravarty sees it, Robinson's critique was different in that it was "fundamentally logical" and directed particularly toward the "theoretical flaws" of standard theory.[30] In her verbal feud with Paul Samuelson and Robert Solow, her target was not these men personally, but the neoclassical economics she thought they defended. Needless to say, their perception of these issues differed from hers.

Bastard Keynesians discovered

Joan Robinson's part in the capital controversy was punctuated with exchanges with Americans she identified as "bastard Keynesians." Her first published reference to bastard Keynesianism occurred in her review of Harry Johnson's *Money, Trade and Economic Growth* in 1962. Her argument was that Johnson was "confronting . . . [Keynes' theory] with its own bastard progeny."

Perhaps she had used this terminology earlier in the secret seminar or maybe in one of her personal letters, where she often first used many of her most striking phrases. But in this review of her former student's and colleague's work, she explained to those beyond the inner circle what she meant. "The bastard Keynesians criticize him [Keynes] in terms of arguments which are purely Keynesian (though formalistic and silly), showing how the effect upon prices of changes in money-wage rates reacts upon liquidity preference and the propensity to consume." She continued,

> The bastard Keynesians point out that Keynes assumed that money-wage rates are rigid—more accurately, that the supply of liquidity is very much more flexible upwards than money-wage rates are downwards. Of course he did. The contemporary world, inhabited by bankers and financiers . . . and managers and trade unionists . . . is not reflected in a model in which money-wage rates can fall indefinitely, or in which the quantity of money remains constant when they are rising.

"But the bastard-Keynesian model is not only silly"; it is also "seriously defective in logic" when it is used "to justify the contention that falling wages and prices are good for trade."[31] Robinson used the term "bastard Keynesian" freely, not limiting it to Americans. She argued, for instance, that James Meade's neoclassical growth model should be classed with bastard-Keynesian rather than pre-Keynesian models.[32]

At Barnard College in New York (March 1976), Robinson assured her audience that she was not using the term "just as abuse." Bastard Keynesians had "artificially restored" Say's Law—that is, the old orthodoxy "against which the Keynesian revolution was raised"—and must be called to account. Say's Law implied that there could not be a deficiency of demand; the bastard Keynesian doctrine takes the rate of saving as knowable and then through fiscal and monetary policy arranges an equal amount of investment, thus restoring Say's Law. "Under its shelter all the old doctrines creep back again, even the doctrine that any given stock of capital will provide employment for any amount of labor at the appropriate equilibrium real-wage rate. Then unemployment occurs only because wages are being held above the equilibrium level."[33] (This, she said, is why the bastard Keynesians were unable to see that high employment and high profits would lead to "continuously rising prices.") However, this governmental restoration of demand in the name of Keynes would in turn lead to rising wages and then rising prices again. There were, of course, American Keynesians like Sidney Weintraub who understood this, "but the bastard Keynesians somehow managed to sweep it under the carpet."[34]

Robinson confessed to having a "sad kind of satisfaction to say I told you so" in regard to the occurrence of inflation, which had allegedly caught the bastard Keynesians by surprise.[35] From the first, the "true" Keynesians were well aware of this problem. She wrote of it in 1936, in 1943, and again in 1958.[36] Even more explicitly, she had analyzed the "inflation barrier" to economic growth in *The Accumulation of Capital*.[37]*

Joan Robinson had clearly earned her right to speak on the issue of inflation which might result from efforts to maintain economic growth and employment levels. Therefore, she felt that the "bastard Keynesians" could have saved themselves much pain and anguish if they had only listened to the Cambridge Keynesians, who accepted the fact that the level of prices in an industrial economy depends primarily upon the level of money-wage rates in relation to output per man employed. Instead, the "bastard Keynesian doctrine, developed in the USA . . . totally ignored this." Yet "it was an obvious corollary from the Keynesian theory of prices that a successful policy of maintaining near-full employment, without any other change in the industrial system, entails money-wage rates rising faster than output per head and therefore a chronic tendency to rising prices."[38]

---

*See Appendix Note 9.3 Robinson's recognition of inflationary aspects of Keynesian policy.

For Robinson, the bastard Keynesians included all those who built models where capital goods were assumed to be malleable or "all made of putty." She particularly liked referring to Solow in this connection. In 1972, when she was weary of the capital controversy, she said,

> There has been a lot of tiresome controversy over this putty. The bastard Keynesians try to make out that it is all about the problem of "measuring capital." But it has nothing to do either with measurement or with capital; it has to do with abolishing time. For a world that is always in equilibrium there is no difference between the future and the past, there is no history and there is no need for Keynes.[39]

Robinson had no doubt about where the bastard Keynesian doctrine came from: it "evolved in the United States, invaded the economics faculties of the world, floating on the wings of the almighty dollar. (It established itself even amongst intellectuals in the so-called developing countries, who have reason enough to know better.)" She thought the worst part was that while "Keynes was diagnosing a defect inherent in capitalism . . . the bastard Keynesians turned the argument back into being a defense of *laisser-faire,* provided that just the one blemish of excessive saving was going to be removed."[40] Robinson condemned Samuelson's alleged role in spreading bastard Keynesianism. The Samuelson textbook *Economics* in the 1970 edition committed this offense,[41] she said, but by his 1976 edition, "Samuelson's faith in macroeconomic policies (but not in the verities of microeconomics) had been badly shaken."[42] Regarding the alleged affection of the bastard Keynesians for laissez-faire and microeconomics as received, she admitted feeling "helpless."[43]

Few economists of this century have been as personal as Joan Robinson in her attacks on individuals. She had learned from the early days of the Circus that there are people behind ideas and that to make a point one must be bold. Samuelson remained ever the gentleman. Solow, who styles himself a Brooklyn boy, was often moved to return her jibes in kind. He said she never treated him better than when he did.

There was a pattern to her verbal aggression. She never attacked someone she considered an inferior; she mostly ignored women; she remained certain that controversy was the way to progress; she spent much time and effort on economists she considered influential and, in the case of capital theory, those she thought were most powerful in shaping American doctrine. Her accusations were widely misunderstood in the United States where the MIT economists she attacked were seen as interventionist Keynesians, advisers to Democrats rather than Republicans.

Joan Robinson ca. 1931

Above left, Paul Anthony Samuelson
ca. 1940, his first year at MIT

Above right, Robert Merton Solow
ca. 1950, his first year at MIT

Right, Edward Hastings Chamberlin
ca. 1928, new Ph.D. of Harvard

Robinson with John Kenneth Galbraith, June 1980

Left, Robinson escorted to the graduation festivities at Harvard, June 1980

Below, Robinson relaxing with Galbraith

Above, Robinson with J. D. Bernal at the Cambridge, England garden wedding reception of Bernal's son, June 1961

Right, Robinson at Harvard, June 1980

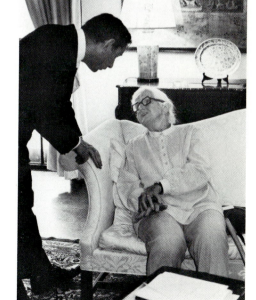

Left, Robinson at Williams College, Fall 1982

Below, Robinson at Barnard College meeting with Edward Nell and Barnard students, 1976

Robinson and Juliet Schor, Williams College, 1982

Joan Robinson ca. 1965

JR

CHAPTER TEN

The Meaning of Capital: Robinson versus Solow and Samuelson

The debate of the two Cambridges between 1954 and 1983 illustrates most pointedly the differences between Joan Robinson and American Keynesians Robert M. Solow and Paul A. Samuelson. The correspondence which has survived reveals the beliefs and personalities of these three leading figures of mid-century economic thought. Through the debate, letter exchanges, and professional meetings, the three became well acquainted. They also became entrenched in their own philosophical positions.

There were two periods of the debate. First was the challenge to the meaning of capital. Second was the reswitching debate. Solow was more prominent in the first period, Samuelson in the second. The debate moved into its second phase without, however, having disposed of the first question. In the first phase, Solow believed for a time that there was substantial agreement between himself and Robinson. She had said that there was no measure of capital; he concluded that that was correct if what one meant was a single measure. Their letters and articles indicate how they differed from that time on over relevance and method. This is the subject of the section on Solow below.

In the second phase, Robinson wrote "the story of what is known as the debate over the reswitching of techniques" for the *Quarterly Journal of Economics* and Samuelson replied. Their surviving correspondence is mainly about the reswitching debate, the subject of the section on Samuelson.

Jousting with Robert M. Solow

Robert Merton Solow was a bright young economist teaching statistics at MIT when he first came to Joan Robinson's attention. (He had earned his doctorate at

Harvard five years earlier.) Solow still has his student copy of her *Imperfect Competition*, which he studied as an undergraduate. As a graduate student he had also read her *Essays in The Theory of Employment* and *Introduction to the Theory of Employment*. After he had begun teaching at MIT, he read her *Essay on Marxian Economics*, a book he thinks of as "devastating to Marxism."[1]

As an undergraduate Solow was much influenced by Wassily Leontief who, he said, "got me to study mathematics." As a graduate student, while a research assistant to Leontief, Solow discovered probability and statistics, "a subject that was not taught to economists at Harvard then. . . . the courses in statistics that were taught were really dreadful; it was a scandal. So I took courses in the mathematics department." Solow claims that as a graduate student, even though Keynesian economics was taught at Harvard, he "was not primarily interested in what you would now describe as macroeconomics . . . but in economic theory, which meant general equilibrium theory." He wrote his dissertation, for which he received the David A. Wells Prize (1951), on the distribution of income by size among families treated as a stochastic process, an econometric treatment.[2]

When he saw Joan Robinson's article, "The Production Function and the Theory of Capital" in 1953,[3] he set himself to working out a model to prove what he thought was her point: he showed to his satisfaction "once and for all that this particular index number problem literally has no solution except under absurdly special assumptions."[4] He then had been dismayed to read her answering note in the *Review of Economic Studies* attacking his effort.[5]

He wrote her a letter trying to explain what he had meant to do. His letter began, "Was it Bernard Shaw who described England and America as two countries separated by a common language?" He then proceeded to answer the issues she had raised in her note: "The title of your article led me to believe that you were looking for some one summary number which could stand for all the various capital goods *in the production function*. And I showed that this simply could not be done." Commenting on some of her other points, he agreed that "the problem of time" presented problems, though he preferred "to put it that the main obstacle is our lack of any decent theory of how a capitalist behaves under conditions of uncertainty."[6]

Robinson replied via airletter with stunning brevity: "I don't think there is any need to bring the nationality question into it as there are many true-born American economists who have contributed to the theory of capital. Also I suppose that American business men are pretty fly at finding the techniques which will maximize profits, which they can hardly do without considering time. Yours sincerely."[7]

Solow was at the beginning of his career; Robinson had a reputation of twenty years' standing when they became joined (or entangled, as he suggested) in this debate.[8] Their correspondence for the late fifties is lost, but at some point, Solow wrote to Robinson suggesting that if they were to continue to call each other names, they should address each other on a first-name basis.

Joan Robinson considered Solow a worthy challenger. She wrote of him, "the brilliance of Professor Solow dazzles more than it enlightens." She must have thought that he might be swayed, because over the next fifteen years, she initiated strenuous discussions with him. Their correspondence is full of warm but sometimes aggressive exchanges. On the personal level they were friendly. When she was about to make her first trip to the United States in 1961, she wrote to "Bob": "I am making out the plans for my visit to the U.S.A. Would you be able to fix me up with some seminars and some dollars for the week beginning March 27th? Perhaps you could drop a word also at Harvard. Much looking forward to seeing you, Yours, Joan Robinson."

Solow replied with plans for seminars both at Harvard and MIT and $250 from each school, and "in addition we will jointly cover the marginal cost of your visit here. Do you want to work that hard during the week?" He added, "I'm looking forward to seeing you." Robinson then asked where she might stay: "I assume that you have some kind of guest house or hostel where I can be accommodated. Would you please let me know to what address I should present myself when I arrive." Harvard was able to provide lodgings at the Dana Palmer House, the university guest house for distinguished visitors.

A hitch in the arrangements occurred. Solow wrote in February,

> Now I have a bit of news in the best-laid-plans-of-mice-and-men department: I have surprised everyone, including myself, by agreeing to go down to Washington for a year and be a handyman at the Council of Economic Advisers. I expect to leave Cambridge [Massachusetts] at the end of this week. So it is possible that the chief abuser will not be here when you come. I shall certainly do my best to pull the strings necessary to get up here for those two days. It would be a pity if we could not get together during your visit; and moreover, I am told that human sacrifices are not nearly so much fun when the victim is out of town.

Solow was not able to return to Cambridge for her visit.

They were not to meet personally until two years later, but they continued to exchange papers and jibes. She wrote in August: "I am going out on a long roam around Asia on September 9th so I fear I will not see your new paper for some time. But if you get it right I will agree with it! Yours, Joan."

Publicly, their exchanges occurred in the 1962 issues of the *Review of Economic Studies*.[9] But private correspondence continued throughout this period as well. On May 24, 1962, Solow wrote to Robinson, "It is my understanding that Lipsey [the editor] is not inviting Rejoinders to Comments—and quite properly, because this nonsense could go on forever. But I should like to say that I think your comments on my paper are a complete red herring." The letter then became edgy:

I'll tell you what the tale is intended to teach you. It has often been claimed that the whole neo-classical apparatus requires, among other things, that capital goods be so instantaneously and costlessly malleable that they can be used freely with more or less labor—you know the sort of thing, you've written some of it. One purpose of my paper was to demonstrate (a) that the apparatus is also capable of dealing with situations in which capital goods are as specific and as rigid in their labor requirements as you please, and (b) that in such situations the log of price-wage-profit relations under competitive profit-maximization is not much changed, and (c) that the usual marginal equivalences continue to hold, with minor reinterpretations. And demonstrate it I did.

Apart from this presumably vain educational intent, I have a real problem in mind. I would like to know something about the rate of return to social saving in the United States now. This can hardly be discovered except by empirical investigation. It is much easier to organize empirical work around a malleable-capital model than a rigid-capital model. So I am anxious to know whether the representation of a rigid-capital world by a malleable-capital model leads to large empirical errors.

Now in order to work out the internal short- and long-run price relationships in a rigid-capital model, I simply assumed away the problem of determining effective demand. And that's your red herring. Effective demand is not a part of the problem I was interested in. Neither, for example, is the determination of the rate of profit or interest—the equivalences I find will hold for any rate of profit, and certainly for the correct rate of profit. So I left such problems aside. Suppose I had taken the time and trouble and had succeeded in grafting a satisfactory theory of effective demand onto the model. The rest of it would have worked the same way. I rather suspect you would then have complained that I had neglected the difference between industry and agriculture, or between men and women, or that I had no theory of the determination of the weather or of the spawning habits of salmon. You'd be right; but who would you be kidding?

Again her response was brief. On May 29, 1962 she answered,

Dear Bob, To me you are a fascinating study:—A clever man who cannot see a simple point. I suppose to you I am just a dense woman. But we have made some progress if you now agree that your model requires the wage bargain to be made in real terms. Yours sincerely, Joan.

Robinson and Solow first met in October 1963 when he went to Cambridge, England to spend his sabbatical leave on a Ford Foundation Faculty Fellowship.

It was Nicky Kaldor who induced me to come to Cambridge. When I told him at the AEA [American Economic Association] meetings that I had a sabbatical to spend at Oxford, he said I was going to Oxford because I was frightened and didn't think I could stand the gaff in Cambridge. You don't tell a Brooklyn boy that he's afraid. I changed my plans and went to Cambridge.

Solow remembered their first personal encounter. He was in the Senior Common Room having coffee when she entered. He knew who she was, but he had not been introduced to her. She was talking to someone else, saying, "I have just returned from China." She wheeled suddenly, pointed to Solow, and said, "and he doesn't even know where that is!"[10]* He was assigned an office in room 23 of the departmental offices in a modern building adjoining the Marshall Library. There he began to receive handwritten notes from Robinson, all on points of economic analysis, which he would answer by hand. (Apparently she threw his answers away in her general clean-up.) Few were dated. Her manner was somewhat patronizing. "Dear Bob, Let us 'try very seriously to avoid talking at cross purposes'. First I will address the question to you that I did to Paul [Samuelson]. When you define the marginal product of labor, what are you keeping constant? J. R."

His reply is lost but it obviously pleased her. "B. S. from J. R. So far so good. It follows that with given means of production in existence the share of gross profit in the value of output depends upon investment and propensity to consume. If you accept this also we can go on to the next point." Once more the reply was satisfactory but lost to us. She continued, "All right. With a fixed supply of means of production in existence, the level of employment, the m.p. of labor and the real wage are determined by effective demand and market conditions (degree of competition). The prospective rate of profit is determined by expectations. You have nothing to add to Keynes at this rate. J. R."

In a handwritten three-page document, inscribed Memo #1 to J. R. from B.S. 29-X-63, Solow said of private and social rates of return, about which she had asked:

> The only way I know of proving this with any generality involves a lot of heavy mathematics. That disturbs me, but only because it makes it difficult for me to communicate to you how it works. (I do not believe that every worthwhile result in economics can be proved in simple English; it is as wrong to believe that economics is in no way like physics as to believe it is in every way like physics.)

Nevertheless, he did try to state such a case in words.

In this way, they progressed to what she called "Points from the Agenda." On November 18, 1963, she proposed her "Agenda for Discussion" to Professors Solow and Arrow. The first point was this: "My objections are to: 1. Overlooking the distinction between long and short period relationships." Solow replied, "I love the judicial way you draw up an agenda. Here are my brief comments:

---

*Both Kenneth Arrow and Solow were Cambridge visitors that year. Solow was invited to be Marshall lecturer.

1. Overlooking the distinction between long and short period relationships. Have I stopped beating my wife? I do not think I overlook this distinction.''

And so on through the six points. Apparently Arrow neglected to take the bait. There remain for scholars to ponder some fifty pages of handwritten or typed exchanges, most of them written by Joan Robinson. There are no personal notes or accusations here. Just economics. In arguments over Harrod's savings, she conceded, ''I have abandoned my rash statement that you *cannot* get off the Harrod knife edge but I maintain that there is no presumption that you can, without altering the technically given real-capital labor ratio (degree of mechanization) which you gallantly assumed to be given and the same for all vintages.''

Much of the surviving exchange took place in the fall when Solow was at Cambridge. After Solow returned to MIT in June, he received another letter about Harrod's saving. He replied in July, ''Since we left Cambridge while most of you were grading examinations, I had no chance to say a proper goodbye. No matter, I'll be back in 4 or 5 years and it will seem as if I had not been away. I wonder if the questions—let alone the answers—will still be the same?'' In August she wrote again, ''I think we were both right. . . . As you remarked before, all this is purely formal. . . .'' She added a handwritten note, ''I fear you are not really interested so don't bother.''

In 1964, Solow was invited to give the Wicksell Lectures at Stockholm. These were published. On January 18, 1965, Robinson wrote to him, ''I much enjoyed your Wicksell Lectures. It is satisfactory to see that when it comes to an actual problem you rely on Keynes and common sense.''

And she continued to follow his career. On July 21, 1970 she wrote about his Warwick lectures:

> I think that if I were allowed to ask one question, all our misunderstanding could be cleared up. In your Warwick lectures in Chapter 3—the vintage case—you assume that gross saving is a ''constant fraction of output'' (p. 50). How is output measured? Presumably in units of the homogeneous consumption good. Then what regulates the prices of the heterogeneous capital goods in which gross investment is embodied (a different vintage each year) in terms of the consumption good?

His reply (lost) must have been unsatisfactory to her. On July 29 she wrote again. ''Sorry! I see I asked the wrong question about your Warwick lectures as all your vintages are made of congealed butter. But the question still is, what is this a parable of if it cannot explain anything except itself—i.e. the butter economy? See you in September.''

The Congress of the Econometric Society which met in Cambridge, England in 1970 staged Robinson and Solow to appear together, he commenting on her paper. She addressed the Congress on ''The Measure of Capital: The End of the Controversy.''[11] Neither the address nor the comments were for immediate publication. While her address was later published, we have only his notes to indicate what he said.

Robinson did not refer to Solow by name in her talk. She gave a history of the meaning and measurement of capital as she saw it, noting specifically that she considered the statistical work which had been done by the assembled econometricians valuable. What she doubted was what the statistics meant in terms of the distribution of income. She claimed that econometricians had been guilty of confusing the two legitimate meanings of capital: (1) capital as a stock of machines; (2) capital as a value in a production function. She argued, "neither concept has anything to do with the interpretation of actual statistics." She added what some might take to be a conciliatory statement: Franklin Fisher of MIT had made a careful study of the issue and determined that an index of physical capital could not be found.[12] He later concluded that "aggregate production functions are not even good approximate descriptions of the technical possibilities of a diverse economy. . . ."[13]

Robinson quoted Fisher in order to make the point, "This leaves the question where it began." But Fisher had made further refinements and had finally concluded that technical relationships, rather than determining labor's share, were representable "because labor's share happens to be roughly constant."[14] Robinson concluded, "It seems then, that the controversy is over. We must agree (though mumpsimus will continue in the textbooks) that marginal productivity of capital in industry as a whole has been shown to be a meaningless expression. We must look somewhere else to determine the laws which regulate the distribution of the produce of the earth among the classes of the community."[15]

Solow carried to the platform the language of their private correspondence: "I want to try to convince you that she is absolutely entitled to end the controversy whenever she wants, just as the author of any work of fiction is entitled to marry off or kill off his characters whenever he feels like, because the controversy has been entirely of her own making, and has been carried on entirely inside her own head."

He went back to the beginning of the controversy.

Characteristically, JR misunderstood, or paid no attention to, or didn't read what I had written (in 1957). She wrote a rejoinder which said very little except that she clearly thought that I was the one who thought that perfect aggregation was possible or necessary. Then I made another mistake. I wrote her a polite letter explaining that she had misunderstood me, and that I didn't think you could count on defining a rigorous stock of capital, but that I didn't think that any serious theoretical issue depended on that conclusion. JR's response was a note that said in its entirety, as I remember, "I see no need to bring nationalities into it." That has been the story of my life and correspondence with JR through dozens of letters since.[16]

Solow and many others in the audience shared a longstanding belief that in many respects "the aggregated model appears to behave well, theoretically speaking." He added, "Obviously an aggregated theory must be *internally* logical; all I mean is that it might give good answers even if it is not a perfect aggregation of the (true?) underlying micromodel." Solow admitted that "the reswitching discussion has alerted us to one respect in which one-capital-good models may be theoretically misleading." But he went on to say, "The practical importance of this failure is hard to judge but obviously there is reason to tread warily." Nevertheless he defended the aggregated model "as a vehicle for empirical work," and he asked, "What competing hypothesis is there? . . . The thing works too well in too many places and too many bodies of data" to be a mere coincidence. "Joan Robinson's alternative suggestion that it all has to do with circularity suggests only that she has no grasp of how you actually go about fitting one of the things to time series." He continued, "Is it worth playing this empirical game? That depends on whether you think of economics as a practical subject or merely a word-game."

During Solow's comment, Samuelson left the auditorium. He did not care for personal confrontation, though he might have agreed with Solow's points. And, of course, the comments were not for publication. Indeed, they were undoubtedly more acceptable in Cambridge on Robinson's home ground than they would have been on American soil. Such comments are ordinary in Cambridge seminars, and one can conclude that Solow had been to enough of these to master what is commonly called "Cambridge rudeness." One distinguished American economist—who had been spending some time in Cambridge, but had no particular interest in the controversy—asked what was going on. The reply was, "Bob Solow is giving Joan Robinson the scolding she so richly deserves."

Solow's comments rolled off Robinson's back. She might even have been pleased to smoke him out at last. Soon afterwards, on September 29, Solow received a note from her inquiring about a reference to a metaphor he had expressed in a seminar at Cambridge. But the correspondence never got much further after that. On October 7, 1970, she asked Solow once more about his "butter economy." She added, "I am glad that you now agree that the 'rate of return' has nothing to do with the pseudo-production function." But she continued, "as you seem to be quite happy stuck in your butter I will try not to bother you any more."

He replied on October 13,

Honestly, I don't like to seem unresponsive; but the truth is that years of going back and forth like this seem to me to have yielded a tape that would sound much the same played backward or forward. Just as a last example, I do not "now agree." I once wrote a paper that proved, in a clan of cases, that the "rate of return on investment," which is a concept having to do with a process *in time* of passing from one possible path to another possible path, is equal to the equilibrium rate of interest, which is a concept having to do with *alternative* possible points on the factor-price frontier. I don't know if this is surprising, interesting, or what. But it's what I proved.

She responded, "The reason why our argument goes round and round is that you have the habit of giving answers before distinguishing the questions." The rest of her letter has to do with four rather involved questions. His reply is lost, but she answered it on November 2, 1970:

I was very happy to have your last letter. If you have kept the copy of my note on continuity you will see . . . that I make the point that you are now making. . . . So there is a small island of agreement for us to stand on. However, I am afraid that it is a very small one. I do not agree that your Dutch lectures were free from butter. They identify the long-period production function with the short-period utilization function, which is possibly [sic] only in a butter world. However, it is nice to agree on one point.

Again on November 19, she wrote, "As we seem to have finished the rate of return, may I take up another question—the length of service life of plant in a vintage model." He answered politely, and she thanked him December 21 for his prompt reply, agreeing on all but one point, and adding, "If you know what the missing equation is, please tell us." Solow replied January 4, 1971 by hand: "As usual, you take my breath away. There is no missing equation," and he cited chapter and verse. On January 11, she answered, "The point is that your equation 33 does not determine anything. There is always one rate of interest which satisfies this equation for each length of life of plant."

Two days later she wrote another letter, calling it a postscript: "The missing equation for the net saving case is $r = r$; the rate of interest is simply given. . . . I suppose your r is something like Marshall's 'reward of waiting' or the 'discount of the future' by owners of wealth. But surely this only works in a stationary state?" His reply is lost but she wrote on March 16, 1971,

Its no use your coming it over me with mathematics because one thing I do know is that if you have an average curve you can draw the marginal to it but if you have the marginal curve there are an indefinite number of average curves (with different constants) which are compatible with it. This is a case in point; net saving is nothing but the increment in the value of capital. To solve the problem you have to have an independent theory of the rate of interest (or as I should call it the rate of profit) and this is what you lack. . . .

On March 23, Solow replied:

I don't enjoy repeating myself, but I'm trying to give you the benefit of the doubt. The *only* way I can make any sense, even erroneous sense, out of what you keep saying is to suppose that you do not understand about simultaneous equations. In my mind, there is no difference between "an independent theory of the rate of interest" and a "determinate system of equations in which the rate of interest is one of the unknowns being determined." You do not ever say which of the equations of Solow, Tobin, et al, you object to, or why you think they have no proper solution. Guess why.

On March 29, 1971, Solow received from her a reprint of her review of his *Growth Theory, An Exposition.* [17] She penned a note, "Dear Bob, I know you do not like being criticized, but you should not take up such exposed positions. Joan." Her review began, "These lectures provide an elaboration of the neo-classical parables (as Professor Samuelson calls them) 'which pretend that there is a single thing called 'capital' that can be put into a single production function and along with labor will produce total output'." She concluded, "How can rules for policy be deduced from a parable that explains nothing but itself? I do not think I will attend the rest of the course."

On April 1, 1971, she raised once again her point about his needing one more equation to determine three ratios. On May 3, 1971, Solow answered: "I write only out of sheer old-world politeness. Please let us stop this nonsense. When the given gross-savings ratio is dropped, the extra equation is given by (38) in conjunction with (36)." The last letter in Solow's file is one from Robinson to him dated, May 10, 1971: "Dear Bob, I agree that it is hopeless so goodbye. Yours, Joan." Solow sent the last three letters to a colleague, adding a note: "Read in order. At last!"

Nevertheless, Robinson and Solow valued their friendship and their ex-changes. In 1979, in an article about the "Misunderstandings in the Theory of Production," she referred to such exchanges as "intellectual experiment." In reviewing her own thought development, she said that she had introduced "a book of blueprints" in her attempts to "dismantle" the neoclassical production function. She added, "From this developed what Professor Solow called a pseu-do-production function. (Bob! I thank thee for that word.)"[18]

Solow and Robinson were to meet once more in the 1970s. Stephen Marglin warned Solow that he had invited Robinson for dinner at the Society of Fellows at Harvard, where Solow is also a member. Solow thought that Marglin wanted to make certain that if he brought Joan Robinson to dinner when Solow was there, Solow would be polite to her. "There was no danger at all. I think Steve sort of thought that if I saw Joan, I would claw the earth, and I explained that I thought of Joan as a friend. In fact, Steve did bring her to dinner and the three of us sat at a small table and had a very pleasant conversation. I thought she was quite subdued at dinner, and I think it was because she was hard of hearing. She was really not her old self."

When Solow was in Cambridge for the 1983 centenary celebration of Keynes, Robinson was in the hospital, possibly in a coma. He asked whether he could go to see her, but was told that she was not having visitors. So the last time he had seen her when she was really herself was at the Congress of the Econometric Society when he had discussed her paper: "She was her own aggressive self, and I wasn't giving an inch, and so it went."

Enter Paul Anthony Samuelson

Joan Robinson and Paul Samuelson first met in 1948. He already knew her work: "I heard Joan Robinson's name for the first time actually from the lips of Frank Knight." Samuelson was given her *Economics is a Serious Subject*. Then in 1934, while still an undergraduate at the University of Chicago, he read her *Imperfect Competition*.[19] Samuelson graduated with a bachelor of arts from Chicago in 1935, earning a master's degree at Harvard the next year. He won the David A. Wells Prize in 1941 for his thesis on the foundations of economic analysis.[20] Samuelson corresponded with Robinson before he met her personally, but there is no record of this correspondence among her archival papers. Samuelson remembers, "We met in Richard Kahn's rooms in the autumn of 1948. She had on red pajamas."[21]

Initially, Robinson thought of Samuelson as a fellow Keynesian. In one of her "Essays 1953," she bracketed him with Kaldor and Kalecki. Her lecture was about the dismay of an Oxford tutor in trying to answer questions from his freshman pupil. His answers are lacking because they are not Keynesian: "But now he has played right into the Keynesian court. Even if he gets a ball over the net once in a while, Samuelson, Kaldor or Kalecki kill his service, so that he never scores a single point. It is a love game to the Keynesian every time."[22]

Part of the reason she included Samuelson as a proper Keynesian was that she had met him personally. He had attended secret seminar discussions in both 1948 and 1952.[23] Perhaps if Robinson had given Samuelson's *Foundations* a careful reading, she might have understood him better right from the beginning. There Samuelson offered a mathematical treatment of what he called the "Keynesian system," where he considered the Keynesian model as one applicable "to problems of business cycles," following models developed by writers "such as Meade, Hicks and Lange."[24] When he wrote *Foundations,* Samuelson was mainly interested in Keynes' consumption function, the marginal efficiency of capital, and the schedule of liquidity preference. But Samuelson was more inclined to follow Walras' discussion of "liquidity preference, *encaisse désirée*, etc. in which Walras "very rightly," in Samuelson's opinion, "continued to believe in what is today called the 'quantity theory'."[25] Samuelson gave Keynes some credit for introducing uncertainty and for contributions to index number theory;[26] but he did not mention any "revolution" in thinking or in policy that might be called for by the publication of *The General Theory.*[27]

Samuelson has consistently followed what he taught in *Foundations*, including the application of Keynesian tools to business cycle theory. I am arguing that Samuelson was thus treating the General Theory as a special case and not as *the* General Theory that Cambridge Keynesians saw it to be. Samuelson corrects me, saying, "I *was* then, and am now, the kind of Keynesian Joan was 1933–1953. This was Joan's 1936 Keynes' system! This is your interpretation, not mine, or Tobin's, or Solow's or Hansen's."[28]

The capital controversy and Robinson's assessment of the American mainstream as "bastard Keynesianism" changed her attitude toward Samuelson. Once the capital controversy was on, Robinson's references to Samuelson became more provocative, that is, more in the spirit of her thrusts at Solow. She accused Samuelson of being one of the economists hawking "pre-Keynesian theory after Keynes." She considered his version of the "pseudo production function" as "an exercise . . . useful for clearing up some fuzzy points in the old theory but it has no application to anything on earth."[29]

Robinson objected to how he measured capital:

> Samuelson's trick of measuring each stock of capital in terms of its own product is of no use, because the physical composition of gross output and the pattern of prices are both different in each economy. He is in error in saying that the elasticity of his curve corresponds to the relative shares of wages and profits in the value of output. I am indebted to von Weizsäcker for the mathematical demonstration of this.[30]

Even when she reviewed works by others, she sometimes attacked Samuelson. For example, B. S. Minhas wrote a book applying one of Samuelson's "propositions." There Robinson found that "the queer methodology nowadays acceptable in our subject is exemplified." She objected to Minhas' assumptions (taken from Samuelson) in his international comparison of factor costs and use. "One cannot but admire the courage with which he leaps from a skyscraper of abstract assumption on to the hard facts. *C'est magnifique, mais ce n'est pas la science.*"[31]

Her summary version of Samuelson's part in the capital controversy is that after her confrontation with him over production functions, he retreated to parables on surrogate production functions. Then he "very handsomely admitted that he had been mistaken. . . . But he mistook his mistake."[32]

Other accusations were sprinkled through her work of the 1960s and early 1970s: "Professor Samuelson took a false step when he tried to identify the quantity of capital-stuff in the parable with the value of capital on a pseudo-production function."[33] "Samuelson's version of the Heckscher-Ohlin theory is still more degenerate," she concluded in an address.[34] She grouped Samuelson with the "neo-neoclassicals" who, "when they began to reconstruct orthodox theory after the upheaval of the 'Keynesian revolution', had evidently forgotten that the problem of measuring capital and accounting for profit as an element in costs had never been solved."[35] Again, "Samuelson was sufficiently candid to admit that the basis of his system does not hold, but the theorems go on pouring out just the same."[36]

Robinson was particularly vociferous about what she considered to be an error in Samuelson's methodology. This technical point was discussed not only between Samuelson and Robinson, but by Harcourt in his *Cambridge Controversies*. Robinson accused Samuelson of committing the error of moving between two points on a plane diagram when in fact a third dimension—time—is required.[37] Samuelson replied that any mathematician knows that a functional relationship is timeless, and quoted Harcourt as vindicating his position.[38] Samuelson took her criticisms seriously, but he held to his views. He was never drawn into the argument, so to speak, but remained on his own ground. From there he replied as a gentleman might: "We all owe Mrs. Robinson so much that there is not the usual sting in such words as '. . . just a bluff' or 'the professors at MIT took over my book of blueprints and tried to . . .'."[39] Samuelson commented, "It is understandable that strong convictions should lead to strong language, as any reader of the 'capital controversies' can document in quantitative detail author by author."[40] This turning of the cheek made Robinson impatient. "Professor Samuelson is kind enough to make me a number of compliments in his comment. I would be more gratified if he would answer my point."[41]

I asked Samuelson if it were the case that Robinson had never understood his eclecticism. "Yes," he replied.

> I think she thought that people like Solow and me were just willful. There are no deaf people like those who will not hear. There was something almost unununderstandable and it had to be, at bottom, something to do with interest, namely a covert ideology or being paid off by the interests, or a kind of selfishness. . . . Earlier I just thought that she thought I was stubborn and didn't like to admit I was wrong when pretty clearly shown to be wrong, just a poor loser.[42]

Did he agree with the Cambridge view that a science moved forward through controversy? Samuelson answered, "My own preference is not for the adversarial procedure. I think it's an expensive, time-consuming thing; but it has a place in the history of science and especially in nominating new ideas which would not in a polite, tea party atmosphere get a hearing."

Is that why he had left the debate of Solow and Robinson at the World Econometric Conference in Cambridge? "I stayed only a small part. I really didn't like it; it was getting . . . there was too much passion in it, and a lot of people were feeling sorry for Joan because Bob was giving . . . as you know she can give out and take. I left as I would leave a bullfight when the bull is being gored. Solow, for once, was aiming hard blows at Joan and many in the audience were enjoying the bloodying."[43]

In this debate, however, Samuelson heard Robinson express the idea that since there was no purely economic determination of the distribution of income, then "the union movement could just come and get it." This was "a power theory," and it worried him as "unrealistic and naive." "I discern very strong forces out there in the real world constraining the real distribution of income." Yet he had searched her writings for her view on what determines the distribution of income in the real world without finding it: "I knew some of the things she didn't believe in, but I didn't know what it was she believed in."[44]

Since Robinson was fond of quoting Samuelson's alleged concession to Cambridge on the reswitching issue, I wondered if she had ever conceded any point to him. "No, I don't recall her ever saying 'by gosh on that point you're right, and I could kick myself' but that wasn't particularly her. On the other hand, I didn't think of her as one who argued for victory."

Correspondence on reswitching*

In spite of all, Robinson obviously admired Samuelson's intellect. For example, she was stimulated to write a paper entitled "Saving without Investment" after reading a paper of his in 1958.[45] Robinson saved (or failed to destroy) correspondence she had with Samuelson during the early 1970s. At the time, she was interested not only in the narrow issues in the capital controversy, but also in what she called "The Philosophy of Prices."[46] The existing correspondence begins with a letter from Samuelson which sets the tone of most of his correspondence with her: "I enclose a more detailed description of what I have been trying to say. By all means show it to any interested party. And if, as is always possible, I have nodded in this matter, please let me know where I seem to have gone off the tracks. Yours, Paul."[47]

There may have been letters lost. Six months later, Robinson wrote, "Many thanks for your amendment. You agree that what Marx called 'prices of production' (when properly worked out) are bourgeois prices. What I was asking is what you now propose to call Walrasian prices based on supply and demand for scarce means with alternative uses. Sincerely, Joan."[48] Samuelson underlined her statement, "Walrasian prices based on supply and demand for scarce means with alternative uses," and wrote his answer at the bottom of the letter: "There is no single model corresponding to the words I've underlined above but in [other work of mine] . . . you will find examples of complete, logically noncontradictory models in which heterogeneous capital-goods' pricing and interest rate determinations are defined over time. Whether these models are realistic or even interesting depends on the eyes of the reader."

At this point, she must have suggested he should reread her article on prices. He replied,

---

*See Appendix Note 10.1 Robinson's view of switching and reswitching.

At your suggestion I reread your 1960 piece, and found it as I remembered it. For 70 years at least students of Wicksell have realized that in a world of constant returns to scale, there is no need for exchange of final goods. I see no contradiction to that in the view of Smith, Ricardo, Sraffa and me—that the equilibrium price ratio of goods readily reproducible at constant costs (and produced in positive amounts) is their cost ratio, without regard to the number of transactions that take place at that equilibrium ratio. Ever, Paul.[49]

Then there is an undated letter on Waldorf Astoria paper but with the return address of MIT written in black ink, asking her to clarify whether Sraffa means "constant returns to scale" when he speaks of "constant returns." In blue ink at the bottom, Samuelson asks, "What else can it mean?" She replied, "Dear Paul, I showed your letter to Sraffa and he replied 'What else could it mean?' For my own part I do not know whether 'scale' applies to a plant, a firm, or an industry."[50] She continued: "I maintain that there are two distinct kinds of prices. While you are now going all out for Sraffa prices, I maintain that there is still a sphere for prices formed by supply and demand, that is where a particular commodity requires particular natural resources," and she quoted his statement that the export of tropical fruits from the tropics is due to the prevalence of tropical conditions there.[51]

At the bottom of this letter, Samuelson typed: "Dear Joan, I went 'all out' for nothing. Strike out any words in our communications that suggested to you otherwise. Ever, Paul." Their letters seemed to cross. Samuelson wrote to her still objecting to being classified with "Sraffa's restricted case." She replied in a typewritten letter: "Dear Paul, The rules of this debate seem to be: 'All statements made by Paul Samuelson are correct, including those which contradict each other'. I am afraid this is beyond me. Yours Joan."[52]

Samuelson replied at length.

I have not asked for a dispensation to neglect logic or common sense. I was only trying to suggest—gently—that your inference was unfounded that I had gone all out for constant cost models . . . to the neglect of more general models. . . . I enclose under separate mail no less than three reprints written in the last year or so that explicitly deny non-substitution theorem conditions; I remind you of my various criticisms of the labor theory of value, and that Stolper and I were the ones who introduced into the economic literature the production box diagrams that deduce concavity of the production possibility frontier and that all my earlier work on factor prices equalization was based (as you were one of the first to point out) on precisely those considerations that you now say I neglect or play down. Over the years I have quoted your work at a copious rate, and as far as I know I have never—even when I disagreed with you—read inferences into them that you had not intended. I shall try to continue to do the same. Ever, Paul.[53]

Robinson took this in stride. She answered, "The important thing is to get the question clear before trying to answer it. Three cases have been mixed up in this correspondence. . . ." and she went on to explain in some detail.[54] She closed with, "I hope this makes my complaint clear. I am most grateful for your patience." But by this time, Samuelson was irritated: "Dear Joan, I feel I am wasting time better spent on other things. Here are my final words on this matter. . . . Please note that I have neither changed my mind about whether Smith is right or wrong or had occasion to do so. . . . Let's turn to more interesting matters."[55]

On April 14, 1972, he wrote her in a more jovial mood: "I used to joke to Bob Solow that the distance between me and Joan Robinson is less than the distance between Joan Robinson and me. His reply was, 'You'll never convince her of that.' Still one lives in hope." Added in a postscript was a fascinating (to economists) note on the "missing equation" she had so often asked Solow for.[56]

> P.S. On the serious question of what are good hypotheses to make to deter-
> mine the 'missing equation' for the profit rate or the real wage expressed in terms
> of any specified goods or marketbasket, any postscript would be too short. There
> is no disagreement that, in a stationary state with only one page of blue-print
> technology which has long been giving to workers only a fraction of the total net
> product, an act of political expropriation that gave the workers collectively
> ownership in the raw materials would successfully result in euthanasia of the
> capitalist class. But Allende will of course face a more complicated model. . . . I
> often analyze minimum-subsistence-wage models, as in connection with the
> transformation problem—but not because I think them realistic or of much
> insight into the laws of motion of capitalism but because so many old-fashioned
> Marxists believe in them. When there are many pages of technology, a once and
> for all expropriation which was shared equally by all workers might well, if each
> worker was subsequently permitted to sell off his share of intermediate goods,
> result after a time in unequal ownership as between the more- and less-thrifty and
> the lucky or unlucky on medical catastrophes, etc. If the system ever comes into a
> new steady state—which I would regard as doubtful—it could be one again [with]
> positive profit rate (not necessarily unique) just high enough and just low enough
> so that the capitalized market value of non-labor resources averaged over people
> of all ages (the retired dissavers and working savers) would work out to equality
> with their cost-of-production total values. In short, Modigliani's life-cycle mod-
> el of saving provides one possible way of finding the missing equation. But there
> are others.

On June 15, 1973, Robinson wrote to Samuelson, "I fear you will think I am nagging, but I wrote this in the hope of enlightening some people on my side of the question. I am submitting it to Q.J.E. [*Quarterly Journal of Economics*] Meanwhile I would like very much to have your re-action."[57] Samuelson answered, "I don't think your piece on the unimportance of reswitching represents any nagging. I read it with interest and profit, and would hope that readers of the QJE will too." He proposed that he should also comment. He wrote, "your paper adds to our too few accounts of the actual process by which scientific ideas get formed, modified, and initiated." He would like to expand his remarks, he said,

> . . . not to controvert your general theses or set any records straight, but to provide supplementary and complementary harmonies and dissonances that the interested reader might also enjoy. This is only a suggestion. If you have some preference for presenting you[r] own viewpoint without complications, I'll be glad within the limits of my time to write you the occasional queries that arise in reading your manuscript. (For example, my memory of my 1965 Summing Up is that, in it I didn't make any *illegitimate* "use of a pseudo production function in describing a process of accumulation through time." But I would not want to trust my memory in so complex a matter. . . . I shall be here all summer, playing tennis and pleasantly engaged in catching up with the research, rejoinders, etc. that piled up while we were in Japan and Australia.[58]

This famous exchange on the reswitching debate was published in the *Quarterly Journal of Economics* in 1975. In her article Robinson offered her review of what the controversy was all about.[59]

Early in the capital controversy, at one of the secret seminars, Ruth Cohen had asked why each technique had a given rate of profit. Couldn't the same technique be subject to different profit rates? Robinson explored this and concluded that with various assumptions as to the amount of labor embodied in an equipment, there might be more than one profit rate. She called it the "Ruth Cohen case," a "curiosum."[60] Later Sraffa integrated time patterns with the same amount of labor and found that "it is perfectly normal (within the accepted assumptions) for the same technique to be eligible at several discrete rates of profit." Robinson thought this circumstance, which seemed commonplace at Cambridge University, was ignored by the "neo-neoclassicals": "They went on as usual drawing production functions in terms of 'capital' and labor and disseminating the marginal productivity theory of distribution."

Then she encountered Samuelson (1961) "on his home ground" and felt she had scored a victory when he admitted that when he defined the marginal product of labor, he kept constant either the physical inputs other than labor or the rate of profit on capital. She crowed: "I found this satisfactory, for it destroys the doctrine that wages are regulated by marginal productivity."[61] She claimed that it was then that Samuelson "retreated behind what he called a surrogate production function."[62]

Robinson observed that "Professor Samuelson found out how to draw a pseudo production function in which the value of capital does not vary with the rate of profit."[63] Her story continued: "For several years, everyone (except Piero

Garegnani) was somewhat baffled by the surrogate production function." Then "a disciple of Professor Samuelson" claimed that reswitching could never occur. The second phase of the debate was on when Luigi Pasinetti pointed out a mathematical error in the supposed proof, and this attracted several others who then explored the question from various points of view. "At the end of it all, Professor Samuelson still thought he could use a pseudo production function in describing a process of accumulation going on through time."

Robinson concluded, "There is no such phenomenon in real life as accumulation taking place in a given state of technical knowledge. The idea was introduced into economic theory only to give a meaning to the concept of the marginal productivity of capital. . . ."[64] She compared two lines of thought—a post-Keynesian approach as this was understood at Cambridge, including contributions by Harrod, Kalecki, Kaldor, and herself; and the pre-Keynesian argument in its "various forms." Walrasian, Uzawaian, and Meadian models were mentioned as "pre-Keynesian models," where "all machines and consumption goods are made of the same physically homogeneous stuff" which is "usually called a one-commodity world."[65]

Robinson's basic accusation was that "the professors at M.I.T. took over my book of blueprints and tried to embed it in pre-Keynesian theory." And this is where she concluded once again that Samuelson still thought he could use a pseudo-production function in describing a process of accumulation going on through time, in spite of the fact that there is no such phenomenon in real life as accumulation taking place in a given state of technical knowledge.[66]

Samuelson's reply suggested that some "possibility of misinterpretation" might arise from the "ambiguity of English speech and grammar." But he added,

> I do not think that the real stumbling block has been the failure of a literary writer to understand that when a mathematician says "y rises as x falls" he is implying nothing about temporal sequences or anything different from "when x is low, y is high."[67]

Nor did Samuelson think either Robinson's or Harcourt's criticism of his method stood. He raised and disposed of the "logical issues" and added,

> In concluding this conciliatory note dealing solely with the logical points raised about my own works, I should say that failure to deal with other aspects of Professor Robinson's account does not mean that I would consider hers an optimal formulation of the issues agreed upon or in controversy. It is valuable as *her* account: from *Rashomon*, we know how different the single reality will appear to different actors in the same drama.[68]

I asked Samuelson whether he really subscribed to his Rashomon theory of economic perceptions. He answered,

I guess at bottom I don't. I don't think that you can be idiosyncratic and selective and say, that's all right in your paradigm, but in my paradigm, it's this, because I think of there being out there a constraining reality. . . . It's the one that calls the tune. But to describe the method of arriving at opinions and truth, I would say that people's gestalts are extremely important. . . . I don't know whether I wrote this down somewhere, I probably did, but I could chat with Joan Robinson in perfect agreement if I talked about something like Mainland China . . . or how you would plan for China—you'd do the highest-yield projects first as long as life was very austere and current consumption was very important and then you'd gradually move on in the absence of innovation to less important projects and so forth. I could almost trap her into describing all that. The moment the capitalistic market came into it then, no, it is all right in China, but not in the markets of the western world.

I took this anecdote to mean that Samuelson believed not that he and Joan Robinson had different paradigms in mind, but only different "gestalts." He added, "I am haughty enough to believe that I understood Joan Robinson but she never completely understood me. She understood parts of me, but she didn't really understand me." And he thought that occasionally she did him an "injustice": "I would get under certain conditions from a curve which represents different steady states the interest rate which prevailed in one of those steady states. She regarded that as an illogical error. . . but it happens to be the case that you can do that in a very limited subset of cases."[69]

On the question of both paradigms and method, Robinson never succeeded in convincing Samuelson, nor vice versa.

JR

CHAPTER ELEVEN

The Sweet and Sour of Befriending Americans

Toward the end of her life, Joan Robinson had a definite opinion about the evolution of American neoclassical thought:

> The doctrines in the United States were derived from the stream of thought elaborated by Robert Clower, taken up by Axel Leijonhufvud, which tried to derive Keynes from the general equilibrium theory of Walras, considered to be the foundation of economics. Clower tried to show that Keynes was not inconsistent with this, that Keynes' theory was merely that unemployment arises from a failure of the generation of equilibrium according to the doctrine of *laissez faire*, that is of the operation of a market system through movements of prices; so that all the old doctrines were reestablished.[1]

This Robinson said in discussion at Kahn's Mattioli lectures, delivered in Italy in June 1978. She was then seventy-four years old. She must have believed in what she was saying, and yet it belies her earlier relations with the two men cited, and their own views as well. The evolution of her opinion is pertinent to our argument that Robinson hoped to influence American economists. When she found she had failed, she might write them off, intellectually, at least.

Robert Clower

Robert Clower was from the American Northwest, and was probably the only Northwesterner Robinson ever knew. (Chamberlin, though born in La Connor, Washington, was reared elsewhere.) Clower is of the same generation as Solow, and was twenty-three years younger than Robinson. Western style, he attended a nearby university, Washington State. Clower received his bachelor's degree in 1948 and his master's in 1949, graduating in his hometown of Pullman. Then he went abroad, where he received another master's degree from Oxford University in 1952. This undoubtedly put him up a notch, for he began teaching at the prestigious private Northwestern University in the mid-1950s. (Clower was awarded a doctorate at Oxford in 1978 when he was fifty-two.)

While at Oxford as a research student, Clower, at the time an admirer of Keynes, came under the influence of John R. Hicks. Clower's first encounter with Joan Robinson was when she attended one of Hicks' theory seminars in 1951 or 1952 and

> . . . nearly gave John Hicks apoplexy. She was dealing with some paper or some book of Hicks', perhaps his *Trade Cycle*, and she kept telling him what he had said. He got pinker and pinker and finally said with much stammering, "I didn't say anything of the sort," to which she replied that if he didn't say it, that it was what he meant to say. He got even more upset. I remembered her from that time as an almost unadulterated bitch. But we took sides, of course.

Later, however, he changed his view of Robinson "considerably."

> I got to know her personally. I was very fond of her. She was the most brilliant woman that I have ever come across, bar none, and was so broad and deep. She had this very tough intellectual side to her, but also this very soft feminine side. It was fascinating to be with her. I was quite a few years younger than she was, but it was something of a love affair, though we were unable to consummate it for a variety of reasons, including my wife.[2]

At one time, Clower was what he now considers "a pretty wild-eyed Keynesian. I was unable to see flaws in Keynes because I worshipped the man so, but that's kind of youthful. Keynes is the first thing I ever read in economics. I read his *Economic Consequences of the Peace* and then *The General Theory* and then back to Marshall, and after that I started doing economics." During the early sixties, Robinson and Clower were very close colleagues, visiting each other and corresponding. "We had a very friendly time from 1962 to 1965. After that, she got a bit fed up with me because I simply could not go along with the generalization of the general theory that was going on in Cambridge." She visited him in 1961 in the United States.* He was back at Cambridge in 1965 and at the University of Essex in the 1960s and "saw a lot of her then. This went on for a few years, but our contacts became fewer and fewer. We simply weren't on the same wave length as before."

Robinson came to consider Clower "a distinguished neoclassical economist." She asked to quote from one of his letters to her to illustrate that such people thought it possible to elaborate the model of an exchange economy "without ever mentioning production."[3]

---

*See Chapter 14.

In 1962, when they were on the best of terms, Clower read a paper at the International Economic Association Conference on Theories of Interest Rates entitled, "The Keynesian Counterrevolution: A Theoretical Appraisal."[4] His argument was that economists had failed to integrate price theory and income analysis. He felt that there was much ambivalence among "professional economists" towards the "Keynesian Counterrevolution launched by Hicks in 1937 and now being carried forward with such vigor by Patinkin and other general equilibrium theorists." He found the profession

> . . . caught on the horns of a dilemma. If Keynes added nothing new to orthodox doctrine, why have twenty-five years of discussion failed to produce an integrated account of price theory and income analysis? If Keynes did add something new, the integration problem becomes explicable; but then we have to give up Walras' Law as a fundamental principle of economic analysis. It is precisely at this point, I believe, that virtually all previous writers have decided to part company with Keynes.

For himself, Clower offered a different interpretation of the formal basis of the Keynesian revolution. His view was that Keynes had brought current transactions into price theory where traditional analysis explicitly leaves them out, so that "Keynesian economics is price theory without Walras' Law, and price theory with Walras' Law is just a special case of Keynesian economics." He concluded that "contemporary general equilibrium theories can be maintained intact only if we are willing to barter Keynes for orthodoxy."

The choice was important, he thought, because general equilibrium analysis is

> . . . a useful instrument for thinking about abstract economic problems. . . . The danger in using this instrument to think about practical problems is that, having schooled ourselves so thoroughly in the virtues of elegant simplicity, we may refuse to recognize the crucial relevance of complications that do not fit our theoretical preconceptions. As Keynes has put it, "The difficulty lies, not in the new ideas, but in escaping from the old ones, which ramify, for those brought up as most of us have been, into every corner of our minds."[5]

And in later papers, Clower has continued to warn of the possible sterility of relying too heavily on Walrasian general equilibrium. Thus it seemed strange that Robinson named Clower as one who "tried to derive Keynes from the general equilibrium theory of Walras. . . ."[6] Asked about this statement of Robinson's, Clower replied,

> No, it's not that I ever thought that equilibrium theory is the foundation of economic analysis. In the 1950s and 1960s, that was the one medium of communication through which you could reach the bulk of the profession. You couldn't

in terms of poetry or Marx and not very much in terms of analogies. Parables or that kind of thing was useful, but it doesn't really carry any weight. The way to get to them is to point out that within their own framework of analysis, there are serious problems that have not really been examined seriously. . . . She thought I was doing really very useful work in communicating with these bastard Keynesians in their own language, and so did I; but I wasn't quite that sure about how things were going, and I proved to be right. All I did was to produce a crazier branch of French economists who do what they call non-Walrasian economics.

Her views at the Mattioli lectures came long after this "honeymoon" period, when Clower had seemed to be doing proper battle with the bastard Keynesians.

As for the accusation that he had tried to derive Keynes from general equilibrium, he replied,

No, I didn't try to derive Keynes, for god's sake, that's crazy. Just the opposite. There wasn't anything in Walras that could possibly get you to Keynes. I suggested that Walras was wrong, and that most of the profession in taking the standard Walrasian maximization assumption constraints as god's truth were simply leading themselves down a blind alley; that those constraints were loose as hell; depending upon what kind of framework you use, you get different results.

Some of Robinson's acrimony toward Clower may have been personal. He said,

I think Joan was partly annoyed with me because I really couldn't take sides on Robertson and various other little in-battles at Cambridge. She was annoyed more than a little bit in 1962 when I became very friendly with Robertson, and also with Sraffa and also Frank Hahn. I simply don't mix with economists on the basis of what they think about political issues. Joan was a bit more careful about these things and in odd ways.

Perhaps Robinson's cooling toward Clower was political as well as economic. Now he is at UCLA, drawn there, he said, because he is "on the same wavelength" as the people there. He explained this to mean that he shares their interest in information/transaction cost approaches. UCLA is "sometimes described" as being dominated by "old-fashioned liberalism in economic policies." Clower said that "they used to call Chicago, UCLA East" and that both schools have been dominated by certain ideas from Hayek. (UCLA was "not noted for hiring strong monetarists.")

Clower remained fond of Robinson over the years. He thought of her as

. . . absolutely professional about economics. Like Harry Johnson, she just lived and breathed economics. But she had this other side to her, political interest and so forth. She just couldn't help getting hung up. I think this goes back to her life as a girl in a very distinguished family, and the behavior of her father—such principled behavior in standing up to a government and keeping silent and taking all sorts of crap and so forth. I think she was so interested in knocking her own class. She had an upper-class Englishwoman's view of the working masses, and they were just that to her. She could never really understand what it was really like to be part of the working class. She had a housekeeper and cook on one side of Grange Road and her husband had his on the other side. Her upbringing made such a difference. She was incapable of talking to people who had no education or breeding. It just didn't go well.

Clower's fondest memories are of Robinson's stay at Northwestern in 1961, her first visit to the United States and one he helped arrange. More about this later.

Axel Leijonhufvud

In 1969 Joan Robinson thought she had discovered another possible ally, a student of Clower's. Axel Leijonhufvud had come to the United States in 1960 for graduate study after earning his undergraduate degree in Sweden at the University of Lund.[7] He was thirty-six years old when Robinson read his book, *On Keynesian Economics and the Economics of Keynes*. His theme was to her liking—"that Keynes' theory is quite distinct from the 'Keynesian' income-expenditure theory," which was being taught as the standard theory in the United States.[8]

Leijonhufvud's book appeared during the period of the reswitching controversy. Robinson may have thought the tide was turning in America. She was pleased to write a favorable review of the book for the *Economic Journal*. "This book comes at a time when for many reasons the neo-neoclassicals are losing their self-confidence, and it is to be hoped that it will give them a salutary shock which will release their energies to tackle the many urgent problems, of theory and of policy, which the Keynesian Revolution opened up but which are still unsolved."

Robinson was amused that "Professor Leijonhufvud treats the 'British Keynesians' as some kind of quaint sect of Old Believers, who, however, preserved valuable traditions that the orthodox have lost. He suggests that we who worked with Keynes were saved from the misunderstandings rife in America because we had the benefit of oral teaching which was not made clear in the book."

She thought that might be so, but that Kalecki had also made a difference in England because he brought imperfect competition into the picture; also, the English had an advantage since they started from the concept of the Marshallian short-period situation. For Cantabrigians, "a short period supply curve relating the level of *money* price to the level of activity (at given money-wage rates) led

straight from Marshall to the *General Theory*." And what seemed most important to her over the years was that the English "had no need to make a detour
through a Walrasian market where all transactions are conducted in kind."
Robinson also observed that Leijonhufvud had toned down the political and social
implications of the General Theory and that "his survey incidentally supports the
impression that the neo-neoclassical scheme was constructed to provide a shelter
from dangerous thoughts, of which we did not particularly feel the need."[9]
Presumably, most American economists would deny that the McCarthy period
had any impact on economic theory, but there was a question in Robinson's mind
that it might have.

In the fall of 1969, the first letters were exchanged between Leijonhufvud and
Robinson. Leijonhufvud had returned to visit Sweden,

> . . . after nine years' study, the first time I could afford it. My book had just
> come out and she was going to review it for the EJ [*Economic Journal*]. I started
> to get a stream of little notes from her as she was reading the book, saying, I've
> now gotten to page so and so, with some comment. I learned only later that this
> was her usual way of communicating with people. I remember that the first reply
> I sent was probably two or three pages single-spaced, and I couldn't keep it up.
> So that was that in correspondence. This long reply of mine she actually used in a
> subsequent book, to my surprise, but I think she had forgotten where she got it.
> Anyway, she reviewed that first book of mine very favorably and helped to get it
> some notoriety. Then off and on during the years, we've exchanged a few letters
> and we've met.[10]

Leijonhufvud visited Cambridge University on sabbatical in 1974 and was
invited to give the Marshall Lectures. He spoke on "Marshall's Method and
Present-Day Neo-classical Theory." He was there for a term and the two of them
went out to lunch

> . . . maybe not quite every week but more frequently than every other week. And
> so we would have long lunches for a couple of hours and then we would make
> other dates to see each other again. I think that she, from reading my early work,
> had decided that I wasn't quite right but my soul could be saved if I would just
> listen to her for a while. And it was clear that when I arrived in Cambridge she
> was all geared up to sort of haul me in. There were a few things I needed
> straightening out on and then I would be in the right camp. And she tackled this
> with great enthusiasm at first and then got rather frustrated with me eventually.

Robinson followed Leijonhufvud's work. In 1977 she wrote,

> Dear Axel, I was very much interested in your piece in the Latsis volume. Of
> course I agree about the relation between Keynes and Marshall. I think the
> distinction between plutology and catallactics is really a distinction between a

process of production and accumulation going on through time and an instantaneous equilibrium in a market. Marshall had one toe in each camp which is what makes his theory confusing. I don't think it is correct to say that the "Cambridge" people have been only negative. We have written several thick books and we have proposed a theory of the rate of profit on capital which no one else has. Hope we shall meet somewhere around the world before too long. Yours sincerely.[11]

Still, in the discussion of Kahn's Mattioli lectures in 1978 Robinson linked Leijonhufvud with Clower as responsible for the faulty American doctrine.[12] Leijonhufvud said that he felt she had not refreshed her impressions of his work, adding, "I don't say she should have spent more time on it."

One of Leijonhufvud's favorite stories is of how Robinson changed her mind about his work. He had written a second book, a collection of papers, which appeared in 1981 when she was nearly seventy-eight years old. One of the last things she wrote was a review of this new book.[13] Leijonhufvud explained,

She correctly perceived that she should be outraged or something; that she should not be outraged but that she should take serious offense at it, but maybe she was not in very good health any more or something like that. She didn't really work through it enough to isolate what it was she ought to hit me on. It's one of my favorite stories—that when she got mad at me over the second book, that she spent half of the review trying to withdraw her favorable review of my first book. That was sort of her temperament.

Robinson wrote in that review,

When I reviewed the earlier book I purported to find some sense in it (which surprised some of my colleagues) but this time I am quite defeated. The arguments all seem to be chopped up into short lengths, then stirred together as though to make soup. The analysis purports to deal with a world of growth with "complete information" apparently about the future as well as the present situation in an economy. "Certain authors," which include me, argue that "a realistic appreciation of the role of ignorance in the human condition must preclude the use of equilibrium models." However this may be, this paper "cannot do without it" (p. 137). But what can it do with it?[14]

Leijonhufvud observed that the "Joan of old" might have written a review showing

. . . where she would agree with me and where she would not. I think at that time she didn't think it was worth her time and energy to work through my stuff and to define clearly what it was that was objectionable to her and what she could live with. I have my own opinions about where it was she should have hit me—what I had to say in that second book on liquidity preference theory—that should be absolutely objectionable to her and to Kahn. On the other hand . . . in the first book she was very happy with my attempt to demolish the Pigou effect.

There was an occasion when Leijonhufvud particularly missed the Joan Robinson he had argued with at Cambridge. On his visit there in 1974, he had found her

. . . a breath of fresh air at Cambridge. I had the feeling that each morning Joan Robinson would arise and brush her teeth and look in the mirror and say that economics is important and it is important to find what's true, or something like that. . . . The rest of the people did not seem to think that economics was all that important. I did not like the intellectual atmosphere there at that particular time.

Robinson was then seventy-one. Nine years later when Leijonhufvud went back to Cambridge for the Keynes Centenary (July 15–16, 1983), he particularly felt her absence. "Clower and myself were playing the role of youngsters. It was really rather a sad affair, because there was no fight in them." "By Royal [Economic Society] decree" Leijonhufvud was assigned the topic, "What would Keynes have thought of rational expectations?"[15]

In an effort to challenge the conference, Leijonhufvud "said something like 'Keynesianism is dead', and nobody was willing to dispute it. Joan Robinson would never have taken it. She was dying, as I said, elsewhere. It was rather sad, but it would have been fun if we could have had one more round, and it might have been worthwhile too."

The aftermath of the capital controversy

The capital controversy stimulated economists of many persuasions to talk about the same things even while they disagreed with each other. The most negative evaluation of the whole affair came from the Cambridge-detractor, Harry Johnson.

Johnson saw Robinson's work in the controversy as "essentially a criticism of the aggregate production function" which had been developed "by J. R. Hicks and R. G. D. Allen at the London School of Economics at the turn of the 1930s." He thought that her criticism "implicitly carries on the Cambridge 1930s myth of a 'revolutionary Cambridge' battling a dinosauric London orthodoxy." But Hayek, noted Johnson, had left London for Chicago by the 1950s and

. . . there was no one left in London either capable of or interested in debating pure "capital theory" with Cambridge. Had it not been for Cambridge (U.S.A.)—I mean MIT not Harvard—responding eagerly to Joan Robinson's challenge to "orthodox" production function theory in order to display its mathematical-economics muscle—Cambridge (England) would have been revealed—even to its own captive student audience—as a voice crying nonsense in an imaginary wilderness.[16]

As for the reasons for the ill-advised participation of MIT, Johnson was of two minds. First,

> Cambridge (U.S.A.) out of a misplaced sense of rivalry, an underestimation of its own intellectual capacity, and an abnegation of its own common sense, chose to engage with Cambridge (England) in debate about these allegedly fundamental issues in theory, and so kept Cambridge (England) in the zombie business. It is a sucker's game for Cambridge (U.S.A.). Nonsense is nonsense, no matter how prestigiously pronounced; so why take it seriously and reconstruct it to the point where you make mistakes yourself?[17]

Second, Joan Robinson and Nicholas Kaldor

> . . . each derives support and satisfaction from the knowledge that there are eminent professional economists in the United States who are prepared to take their arguments seriously, little realizing that if they did not exist it would be necessary for American economics to invent them to meet its own need for an orthodoxy against which to demonstrate its own scientific superiority.

Johnson's argument was that "a methodology requiring an orthodoxy to assault" can stultify discovery of new and important truths. He attributed this "baneful influence of concern about orthodoxy" to the identification of Keynesian economics in Britain "with left-wing or at least Labor Party politics, and the politicization of economics that it has entailed."[18]

Thus Johnson would have had it that Robinson led the assault on traditional capital theory to achieve left-wing ends. MIT responded to show its mathematical muscle and superiority. Presumably, from Johnson's point of view, the other participants were mere dupes. This criticism does finger that deep belief at Cambridge that controversy is the source of progress. It also raises the question whether any "progress" was made in the capital controversy.

There was some impact on individual American economists which may represent a harbinger of the future. Martin Bronfenbrenner, whom Sidney Weintraub characterized as not only a "gifted contributor to many spheres of economic literature," but also "an unreconstructed adherent of marginal productivity theory,"[19] was finally impressed by the importance of the controversy. The "Two Cambridges" controversy, as Bronfenbrenner saw it, "is a root-and-branch attack upon the neoclassical orthodoxy of the century beginning in 1870. . . . Distribution theory lies at the center of this entire onslaught. Inexcusably as I now believe, I underestimated the attack's importance in my own book, misled by its late–1960s detour into peculiar special cases—double-switching, reswitching, and so on.''[20]

Bronfenbrenner recognized that many objections, ''both theoretical and statistical,'' had been made, particularly against aggregate production functions, but he persisted in arguing that in dealing with long-term problems,

> . . . it may become quite legitimate to make the assumptions to which Cambridge objects so persistently—to treat ''physical capital'' . . . as a homogeneous mass of ''machines,'' ''jelly,'' ''meccano sets,'' or Mrs. Robinson's own favorite, ''leets,''(''steel'' spelled backwards). The only restraint required is the standard equilibrium one, which is that the marginal productivity of $1 worth of Machine A in a representative firm of Industry 1 should approximate that of $1 worth of Machine B in a representative firm of Industry 2.[21]

Thus, as Clower had noted, when asked to choose between Keynes and equilibrium theory, American economists would more readily forego Keynes. And it was Robinson's repeated accusation against Robert Solow that he had allegedly retreated into a one-commodity world in order to save the orthodox theory. In the same vein, Robinson's quarrel with Samuelson was that he ''repudiated J. B. Clark but continued republishing his text-book just the same.''[22]

The Cambridge view was that Americans were imprisoned by an unshakable belief structure. Phyllis Deane paraphrased Samuelson's beliefs:

> Until the laws of thermo-dynamics are repealed, I shall continue to relate outputs to inputs, i.e. to believe in production functions. Until factors cease to have their rewards determined by bidding in quasi-competitive markets, I shall adhere to (generalized) neo-classical approximations in which relative factor prices are important in explaining their market remunerations.[23]

Robinson, in her review of C.E. Ferguson's *Neoclassical Theory of Production and Distribution,* called attention to his reliance on ''belief.''[24] Ferguson wrote, ''The question that confronts us is not whether the Cambridge Criticism is theoretically valid. It is. Rather the question is an empirical or econometric one: is there sufficient substitutability within the system to establish neoclassical results?'' Ferguson had stated in his preface: ''Until the econometricians have the answer for us, placing reliance upon neoclassical economic theory is a matter of faith.''[25] Robinson could make her point by quoting him directly in her review.

By 1977, Bronfenbrenner could see more importance in the Cambridge University views, but for others, faith may continue to obscure the damage done by the Cambridge criticism.

During the height of the controversy, the International Economic Association held a Round Table Conference on the Theory of Capital at the Island of Corfu,

Greece, September 4–11, 1958. Samuelson and Solow were among the twenty-six invited participants. Robinson was not. Austin Robinson explained:

> You ask why Joan did not participate in the IEA meeting on the theory of capital. I think one has to remember that those conferences were limited to a very small number of people. We made it a rule not to exceed thirty-five participants if we could avoid it. The purpose of the IEA in these specialist conferences was to achieve a real meeting of minds. Thus one could only invite three or four people from any one country, however distinguished they might be. At that conference, if I remember right, we had Nicky Kaldor, John Hicks, and Piero Sraffa from this country, as well as myself as one of the officers of the IEA. That was our fair share of the total of participants. At that particular time I think the others all had at least as strong claims as Joan to being expert in that field. In retrospect it may now seem wrong, but at the time I do not think that Lutz was greatly at fault. It was he who made the program and suggested the participants. . . .
>
> Since I dictated the above I have got hold of a copy of the volume that reported the meeting on the *Theory of Capital*. I now realize that the English contingent included also David Champernowne, who made an important contribution to the conference. There are many references in the volume to the work of Joan, and you may be right that she ought to have been there. But we were very scrupulous at that time about not asking the same people year after year to conferences on different subjects. With small numbers of participants we were very anxious indeed to have a rotation of the people concerned and Joan's participation in the *Monopoly* conference may possibly have affected the question of whether she should be invited.[26]

Joan Robinson was, however, at the 1970 World Econometric Conference held in England, where she announced "The End of the Controversy" and then faced Solow.[27] In her address she relied on the work of Franklin Fisher of MIT to establish that "the pursuit of the will-o'-the-wisp of an index of physical capital should be called off." That Robinson quoted a professor at MIT approvingly would appear as some kind of détente in the debate. (This is the address which Solow had commented on.)

There was the second "ending" of the controversy in the set of exchanges between Robinson and Samuelson on "the unimportance of reswitching" in 1973–74.

But Johnson's question remains. Had these bright lights of the profession made good use of their time? I asked Samuelson whether he thought so. He answered, "I thought the work of Joan and Piero Sraffa and some others was constructive work. There were certain complications in the theory of heterogeneous capital which mainstream economists had not noticed. Criticism—it's not a pejorative word, and the act of criticizing is a constructive act."[28]

Solow said his interest in capital theory had come from a concern with growth economics. He thought of the controversy as sort of a period piece:

> I think [the capital controversy] attracted a certain amount of attention, and it did serve in the late sixties and early seventies during the Vietnam War, when there was a lot of left political activity. It was useful that there was intellectual activity going on that seemed to have a political aspect to it. And it may have, the existence of that literature, might have induced some number of graduate students or undergraduate students in economics who were sort of unhappy with the culture and the society to question the assumptions of orthodox economics farther than they might otherwise have done. But I think that it turned out to be unsuccessful in that what we are left with now is that the large majority of the profession and their students accept without thinking the assumptions of standard Walrasian economics. And a much smaller minority, which questions the wrong assumptions.

What are the wrong assumptions?

> Well, they follow Joan instead of following Keynes (she would kill me for this), because I think there's absolutely nothing Keynesian about Joanian economics. As I said, she would murder me if she were here, but Keynes was an icon, not anything else for her. There's nothing in *The Accumulation of Capital* or *Exercises in Economic Analysis* or in any of those papers which strikes me as having a genuine root or inspiration in Keynes. I have tried (in not yet published lectures given at the University of Birmingham, 1984) to make of the notion of animal spirits what I think Keynes wanted to make of it, but Joan never did. She got the word or phrase from the General Theory, but I don't think there's anything Keynesian about her. I think it's too bad from my point of view that the students who by natural inclination, experience, or whatever, are or were willing to question the assumptions, got pushed down Joan's line rather than asking themselves, "How do we make Keynesian economics?"[29]

Leijonhufvud said he thought controversy had its place. "I think long controversies are particularly interesting but doing normal science isn't sufficiently interesting to me. When I watch two giants like Milton Friedman and James Tobin for twenty or thirty years, and after all that time they cannot agree on the statement of the issues and how they would be resolved. . . ." As for the capital controversy, he remembers a conversation where "Joan herself said to me that they had gone off on the wrong track in making that the issue. I'm not sure whether she meant that it was the wrong tactic or that it was the wrong path to take in trying to have it out with American neoclassicalists. I remember very well when she said that. No, that controversy too was of some interest." Clower said simply that while the controversy was worthwhile, "capital theory is a worthless branch of the literature, as taught."[30]

Since a central focus of Robinson in the debate was an effort to escape from Walrasian equilibrium, it seems important that both Clower and Leijonhufvud (but not Samuelson and Solow) now say that Walrasian approaches are blind alleys. In the article about which Joan Robinson wrote her admiring letter to Leijonhufvud in 1977, there is a footnote she might particularly have liked:

> . . . It has in fact long been apparent that some of the most accomplished and admired contributors to neo-Walrasian economics do not attach to its models the substantive belief that "the world is like that." In particular—and quite contrary to the allegations of the "new Cambridge" economists (whom one must nonetheless credit with being out far ahead of the pack in arguing the fundamental irrelevance of neo-Walrasian general equilibrium theory to Keynesian economics)—the major contributors to this program obviously have no ideologically based attachment to it whatsoever. Indeed, the "typical" neo-Walrasian (loosely speaking) tends to be an "interventionist" in matters of socio-economic policy. . . .[31]

This is an irony which caught the attention of both Harcourt and Tobin—that in the capital controversy, the main adversaries were not always in opposite political camps. And to add to the muddle, Leijonhufvud's note continued, "the 'Chicago school' (equally loosely speaking) known for its 'anti-interventionism' is notable also for its critical opposition to the neo-Walrasian mode of theorizing."[32]

Galbraith's suggestion that economists hang onto the life views imprinted on them in graduate school may explain more than Joan Robinson's suspicion of latent class interest. In my opinion, Samuelson's Rashomon theory of economic perception, even though he junks it, stands as a critical key to comprehending the capital controversy.

$$JR$$

CHAPTER TWELVE

The Mature Years: Beyond the Capital Controversy

Joan Robinson did not spend all of her time and energy on the capital controversy. Her interests continued to broaden, though most of her technical articles did indeed concentrate on the exchanges on capital theory. She turned fifty in 1953, the year she published ''The Production Function and the Theory of Capital.'' During the decade 1950–1960, she brought out two volumes of her collected papers (1951 and 1960, Volumes 1 and 2); *The Rate of Interest and Other Essays* (1952); a short pamphlet, *On Re-reading Marx* (1953); and her *Accumulation of Capital* (1956). Before she was sixty, she had added *Essays in the Theory of Economic Growth* and *Economic Philosophy* (both in 1962). There were the *Monthly Review* articles as well. This period, known for the capital controversy, was thus an especially productive one. How remarkable this is in comparison to, for example, her rival Chamberlin!

As her ancillary work became less technical, it became more interesting to the general reader, including many economists who were either unable or unwilling to wade through the articles which made up the capital controversy. Robinson was not only the most important female economist in the world, but one of a small circle of world-renowned Western economists. She continued through her sixties to demonstrate mastery of a broad range of issues and techniques.

The reception of her work in economic journals continued to vary. The English reviewers mostly liked and understood her.[1] American reviewers regretted her use of literary rather than mathematical techniques, considering literary forms ''less rigorous.'' Both British and American economists challenged her political views, accusing her of naïveté or worse.

Her first volume of collected papers, printed in 1951, covered the wide range of early interests: imperfect and perfect competition, the issues raised by *The*

General Theory, a consideration of Schumpeter's *Capitalism, Socialism and Democracy*, and Harrod's dynamics and a theory of planning. G. L. S. Shackle exclaimed,

> Can it not be said that economics, whether by "historical accident" or through inborn temperamental aptitude, is predominantly and especially an Anglo-Saxon and Scandinavian subject? . . . These thoughts were prompted by the book under review. Its author is a notable iconoclast, a strong exemplar of self-determination in economic thought, one of the most ingenious and subtle thinkers that our discipline has produced in modern times. Yet she is a main pillar of the recent Cambridge tradition, one of the torch-bearers of Keynesian economics, that is, of the modern orthodoxy, and a superb expositor of Marshallian doctrines.[2]

Shackle's only objection was to a few articles of a "more polemical and more political turn," and he asked, "Would it be unfair to suggest that about some of these latter there is a faint aura of the fairy story, where every character is either deepest black or purest white, a wicked apologist of *laissez-faire* or a noble victim of it, the stark contrast being relieved only by the presence of that *éminence grise* the higher Civil Servant?"[3]

From Stanford University, Kenneth Arrow wrote, "Any publication of Mrs. Robinson's is a happy event, and this is no exception." But he felt his task complicated by "the author's own review, in the form of a preface, where she deplores the emphasis in her earlier articles on static analysis." This seemed to place the present book at "a low place in the author's affections."[4]

Arrow particularly admired her "excellent exposition" of the classical theory of international trade, and thought her inclusion of "Beauty and the Beast" was "by itself worth the price of the whole book." But the "most striking impression which an econometrician derives from these papers is Mrs. Robinson's antagonistic attitude towards rigorous theoretical analysis." He felt that even in the most theoretical works of her "static" period, she had failed to set forth the assumptions and she had left him worrying whether all the relevant factors had been taken into account. "That these fears may not be groundless can be seen in the essay, 'Rising Supply Price', where, in a postscript, it is noted that Keynes pointed out the omission of an important element of the problem."[5]

Arrow added that while Robinson had not particularly cared for the article, he felt that "this article, reworked in a more rigorous fashion, would seem to be a very useful addition to the literature on linear programming." This comment suggests that "Joan I" could have remained popular with American mainstream economists even without the math. At bottom, it was her choice of problems and method which separated her from the American mainstream.

Arrow was also struck by her statement, "The English distrust theory, for a theory may be wrong, and the more logically it is followed out, the worse the confusion that results."[6] He could agree that "ideas are far more important than rigor," but that "the justification of mathematical methods is not the superior analytic skill of the performance but the increased possibility of discovering relevant factors and their relation to a problem."

He was also on guard for Robinson's political theme, which he took to be the "necessity of planning." He noted that she stressed the imperfection of the market mechanism and at the same time she pointed out the many unsolved problems in planning an economy. He felt that she "seems to have great confidence in the ability of government officials to learn by doing," and he slyly wondered if the current (1953) British experience had confirmed this confidence.[7] Some of these ideas were recurrent themes. Lawrence Klein, in reviewing her *Accumulation of Capital*, had noted that some of her models were simply verbal expositions of "long familiar results in the theory of linear programming."[8]

Whereas Robinson's first volume of *Collected Economic Papers* had been "culled from the work of more than twenty years," her second volume, which came out in 1960, was primarily work published during the previous five years. Volume 2 showed again her wide range of interest: problems of development under capitalism and socialism; "scholastic" articles on growth and capital; and assorted articles on imperfect competition, interest, and employment, including some attempts to link these "to the requirements of a type of economic analysis which has freed itself from the need to assume conditions of static equilibrium."[9]

The *American Economic Review* printed a harsh review of her Volume 2 which is of particular interest. Martin Bronfenbrenner, then at the University of Minnesota, found, "The whole is strongly controversial, marked by the animus of Mrs. Robinson's recent work against the Marshallian tradition of her upbringing. Her allegiance to the Keynesian Left continues more Keynesian than Keynes, to the extent that the master, rewriting today his last essay on the U.S. balance of payments (with a postscript 'I told you so!') might well include a footnote on her forced paradoxes in his famous reference to 'modern stuff gone silly and sour'." Referring to Robinson's political views had apparently become *de rigueur* for American reviewers. (Several American economists interviewed by the author expressed a belief that if Robinson had been invited to the United States during this decade of the McCarthy era, she would have been refused a visa.)

Bronfenbrenner thus offered two opinions that became common. One was that Robinson owed her initial reputation "and perhaps (if I may hazard a guess) the greater part of her permanent reputation as well" to the static theory of imperfect competition which she now minimizes. The other was that had Keynes lived, he might have included her work among the "modern stuff gone silly and sour." Bronfenbrenner decried "the outspokenness of Mrs. Robinson's various positions, and her intolerance of opposition particularly from academic sources." Was it her adversarial style or her views which bothered him?

Yet he agreed that her case against Marshallian orthodoxy had its points. Orthodoxy did assume static conditions in a growing economy and more explicitly neglected capital growth in its static theory of price and distribution. But "it is the contention of most of us that most of the time Marshall's slip makes no difference whatever to Marshall's problems."

Bronfenbrenner also conceded she might have been right in her attacks on the theory of capital and on production theory generally. "It is accordingly easy to tear down the impressive structure erected on these shaky foundations. But Mrs. Robinson has little to replace it with, and more important, she again fails to show us what real difference our ambiguities make."[10] Since the efforts to generalize the General Theory were well underway, Robinson might have thought this criticism unfair. As earlier mentioned, some years later (1976), Bronfenbrenner decided that he had "inexcusably . . . underestimated the [Cambridge] attack's importance."[11]

Chicago's *Journal of Political Economy* carried an ambivalent review of Volume 2 (listed there as Volume 1). Hyman P. Minsky found her first few articles "frequently marred by political naïveté and casual errors of fact." Even so, he thought the content of these articles important. Another paper he termed "interesting, although in places outrageous."[12]

In 1960, Robinson also published her *Exercises in Economic Analysis*, which was directed toward teaching Cambridge economics to students. Robert Clower found the book charming and provocative as an introduction to economic theory, and a "vastly more significant contribution to the existing literature than its size or title might seem to indicate." However, he complained that "like most English economists, Mrs. Robinson apparently finds it difficult to take seriously the writings of Continental and American scholars." Clower particularly objected to her proceeding "as if the 'nature of Reality' dictated the use of particular theoretical models to describe particular concrete situations."[13] Robinson visited Clower at Northwestern University the same year this review appeared.

G. D. N. Worswick of Oxford reviewed *Exercises* in concert with an American textbook: *Cases and Problems in Economics* by J. S. Duesenberry and L. E. Preston. Worswick preferred the American approach, which emphasized quantitative relationships using real examples. Robinson's exposition was pure theory in verbal form, and relied on leading the student to draw diagrams for himself. Worswick thought it might require some prior knowledge of economics even to follow her "do it yourself" kits.[14]

The final book Robinson wrote in her fifties was *Economic Philosophy* (1962), which became very popular in America. She subtitled this book, "An Essay on the Progress of Economic Thought." In it she called for us to "find the roots of our own beliefs" and to attempt to distinguish ideology from science. This was necessary because economics, which was really "a branch of theology," had been trying to "escape from sentiment and to win for itself the status of a science."

Robinson was in favor of this effort, but it would require that economists face up to their own ideologies and learn how to dispose of old and outdated theories.

Robinson said in a much quoted sentence, "The lack of an agreed and accepted method for eliminating errors introduces a personal element into economic controversies. . . ."[15]

One of her North American reviewers, William D. G. Hunter of McMaster University, Canada told us what Robinson did not—that "*Economic Philosophy* started life as one of the series of Josiah Mason lectures endowed by the Rationalist Press Association and delivered to an adult education class."[16] This shows another facet of Joan Robinson's life—her unsparing efforts to teach economics to people of all backgrounds.

Another stimulus to the writing of *Economic Philosophy* was probably Gunnar Myrdal's visit to Cambridge as the Marshall lecturer in 1950. At that time he had lectured on and had later published his *Political Element in the Development of Economic Theory,* to which Robinson refers in *Economic Philosophy*. She had probably been developing her ideas along Myrdal's lines for some years, perhaps trying to explain to herself why the reaction to her work by American economists had been so violent.

Robinson went after the fundamental philosophy of economists, alleging that "one of the great metaphysical ideas in economics" was associated with "the word 'value'." She concluded that "value" as used by the classical economists had no operational content. Then there is the word "utility," a concept employed by neoclassical economists. According to Robinson, utility was "a metaphysical concept of impregnable circularity," that is to say, "*utility* is the quality in commodities that makes individuals want to buy them, and the fact that individuals want to buy commodities shows that they have *utility*."[17]

She argued that the Keynesian revolution had challenged this structure. At that time, she was rather hopeful of the strength of the revolution: "The Keynesian revolution has destroyed the old soporific doctrines, and its own metaphysics is thin and easy to see through. We are left in the uncomfortable situation of having to think for ourselves." The "fresh question" of long-run development forced a realization that neither neoclassical nor Keynesian short-period analysis was adequate to the task.[18] Then she asked the question: "With all these economic doctrines, decaying and reviving, jostling each other, half understood, in the public mind, what basic ideas are acceptable and what rules of policy are derived from them?" She concluded that all economics is rooted in nationalism, the "one solid unchanging lump of ideology."[19] And seemingly because this is so, Robinson's optimism was tempered:

> Perhaps all this seems negative and destructive. To some, perhaps, it even recommends the old doctrines, since it offers no "better 'ole" to go to. The contention of this essay is precisely that there is no "better 'ole." The moral problem is a conflict that can never be settled. . . . All the same we must not abandon the hope that economics can make an advance towards science, or the faith that enlightenment is not useless. . . . The first essential for economists . . .

is . . . to combat, not foster, the ideology which portends that values which can be measured in terms of money are the only ones that ought to count.[20]

Economists of all persuasions found the book profoundly disturbing. Kurt Klappholz, reviewing for *Economica*, saw her theme as rather similar to Gunnar Myrdal's *The Political Element in the Development of Economic Theory*. Both wrote on "the manner in which economic theory, from Smith to the neoclassics, was used to bolster the 'ideology' of *laissez-faire*."[21] Klappholz found it also an essay in methodology, particularly "the arguability of metaphysical statements and moral judgements." He was disturbed that Robinson's argument implied "there can be no scope for a critical, or rational, appraisal of the merits of any economic system," though he felt she stopped short of drawing this conclusion.*

For a change, her reviewer in the *American Economic Review* was someone who might have been expected to be more sympathetic to her notions—Paul Baran of Stanford University. But Baran found her *Economic Philosophy* a book of despair. He thought her question was "What is the use?" in the face of the arms race and the desperate needs of two-thirds of the human race. "It is this melancholy question that dominates the compact, witty, and suggestive little book under review which might well be called 'A Brilliant Woman's Guide Away from Economics'."

Baran relied on Marx for a more optimistic view, and rejected what he saw as Robinson's stance: "the bitter characterization of economics as a never-ceasing, self-propelling sequence of misconceptions, metaphysical vacuities, and partial pleading."[22] Harcourt believes that toward the end of her life she did hold these views.[23] Baran also believed that Robinson was herself caught in metaphysics when she emphasized "ideas" rather than "interests." He concluded, "the trouble with economics is not that it does not yet 'know enough' as many of its practitioners love to repeat. Its fatal shortcoming is that it does not incorporate in its knowledge the understanding of what is necessary for the attainment of a better, more rational economic order." Baran's review is of especial interest since he saw Robinson's disillusionment with economics before she publicly admitted it.

Economic Philosophy was reviewed in the *Journal of Political Economy* by George J. Stigler, then of the University of Chicago and, like Friedman, a member of the Mont Pelerin Society. Stigler found in the book such a "number of remarkable new errors" that he thought it best to view it as simply "an expression of her own philosophy."

Stigler worked up a picture of "a superior logician contemplating a world with much want and evil, after studying some books on the formal theory of economics." He accused Robinson of roaming "freely, and indeed blithely and often

---

*Clarence Ayres also made this point in a letter to Robinson. See Chapter 14.

irresponsibly, over an immense range of analytical and policy questions.'' In effect, he accused her of being cut off ''from two generations of immensely varied and instructive empirical research'' and of having thought that ''economic history had no relevance to economic theory B.K.,'' that is, before Keynes. He wanted to rely on empirical evidence that there is no general tendency ''to overshoot equilibrium in competitive industries.'' He concluded that ''a logician is a wondrous creature,'' but cannot distinguish between large and small errors, while ''an economist can.''[24] This is the only instance I know of where an American economist went so far as to write Joan Robinson out of the economics profession. Robinson must have concluded that Americans of whatever ideological persuasion are difficult to please. Yet even Harcourt thought Robinson was guilty of ''undue concentration on the interests and writings of English, especially Cambridge economists.''[25]

Kenneth Boulding reviewed *Economic Philosophy* for the sociologists. He delighted in her aphorisms, but he had one or two bones to pick. ''Mrs. Robinson quotes Gerald Shove as saying that Maynard Keynes 'had never spent the twenty minutes necessary to understand the theory of value'. One wishes that Mrs. Robinson had spent an extra ten minutes in understanding it thoroughly.'' Boulding thought Robinson was ''selling economics too short'': ''Mrs. Robinson has the same kind of prejudice against exchange that Milton Friedman has in its favor. . . . If Milton Friedman believes in economics too much, then Mrs. Robinson believes in it too little, so perhaps they should get together—with the sociologists to mediate!''[26]

William Jaffe of Northwestern University had a different view. He thought Robinson fulfilled the main purpose of the book, which was ''to sort out the mixture of ideology and science in economics, without prejudice to either ingredient.'' Rather than finding her message one of despair as Baran had, Jaffe noted that hers was an appeal to economists to combat rather than foster crass materialism.[27]

In her seventies, Robinson remembered the 1950s as a decade when ''in Cambridge, the Keynesian revolution was being consolidated and expanded.'' Of her shorter works, she felt that the essay, ''The Generalization of the General Theory,'' and the seminal article, ''The Production Function and the Theory of Capital'' (1953) were important; that during this decade, she ''was always hankering after the story of accumulation without new inventions,'' and that it all inevitably led to the ''endless dispute with the neo-neoclassicals'' in the 1960s.[28]

This statement of hers refocuses her life as she saw it in the early 1970s—a continuing process of generalizing the General Theory. Without disowning her *Exercises*, her pamphlets on China, or her *Economic Philosophy*, she apparently viewed them as of minor importance—works for students rather than for colleagues. *Economic Philosophy* was, however, considered in the United States as one of her most interesting and influential works.[29]

Broad themes in her sixties

The broadening of Joan Robinson's interests was immediately apparent with the publication of Volume 3 of her collected papers in 1965. The papers were "gleanings from the last five years, except for two pieces which have strayed in from an earlier period."[30] One group of papers came from travels she had made to India, China, and Korea, originally published in such journals as *Monthly Review* and *Political Quarterly*. Another group was concerned with aspects of Marx, while still another showed her continuing interest in Keynesian questions.

The first ten articles contained the meat: "mainly controversial discussions of basic economic theory," including capital theory. Undoubtedly she thought of these ten as representing her major work of this five-year period. One of these, however, was an older article, "Teaching Economics," always a serious concern of hers. In 1974, looking back over this period for her second edition of Volume 3, Robinson observed that she found "something baffling about our endless dispute with the neo-neoclassicals."[31] She attributed the differences in the papers in Volume 3 as compared to Volume 2 mainly to the influence of Sraffa's *Production of Commodities by Means of Commodities*.[32]

H. Uzawa, reviewing Volume 3 for the *American Economic Review*, discerned in the technical essays helpful insights into the conceptual framework of her larger work, *The Accumulation of Capital*, a book which had been found difficult. He listed among these (and I paraphrase) her emphasis that theory must be based in some broader historical perspective through a macroeconomic approach to production, accumulation, and distribution; her questions about the nature of capital; her reliance on the urge to accumulate (animal spirits) as the basic determinant (together with thriftiness) of the level of investment and the rate of profit; the crucial importance she placed on the role of entrepreneurs in investment decisions; and her concern with the adverse effects that the mechanism of laissez-faire capitalism has brought upon the welfare of the society.[33]

In spite of the variety of subjects in Volume 3, Eprime Eschag of Oxford, reviewing for *Economic Journal*, was able to find a common theme in the "criticism of orthodox, respectable and generally accepted opinions."[34]

Economics: An Awkward Corner

Robinson wrote *Economics: An Awkward Corner* in the summer of 1966, "when current happenings provided a painful illustration of its main thesis," which was that "the notions of *laisser-faire,* that business men know what is best, are contradicted by the evident need for planning to maintain 'a high and stable level of employment'." The major problems she saw at the time were those of inflation and imbalance of international payments. At the time, Scotland and Northern Ireland had high unemployment rates, but this had not yet happened in England. Robinson claimed that it was "impossible to understand the economic system in which we are living if we try to interpret it as a rational scheme." Instead, "in every age economic life has been a scene of conflict and compromise, defended by rationalizations that did not fit with experience.''

Many of the difficulties were due to "partial laisser-faire," though that is greatly to be preferred to total laissez-faire. After analyzing the general problems, including international finance, employment, and growth she offered recommendations, the chief of which was that the state should become the "rentier," the chief owner of capital, though not its manager or controller. She admitted that this was "a drastic remedy."[35]

While not a standard American economics journal, *Science & Society* did review this book. M. E. Sharpe, who would in the next decade become the publisher of the *Journal of Post Keynesian Economics,* understood Robinson's argument that "full employment and growth, while preferable to unemployment and stagnation, do not make sense as objects of policy in and of themselves." There remains the old question of what employment is for. *Economics: An Awkward Corner* analyzed British problems, but Sharpe thought it should have been taken more seriously by American economists. He added prophetically that "by the time a balance of trade crisis arrives, the problem is all but unmanageable."[36]

Eschag reviewed *Awkward Corner* for the *Economic Journal,* finding the book's chief merit the "bold handling of certain fundamental economic and social issues." She feared, however, that "many economists are either too deeply engrossed in their complicated but limited technical studies or are too nervous and timid to concern themselves with these important issues." Eschag linked Robinson and Galbraith as being willing to take the time for such work but also as having the "irreverence to pose certain basic and, at times, embarrassing questions on the present system of 'partial laissez-faire'."[37]

Reports on China and *Economic Heresies*

Robinson's *The Cultural Revolution in China (1970)* and her *Economic Management in China* (1972) were both pamphlets, based on trips she had made to China.[38] Of *Economic Management in China* Robinson said, "These notes can offer no more than a scrappy and impressionistic account" of the management emerging in the " 'struggle and criticism' of the Cultural Revolution." She was opening up questions to "inspire more adequate investigation by others who have the language and the background that I lack."[39]

Economic Heresies is a systematic comparison of the different streams of economic analysis as Robinson viewed them. She saw herself as reexamining the "old-fashioned questions."[40] For example, she compared the stationary states of Walras and Marshall; the interest and profits of Walras, Marshall, and Keynes; various nonmonetary and growth models; even the Chicago School and Keynes. After her examination, she concluded, "We can surely agree to start again where Keynes left off. Who wants to deny that the future is uncertain; that investment decisions, in a private-enterprise economy, are made by firms rather than by households; that wage rates are offered in terms of money, or that prices of manufactures are not formed by the higgling of a perfectly competitive market?''

Her plea was for models which were relevant to actual problems and which took account of the mode of operation of the economy to which they referred. '''Pure theorists' sometimes take a supercilious attitude to 'structuralists' or 'institutionalists'. They prefer a theory that is so pure as to be uncontaminated with any material content. Was Keynes an institutionalist? He took into account the institutions of a nation-state, of the organization of industry, the banking system and the Stock Exchange as he saw them.''

Robinson noted that there had been changes in both ideology and institutions since Keynes' day. Yet old problems like poverty had not been solved and new problems like the armaments race and ''making the planet uninhabitable'' had arisen. She thought it the duty of economists to enlighten the public about the economic aspects of these menacing problems. She argued that neoclassical economics would be of no help in doing so.[41]

Two friendly reviews of *Economic Heresies* appeared in the United States, though not in the mainstream economic journals—the government publication, *Monthly Labor Review,* and the *American Journal of Agricultural Economics.* The reviewers admired her attacks on the ''new orthodoxy'' and cheered on her admonition that time must be brought into the theoretical picture and that the question must be asked, ''what form should employment take.''[42]

The Canadian review was by A. Asimakopulos at McGill University, who had studied at Cambridge and who is mentioned in the preface of *Economic Heresies.* He thought it such a valuable book that it ''should be required reading for advanced students in economics.'' Asimakopulos was altogether sympathetic to Robinson. He felt she had been fully vindicated in the capital controversy, and he valued her critique of neoclassical approaches to economic theory.[43]

Stephen A. Marglin of Harvard was asked to review *Economic Heresies* for the *Economic Journal.* He agreed to do so ''because Joan Robinson is one of the two members of her generation who helped me to see orthodox micro-economic theory . . . for what it principally is, an ideological defense of capitalism.'' Marglin did not believe that orthodox theorists see themselves as ideologues:

> Quite the contrary: my teachers presented orthodox theory as a bag of neutral tools, as easily applied to criticism of the *status quo* as to its defense. . . . Yet, the results would hardly be different if a conscious conspiracy were afoot. In the United States, at least, major universities barely tolerate dissent and criticism. If one post is conceded to a house radical, the orthodox establishment considers its obligations to diversity adequately discharged. The market place of ideas is in fact about as free and competitive as other major markets.

Marglin welcomed *Economic Heresies*, but added some critical comments, particularly of Robinson's reliance on ''animal spirits'' to account for differential growth rates.[44] Thus the *Economic Journal* review was by an American who considered himself a heretic.

The review in *Economica,* however, was by someone from another camp. F. H. Hahn was then at the London School of Economics, although he had been on the faculty of Cambridge since 1960. Hahn wrote a spirited review, almost as though he had understudied her style of attack. "I will not comment on her exposition of the Robinsonian orthodoxy. . . . The certainties, the intemperate and patronizing tone, the magic formula and magic phrases . . . and the lack of comprehension of what it is good modern theorists are saying." He found the book depressing. "After all, Professor Robinson is a great economist." He did not deny a "kind of crisis in economics at present." He thought the "gap between theory and fact is far too large, and in some sense becoming larger. . . .Many of us are aware of these difficulties, and we can only beseech Professor Robinson . . . to believe that the reason why we do not endlessly discuss them is that we have not yet found an alternative precise route which points to salvation. . . . At the moment all this is fit for after-dinner conversation only."[45]

The fact that three prominent economists, Asimakopulos, Hahn, and Marglin had written such different reviews is an indication of how controversial the views expressed in *Economic Heresies* were (and are) among economists.

James Tobin, who was to win the Nobel Prize in Economics in 1981, wrote a review, not so much of *Economic Heresies*, but of Joan Robinson herself for the social science journal *The Public Interest.* He entitled his review "Cambridge (U.K.) vs. Cambridge (Mass.)." Tobin linked Robinson's Ely address in New Orleans in December 1971* and *Economic Heresies* as having the same thesis: "the retrogression of economic theory, especially in the hands of American practitioners, since the Second World War."

He felt her charges that the economics profession had failed to respond to problems were old hat, in that this was the common plea of "the growing numbers of radical economists." But he also wrote, "Probably Mrs. Robinson is just unaware of the volume of research over the past 10 years on poverty, inequality, pollution, population, conservation, externalities, and public goods. A theorist *par excellence,* she pays no attention to the empirical studies and policy applications that constitute the great bulk of the economists' output."[46]

This criticism missed her point that orthodox theory must reflect these applied discoveries. During the 1960s and 1970s, there appeared new university texts in applied fields which took into account cultural, political, and evolutionary factors. But these ideas were not being introduced in traditional theory texts, nor into theory itself.[47]

Tobin thought much of *Economic Heresies* was devoted to Robinson's running battle with Samuelson and Solow: ". . . she regards neoclassical growth theory, particularly as developed in Cambridge, Massachusetts, as the culmination of

---

*See Chapter 14.

everything that has gone wrong in economics." He noted that Samuelson was condemned "for his part in constructing a 'neoclassical synthesis' of Keynesian and pre-Keynesian theory. She regards this as a step back to the defense of orthodoxy." Tobin objected because he saw Samuelson in a much broader context, including that of his work in the theory of public goods, "well known to American undergraduates but evidently not to Mrs. Robinson."

Tobin defended Solow's use of the marginal productivity theory of the distribution of income. Solow "has never attached any ethical content to marginal productivity, and as a member of Presidential commissions on technological unemployment and income maintenance, he has been a proponent of government intervention to diminish poverty and inequality." Tobin noted that "like Galbraith on this side of the Atlantic, she regards modern capitalist enterprise as neither competitive nor profit-maximizing. (This plus a generally iconoclastic stance toward the economics profession, is about their only similarity.)" Then Tobin conceded, "if this empirical observation is right, it would indeed be difficult to sustain marginal productivity theory in any very rigorous form."

Even if Robinson were right about economic theory, said Tobin, he would find it incredible "that faulty articles on growth theory in esoteric journals are responsible for the ills of the world, or even for economists' failures to solve them." In his opinion, "the intrinsic difficulty of the problems, not bias or error or even neglect by economists, is a more likely explanation of delay in solving them."[48]

In this review, Tobin made one important concession: "I believe she is right to object that Walrasian general equilibrium, even when enlarged to postulate markets in all commodities in all contingencies at all future dates, is no real solution." Robinson must have been pleased with this.

In 1965, when she was in her sixty-third year, Robinson was elected to a Chair at the University of Cambridge, recognition that had been a long time coming. She delivered her Presidential address to Section F (Economic Studies) of the British Association for the Advancement of Science in 1971. That same year, Robinson was invited to give the Richard T. Ely Lecture to the American Economic Association, a signal honor from the point of view of Americans. Within the profession, as her honors arrived, her influence had waned, a not uncommon experience.

Trying to "ring through" in her seventies

Joan Robinson spent her seventies "trying to ring through." She traveled extensively, gave lectures, wrote two new books, numerous articles, and brought out Volumes 4 and 5 of her collected works. Her formal teaching career came to an end in 1970, the year she was sixty-seven years old. The department where she had given her first lecture in 1931 was now huge and her influence diminished.[49]

In 1971 Robinson was asked to give up her private office and to join other senior staff members in a shared office. She took this unwelcome move as a signal to throw away much of her correspondence. As Austin Robinson observed, "Joan was a great destroyer." A graduate student was present when, in a great flurry, she threw out the correspondence of the capital controversy. He wanted to save the "waste paper" but was in no position to do so. He hastened to the visiting Paul Davidson's office* to tell him. There was no one up to stopping her. She said, "No one will ever write a biography of me as they are writing of Keynes."[50]

Her work went on. With John Eatwell she wrote a full-scale textbook which she hoped would be adopted widely in the United States, competing with Samuelson's *Economics. Introduction to Modern Economics* integrates Robinson's views of the development of economic analysis from the classical economists to the present. The economist's tools are applied to problems ranging from those associated with "socialist planning" to those of the capitalist nations. Among the problems of capitalist nations she discussed were armaments, employment, and growth; those of the socialist nations were the same but also included agriculture and reform. Problems of the third world included foreign trade, underdevelopment, capital inflows, and population.[51]

Robinson's second book in this period was for the Modern Cambridge Economics Series (which she continued to edit with Phyllis Deane and Gautam Mathur), entitled *Aspects of Development and Underdevelopment.* This handbook successfully integrates theory and her sage observations on problems in real economies.

Introduction to Modern Economics is Robinson's only book written with a collaborator. She confidently expected that McGraw-Hill would publish it in the United States as well as in England. With some disappointment, Robinson wrote to Alfred Eichner,† "[W]e were foolish enough to allow ourselves to get committed to them before we found out that McGraw-Hill USA had been frightened off by the leaders of the economics profession and was merely taking 3,000 copies of the UK edition."[52] Nor, apparently, did McGraw-Hill promote the book in the United States. Robinson asked Eichner to get the book into the hands of American students while she tried to arrange for American publication. She had high hopes: "I am eagerly looking forward to see how Robinson/Eatwell is going to be received."[53] She was modest: "I expect everyone will have some points of disagreement with the book. . . . We did not intend to lay down the law but to get discussion going."[54]

Eichner, who was very grateful to Robinson for help she had given him on a manuscript, wrote her a word of warning: "Unless the book is somewhat refurbished so as to conform more to the American style, rather than the English style, of teaching elementary economics, I am afraid that Americans, even with the best of intentions will find it difficult to adopt it for their courses." He also told her an "awful" tale. Ed Nell had asked a local bookstore to obtain copies of the book for

*Paul Davidson was visiting Cambridge University that year.
†See Chapter 15 for more of their correspondence.

the upcoming American Economic Association convention. The bookstore had sent someone to get the books newly unloaded from the ship and had prominently displayed a copy in the store's window. "However, when some students went in to try to purchase the book, they were told that it couldn't be sold to them. It seems that McGraw-Hill (USA) was unable to tell the bookstore what the book cost, so the store did not know what price to charge."[55]

Robinson asked Eichner to explain his reservations about the text. He replied that it was at the pedagogical level that he saw problems. "As useful and helpful as the book may be to someone already well trained in economics, it is not a usable teaching instrument. . . . it would leave an American undergraduate, and indeed most graduate students, somewhat bewildered."[56] Robinson answered, "Robinson & Eatwell is being used in a few schools in North America so we shall have to see how it goes. I think the neo-classics will collapse in Europe before they do in the U.S.A."[57]

By the time this textbook appeared, *Econometrica* and the *American Economic Review* had discontinued book reviews. The institutionalist *Journal of Economic Issues* published Karl de Schweinitz, Jr.'s review. He began with a summary: "A giant among neoclassical economists, Joan Robinson for years has been taxing neoclassical economics for the unreality of its assumptions, the triviality of its theorems, and its capitalist apologetics." Nevertheless, in an otherwise favorable review, de Schweinitz concluded that *Introduction* was "best suited for students who already have a knowledge of the historical and institutional background of contemporary economies, some understanding of the methodology of the social sciences, and the intellectual toughness to follow tightly reasoned verbal arguments."[58] Once again, Robinson had written a book too difficult for her audience.

David Houston, writing for the *Sloan Management Review*, felt that Robinson and Eatwell had produced a "genuinely different approach" to the introduction of economics. He thought it might be "well-suited for a small class of intellectually oriented students" and to some extent it reflected "the differing level of university students here and in England."[59]

The *Economic Journal* review also was written by an American—John G. Gurley of Stanford University. Gurley found *Introduction* a difficult book for beginners. He thought it had some other faults, such as being weak on contemporary institutions. But he liked the economics in it. In his opinion, this text would "much better prepare the coming generation of students for understanding and solving the real problems of the world than neo-neoclassical economics ever can. . . ."[60] Gurley was by this time considered a heterodox economist.

Another review appeared as an article in a collection of essays. Canadian Robert Needham announced that the text was "long overdue." He thought it "fairly accurate . . . to say that in the last twenty years or so her [Robinson's] main involvement has been in fighting battles . . . with the leading neoclassicals [rather] than with presenting simply and systematically the Cambridge view."

Needham felt that North American economists had not given her work the attention it deserved, primarily because they had been trained in a tradition signified by Samuelson. He added, "it is rare to find a continuous and meaningful attempt to deal with the history of economic doctrine in any other way than that which is consistent with received neoclassical dogma."

Needham thought specialization led economists to become "indoctrinated in the ways of a profession dealing with worlds and small aspects of worlds that have never and will never exist." Furthermore, "university education does little to train students to think critically of their world and how to change it." He found the teaching of Galbraith, Myrdal, Robinson, and Benjamin Ward exceptions to this rule. However, "the indoctrination process for priest and novice alike does not allow one to dwell long on heretical points of view, however different, challenging, downright disturbing, and somehow amazingly refreshing they may be. In fact for success in the profession one is best advised to forget about social relevance."

To counteract this, Needham adopted *An Introduction to Modern Economics* and taught what he called "the Cambridge paradigm." He termed this "the beginning of an attempt at grass-roots articulation and discussion." Needham found the text more difficult for both the students and the professors than an ordinary text. Robinson and Eatwell used a "terse style" in order to "force understanding by making it necessary to figure it out first hand." But Needham also found the text more relevant and better preparation for dealing with practical research questions, and even for undertaking employment as an economist.[61]

American Frank Roosevelt, writing in the same collection, saw *Introduction* as representing "the Cantabrigian Approach," one he considered inferior to that of Marx.[62] Roosevelt admitted that radicals had been attracted to the Cambridge school because of its "fame by attacking some of the central concepts of neoclassical economics."[63] But Cambridge was guilty of "commodity fetishism," because it continued, as does mainstream economics, to separate the physical from the social aspects of production.[64] Roosevelt was particularly put off by "the sympathy which Robinson and Eatwell have for managers." He accused them of losing sight of the idea of socialism as a system of workers' control. Robinson, he concluded, was "naive—especially with regard to the benevolent character of the state." Her remedies, which seemed to him to be "'state capitalism', would leave people still performing alienated labor under the direction of an autocratic elite." He thought Robinson not only did not understand socialism but did not know what was wrong with capitalism.[65]

Robinson's other new book of this decade was one of her most readable. *Aspects of Development and Underdevelopment* was directed toward the intelligent undergraduate and interested general reader. Not a survey, it attempted "to throw some light upon the question of why a quarter of a century of 'development' has produced results so different from what was proclaimed to be its object."[66] Robinson was concerned with how unhelpful some western economic concepts, for example Gross National Product, are in dealing with the third world. She discussed problems of population, the "modernization of poverty," planning, dependence on primary commodities, the misdirection of aid and loans, and the arming of the third world. She was not optimistic. All the economist can do is "to remove some illusions and to help whoever is willing to look to see what their situation really is."[67]

Kenneth P. Jameson of the University of Notre Dame reviewed *Aspects* for the institutionalist *Journal of Economic Issues*, along with a review of a collection of articles entitled *Toward A New Strategy of Development.* He found some important similarities. For example, both works included an analysis of the "role of the military in development, a subject omitted from most economic development treatises."

Another similarity he found was a profound pessimism. He quoted Robinson's conclusion: "While population is still growing, though at a slightly decelerating rate, the arms race is continuing at an accelerating rate and the spread of commercialism is destroying human values everywhere, it is not easy to take an optimistic view of the situation of the Third World today."[68] By the time Robinson wrote *Aspects*, economic development was no longer a popular topic in the United States. I asked the Indian economist S. Chakravarty why he thought this was so. He felt that American economists tend to lose interest in problems which cannot be easily solved.[69]

Except for these two volumes, the work Robinson published during her seventies consisted of collections, reminiscences, and papers with reflective views, such as "The Unimportance of Reswitching." There were four volumes of articles, two of them in paperback, making her work available to students.[70]

Marc Vandoorne of State University Center, Antwerp, reviewed Volume 5 of her collected papers for the *Economic Journal* and found "the message of this, her last collection, was that 'the Keynesian revolution still remains to be made both in teaching economic theory and in forming economic policy'."[71] Vandoorne was impressed most of all by her argument that morality should be brought back into economic and social thought.

Joan Robinson was seventy-one years old when she made the commencement address at the University of Maine entitled, "Morality and Economics," which so moved Vandoorne in its published form. Her ultimate attack on orthodox economics was straight from the moral sciences. She said,

> I want to speak about the philosophy of economics. It is an extremely important element in the view of life and the conceptions which prevail in this country. Freedom is the great ideal. Along with the concept of freedom goes freedom of the market, and the philosophy of orthodox economics is that the pursuit of self-interest will lead to the benefit of society. By this means the moral problem is abolished. The moral problem is concerned with the conflict between individ-

ual interest and the interest of society. And since this doctrine tells us that there is no conflict, we can all pursue our self-interest with good conscience.

Adam Smith's phrase, the "invisible hand," had become a central doctrine of orthodox economics, in spite of much evidence that the "doctrine of the free market—the pursuit of self-interest—has worked out to the disadvantage of society." Robinson objected to associating this doctrine of selfishness with Adam Smith, who had shown in his *Theory of Moral Sentiments* that he relied very much upon morality and that he "took it for granted that there is an ethical foundation for society." It was Robinson's hope that "the moral consciousness which has grown up in modern times in the youth of America, which has led them to protest against the unequal balance prevailing between morality and the market . . . will find that the doctrines of Adam Smith are not to be taken in the form in which your professors are explaining them to you."[72]

Robinson twice referred to Kenneth Arrow (a Nobel laureate since 1972). He was, she said, a "great exponent of orthodoxy" and a "great exponent of the mathematics of the market economy." Yet even Arrow had said that "the idealization of freedom through the market completely ignores the fact that this freedom can be, to a large number of people, very limited in scope." She agreed with Arrow that "the invisible institution of the moral law" was necessary to society.[73]

The capital controversy had continued to depress her during her seventies. She penned "Still Further Thoughts, April 1979" on the "Debate: 1970s." "I feel frustrated by our round of papers because no-one answers me either yes or no. . . . The argument started with my attacking what I believe to be a fundamental, indeed fatal, flaw in neo-neoclassical methodology. . . . After several vain attempts to ring through, I shall in future leave Samuelson to rot in peace. . . ."[74]

JR

CHAPTER THIRTEEN

Her "Great Friend," John Kenneth Galbraith

The close personal friendship between Joan Robinson and John Kenneth Galbraith stretched from a first acquaintance during Galbraith's year at Cambridge in 1937–38 until her death. A shared view of economics, especially American conventional economics, united them. Galbraith, at six feet eight-and-a-half inches, towered over Robinson's five feet seven inches, but in physical stature only. He found her "wonderfully independent and formidable" and considered her his "much admired friend."[1]

Galbraith, born in 1908, was five years Robinson's junior. He grew up, as she had, before World War I, but there the similarities end. Galbraith was born in Iona Station, a farming community in what he calls "Scotch" Canada. He writes of a "deeply valid appreciation of the nature of manual labor" from his boyhood on a farm: "A long day following a plodding, increasingly reluctant team behind a harrow endlessly back and forth over the uninspiring Ontario terrain persuaded one that all other work was easy."[2]

With a background so different from Robinson's, Galbraith nevertheless arrived at opinions of the world and economics which were similar to hers. After attending agricultural college, Galbraith made his way to the University of California at Berkeley on a fellowship. Economics at Berkeley during the 1930s was distinctly heterodox. Galbraith came under the influence of Leo Rogin, who "years before the Keynesian revolution . . . was discussing Keynes with a sense of urgency that made his seminars seem to graduate students the most important things then happening in the world." Galbraith also studied Marshall with Ewald Grether, "who taught with a drillmaster's precision for which I have ever since been grateful." He was also influenced by Thorstein Veblen's books, which were "still being read with attention in Berkeley in the thirties."[3]

The depression was much on the minds of the youthful scholars at Berkeley, as were possible political solutions to economic problems. Galbraith remembers his colleagues and friends among the graduate students as "uniformly radical and the most distinguished were Communists." He feels his agricultural background separated him from the Marxists. (He also confesses a weakness for enjoying "the corrupt system" even then.)[4] By 1934, when he was twenty-six years old, Galbraith's life pattern seems to have been established: a life of public service; academic effort in teaching and writing; and political activism.

One can see a glimmer of how he would like to be remembered in his review of Keynes' *Collected Writings:* "Keynes rejected specialization. . . . In no necessary order of importance his pursuits included the following: his public career in the treasury during two wars; his long association with King's College, Cambridge, of which he was the highly successful and, as speculator one must believe exceptionally lucky, bursar; . . .the chairmanship of a major insurance company; journalism; support for the arts, . . ." The point was that Keynes used all these experiences to aid him in understanding economics. In Galbraith's opinion, "Whatever the case in other disciplines, there can be no doubt that in economics, specialization is the parent not only of boredom but also of irrelevance and error."[5]

Galbraith visited Cambridge University for scholarly work on three separate occasions. The first was in 1937 when he arrived as a Social Science Research Fellow, on Rockefeller money.[6] For him, 1937 was a year of far-reaching decisions. He became an American citizen, married Catherine Merriam Atwater, with whom he has "lived happily ever after," and sailed for Southampton to spend his year at Cambridge. There he met Joan Robinson for the first time. Galbraith said,

> My acquaintance with Joan Robinson extended from early autumn of 1937 until the time of her death, a matter of nearly a half century, and I suppose I met her in the first days or weeks of the autumn term in 1937. I had gone to spend a year at Cambridge with the expectation of seeing and working under Keynes, but that was the year of his first heart attack, and he never showed up at the university all that year. I spent the year with Joan Robinson, R. F. Kahn, and Piero Sraffa, all of whom were intellectually very close to Keynes, and there was very little that I missed, because we talked about him all the time.[7]

The Cantabrigians he remembered most fondly from that year were Piero Sraffa, "one of the most leisured men who ever lived," and Michal Kalecki, "the most innovative figure in economics" that he ever knew.[8] Galbraith had arrived during the era of frequent Keynesian "conversions," but he was already acquainted with the General Theory, and had been made ready for it by his observations of the depression and also by his Berkeley professors. At first, Galbraith was drawn into the excitement by Keynes' "friends, students, and acolytes." Later, his long-term attitude toward theorists prevailed: "I penetrated the thicket of technical controversy surrounding Keynes's work and became one of the acknowledged oracles. I also learned that this accomplishment, though it served indispensably for gaining the respect and attention of other economists, served negligibly as a guide to practical action. This is true of nearly all sophisticated elaboration in economics."[9]

At the time of Galbraith's first visit, Joan Robinson had just published her *Essays in the Theory of Employment* and was writing her *Introduction to the Theory of Employment*. Galbraith's wife Catherine said that there was some amazement at Joan Robinson's having produced a book and a baby in the same year. Galbraith thus was fully acquainted with these books. He has continued to refer to her in his written work, however, mainly in connection with her *Economics of Imperfect Competition*.

During this first English sojourn, Galbraith regularly went to London, where he attended Hayek's seminars and became acquainted with Nicholas Kaldor, who was then teaching at the London School of Economics. Their friendship was strengthened after World War II, when Galbraith was put in charge of the overall economic assessment of the German mobilization effort and hired Kaldor on his staff.[10]

In the early fifties, when Joan Robinson was hard at work generalizing the General Theory, Galbraith took up the thread of Cambridge again, dining with Kahn in 1955 in Geneva, traveling with the Kaldors in India, and arriving in Cambridge in 1956 to occupy the Kaldors' residence in their absence. He was writing *The Affluent Society* at the time and attended neither the secret seminar nor the Sunday walks. Galbraith recalled: "I remember the Sunday walks. I remember walking over from the Kaldor house to the backs and encountering Joan and Kahn just starting out to walk. I asked them where they were going, and they said 'To London and back' or something of the sort."[11] Galbraith found Kaldor's lovely house and splendid library very congenial to his work on *The Affluent Society*.

By 1956, Galbraith's interests in economics were far from theirs, and their friendship was based more on politics than on economic theory. Galbraith remained the quintessential North American pragmatist who could not be lured into the joys of the capital controversy, and he was apparently not urged to attend the secret seminar. Yet there was respect between Robinson and Galbraith. Galbraith asked her who the good young economists were at Cambridge University. "She looked at me sternly, which in her case could be very stern indeed, and said, 'My dear Ken, we were the last good generation.'"[12] Galbraith and Robinson shared other friends beyond Cambridge, especially the Myrdals. They also had acquaintances in common. One was John Strachey, who had piqued Robinson about her ignorance of Marx in the mid-thirties.

Galbraith's third extended visit to Cambridge was in 1970, when he came at R. A. Butler's invitation. Butler was now Master of Trinity and Galbraith was invited as a Fellow, settling "into comfortable rooms in Nevile's Court." There he worked on *Economics and the Public Purpose*.[13] This visit came at the end of

Joan Robinson's teaching career and just before Galbraith's election as President of the American Economic Association.[14]

Galbraith set about choosing the person who was to give the honorary Ely lecture (the only patronage of the position, apart from formulating the program for the annual meeting). "I never had any hesitation. I immediately chose Joan; the only person that I would have chosen if Joan had not been available was Gunnar Myrdal." This was a singular honor, an opportunity to present a formal address to a prestigious group. Taking it in her stride, Professor Robinson welcomed the forum as an opportunity to berate American economists about the dreadful state of the profession.*

There is no lengthy correspondence between the two friends. Only one letter of Galbraith's survives in Robinson's archival collection. He thinks there probably were not many. ("I am a poor letter writer. I don't sit down and write long letters. Very few writers are letter writers.")

The extant letter is a copy of one addressed to Harold W. McGraw, on November 30, 1973, challenging McGraw-Hill for allegedly reneging on an agreement to publish an American edition of her textbook (written with John Eatwell). This was to be her invasion of the American undergraduate classroom with what she called the modern economics, but McGraw-Hill published it only in England. Galbraith wrote, ". . . someone recently told me that, following the adverse reaction of some scholar of the Harding era in Ohio, you have decided not to press [her book]. I never quite credit these rumors, but do reassure me."[15]

From the point of view of the English, Galbraith fits their stereotype of an American institutionalist. John Veazey argued that Galbraith had "revived" American institutionalism from its dormant state, created when the "refugees . . . overwhelmed the native American institutionalist school."[16] Galbraith demurred that Veazey's allegation is a "marked overstatement. . . . The institutionalist school had far more important figures and far more devoted figures than I've ever been. Clarence Ayres, for example, and Wallace Peterson."[17] The English had been aware of such an American school, at least since the publication of Lord Robbins' *Essay on the Nature and Significance of Economic Science* in 1932. Robbins had written, "And now we have the Institutionalists. . . . and in recent years, if they have not secured the upper hand altogether, they have certainly had a wide area of power in America."[18]

Galbraith admits to having been associated generally with the founding of the Association for Evolutionary Economics (an avowed institutionalist association which purports to carry on the post-Darwinian work of Veblen), and of having been asked to be its president. However, being president of the American Economic Association was quite enough. He has simply gone his own way. Galbraith is on record as considering Veblen "the most interesting social scientist the United States has produced."[19]

---

*See Chapter 14.

The relationship between Robinson and Galbraith was predominantly a friendly rather than a professional one. Robinson's professional effort was directed toward pure theory, which Galbraith thought useless at best.[20] Since Galbraith's economics was also anti-orthodox, he did not give Robinson grounds to establish her adversarial stance toward him, but she was not uncritical. When she reviewed his *American Capitalism* for the *Economic Journal,* she saw his thesis as contrary to hers in the *Economics of Imperfect Competition.* There she had "debunked" the prevailing orthodoxy, which claimed that the worker received the value of his marginal product, "though perhaps Professor Chamberlin did not see it like that." In her debunking, she felt her work had "hacked through" a "prop to *laisser-faire* ideology."[21]

Thus she objected to Galbraith's argument of countervailing power. Galbraith had accepted the idea that competition is incompatible with the conditions which prevail over larger areas of modern industry, but he had proposed an "alternate defense" for American capitalism. He argued that American capitalism generates within itself a corrective to the concentration of economic power in large firms through the development of the countervailing power of big government and big unions. This, she said, was "rebunking *laisser-faire.*" She enjoyed what she found to be a "shrewd, witty and forceful" argument addressed to "wider circles than the professional economists." However, she doubted that Galbraith would be "altogether welcome" as an ally to orthodoxy. Was he too candid or too cynical? She couldn't decide.[22]

In addition to this review, Robinson referred occasionally to Galbraith's books. In her *Economic Philosophy* (this would be after Galbraith's second sojourn at Cambridge), she saw in *American Capitalism* more than a rebunking of laissez-faire. Now it was a legacy of the discussion set off by her *Imperfect Competition.* By giving the trade unions the social role of restoring wages to an acceptable level through countervailing power, Galbraith was recognizing the efficacy of her thesis that workers' wages had been depressed by monopoly employers.[23] In this context, Galbraith's thesis was the best defense of capitalism as an economic system. But she accused Galbraith of being a "disciple" of Schumpeter in this line of argument. "They provide a tough, cynical and intelligent defense of capitalist rules of the game which is far more effective than the soft, sophistical special pleading of the orthodox school."[24]

Though a personal friend, Robinson always saw Galbraith not as himself, but in relation to some other tradition. For example, she thought of him as in Chamberlin's debt somehow, since Galbraith made a great point of the fact that "under oligopoly price competition ceases to operate," that is, competition takes other forms, such as advertising. Robinson concluded that Galbraith was only contrasting the theoretical failure of capitalism with its practical achievements. "After all this debate the beautiful simplicity of the doctrine that *laisser-faire* capitalism has a natural tendency to produce the maximum possible benefit for the community can never be restored. . . ."[25]

Robinson saw *The Affluent Society* as a demonstration of how the *"laisser-faire* bias that still clings around orthodoxy also helps to falsify true values." She quoted one of Galbraith's most memorable descriptions: "The family which takes its mauve and cerise, air-conditioned, power-steered, and power-braked car out for a tour passes through cities that are badly paved, made hideous by litter, blighted buildings, bill-boards" and so on. She added, "We have not quite reached that stage here, but we are well on the way."[26] Another of Robinson's favorite Galbraithian epigrams was his "private affluence and public squalor," which she referred to again and again.[27]

In a symposium of economists published by the *Monthly Review* on the subject, "Has Capitalism Changed?" Robinson again showed her preference for Galbraith's *Affluent Society* over his *American Capitalism* when she responded, "Galbraith would have done better to draw upon his *Affluent Society* for a contribution to this [symposium] volume rather than from his earlier and more soothing work."[28]

Robinson's view of *The New Industrial State* was essentially that Galbraith "sets out to substitute for Marshall a picture, based on general observation . . . of the behavior of giant firms." His account "appears plausible or, at the very least, worth discussing, but it has no success as an ideological doctrine."[29] Robinson, now in her seventies, felt Marshall's theory that there was an upper limit to the size of firms was "one of the fossils of the nineteenth century doctrine that has been carried down till today in mainstream teaching." She noted, with irony, that since Galbraith "writes in a bright, readable style, his views need not be taken seriously." She meant, of course, that he would probably not be taken seriously by the economics profession.[30]

Her greatest compliment to Galbraith was paid in her review of Robert Lekachman's *Age of Keynes*. She objected to Lekachman's patronizing attitude toward Galbraith. Lekachman, she wrote, "fails to remark that Galbraith alone has drawn the moral from the General Theory—once we accept the idea that there ought to be full employment, the question follows what should employment be for." She felt it was evident that there had been "a disastrous failure in *public* spending," a point Galbraith had long argued.[31]

Galbraith, on the other hand, was rather more chary with his references to his friend Joan Robinson's work. From reading his books, one might suppose that she had never written anything except *The Economics of Imperfect Competition*, which he always bracketed, in references, with the work of his Harvard colleague, Chamberlin. In his 1975 biography, John S. Gambs complained of Galbraith's being stingy with acknowledgments. Not only was Robinson's work not mentioned, but Galbraith also ignored Clarence Ayres, Gunnar Myrdal, and Allan Gruchy, all of whom he knew personally.[32] David Reisman also accused Galbraith of "overstating the novelty and originality of his own contribution."[33]

Surely Galbraith's style precludes academic acknowledgment, and he offers no excuses. His books are directed neither toward establishing a cult nor toward an exclusive academic community. He has admitted to having inherited from the farming community the affliction of "a serious sense of inferiority," which leads one to "assertive compensation" coupled with "an aggressive feeling that I owed it to all I encountered to make them better informed."[34]

Citing references would have required that he work in an entirely different way, and perhaps at less congenial places than Kaldor's house, Nevile's Court at Trinity College, or Gstaad, Switzerland. Checking footnotes is competitive with productivity. An estimated output of Galbraith's work between 1959 and 1968 included eight non-fiction works, a novel, thirty-two magazine articles, fifty-four book reviews, thirty-five letters to the editor, eight introductions to books, and numerous lectures and major speeches for Lyndon Johnson and John, Robert, and Edward Kennedy.[35]

Galbraith's views about Robinson's early work changed over time. In the 1930s, his view of the economy was derived from the "classical orthodoxy of Alfred Marshall as modified by the recently published work of two young economists."[36] However, in the postwar situation he could see "that the analytical task would appear to have failed because oligopoly . . . has not yielded to the kit of tools long employed for the analysis of the competitive market" which had come to include imperfect competitive tools.[37] Galbraith had decided by 1948 that the Robinson-Chamberlin analysis had "only substituted a new set of frustrations for the old ones."[38]

Galbraith believed that economics had become obsolescent by failing to take account of the absence of price competition, and his several works were directed toward reaching beyond "the obstinate orthodoxy" to a general public which might understand this point. This was part of what Robinson saw as a legacy of imperfect competition.

One of the ideas Galbraith especially admired was Robinson's notion of "disguised unemployment." While in India, it occurred to him that the fifty ambassadors (including the High Commissioners from other Commonwealth countries) represented a "spectacular example" of disguised unemployment.[39] He also recognized Robinson's ability to turn "Keynes's ideas into accessible English."[40] Coming from Galbraith, this was the highest of compliments, as he has some pride and competence in the matter of style.[41] Galbraith thought that even "the idea of *The General Theory* could have been stated in clear English," had Keynes taken the time.[42]

There were two areas where Galbraith and Robinson had a comfortable meeting of the minds. One was the necessity of criticizing "conventional" or "standard" economics. In the Keynesian tradition, Robinson first took Marshallian-Pigouvian economics as a point of departure, later switching her sights to the American "bastard Keynesians." Galbraith used Samuelson's economics as his target. He might have helped to convince Joan Robinson of the validity of this point of departure insofar as American economics was concerned. To a degree, Robinson shared Galbraith's belief that "the problem of economics . . . is not one of original error but of obsolescence."[43]

The other area was the diabolical nature of the arms race. On this issue they were in complete agreement. Galbraith said, "If we fail in the control of the nuclear arms race, all of the other matters we debate in these days will be without meaning."[44] Robinson, expressing concern that America would "rather blow the world up than allow someone else to lead it," concluded "until that mood passes, there is nothing else worth discussing."[45]

Both were politically active in opposing the arms race. Robinson gave one hundred pounds to help found the Cambridge nuclear protest efforts, and made her pilgrimage to the Mormon country of Utah to speak for peace even when her doctor advised her strongly not to make any trip by jet. There was a third matter sometimes discussed between the two friends—that the way to criticize neoclassical and equilibrium economics was from "an absolutely solid position in the classical tradition." Galbraith said of Robinson, "Nobody could accuse her of being a critic of conventional economics without having understood it. She was acknowledged to be a master of the structure which in terms of power, in terms of distribution of revenue, in terms of expropriative tendencies, she was criticizing."[46]

Both Galbraith and Robinson shared a strong orientation toward what economists are fond of calling the "real world." But Galbraith thought Robinson had another motivation which was also important:

> Joan began with a strong suspicion of the establishment view as being, as Marx said, generally a reflection of interest rather than reality. I've always thought that she was right in this with some modification. I've always thought that the establishment view had an enormous debt to the past. Economic institutions, economic processes change while economics committed to the psyche of scientific method and the implication therefore that there is an unchanging truth, unchanging matter as in physics or chemistry has an inbuilt tendency to obsolescence. And I have always felt that more strongly than Joan. I think she always felt that it was an expression of ruling class interest, with which I would agree, but which I would modify by the commitment of people to the scientific mystique. And also the more practical commitment of a good many economists to keeping for their lifetime what they learned as graduate students. Many economists are very economical with intellectual effort and don't like to see their beliefs modified by time. Joan had a certain instinct to comfort the afflicted and afflict the comfortable which I have always found highly sympathetic.[47]

Linked by such shared suspicions, talents, and beliefs, Galbraith and Robinson enjoyed a friendship of many years.

JR

CHAPTER FOURTEEN

North America in the Sixties: Visits and Exchanges

Before World War II, Robinson's travels had been more personal than professional. First there were those years in India with her husband, and then some mountain climbing expeditions to Switzerland.[1] After the war, she was an avid traveler. She particularly enjoyed visiting India and China and other developing nations. Her enthusiasm for China was considered scandalous by some, but the record is that Robinson asked hard questions wherever she went. Her visits to the United States during this postwar period were just a minor part of her travel, but they are important in the history of economic doctrine. There is universal agreement among those she visited that her main objective in coming to the United States was to spend time with her daughter and grandchildren in Canada without spending too much money. Americans were not offended by this. She had many more invitations to visit campuses than she accepted.

Before her daughter moved to Canada, Robinson probably did not wish to visit the United States. Clarissa Kaldor* wrote to Robinson from Squaw Valley, California on January 2, 1960, "Susan Thomas reports that you can't believe that we really like America—it's extremely difficult to put across why." Then Clarissa Kaldor described what it was like to be near Squaw Valley, "6000 feet up in the Sierras, 200 miles from San Francisco and Los Angeles, but connected by enormous roads kept free of snow" in a modern lodge "crowded with the sporting young," where

> . . . the young are dressed extremely well and attractively—it is completely democratic, nothing posh, no waiters, all cafeteria—you can spend money, a steak costs $4.50 but nearly everyone has hamburgers for 60 cents and stay at

---

*Clarissa was the wife of Nicholas Kaldor, who was visiting the University of California at Berkeley in 1960.

cheap motels or cabins near and drive in (as we do, 15 miles along superb roads). It is all exhilarating, and all values are not cockeye. For instance, one of the enjoyable things about the USA is the variety of paper backs (including Penguins but many, many more). . . . It is very nice to live in a country where the majority are able to live a good life—and people are really happy and hence very nice, unfussy, unpompous and easy going. It is an endlessly fascinating, not well documented country and as one world traveler to another I can't recommend it too highly. It's really important and changes the "image" just as India does.[2]

1961 swing through the States

Robinson was invited to address the Midwestern Economic Association and to consult on Liberia with Robert Clower at his home campus, Northwestern University. She accepted. Both Clower and Davidson believe that she had probably not been invited before because there was some fear that the State Department would deny her entry. With President Kennedy in the White House, there was no trouble. In fact, Robinson praised the officials in London who arranged for her papers for this first visit.[3]

She asked Solow for help in arranging a stopover at Cambridge. He had set up the en route visits to Harvard and MIT. She again wrote to Solow, "I am proposing to arrive at Cambridge Mass., on Tuesday the 28th March and leaving for Toronto by the night train on Tuesday 4th April (I assume there is a night train)." She wanted to visit her daughter. However, she was going to give full measure for her $250: "I was proposing to offer you two seminars on the Use and Abuse of the Production Function. I think we should have two because I am sure we shall get in a thorough muddle at the first one."[4] Solow replied, "What will you bet that one of us will be in a bigger muddle at the end of the second seminar than at the beginning of the first?"[5]

Robinson never mentioned her reception at Harvard, but in "Reminiscences," written in 1977 when she was seventy-four years old, she gave a long account of what happened at MIT.

In 1961 I was invited to take a couple of seminars at MIT. I chose the subject: The Use and Abuse of the Production Function. During the first session, I asked Samuelson: When you define the marginal product of labor, what do you keep constant? For a moment, he was quite disconcerted, and then started off on some baffling rigmarole. I cut in: Paul, I asked you a simple question, can't you give me a simple answer? He replied that he would have to think it over. This scene was long remembered by the students at MIT who witnessed it.

Samuelson turned the joke against himself. He put round a paper next day as follows: Thursday at 4.40, Mrs. Robinson asked the question. Professor Samuelson: Well I mean to say, the Kings of England were William the First, and William the Second. . . . Mrs. Robinson: Come, come sir, answer the question!

Friday 6.30 a.m. (implying a sleepless night) the answer is that either you keep all physical inputs constant or you keep the rate of interest constant.

Robinson concluded her report of this encounter, "It was great fun to tease Samuelson, but this debate took attention away from the main issue."[6]

After visiting in Toronto, Robinson went to the Midwest, staying at Clower's home in Evanston, Illinois. Officially, Clower had brought Robinson over as a consultant on the Economic Survey of Liberia. "Just a boondoggle," he says, to pay for her honorarium and her travel. She arrived at Northwestern "full of the problems she had given Samuelson" and stories that she had had Samuelson "do some recanting." After her visits in the United States, Robinson was scheduled to go to Cuba via Mexico. Clower said she was "full of revolutionary fervor for new blossoming societies. I found that very interesting."[7]

Clower got to know her "other side."

I squired her around to various places. We must have been together almost constantly for ten or twelve days. I didn't let her out of my sight until I sent her up to visit what she called the hippopotami—that's the people wallowing around out in the sticks. She included the people in West Lafayette, Indiana partly in that category: I think she was surprised to find a powerful department at Purdue. The real hippopotami to her were the types that I had grown up with at Washington State.[8]

Robinson visited Clower's alma mater in Pullman, Washington. "She went out there and talked because I had arranged it. She loved the people but she found them really rather dim."

She had other adventures in the Chicago area. Her address before the Midwestern Economic Association was a great success. Afterward, during a question period, someone asked a question that Clower said

. . . sounded like an almost personal attack on Joan, something like that he was glad to meet the person who had written a book which had provided so much torture for them in graduate school. He thought he was complimenting her. Joan's answer was, "Yes, I am always glad I wrote that book because that way I didn't have to read it." He then came back with something else, and the whole audience (she looked, at that particular address, something like a grandmother) just sort of rose and five or six people just kind of pushed him down in the chair. They didn't want this kind of thing. She was regarded as really one of the sages of the profession. She gave a *great* talk and she fielded the questions. We were so fascinated.

Clower and others showed Robinson the town. They took her to night clubs. "She was great in night clubs. She liked to dance. She could really kick up her heels.'' Once they took her to a strip tease. ''I don't think I suggested that but probably Bob Strotz, who became president of the Midwestern Economic Association, did just to shock her. But nothing shocked her. She didn't find it very amusing.'' Robinson was fifty-seven at the time of this visit. Clower found her very attractive, thought she was more like forty and ''very vigorous.''

Robinson also visited the University of Chicago, where her former pupil and colleague Harry Johnson was teaching. Johnson once said that as far as Robinson was concerned, ''you got used to the image that she was not recognizable as a female of the species and did not behave like one, and that was one of the main lessons one had to learn.'' He invited her to talk to his students. ''They looked at her and decided, 'Well, we'll certainly show this old grandmother where she gets off.' After they picked their heads up off the floor, having been ticked off with a few well-chosen blunt squelches, they took a much more respectful attitude.''[9]

After visiting the hippopotami in Washington State, Robinson stopped at the University of Colorado. Leslie Fishman* said she stayed less than a week, but that she did participate in their World Affairs week, wherein some sixty or seventy political and academic luminaries are invited to discuss the major issues of the day. Clifton Grubbs,† a young faculty member, was ''appointed to be her chauffeur and see that she was properly entertained.'' Grubbs had studied at the University of Texas under Clarence Ayres. He told Robinson that what she was saying, her current thinking, had been written and discussed by Ayres a long time ago. He gave her a copy of Ayres' *Theory of Economic Progress* on the promise that she would read it.[10] And she did.

The Texas connection: corresponding with Ayres

Joan Robinson's reading of Clarence Ayres' *Theory of Economic Progress* led to a correspondence between them which highlights Robinson's openness, her suspicion of American intellectuals, and the philosophical distance between her and American institutionalists. It also shows how lighthearted she could be in argument.

When Robinson first heard of Ayres' *Theory of Economic Progress* it had been in print for seventeen years. Without the catalyst in the person of Clifton Grubbs, some of the pages and arguments in Robinson's *Economic Philosophy* might have been different. In any event, her book would have interested Ayres, much of whose teaching and training was in philosophy. Ayres was delighted to receive a request from her publisher for permission to quote 103 lines of *Theory of Economic Progress*.[11] He immediately wrote to ''Mrs. Robinson'' that ''This would have been a complete and inexplicable surprise if I had not had a letter from Cliff Grubbs late last spring in which he said he had been propagandizing you while

---

*Fishman is now at the University of Keele, Staffordshire, England.
†Grubbs is now at the University of Texas, Austin.

you were in Boulder. Any book with such a title would capture my attention; and such a book coming from you would in any case have aroused excitement. But now I feel like the prisoner in the dock while the jury is out."[12] Unlike most of Robinson's American correspondents, Ayres was older than she, by twelve years.[13]

Robinson must have written Ayres two letters which do not survive, for in October he thanked her for "both letters," expressing delight that she found *Theory of Economic Progress* "worth reading," for "yes, it has been ignored. That's obvious, and in any such situation I'm tempted to assume a conspiracy. It's always easier to think other people wicked than to credit them with being as stupid as the facts suggest. But I'm afraid the academic mind is just as prone as any to follow well trodden paths."[14]

Thus began a correspondence between two kindred souls, anti-establishmentarianists within the profession of economics as well as in the general world. Robinson saved five of Ayres' letters to her, and he saved two of hers. But their similar attitudes toward mainstream economics did not mean that there was no room for debate between the two.

What had interested Robinson about Ayres' *Theory of Economic Progress* was that he had offered an alternative explanation of the origins of industrial capitalism to the traditional Weber thesis of the influence of Protestantism or to Sombart's "theory that it was all due to Catholicism." In answer to the question of why the industrial revolution had occurred in Western Europe, Ayres suggested that the Mediterranean area offered a frontier condition, where ideas from older societies were introduced but where religion had only a "weak hold" over society, thus allowing for technological progressiveness. Most importantly for Robinson, Ayres offered an alternative to Walt Whitman Rostow's notion that industrialization "begins as a reaction to national humiliation."[15]

There had been some early correspondence between Robinson and Rostow about economic growth. In the course of writing a short book on the subject, Rostow had read some of her early manuscripts (before *Accumulation)*, which he had found "immensely interesting and valuable." He decided, "The difference between our methods is evident enough: I am trying to ask what determines the rate of growth primarily; and only secondarily, why is a growing capitalist system inherently unstable." This had led Rostow "into the murky region of the social framework of the economy."[16] Rostow had also sent Robinson part of his manuscript of *The Process of Economic Growth*. He confided,

I am convinced that economists of our generation are, at their own initiative, going to be forced to forge formal links between economics and the general analysis of society. We cannot treat the size and quality of the working force as exogenous and the scale and character of the flow of innovations, and still be relevant to some of the main issues of our day; nor can we rely on the historians and sociologists making the links for us.

Rostow added: "I hadn't realized it until I came to write the chapter (II), but this means that we must make up our minds about Marx' general theory of society. It has, virtually, no competitor. In formal terms we all thoroughly fudge our view of the inter-relations among economic, social, and political factors." And he paid her a compliment:

> Being a reasonably well brought up young man with a decent respect for accumulated knowledge, lore and concepts, I've worried some about whether or not more may be lost than gained by trying to bring formally into the analysis non-economic motivations. On balance I've concluded that it cannot be avoided. So, to this point, I have found your mode of exposition far more rewarding than the econometric models based on the multiplier-accelerator; and the Vicissitudes are all real to me and the discussion of them valuable and fresh.[17]

Nevertheless, when Rostow made up his mind about Marx,[18] it did not please Robinson. It was not uncommon for her to challenge intellectual adversaries in her books, and if she was using Ayres to attack Rostow, Ayres was nevertheless delighted at the attention. She cited Ayres' views with approval, implying that his explanation of patterns of economic growth was better than Rostow's. She admired Ayres' conception of "great inventions" as being "essentially new combinations of tools devised for different purposes."[19]

Ayres, however, was more interested in her arguments in *Economic Philosophy* on the nature of value. He had spent years of teaching effort on this subject, and his new book was about values.[20] He was disappointed in her views. She had argued, "Any economic system requires a set of rules, an ideology to justify them, and a conscience in the individual which makes him strive to carry them out."[21]

He objected to her argument that "a society cannot exist unless its members have common feelings . . . an ideology." Ayres thought she was implying that tribal feelings (conscience) and their rationalization (ideology) are the "sole source of 'rules'," that is, "of value judgments and so of social, political and economic systems." He accused her of dismissing value as having no operational content, as being "just a word."

Ayres' whole life was spent arguing that there are such things as rules operationally determined, rules that are more than ceremonial in origin or character. His philosophy was very much influenced by John Dewey and his economics by Thorstein Veblen. Ayres pointed out to Robinson that one Britisher did insist that "value" had operational meaning—Jacob Bronowski, who was influenced by Charles Peirce and William James. Ayres added, "Adam Smith was quite right in trying to establish a connection between value-in-use and value-in-exchange. He was wrong only in thinking that the connection which the market establishes is a satisfactory one."[22]

Robinson, on the other hand, had not spent her life thinking about values.

Instead, she was attacking what economists call price or value theory. Her interest was in dismissing value theory rather than in developing any operational notions of it. To her, one of the great metaphysical ideas in economics was expressed by the word "value" and she was all for minimizing the reliance on metaphysics and getting on to a science with testable hypotheses (as distinguished from metaphysically derived hypotheses). She had used some of Ayres' ideas but not all of them. She was not ready to adopt instrumental value theory or the possibility of a "self-correcting value judgment."[23] Robinson's target was the price theory maximization solution associated with a competitive market. In her book, she had concluded that it was better to reduce "value" to a word, and she held to that.[24]

Ayres tried to explain. Admitting that every social system is permeated with questions of conscience and ideology, he insisted that many value judgments were in fact operationally based. He offered "rules of the road as a case of organizational procedures which are not of 'ceremonial' origin or character. They are technological in origin, and technological in substance." He suggested that "even the rules about killing people" may contain some "technological (or factual) content." While the tribal nonsense may vary, "isn't there a central core of facts like that of the irreversibility of death in all tribal systems, and isn't it that (rather than tribal sentiments and rationalizations) which no social system of economy can exist without?" Ayres was "making no claim to superior acumen." He attributed his ideas to having been exposed to John Dewey in his student days, "and it took."[25]

Robinson's replies to these 1961 letters have not survived, but twelve days later Ayres exclaimed, "The focus sharpens! You say '. . . (l) it is impossible to show by a merely (sic!) rational argument why the individual should keep the rules—see the passage about voting. . .'." Robinson had argued there that while one vote may be decisive on a small committee, it will not matter in a general election. So, while "it is certainly right that everyone should feel that it is his duty to vote," nevertheless, he cannot be persuaded "by reason." In her example she insisted that moral feelings "are not derived from theology or from reason."[26] Ayres felt that in the voter example she had "chosen a particularly weak obligation to 'prove'" her point. What about a "stronger obligation: . . . If you drink, don't drive."

This was a particularly American example to have chosen, and must have left Robinson quite cold. She was living on Grange Road near Cambridge University, and probably seldom rode in an automobile. (Ruth Cohen says she does not remember that Joan Robinson ever drove a car.) For Ayres, the rule expressed general recognition that a drunk driver is a menace to all members of the community: "This fact is operationally established by constantly repeated experience. The rule and law . . . rest on this fact alone." He admitted that people might feel strongly about drunk drivers and that it could be argued that such feelings result from tribal conditioning and thus there were possibly "irrational" sources, but "it aint so! . . . Some rules are operational in origin and intent, and some feelings derive from a correct apprehension of the facts.'' He hastened to add that he was paying her ''the highest compliment I know of'' in arguing with her; that ''it is quite futile to discuss these issues with our colleagues who employ the most recondite mathematics to ascertain how many utilities can be balanced on the point of a value.''[27]

Again her answers are lost but Ayres, in his third letter to her in November, concluded ''we seem to be playing tag.'' He wanted to ''revert to the issue'' that ''we do make 'value judgments' for which logical (technological) justification can be given by reasonable arguments.'' He wanted to understand her: ''I suppose you capitalize Good Thing by way of suggesting that it is a 'metaphysical' concept for which no rational explanation, let alone justification can be offered though seemingly we can't get along without such fancies.'' However, he emphatically denied that ''conscience so conceived is a technological necessity.'' He also countered with the admonition that ''your judgments of full employment and stable money'' were clearly judgments for which logical justification could be given.[28]

Apparently Robinson wrote him again on July 9 and September 16. He replied: ''Since you invite resumption of our correspondence—here goes.'' Robinson had suggested a ''test question'' of how could you ''convince a citizen who is stupid or slack or both that he ought to vote.'' Ayres countered, ''this may be an effective debating trick but it isn't effective thinking.'' They were back to Go, miles apart philosophically. For the moment they might be viewed as separate planets circling the sun, seemingly in some rough concert but really making paths of their own—from different origins and toward different destinations.

But the questions Ayres and Robinson raised still plague the student of economics, including the question of the source of rational decisions and value judgments. Ayres stated his position on what he called ''the spiral of human consciousness: . . .we do in fact make value judgements (for good and bad, right and wrong) and define values on the basis of knowledge and understanding of facts. . . .'' Our being unreasonable

> . . . doesn't seem to me to invalidate reason. Do you really think it does? Do you really think that civilized human behavior (e.g. the effort to achieve full employment) is an elaboration of crow-like animal instincts,* or tropisms, or reflexes, or something? . . . To my mind what is wrong with [the classical tradition in economics] is not that it is pre-occupied with ''value.'' The trouble is that it has tried for several generations to establish a valid conjunction between value and price, thereby validating the commercialism into which Western society has drifted.

In this same letter Ayres confessed that certain items in *Economic Philosophy* ''astonished and dismayed'' him, in particular her (1) animal analogs, (2) her

---

*Robinson had referred to rook behavior in *Economic Philosophy,* 1962a:6.

evocation of 'conscience', and (3) her "apparent dismissal of value judgments as having no general intellectual validity." He admitted that he had attacked her on (3) since it seems to run through the book and to be a position widely held by scientists and social scientists. Then, to his further dismay, he found that she "really seemed to be taking the crows seriously, and that [she] seemed to attach genuine significance to 'conscience'."[29]

Robinson's and Ayres' differences were philosophical in nature. She was the inheritor of a long tradition of English exploration of ideas. With the exception of G. E. Moore, these were the same philosophers who influenced the "classical tradition" in economics.[30] Ayres, with a deeper interest in philosophy than Robinson had, was of the American pragmatic tradition of John Dewey, Charles Peirce, and William James. Yet both Robinson and Ayres, in their own ways, wanted to challenge the classical tradition and its dependence on the rational economic man. She burrowed from within. Her first book, *The Economics of Imperfect Competition*, had attacked the marginal productivity theory of income distribution. Ayres attacked the classical philosophical underpinnings. He was in the less advantageous position, having bypassed the traditional training of economists. But they both eventually shared the uncomfortable knowledge that the issues each had raised in regard to value theory in economics had been largely ignored by the economics profession.

In *Economic Philosophy,* Robinson had not only moved against the classical tradition but had introduced some of the recent (c. 1950s) developments in the philosophy of science, developments which were *au courant* at Cambridge in the post-World War II years. She cited Karl Popper for his "criterion for propositions that belong to the empirical sciences, that they are capable of being falsified by evidence."[31] Robinson continued to insist throughout her later work that only by testing hypotheses could economics expect to move forward. Perhaps her former student and critic, T.W. Hutchison, was correct in saying that she was not herself producing, even in some of her best work, the testable hypotheses she was demanding.[32]

On other philosophical topics, Robinson had said, "Keynes took up the study of the theory of probability under the influence of Moore's ethical system, which taught 'the obligation so to act as to produce by causal connection the most probable maximum of eventual good through the whole procession of future ages'." She added there that even a correct theory of probability "would not have provided a very handy manual for conducting daily life." Again, she was imbued with the idea that what separated economics from science was our own ethical systems, a proposition that Ayres certainly could not accept.[33]

In 1968 the correspondence resumed briefly when Ayres wrote to compliment Robinson on her "little book on Britain's 'Tight Corner',"[34] and to mention a student who was applying to Cambridge and for whom he had written a letter. This series of letters foundered on politics, a topic which they had also discussed in earlier letters. Robinson was known by close colleagues for having a "stereotype of Americans."[35]

In the earlier series, Ayres closed his November 1, 1962 letter with a query: "Why are you so bitter about the USA? Granted there is a hole in the doughnut, there is also a doughnut around the hole." Again, on November 12, "Your judgment of the Solomon figure is a honey; but in applying it, you have left out the missiles. It works better if we suppose the missiles are the baby, Castro the foster mother, Khrushchev the real mother, and Kennedy the Solomon who proposes to dismantle the baby." On November 28, he asked her, "What official line on Cuba am I swallowing?" When the correspondence resumed a year later, Ayres did not mention politics.[36]

When Ayres wrote her in 1968 about her *Economics: An Awkward Corner*, he objected to her "closing crack about 'the American crusade'" against communism.[37] Robinson had written,

> . . . we could set about to make a country where all can be comfortable, cheerful and free to follow their fancies. This is a selfish ideal. Democracies are selfish. They think of the nation, not of the world. Two menaces hang over the world today—the rise of population ahead of economic development which is spreading desperate misery in the southern continents, and the American crusade against communism, which threatens worse horrors than it is already perpetrating and meanwhile prevents each economic system from settling into peaceful co-existence with the other and using its resources to meet its urgent needs.[38]

Robinson replied to Ayres: "I was very pleased to know that you share my enthusiasm for my quotation from Keynes' Economic Consequences. I was surprised that you objected to my remark about American foreign policy—I thought everybody had now come round to my view."[39]

Ayres responded,

> Curious that you and I should have argued all one year about Thugges and thalidomide babies without ever crossing swords about the U.S.A. and the U.S.S.R. However at that time I, at least, did consciously avoid it, because I felt that any mention of that issue might terminate the discussion. But I couldn't mention your book (which I wanted to do for other reasons) without rising to your challenge. OK: so be it. It has always seemed to me that a distinction can (and should) be made between "communism" as a socio-economic ideal and "class war" as the road to it. Similarly, it seems to me that a distinction can and should be made between Soviet ideals and the apparatus of "party" dictatorship. A similar distinction likewise can (and should) be made between the democratic and equalitarian ideals of Western countries (including Britain and the U.S.A.) and the apparatus in which they have been historically involved. Perhaps both power structures are most unlovely in their foreign policies and actions. The

export of democracy has produced some very unlovely scenes—in Latin America, India, and elsewhere. But I would rather have taken my chance in the India of Clive or Warren Hastings than in any one of the "People's Democratic Republics" the U.S.S.R. has set up.[40]

Robinson replied,

I fear that once more I must accuse you of a non-sequitur. In what way does the evil of Stalinism justify the U.S. in imposing or supporting military dictatorships in Asia and Latin America, and now they have started on Europe with Greece. In my view, the cold war and the re-arming of Germany contributed a great deal to the tough policy of Stalin and its revival now.[41]

Ayres answered,

Dear Joan. . . . Life is full of non sequiturs. And after all, it's the sequiturs that get us into trouble. The USSR party dictatorships were only following the logic of power in checking the growth of liberalism in Russia and in Czechoslovakia. But why call it Stalinism? Poor old Stalin—the sacrificial goat of the party dictatorship. American capitalism is evil. German re-armament is evil, and Greek military dictatorship is evil. Therefore American capitalism is responsible for both. Or better, the CIA. Magic letters—which, I am delighted to note, you haven't used. My gauge of the potency of the CIA is the Bay of Pigs.[42]

This was the last letter of record. They were not totally at odds. Ayres had written in his next to last letter a statement with which they could both agree: "In the meantime we may wipe each other (and everybody else) out in a holocaust of atomic fusion. That, too, will be regrettable. You and I at least can regret it in advance."

Visiting professor in the 1960s

The 1960s were a time of turmoil in the universities of the United States even before the Vietnam War. In the Free Speech Movement, the students at the University of California at Berkeley objected to the rule that no politicians (including candidates for governor or President) were to be allowed to address campus groups. As the Vietnam War became more controversial, so did the military draft, and students began to argue that there was little of what they called "relevance" in their curriculum. This was painfully evident to students of economics, and on many campuses, economics students were in the leadership of what was called "student unrest." Joan Robinson spoke over the heads of their professors to these students. Although now in her sixties, she reached a zenith of popularity as a speaker, and she gave generously of her time.

In 1965, she again visited the University of Colorado, where she gave many seminars on growth theory, the capital controversy, and methodology. Leslie Fishman has said, "It was a glorious week and the staff and postgraduate students who attended were suitably thrilled. . . . My most vivid recollections involve the enthusiasm she showed for the Rockies and the surroundings, as well as the frugal but enjoyable and nutritious vegetarian diet that she followed, laced with an appreciation of good whiskey."[43]

Robinson turned down more invitations than she accepted, and seemed most likely to go where she knew the people who were inviting her. Others she would sternly decline, so that they were aware of their presumption.[44]

Her favorite invitations came from students rather than from colleagues. She was invited by the Associated Students of Stanford University to visit there, her honorarium to be paid from student funds. This invitation came about when Michael M. Weinstein, an undergraduate in economics, was elected head of the parliamentary arm of the student government. Denis Hayes was president of Stanford Associated Students.

Weinstein was interested in responding to the complaints of the students that their curriculum needs were not being met by the university itself, that they should have a broader picture of the world than they were getting. Some of the graduate students in economics suggested that Joan Robinson be invited. She came for a stay of six weeks beginning April 8, 1969. The department of economics supported the visit. Lorie Tarshis, a former student of Keynes, was chairman of the department at the time. Robinson was offered an office and affiliation with the department; she accepted the office and declined the affiliation. Nevertheless, the courses which she offered were given credit in economics.[45]

Robinson's honorarium, according to Weinstein, "was a mere fraction of opportunity cost." He thinks that she turned it all back to the student association so that they could arrange other educational programs. There were no enrollment limitations, and according to Weinstein, her classes were very well received. Weinstein does not remember that she required any special care or treatment. She lived either in a dormitory or a building something like one and took her meals with students in dorms. She had friends among the faculty and made friends among the students. She had been invited, he said, because of "the content of her writings, her impeccable credentials, thoughts and research, and because she was an iconoclast." At the time, the economics faculty seemed "conservative and homogeneous" to the students. According to Weinstein, students felt a need for someone to tell them they were not idiots if they questioned received learning.[46] They were not disappointed. When students were demonstrating at a Stanford research laboratory, Robinson went there to teach her classes as an act of solidarity.

Robinson is remembered as "a character" in the best sense of that term. Once she invited Weinstein and a close friend to be her guests for dinner and to attend an opera. They arranged the time for dinner and picked her up and started for San

Francisco (about forty miles from Palo Alto). Five miles out of the city, Robinson asked, "Why are we here?" They said they were going to the opera. She said, "I meant the Stanford opera." She had this "otherworldliness, was on a different wavelength from other people, and in this she was very charming."[47]

Weinstein went on to MIT to earn his doctorate and is now the chair at Haverford College (Pennsylvania). I asked him if Joan Robinson had had a lasting influence on the students at Stanford. He thought that few of them actually adopted her view of economics, though they remembered her for her critical discussions. His fantasy was for Robinson and Solow to be given a joint Nobel Prize, at which point they would have it out on the platform. He thought of her in 1969 as a "feisty individual."

After this invitation, Robinson thought there should be others from students in the United States. Sidney Weintraub, who wanted her to come to the University of Pennsylvania, asked her, "What are your plans for Fall 1972–Spring 1973? I know your preferences on this, but I just am in no position to facilitate an invitation from students. I am not aware of how such a budget authorization would work though if this was a precondition, I'd raise some queries."[48] According to the departmental chairman at Pennsylvania, Robinson never did visit there.[49] Weintraub wrote her again the next year, "You will be interested in the fact that I am being 'petitioned' by our second year graduates to offer a course built about your 'type' views: they are in near rebellion at the econometrics and math-econ to which they have been subjected by our substantially MIT crowd."[50]

Robinson was to become more acquainted with this rebellion during her other visits in the 1970s.

The Ely Lecture caps it all

The 1970s saw another phase of Professor Robinson's relations with Americans. First, she was to address the whole profession at the annual meeting of the American Economic Association in New Orleans. Second, she was to become closely allied with a group of economists who were Keynesians and who agreed with most of her arguments on neoclassical economics.

Galbraith's invitation for Robinson to deliver the Richard T. Ely Lecture came during the year of her formal retirement from teaching. She felt the capital controversy was behind her and had announced this view at the Econometric Society Meetings in Cambridge in 1970. She was disillusioned over the failure of Cambridge economics to influence American economics, and was at the time working on her textbook with Eatwell, which she hoped might at least reach undergraduates through the more adventurous of the younger faculty. She knew from her invitation to Stanford and her addresses at other campuses during the 1960s that she had an audience among the young in America. Now she was to address the profession itself, an address which would be carried in the major journal, *American Economic Review*.

Joan Robinson was a fitting choice. The American Economic Association began in 1885, Richard T. Ely being among the founders. Originally the Association was "a protest against the narrow conventional English economics as well as the traditional self-satisfied political and social ideas in America."[51] So Robinson was to address a society which had been born of controversy over some of the issues which she now raised.

Before the evening address, Robinson was invited to come to Galbraith's rooms for a cocktail. Jan Kregel, who had been her student at Cambridge, accompanied her and then took her to the Rutgers University cocktail party. The Davidsons then took them to dinner.[52]

Paul Davidson remembers the dinner this way:

This was six o'clock in the evening and she was to speak at eight. And in New Orleans most of the restaurants don't get busy until eight. She also had these strange eating habits and you had to be careful about what she would eat and what she wouldn't eat. In the Fairmont Hotel they had this smorgasbord, so she could pick and choose whatever she wanted. So we went there. We were the only table at the time we went in. And you know you wait on yourself. While we were eating, in walk about a dozen people—Samuelson and his wife, Arrow and his wife, the whole establishment, and they take a huge table, and we're the only two tables in this whole dining room. And of course they have to walk right past us to get to the food. Obviously they were eating early in order to hear Joan Robinson's lecture. Otherwise, why eat at that time? Well, they walked past us and back, and not one of them said, "Hello, Joan," or stopped and said, "Hello, we're here to hear your speech." It was like two independent people who didn't know each other.

And it's true the room was dark, but you can't miss this woman with the shocking white hair, so they must have known who she was, even though her back was to them when they were sitting. Not a word was spoken between her and them. And we must have overlapped by forty minutes. You had to walk back and forth for each dish that you had. So that was an indication of her relations with people. My wife said, "Well, why didn't they come over and say something?" I told her, "I think they were afraid she might cut them cold, just ignore them. That would be very embarrassing." I mean she was a terrible woman in that sense. She had no qualms about being rude if she wanted to be.[53]

At eight, Robinson faced a full house and a distinguished one; Tobin said "she had the prime-time audience appropriate to her towering stature in the profession."[54] Galbraith thought he had never seen so many people at an Ely lecture. Her address was entitled, "The Second Crisis of Economic Theory." Her attack was immediate: "When I see this throng of superfluous economists—I am using that word, of course, in the Shakespearian sense—I am reminded how much the profession has grown since the 'thirties and how many more there are now to

suffer from the second crisis than there were to be discredited in the first."[55]
Tobin wrote, "Mrs. Robinson is always eloquent, and she is formidably eloquent
when charged with righteous anger. The targets of her indictment loved every
word."[56]

The second crisis in economic theory, she argued, came, as did the first, from
the failure of economic theory to deal with real world problems. The first crisis in
her lifetime was when orthodox theory could not provide any explanation or
program to deal with the great depression. The second crisis, which grew out of
the first, was that economic theory once more "had nothing to say on the
questions that, to everyone except economists, appear to be most in need of an
answer," namely, (1) what is full employment supposed to be for, and (2) how are
the fruits of production to be distributed among people.[57]

Tobin, in a criticism of the address, called attention to ongoing empirical
research as the answer to her allegations. But the question that Robinson was
raising was not whether economists neglected empirical studies in these areas, but
whether received economic *theory* was adequate to deal with the problems.
Actually the American Economic Association had debated a similar proposition
the year before.* Not surprisingly, Gurley and Solow had come down on different
sides of that issue.

In the capital controversy, Robinson had attacked neoclassicism for its methodological and logical problems. In the Ely lecture, she attacked it for its failure
to provide answers to meaningful questions. Tobin reported, "Since her main
complaints were against abstract theory, perhaps each listener was glad to hear a
speaker with impeccable theoretical credentials tell off those *other* fellows who
clutter up the journals with fancy models and mathematics."[58]

In 1977 she would address American economists again, in their *Journal of
Economic Literature*. This time she would ask pointedly, "What Are the Questions?"[59]

---

*See Appendix Note 14.2 American Economic Association (AEA) debate.

JR

CHAPTER FIFTEEN

Robinson and the American Post Keynesians

After her discovery of bastard Keynesianism, Robinson had learned through correspondence and through her visits to the United States that there were also American Keynesians of another sort. These scholars cherished her work and admired her attacks on the mainstream. In the late 1960s a correspondence developed with two of them: Paul Davidson and Alfred Eichner. Davidson first wrote to her in 1967, Eichner in 1969.

Through her acquaintance with them, Robinson came to realize how isolated these Americans were in their own country. This knowledge led her to play a role in the founding and naming of the American post Keynesian journal, and to become a rallying focus of American post Keynesians. Through patient criticism, she strove to bring their work into harmony with the Cambridge tradition, the better to provide an alternative to neoclassical economics. She even plotted with them to crash established American journals with post Keynesian articles.

Paul Davidson initiated correspondence with Robinson by sending her a paper he had written on the demand for finance.[1] She replied,

> Many thanks for sending me your paper. I broadly agree with your treatment of the role of money in growth. It is depressing that a man as enlightened as Tobin should set up such a ridiculous model. I do not know why you say that the Keynesians neglect money in relation to investment. I think they have been rather at fault in exaggerating the importance of the rate of interest. What has been entirely lacking until recent times is any theory of the rate of profit. This I feel you do not really deal with. I see that you refer to my Essays in the Theory of Economic Growth. What is your reaction to the theory of the rate of profit which I am trying to work out . . . ?[2]

At the time, Davidson was thirty-six years old, and Robinson was sixty-three. As others had done, he answered with a four-page single-spaced letter.

Davidson came to economics via biochemistry with a thorough training in the sciences, including experimental design, so that mathematics was a natural language for him.[3] While working on his doctorate in economics at the University of Pennsylvania, Davidson came under the influence of Sidney Weintraub and became acquainted with Robinson's work. In a course in recent developments in economics, Weintraub took his students through *The Accumulation of Capital*. Davidson's background thus did not include indoctrination in neoclassical paradigms, though, of course, neoclassical models and theory were part of the curriculum.[4]

Robinson's response to his long letter was written by hand on one of the blue "air letters" she customarily used.

Dear Prof Davidson, I find your objections as hard to understand as you do my writings, e.g. *Essays* p. 10. Surely if technical conditions, thriftiness conditions and the rate of investment are given, effective demand is determined. Certainly there is no guarantee of full employment. In *Accumulation* p. 50, I am chasing a distinction between the increment of capital being planned and the rate of investment week by week—carrying it out. The main point however is the rate of profit. The classical theory is ok provided that the real wage is given by subsistence. The neoclassical theory is a mess (as Samuelson has now admitted by implication). Why do you not accept our theory? If you agree about "animal spirits" surely accumulation is the causal factor and the rate of profit is determined by it. However in my last book of Collected Papers (Blackwell, Oxford Volume III) I give A Reconsideration of the Theory of Value that tries to go deeper. Yours Joan Robinson.[5]

Davidson did his homework and replied in another four-page single-spaced letter which concluded,

I hope I have explained why I hesitate to embrace the "Cambridge School" theory entirely. That it is an improvement over Samuelson's neo-classical muddle I have no doubt. Nevertheless more must be done about (1) explaining margins and (2) associating the rate of profit with all components of effective demand and not only accumulation.[6]

Missing is a letter which Davidson remembers as a "kind comment" from Robinson regarding his "A Keynesian View of Patinkin's Theory of Employment."[7]

Davidson replied to Robinson January 29, 1968, agreeing that

. . . a point by point discussion of these matters . . . would be exceedingly fruitful. . . . I am constantly reminded of the caveat, in the Preface to *The General Theory*, about what foolish things one can believe if one thinks too long alone. (I have tried to generalize this to suggest that the MIT group can believe foolish things although not alone—because they converse only into human echo chambers.)

Davidson read the reprints she had sent him and thought,

> As far as marginal productivity is concerned—I think the first issue is to examine the question as to whether marginal productivity is (1) a theory of imputed prices, or (2) a theory of income distribution or (3) both. . . . It is not difficult to understand why, under the neoclassical assumptions of perfect competition and perfect knowledge, items (1) and (2) were taken to be equivalent (in the long-run at least). Once it is generally recognized that the theory of imputed prices is separated from distribution analysis, our profession will go a long way in accepting a theory of aggregate income distribution for the market sector of modern economies, which is not rigidly tied to marginal productivity. As long as the high priests of U.S. economics continue to provide incantations about income distribution being determined by the marginal productivity of the holy trinity of land, labor, and capital operating under the divine auspices of Euler's theorem, little progress will be made. Nevertheless I do not want to throw marginal productivity out completely. . . .[8]

Davidson was clearly on Robinson's side in the reswitching arguments and wrote of this in the same letter:

> The dated labor argument and problem of switching seems to me to involve the MIT people into the type of fallacious argument that Keynes was trying to destroy in Chapter 16 of the G.T.—namely that lengthy processes are physically efficient merely because they are long. When Samuelson gave a seminar on reswitching at Rutgers (in May 1967), I called his attention to this chapter and particularly to the Keynes quote on p. 215 about not devising "a productivity theory of smelly or risky processes as such." Surprisingly, Samuelson indicated he knew nothing of the contents of Chapter 16—at which point I suggested that pp. 215–17 might be more vigorously studied at MIT than pursuing this logical exercise of switching *ad nauseam.* I fear Professor Samuelson did not appreciate this suggestion. And so Samuelson, like Cournot, continues to be "the great parent of so many brilliant errors based on false analogies" between economics and mathematical systems.

Davidson then recommended Jan Kregel as a student interested in writing about Cambridge economics.

Davidson had an idea which bothered Robinson. He thought that Keynes of the *Treatise* was arguing from a Marshallian period analysis, while in at least some chapters in *The General Theory,* Keynes was using a Walrasian framework. She wrote him, March 7, 1968, "As you know I do not sympathize with the attempt to build up a theory of capital accumulation on the basis of Walrasian prices and I think that in that chapter Keynes had fallen into the error of identifying the marginal productivity of investment to society with the rate of profit." And she still thought Davidson's system was lacking a theory of profits.

Davidson agreed about his lack of a theory of profits, but he questioned her "belief that the determination of the rate of profit is 'essential' to the question of long-run growth."[9] He was most appreciative of her "stimulating responses to my earlier letters. I think I have already greatly profited from our correspondence and I do look forward to future discussions."

Robinson replied, "I am distressed to find we still disagree so much. . . . You cannot conceive the quantity of capital apart from the rate of profit. This is just what Sraffa and I are going on about. Even Samuelson now admits it, though he evidently hasn't taken in the point. Yours in hopes of better understanding"(May 8, 1968).

Davidson continued to send her his offprints. She wrote,

> I was very much puzzled by your saying that the price system in the General Theory is based on Walras. None of us were in any way influenced by Walras and when Hicks came out with a modernized version it was immediately seen to be full of contradictions. The basis of the General Theory is the short period of Marshall. . . . I am a bit puzzled also by your interpretation of the Treatise. I am arguing about this with your young man Kregel. I hope I will get him to see things from my point of view (November 12, 1968).

Davidson assured her that he had not meant "to imply that the Walrasian general equilibrium approach was explicitly underlying *The General Theory.* . . . Nevertheless, the *Treatise* follows Marshall more closely . . ." (November 26, 1968).

They also had exchanges about Kaldor's neo-Pasinetti theorem. Robinson concluded, "I am afraid that Kaldor has the tendency to confuse the analysis of comparisons with the analysis of a change taking place at a point of time" (December 4, 1968).

Davidson replied, "I realize that you are comparing two positions, while I, like Kaldor, am trying to analyze a change which is taking place—but surely there must be some connection between these two approaches" (December 11, 1968).

Davidson and Robinson had several other exchanges, all in good humor and all making independent and penetrating points. But there were still misunderstandings. Davidson was undoubtedly thinking of himself as a Keynesian at this point;

Robinson was thinking of herself in the new Cambridge tradition, which she called "Anglo-Italian."* On September 3, 1969 Robinson wrote,

> I was quite dumbfounded at your saying that I believe the propensity to save has an influence on the rate of growth. This is precisely the opposite of what I have believed and proclaimed for years. The "Anglo-Italian" theory is that the propensity to save has an influence on the rate of profit. I think the real difference between us is that you have never brought the rate of profit on capital into your system of thought.

Davidson replied, "I despair to think that communication at such distance may merely encourage misunderstandings and accentuate differences. Let me therefore try to reformulate my comments on this 'Anglo-Italian Theory'" (September 15, 1969). This required five single-spaced pages.

Robinson answered, "The purpose of the Anglo/Italian theory is to show the determination of the rate of profit in the study of steady growth. It seems to me that you object to the question rather than to the answer. . . . I do not know why you are so worried about finance . . ." (September 22, 1969).

Davidson's rejoinder was,

> Perhaps I am overemphasizing the "finance" aspect of growth. But is it correct to assume "proper behavior by monetary authorities" in a free country such as the U.S. or U.K.? With interest rates at historic highs, and with modern quantity theorists such as Friedman and Harry Johnson providing widely-publicized guidelines for central bankers, I am not optimistic about the monetary authorities behaving properly . . . (September 24, 1969).

Robinson replied with two papers and this comment: "I also am not optimistic about the monetary authorities behaving properly but surely it is necessary to work out what the proper behavior would be . . ." (October 2, 1969).

They continued to correspond. Robinson had visited the States, and Davidson had been to a conference in England, but they still had not met. Davidson concluded from their discussions of the "Anglo-Italian" theory that "uncertainty is not only the keystone of the Keynesian short run analysis of unemployment, but it is also the foundation of the Anglo-Italian theory of growth" (November 14, 1969). On November 20, 1969, she wrote, "I am very glad that you feel that we are getting together, though the main point still seems to be rather obscure." Robinson pursued the correspondence even when she was in Canada, and they exchanged comments on each others' comments.

---

*See Appendix Note 8.3 The New Cambridge edition and the Anglo-Italian School, 1949–1975.

Much of their discussion was about fundamental modeling techniques. Davidson wrote,

> I have no fundamental methodological objection to the Anglo-Italian approach of initially extrapolating from all complications. . . . In fact the Anglo-Italian approach has provided a tremendous service by showing the foolishness of the neoclassical view of steady growth. This is no small accomplishment and I certainly do not wish to detract from it in any way.
>
> What I do fear, however, is now that a seemingly mortal blow to the neoclassicists has been delivered, creating a tremendous redundancy in the human capital stock on this side of the ocean, the American school will try to restore its capital values by drawing the Anglo-Italian school into an endless controversy as to which of the two simplified unrealistic models—the Cambridge, Massachusetts or the Cambridge, England one—is least unrealistic . . . then the human capital losses implicit in modifying the mythical model to take into consideration real world complications will discourage the students of the victorious school of thought, for they will find the development of marginal variations on the same mystical theme of steady state growth to be professionally more profitable" (December 15, 1969).

Meanwhile, earlier that year (February 12, 1969), Robinson had received a letter from Alfred S. Eichner, a young faculty member at Columbia University, who sent her his article on oligopolistic pricing.[10] On February 25, she replied, "Looking forward to meeting you."[11] They met when she visited Columbia in March, and Eichner sent her other papers of his. Her response was, "I am very glad to find some one who finds that I am some use." She began by teaching him English economics. Once she commented, "I think you are misled by my giving the dynamic theory to 'Marshall' and the static to 'Pigou'. Both are in Marshall as well as a lot else. You must remember that Marshall *was* economics at that time. The boyg that Keynes was attacking went under his name." (This is in her handwriting on Eichner's manuscript. She liked the word "boyg" and used it often, apparently to refer to a morass of circular reasoning.)

Eichner was working on "a comprehensive alternative to what now passes as the conventional wisdom in economics."[12] He sent her chapter after chapter of his manuscript. She made detailed comments, drew diagrams. He wrote, "You cannot realize how much I value and treasure [your comments and criticisms]. . . ."[13]

Once she mentioned, "I am bringing out *Imperfect Competition* with a new Preface in which I repudiate the old nonsense." While critical, she was encouraging and wrote to him, "I am very pleased indeed that you should be working on these lines in the citadel of neoclassical static theory" (September 5, 1969). Referring to her own work, she said, "I think this will be made clear in other papers in my projected book, which I shall call Some Old Fashioned Questions in Economic Theory" (April 11, 1970). This book was issued as *Economic Heresies*.

Robinson was pleased with Eichner's progress: "I was very pleased to know that you have seen the point of my Accumulation" (May 4, 1970). She scolded him at times: "The neoclassicals are notorious for sloppy methodology and we should be more exact. I think it is necessary to separate the general talk about how firms behave in reality from a tight model on stated assumptions. You seem to slip from one to the other without marking which is which" (June 9, 1970). She was personal: "I am here visiting my daughter's family and have switched off being a professor to being a granny" (June 12, 1970). She was to the point: "I fear you do have a blind spot about TIME owing to neoclassical miseducation" (April 24, 1971). She was often shocked: "I was quite stunned by your letter. Certainly there is a deep misunderstanding. How could you possibly think that I hold that past saving out of profits determines present investment? Did you think I have joined the pre-Keynesian camp" (July 20, 1971)?

Another issue arose. What should their type of approach be called? In a criticism of Chapter VI of his manuscript, undated, she used the term "post-Keynesian writers and analysis," but usually she used the term "Anglo-Italian" during this period. Eichner raised the question: "Incidentally, I note that Harcourt in the most recent JEL refers to it as the neo-Keynesian model" (undated letter).

Eichner said that his own efforts were to provide a microeconomic foundation to the macroeconomic theories of the "Cambridge neo-Keynesians," adding, "Perhaps you might be able to clarify for me how the group should most properly be delineated. Should they be known as the Cambridge neo-Keynesians, as I have been wont to term them, or as the Anglo-Italian school, as you refer to them in your last letter?" (This letter, undated, was in answer to hers of June 9, 1970.) Eichner argued that the term "Anglo-Italian" would never catch on in the United States. By April 6, 1971, he was using "post-Keynesian," while Robinson (April 16, 1971) continued to use "Anglo-Italian." Eichner promised her that he "would not refer to it again as the neo-Keynesian theory."

Kenneth K. Kurihara in 1954 had written a book entitled *Post Keynesian Economics*, but the term was then lost for years.[14] It reappeared as a subtitle in Kregel's 1973 book.[15] In 1971, however, there was still some groping for what this school of thought, if it were one, was to be called. Eichner pointed out that it was significant that Kregel did not use the term in his 1971 book, *Rate of Profit, Growth and Distribution: Two Views*, when the latter was working closely with Robinson.[16]

There was a new development when Davidson expressed an interest in spending a year at Cambridge studying the "Anglo-Italian" approach.[17] He was invited as Senior Visitor for 1970–71. Meanwhile, he conceded, "I am still at a loss to respond to your basic question. 'What determines the overall rate of profit on capital as a whole?' " He was looking forward to his visit to Cambridge as an "unusually challenging, stimulating, and rewarding experience" (March 2, 1970). The experience would also have its difficulties.

Robinson replied,

> Your last letter makes clear to me there is a very fundamental difference in our points of view. You think of a dichotomy between "real" and "monetary" factors, and you assume in a "non-monetary" economy the "real" factors would get into equilibrium. To me the most important thing about the General Theory is that it broke down the dichotomy and showed money as one institution in the actual economy. The idea of a "real" economy in which saving consists of buying machines seems to me to be total nonsense . . . (March 6, 1970).

But she sent another essay to explain further what she meant, and opened the letter with, "I think it is time we stopped Professoring each other. I am very glad to know that you are going to be in Cambridge next year." To make certain that the discussion might "go on satisfactorily," she then sent him twelve "points," reminiscent of the Solow "agenda" (May 7, 1970).

Davidson answered that he was "perfectly comfortable with the list of twelve. I believe that the difference between us ultimately revolves on two aspects: (1) questions of emphasis, and (2) whether certain institutions which have functions in an uncertain world can be made to play roles in economies which are, by hypothesis, experiencing smooth development." He was "reasonably confident that our discussions will go on satisfactorily and profitably" (May 21, 1970).

Upon arrival in Cambridge, Davidson settled in to share the faculty office assigned to Kahn. (Kahn mainly used his spacious rooms at King's College as both home and office.) The first thing Davidson did was to hand Robinson the outline and Chapters II through X of his manuscript entitled, "Money and the Real World." Their relationship immediately worsened.

Davidson recalled,

> . . . she got to Chapter V, I think, and she came back to my office and she came around the desk and said, "You are trying to destroy everything that I worked twenty years to build. I don't want to talk to you any more." And for weeks we wouldn't talk, but . . . every morning she would leave an essay: "How do you explain: . . ." and the paper would be blank. Like an undergraduate she would set me an essay question. I would write out the answer and put it on her desk when she wasn't in the office. And I would come back and find a paper which would say (1) why that point was wrong and (2) why that point was wrong. And

so we had a whole series of essays between us, where I'm trying to explain something and then she's telling me why I'm wrong about it.

I asked Davidson if this had not bothered him. He said, "I have a thicker skin than most people. It didn't bother me as long as I was learning something from the process; I was sorry that I wasn't getting along with her but that didn't really bother me."[18]

By January, Robinson was saying, "we seem to have gone right back to the beginning. . . . Will you, moreover, admit the notion of a tranquil economy to provide a bench mark for analysis? If so, we can get going again" (January 1, 1971). Davidson replied the same day, "Yes let's get going again!" And they did. On January 16 he asked her for comments on his Chapter XIII, which was about Kaldor's neo-Pasinetti theorem. She complied on February 18 and he answered her numerous objections. And so it continued through the year.

Davidson was invited to give a mathematical seminar for a group at Churchill College. He was told who would be there and was asked if there were others he might like to invite. "How about Joan Robinson?" asked Davidson. "You don't want to invite her," he was told. He replied,

Well, she invited me to Cambridge. I think it is just polite that we do it. [His host] kept saying, "No, you don't want to invite her," that she would mess up the whole thing. I kept insisting, so finally he said, "Well, I've warned you, but we'll invite her." And he was right. I got up to give this talk on the neo-Pasinetti theorem and Joan is there with Richard. I don't get thirty words out when she suddenly stands up and says, "Now wait a second. You're all wrong." And she goes up to the blackboard and takes fifteen minutes explaining why I'm all wrong. She had read the paper because I had given it to her. And after she finishes and makes a complete shambles out of this, she says, "Come on, Richard," and she picks up and walks out. Without waiting for me to respond or anything. She had used about twenty or thirty minutes of this talk, so I put the thing back together again as best I could in the remaining time. They said, well, we told you not to invite her.

Several years later, Robinson wrote to Davidson that she had changed her mind and agreed with his point (August 17, 1973).

1971: A U. S. post Keynesian movement emerges

Robinson wrote to Eichner on March 23, 1971, "I am expecting to be in Columbia for a fortnight in November. Will you still be there?" and on April 24, "I believe it is the students not the faculty who are responsible for my invitation to Columbia." Anwar Shaikh and other graduate students, following the upheavals the previous spring over the Cambodian invasion, had urged her to visit Columbia.[19]

Columbia was the last stop on a tour that had included Harvard and MIT and would finally end with her attendance at the American Economic Association meetings in New Orleans in December. Her friend Luigi Pasinetti was at Columbia that year as a visiting professor. Robinson's lecture was delivered in the largest lecture hall Columbia had, one which held almost a thousand people. Eichner was no longer on the Columbia faculty, but he was still involved in research there and he attended the lecture. These are his recollections:

> Because of the political sensitivity of the period—you know there was fear of students taking power—it was a very strange period. Joan did what I suspect she did at every other university. She began by looking out over the audience. In the audience was Phelps, a well-known neoclassical economist, and she said, "Is there anybody here who will defend neoclassical economics?" And of course, no one responded. She then delivered her usual criticisms of the orthodox theory. Afterward she went upstairs to the office which had been provided for her.
>
> Luigi Pasinetti and I joined her in that office, and we began by saying what a terrible situation it was, with not a single well-known member of the profession willing to defend the type of theory the students were being forced to use in their dissertations. Joan had completed a tour in which she had, in her view, challenged the leading figures in American universities to defend what they were requiring students to do. In the meantime, she was hearing complaints and criticisms from students of how they were constantly being forced into the intellectual straitjacket of having to estimate some variation of a neoclassical growth model and how, if they tried to protest or follow a different course, they would find all their support being withdrawn. This was the dilemma.
>
> We came upstairs and we talked about what a terrible situation it was and what could be done about it. At this point, I said to Joan, "Why don't we try bringing together, at the meetings coming up, all the people who might be sympathetic and let's see if we can agree upon some program or course of action that might remedy the situation." I then drafted a letter which Joan signed. Joan was asked to supply a list of names of all the people she knew, including a number of people who became prominent among the American post Keynesians. I supplied the names of people that I knew as well. From this, we put together a list of about twenty to thirty people. We sent out invitations asking them to join us for a dinner session the night before Joan gave the Ely lecture. We arranged for a hotel room and we sent out for sandwiches, a very informal process. We got together and we discussed it, this group of us, including a large number of people that I had never met before.

This group was not yet known as "post Keynesians," for the choice of a name was still to take some time. Eichner said the meeting was "very traumatic," because it was the dinner period, and Robinson was scheduled that night to give a lecture to the Union of the Radical Political Economists (URPE). Seventeen people attended the dinner meeting, several of whom were members of URPE.[20]

Eichner said,

> Joan then gave this absolutely brilliant, satirical lecture on Marx to URPE. It was a very clever put-down of Marxian theory. At which point, Jan Kregel, Bob Harris and I took Joan Robinson out and I'll never forget walking down Basin Street. There was this woman on a swing—bare-breasted. As we walked by, she was swinging out, and it sort of confirmed everything Joan found unpleasant and terrible about the United States. We went to this bar where some woman was playing this organ. She must have been the owner, because that is the only way she would have been permitted to play this organ. We were sitting around, but the noise was so great it was impossible to hear. The next thing we knew, Joan was slumped on the table. We said, "Oh, my god, she's overdone it." But then the music stopped, and she woke up. She had just gotten bored and gone to sleep. It was the typical way in which Joan would handle a situation when she got bored. She would simply go to sleep and rest up for the next occasion. The next night she gave the Ely lecture.

Eichner reported to those who had attended the dinner meeting that he thought there was one small piece of common ground in the discussions—"the feeling that the *American Economic Review*, among other journals, is not likely to publish the work of those in the room—or the work of others who fall outside the mainstream of American economics." He proposed sending a letter to Galbraith, current president of the American Economic Association, to ask that he take steps to "broaden the base from which the *AER* draws its materials."

Joan Robinson embraced this cause with enthusiasm. In an early letter to Eichner (October 2, 1969) she had remarked, "I have been working on these lines now for twenty years but I think that I have been treated to a conspiracy of silence in the United States." Thus began a long story of trying to place post Keynesian articles in the leading economic journals, with Robinson cheering on the sidelines.[21]

Robinson wrote to Eichner (January 3, 1973), "What happened about Shaikh's Humbug article? It would be a very suitable case to agitate about the way good articles are suppressed."[22] Eichner replied that Shaikh's article would be in Edward Nell's forthcoming book (February 15, 1973). Robinson objected, "I think it is a great pity not to try Shaikh's article on the *AER*" (March 28, 1973).

She was not ready to give up hope, and wrote Eichner again,

> I think you take too gloomy a view of the situation. There will soon be lots of books coming out on our side of the question and this will provide ammunition

for people who are fed up with having to teach what they don't believe in. There is no hope of shifting the old guard but I think the students will be on our side and we will have to work it through them. (July 11, 1973).

She was thinking of the forthcoming Robinson/Eatwell text as a new beginning.

But the next year, she confided, "I suppose you know that Shaikh's Humbug article was published in Review of Economics and Statistics as a note not an article, and that Solow's reply was not shown to Shaikh . . . nor was he given the usual right of replying. This is a very clear case of bias in the journals and I think you should make the maximum fuss about it. Solow's reply is evasive, silly and abusive as usual."

She added, "On this side the anti-neo-classical movement is going on pretty well but it is still knocking its head on a stone wall in the United States" (June 21, 1974).

Eichner explained that the *Review of Economics and Statistics* was not under the auspices of the American Economic Association and thus not subject to any pressure from that quarter. She replied, "I should have thought that we could take up the cudgels for Shaikh. Surely the A.E.A. covers the profession as a whole not just its own journals" (July 10, 1974).

Meanwhile, Robinson encouraged Eichner to submit his book to the Cambridge University Press, which did publish it along with some other post Keynesian works. Eichner shared with her the comments of referees on an article he and Kregel had submitted to the *Journal of Economic Literature*. She commented, "The referees notes on your paper are really passed [sic] the limit. . . . I really don't understand the American situation and I cannot advise you . . ." (October 23, 1974). But she admitted that "I quite agree with Feiwel's remarks about me— I am a red rag to most editors. You can plug Sraffa and Kalecki" (December 11, 1974).

Eichner organized a seminar to meet monthly in New York, and though it was soon discontinued, the fact that there was some constituency came to the attention of Sidney Weintraub at Pennsylvania. As Eichner put it,

Sid Weintraub had become enormously enthusiastic. I don't think he was in New Orleans, but he had become more and more interested in what Joan was doing and more and more willing to identify himself with Joan and with seeing her as someone that he could make common cause with. And Sid had this vision. He really believed that it was possible to set up a journal, and that was what he should do. And he wasn't discouraged by the fact that we couldn't get the seminar going. Once the seminar collapsed—it was too hard doing it once a month—we set up a conference, and we held it here at Rutgers. That conference was enormously successful. We brought in people from all over the Eastern

United States. Sid said, "We've got to form a journal. I'm going to ask Ken Galbraith for some money," and so Sid raised the money.

Through contacts with M.E. Sharpe, who had become interested in Eichner's and other post Keynesians' work for his *Challenge* magazine, a deal was struck, and the *Journal of Post Keynesian Economics* (JPKE) was established. The journal settled once and for all what the movement should be called. On September 13, 1978 Robinson wrote to co-editor Paul Davidson, "Many thanks for sending JPKE no 1. . . ."

In the past six years, Robinson had seen some signs making her optimistic about the final outcome of her battle with the neoclassicals. On June 17, 1975 she wrote Eichner,

> I think we can take some comfort from the fact that the critics (and this includes Solow in the Times Literary Supplement) have now conceded the validity of the post-Keynesian arguments. They have withdrawn to a second line of defense— that the post-Keynesians haven't yet run statistical tests of their theories and that in any case the theory has no significant policy implications. Time and further work will break down this line of defense, too.

But on July 14, she admitted, "I have just returned from my world tour. . . . Solow seems to be singing 'That old time religion is good enough for me', but I do not know for how long they will be able to maintain this position."

> The new journal began splendidly. Davidson wrote to tell her: I am pleased that the JPKE continues to grow in subscribers beyond my wildest dreams. When Sidney Weintraub and Ken Galbraith first approached me with the idea of starting this project, I was highly skeptical as to whether we could get more than 400 or 500 subscribers in the first year and, perhaps 1,000 in three years. With only two issues out, we are well over the 1,600 mark. . . . The publisher . . . seems to be exceedingly happy about the way subscriptions are rising. It must mean that Sidney and I made a bad deal and the publisher is making a good profit already. . . . Perhaps, there really is a constituency out there looking for new ideas (May 3, 1979).

Thus, as Joan Robinson was retiring from teaching at Cambridge University, her influence in the United States was taking a firmer hold, perhaps not where she had willed it—at Harvard and MIT—but not quite out in the sticks with the hippopotami either.

Growing closer to American post Keynesians

Robinson's correspondence with Davidson had dropped off after his year at Cambridge, but their friendship continued. Davidson believes it was strengthened by her disillusionment with developments at Cambridge. In August 1973, Robinson wrote, ''I did not write to you about your book because I was put out at your making me say the exact opposite of what I have been teaching for 30 years. . . . However, I agree with you that Nicky's Neo Pasinetti theorem is no good. I regret that I tried to rationalize in my *Heresies*'' (August 17, 1973).

In the late seventies, about the time she started to disagree with one of the Italians, Pierangelo Garegnani, Davidson began to get a series of friendly letters. ''Where is Jan Kregel both geographically and mentally?'' she inquired, adding that she hoped the ''Post-Keynesians'' were doing well (April 17, 1978).

Davidson had her down to Rutgers after her Gildersleeve lecture at Barnard in March 1976. She wrote that she had ''much enjoyed meeting your chaps. . . . Your review of Shackle is excellent. We are really beginning to get on!'' (Received from Canada April 12, 1976.) Davidson had sent some students to pick her up in New York City and to drive her to Rutgers where both he and Eichner were teaching,

> . . . because you know she just couldn't take public transportation. She was always too helpless for a very strong woman; it was always amazing how she could get people to do almost anything for her. But the students who drove up said they had a fantastic time driving back down with her in the car. For her address we had the largest turnout we have had for any speaker, at least during the fifteen or twenty years I have been here. We must have had over 250 people with notice of maybe only ten days.

Robinson was exceptionally accommodating. When writing a piece for the proposed journal (JPKE), she offered to tone it down ''if my aggressive line will put your board off'' (December 1, 1976). She expressed a liking for one of Davidson's papers and hoped he would ''put the same points where they will be read in the U.S.A.'' (July 3, 1978)

In the first issue of the *Journal of Post Keynesian Economics*, Davidson had an article about ''crowding out,'' a subject they had been arguing about over the years. She wrote, ''I like your piece about 'crowding out'. This ought to settle the matter. But when, as now, the inducement to invest is low, neither shortage of finance nor of savings has anything to do with the case'' (September 13, 1978). Davidson believes that this seeming change of heart was due more than anything else to Robinson's growing disenchantment with the Italian branch of the Anglo-Italians. While some of the American post Keynesians had gone in the direction in which Robinson was pointing—the emphasis on expectations—Garegnani was following what he considered to be the Joan Robinson of 1971, emphasizing the long period.[23]

Davidson believed that

> . . . in the mid-seventies she began to realize that her real friends were really the American post Keynesians and not the Sraffian post Keynesians. But it was very late in her life at that stage, and I think she had some trouble because it suggested, at least to me, that a lot of her work, which she had striven for, had gone in the wrong direction with the Sraffians. And you can see it in our earlier correspondence. I keep trying to drag her into the question of the role of money and she keeps trying to drag me into what she calls the wages and prices economy, the Sraffian economy while I was in Cambridge.

In 1979 there was an effort to have Robinson "testify" before the Joint Economic Committee of the United States Congress. Unfortunately, "owing to a chapter of accidents," this did not come off.[24] Davidson commented, "I truly regret that the Joint Economic Committee did not schedule you for hearings. I think it would have been a breath of fresh air in Washington" (May 3, 1979).

Americans of Davidson's persuasion always appreciated Joan Robinson. Clearly Robinson had more esteem for them after she had met with the American post Keynesians in 1971, and had come to realize their frustration and isolation within the profession. In her last years she knew that there were some American economists who both comprehended and admired her fifty years of contributions to economics.

JR

CHAPTER SIXTEEN

North America
in the Seventies:
Lectures and Honors

Joan Robinson continued to receive invitations to visit the United States through the late 1970s. After the disappointment over the failure of McGraw-Hill to publish an American version of her text with Eatwell, and after the disillusionment over the capital controversy, Robinson had nevertheless found many Americans with whom she could empathize.

1975: Morality in Maine

In 1975, Robinson delivered the commencement address at the University of Maine at Orono.[1]

Generous as always with her time, she spent several days on campus prior to commencement, conducting seminars. Arrangements for her visit were made by Professor James Clifton, who had had extensive correspondence with her concerning his research.[2] Robinson is remembered in Orono for graciously providing opportunities to those faculty members who wished to discuss their interests with her. While there she saw her Girton College roommate, Una LeBoutillier—a reunion after many years. Her topic was "Morality and Economics." We can picture her, a striking woman of seventy-one years, white-headed, with those penetrating blue eyes looking out over a hushed audience saying, "I want to speak about the philosophy of economics." She gave the address which so impressed Marc Vandoorne when he reviewed her *Collected Economics Papers*, Volume 5.[3] In it, she attacked the branding of Adam Smith as a simplistic promoter of self-interest, when really Smith had taken for granted that there must be an ethical foundation for society.[4]

1976: Gildersleeve lecturer at Barnard

In 1976, Robinson was appointed a Virginia C. Gildersleeve lecturer at Barnard College. She spoke at Barnard's Altschul Hall at 4 p.m. on March 2 on ''The Age of Growth.'' The Gildersleeve professorships were provided to bring outstanding women to lecture at Barnard. Robinson was nominated by the economics department especially on the recommendation of Sylvia Hewlett.[5] The department of economics at Barnard recommended Robinson to the alumnae board both on the basis of her impressive academic qualifications and as ''an ardent feminist.''[6]

The characterization of ''feminist'' was a little off the mark. Hewlett confessed,

> I couldn't understand why she wasn't at all interested in being a feminist, being such a strong woman herself. I could see her being impatient with some of the contemporary movements, but to reject feminism, the whole shebang, I found hard to understand. She always said, for instance, that she felt that she was as good as a man and that she had had as many chances as a man. But she clearly didn't. Look at her life. She got the chair in economics when her husband relinquished it, despite the fact she was always more prominent and better known than he was. A very glaring example of the kind of disadvantages that women labored under all those decades.
>
> I tried to make her talk about her early womanhood and she remembered certain things. For example, one reason she was so fond of India was that it was a very happy period for her, I mean personally happy for her, going to India as a memsahib, and I wonder whether her marriage was good at that point. She remembered that as a kind of golden period and it rubbed off on the whole country. On the whole I think she felt very inadequate as a woman. She told me once that her daughters were real women; they could cook two hot meals a day for their families and that was something she couldn't do. I found that very odd. Any suburban housewife can put together two meals but not many people have contributed to scholarship and to policy what she has. She was brought up in a very upper-class setting and was totally dependent on servants, had been all her life, couldn't boil an egg.
>
> But what surprised me was that she felt this was a matter of shame, not for socialist reasons, but because she couldn't perform the ordinarily womanly things. Part of it was she had a lot of problems in seeing herself as a woman, and she couldn't face, or talk about the kind of personal things that really come out of being a woman. She was very proud of her professorship. For instance, I was to introduce her at a cocktail party off Fifth Avenue. Joan and I worked on her introduction for this very socially prominent occasion. She didn't want to be called Joan Robinson; she wanted to be called Professor Robinson. It was a label that mattered to her more than anything.[7]

As usual, Robinson gave full measure to Barnard. She delivered the lecture, met with the Barnard Economics Club on "China in the 1970s," discussed "Ideology and the Theory of Income Distribution" at a Graduate Students and Faculty seminar, gave a luncheon talk on "Cambridge in the Thirties," and addressed the economics department on "After the Capital Debate," in addition to several social events. Generally Hewlett took care of her in between, entertaining her as a guest in her home. For these occasions, Robinson "took great pleasure in wearing outlandish Chinese gowns and looking really rather dashing for an elderly woman, which is what she was. [Robinson was seventy-two years old.] And she really had some flare for caring for her appearance." Hewlett gathered from Robinson herself that she had not always felt herself to be an attractive woman. And then there was the remark by Maurice Dobb, who in interview confessed that he didn't like Robinson's legs. Hewlett believed that Robinson felt she could compete on intellectual fronts but "not as a woman."

1978: "The economics of destruction" in Toronto

In 1978, Robinson was invited by D. E. Moggridge and S. K. Howson, both former students, to give a lecture on the Scarborough Campus of the University of Toronto. She also visited York University at that time. At noon, she addressed a group mainly of undergraduates on "The Economics of Destruction." One member of her audience, Hal Kursk, took notes and later discussed and corrected the work with Robinson. It was published in the *Monthly Review* after her death (October 1983).[8] She was now seventy-five years old and increasingly disillusioned. She was convinced that Keynesian economics, in promoting full employment ideals, had contributed to the arms race, "owing to the inhibition to spend money on welfare and unemployment." She was no longer optimistic. She began her talk this way: "We are sitting around discussing ideas totally beside the point. The important question is not whether the rate of inflation is high or low or can be brought under control but whether our generation will succeed in destroying the world." She concluded, "Economics should begin to address the important issue of our impending doom."

1980: Honorary doctorate at Harvard

In 1980, Harvard University gave Joan Robinson its highest tribute, the honorary Doctor of Laws. She was among a particularly notable group, which included Walter Cronkite, Anna Freud, Octavio Paz, and Helen Frankenthaler.[9]

Robinson arrived using a cane, and for the ceremony wore white slacks and a white overblouse. She was joined in the festivities by her old friend, John Kenneth Galbraith, who remembered the procession as one occasion when economics was not discussed. The Harvard University *Gazette* reported the committee's accolade: "With insight and elegance she has examined the imperfections of the market and revealed the inconsistencies of poverty and wealth, scarcity and abundance.''[10]

She was pleasant and subdued, a little hard of hearing.

1980: Inflation and crisis at Notre Dame

In September of 1980, Robinson visited Notre Dame to lecture on ''Inflation and the Economic Crisis'' (according to notes in her archival papers). She had some advice for ''this university within a few miles of Chicago.'' She thought they should study the antidevelopment, at the same time as they studied the development, of economic theory. ''Milton Friedman is quite clever, I shouldn't say clever, but cunning. He has allowed enough loopholes in his theory to make it tautological.''

Robinson warned that economists too often mistake a symptom for a cause. She quoted Nicholas Kaldor (whom Prime Minister Harold Wilson had appointed to the House of Lords), saying that Kaldor was ''trying to educate the House of Lords: The explanation that he puts forward is that the quantity theory is being used as a cover for a policy that really consists in attacking the trade unions.'' Actually it is not a very clever idea to reduce output as a way of stopping prices from rising, she said. ''If inflation is primarily the result of a class war, which this argument seems to show, while the United Kingdom's government policy is seriously threatening to destroy British industry, surely the sensible thing would be to arrange an armistice.''[11]

In her talks, Robinson never pulled her punches.

1981: Peace in Utah

In 1981, against doctor's orders, Robinson accepted an invitation to give the Tanner Lecture on Human Values at the University of Utah in Salt Lake City.[12] Advised to do no flying at all, she did fly to the continent and was accompanied cross-country on Amtrak by John Eatwell, who saw to her welfare. She gave two lectures and participated in a panel discussion.

The first lecture was on ''The Arms Race,'' the second on the relationship of the arms race to the ''problem of effective demand and employment.'' On the panel she was faced by ''two leading figures from the arms control field'' and public questions. The lectures were free and the public was invited. She was the third Tanner lecturer, the first two being Lord Ashby in 1979, and Wallace Stegner in 1980.

Robinson's archival papers show that she worked diligently on her addresses. She was direct in her comments, criticizing Margaret Thatcher's acceptance of a campaign to get the Dutch to allow new nuclear missiles in the Netherlands. Robinson warned, ''The nuclear weapons that are now being developed cannot provide defense. If they are not to be used for aggression, they could only be used for revenge." She told the audience about a false alarm set off by a flock of geese in Cambridgeshire where there are missiles. She characterized the era as one carried on by the "momentum of research and development"; by "self-righteousness and mutual distrust induced by the atmosphere of a war of ideology." She called for fairness in the arguments over Hiroshima, noting that her friend and colleague, Professor Tsuru, had told her that "his judgement is that resistance by the Japanese army would have been desperate and would have taken at least a month to overcome, with heavy casualties." But now, she said, "instead of deterrence we have competition in terror."

In her second lecture she brought economics to the forefront: "It is not a limitation of useful ideas or schemes for investment projects but the religious belief in laisser faire in the Western World that stands in the way of systematic employment policy." She mentioned the supply-side economics of the Reagan administration as a case in point. She thought it tragic that before economists had explained how to solve unemployment problems, Hitler had already discovered how. Now she reported that Kaldor had discovered the work of H. P. J. Rüstow, who was an independent discoverer of the theory of employment. Rüstow had worked out how to subsidize investment with tax credits and work-creating schemes for the Weimar Republic. She concluded, "it is tragic that Brüning failed to eliminate unemployment. . . . But in the last resort, it is not the politicians, but the economic theorists who are to be blamed for the adoption of the wrong policies."

For her third lecture, Robinson wrote that "since the United States has a religious belief in the private enterprise system and does not want to make use of what one might loosely call Keynesian policies, policies of having a budget deficit in order to keep up the market and keep up the employment," deficit spending resulted in contributions to the arms race. This was so in America "because you are not allowed to do anything that is helpful to people." She thought the problem serious enough to say that in a war, though the Chinese would survive, "our heritage would be destroyed and life would be impossible. . . . Our famous western civilization is in peril. And that is a much bigger problem than inflation."

Furthermore, she noted that the arms race aggravated inflation: "If your expenditure which is boosting effective demand is expenditure on armaments, then there is nothing coming forward to increase the supply of goods and services and so to mitigate the inflationary effect of investment expenditures."

1982: Reading Ricardo at Williams College

Robinson made her last visit to the United States in 1982. Again, she had been advised against flying. But she welcomed the chance to talk with American students and to visit her daughter and her family in Canada. Gordon Winston, who corresponded with her, suggested her as a Bernhard Fellow, a college-wide fellowship at Williams College. In the spring of 1981, when she agreed to come, she was in reasonably good health. While she was given a fee befitting a distinguished visiting professor, her expressed reason for coming, according to Winston, was that she was interested in reaching undergraduates beyond the influence of their mainstream professors. She arranged to stay until Thanksgiving, though the term did not end until December. She had been warned of the "treacherous conditions" of a New England winter.

Juliet Schor, a member of the department of economics, was appointed to help her with "the Americanization of things," to attend her classes, and then take them over after Robinson's departure.[13] Two students, one a man and one a woman, were hired to keep a close eye on her. She was given a place to stay, boarding with students. According to Winston, Robinson made a powerful impression, not so much because of her ideas, but because of her person: "She still had at times awesome intellectual power and always personal command."

Robinson was very popular with her younger colleagues and students. What impressed Schor most was her intellect:

> She was like brain matter; her intellect dominated her personality so much; yes, she loved her grandchildren and all that, but she was consumed by intellectual activity. She couldn't abide small talk—that was another reason that some people found it hard to be with her. Usually people are engaging in small talk and she had no interest in it whatsoever.[14]

Schor and Robinson got along very well. Robinson considered Schor "an intellectual comrade, which was very important to her."

Schor found Robinson to be "really very Keynesian. She was a Keynesian Keynesian. She basically thought, she still thought Keynes and Kalecki, that's where it was at." I asked Schor if she thought Robinson's leftist tendencies showed up in her theories. Schor answered,

> It's rather difficult to locate a rigorous theoretical distinction between capitalists and workers and a conflict over the surplus. She did have conflict in her head— some kind of conflict, although she also had a mark-up pricing model. But I think she basically had a view that the wage is determined by the class struggle, and that it is exogenous. However, there are a lot of things that Marxist economists are concerned about that she was not interested in, such as questions of the labor process or discrimination.

Schor continued,

> Her visit was a bit hard for me because I was very busy at the time and it was a tremendous commitment which just fell into my lap. But I found her to be very

sweet. I can't understand all the things people have said about her. Perhaps she was a "hard" personality to other people, but I didn't find her to be like that.

The two students who took care of Joan Robinson would take meals with her if Schor didn't. Robinson took breakfast herself, and lunch usually with Schor. Sometimes the students would take Robinson to events she wanted to go to. According to Schor, "She always wanted to go. She was very active." Robinson was very fond of one of the best economics students, a woman.

> Joan went up to this student and put her hands on her shoulders. She shook her and said, "Whatever you do, promise me you won't go into economics." She really felt that it was a great mistake for young people to go into economics. I think she felt that way about me too—that it was unfortunate I had chosen this field.

Had Robinson suggested alternatives? "No. What she was interested in at that time was politics, really. The nuclear movement." But she still wanted to work? "Oh, yes. She was reading Keynes and Sraffa's edition of Ricardo—that was her intellectual plan. She said she was not going to write any more because she had already written everything she had to say. She was just going to read. She had just finished 'Economics and Ideology', which was her last paper. She gave a seminar on that paper."

I asked about Robinson and feminism. Schor said,

> She did not believe in feminist ideology. I would put it that way. She did not identify herself as a woman. She very strongly wanted to be considered as a person of no gender. Over and over again she made that point; and there is nothing that irked her more than people saying, "She is the greatest woman economist." It's odd; I wouldn't say she didn't like women because there were certain women she very much seemed to like, so it was a mixed bag. Now, I would never say she wasn't a feminist, on account of what she did and who she was. I say this even though she didn't have respect for the fact that she did it as a woman. But, deny it as she did, it had a tremendous impact in her life, the fact that she was a woman. She knew that.

Did she know that?

> Well, she knew she was discriminated against. And she did feel very warm toward her role as a woman in some ways, but in other ways she was very male-identified. Her favorite of the students was a young man who unfortunately wasn't very good in economics. She wrote me a letter saying something like that—that it was unfortunate that her "favorite pupil is very inarticulate, but I think not mistaken."[15]

When Robinson left Williams College to visit her daughter, she wrote,

> Dear Julie, I have arrived here ok and find the family well. Would you please thank my class for the memento of Williams they gave me. Two or three of them I feel will be friends and I wish them all luck—their own way. Keep in touch and let me know where you fetch up. With grateful thanks for all your care and help. Joan.[16]

In December, still in Canada, Robinson urged,

> Please encourage any one who wants to keep in touch with me to write to Cambridge (I hope this includes you!). . . . I am sorry I am so disorganized now that I cannot write coherently (or legibly). I hope we can keep in touch. Thanks for all your kind care without which I could not have survived.[17]

From Cambridge, Robinson wrote in January, ''I hope you received the mark list. There were two names for which no papers appeared. On the whole I was pleasantly surprised. I think I have succeeded in sowing a little seed, which you must water and protect. Why don't you ring me up on a Sunday (when it is cheap)—01144–233–357548? It is easier for you to hit off the time than for me.''[18]

Robinson had told Winston that if she had realized ''how slowed down'' she was, she might not have come. But clearly she made good friends at Williams and is remembered there with fondness. Schor talked to her in Cambridge: ''She called me up just before she had her stroke. She was very unhappy when she got back; she felt disoriented and alienated.'' Schor feels that the plane ride back may have had something to do with Robinson's deterioration, possibly inducing small strokes. Stephen R. Lewis, Jr. of Williams College wrote, ''We were surprised to learn when Joan was here that Williams was the only place other than Cambridge that she had ever done anything besides a visiting lecture or two. We're pleased with the distinction.''[19]

Her longest stay also proved to be her last.

JR

CHAPTER SEVENTEEN

What Are the Questions?

"What are the questions?" asked Joan Robinson in her seventy-fifth year. She was addressing the members of the American Economic Association through their *Journal of Economic Literature*.[1] She had already announced the second crisis in economic theory in New Orleans in 1971, and had been lecturing over the world on the "disintegration of economics."[2] She felt that "there are no consistent and accepted answers to the questions that were . . . raised" in the 1930s, the so-called years of high theory; that the "great mass of work that has been done since and the proliferation of academic economic teaching has been little illuminated by the ideas that emerged at that time."[3]

Surely she was correct. Schumpeter had written in 1934, in his review of her *Imperfect Competition*: "A book of such range and power always leaves our minds with a question. Having been carried so far by this Virgil, where shall we go now?" Answering his own question, Schumpeter wrote:

> First, the element of time must be got hold of in a much more efficient manner, if for no other reason because what people try to maximize is certainly gain *over time*. . . . Second, the element of money cannot any longer remain in the background to which long and good tradition has relegated it. We must face the fact that most of our quantities are either monetary expressions or corrected monetary expressions. . . . Third, we probably all agree that our equilibrium analysis is really a tool for the analysis of chronic disequilibria . . . and this means that we must build the economic cycle into our general theory. Fourth, in some lines of advance the time has probably come to get rid of the apparatus of supply and demand, so useful for one range of problems but an intolerable bearing-rein for another.[4]

Ironically, these matters, mentioned in a review of her first major work, were in fact the goals she worked toward during the next fifty years, that is, until her death in 1983.

In 1977 she thought that the "lack of progress" might be connected with the origin of the new ideas themselves—that they were thought to be part of "a purely intellectual movement," by Shackle, for example. In her view, the years of high theory "arose out of the actual situation of the thirties—the breakdown of the world market economy in the great slump." At the moment that one began to discuss actual problems, questions of policy arose, these involving politics and thus ideology. For Robinson, "there is no such thing as a 'purely economic' problem that can be settled by purely economic logic."[5]

While laboratory sciences proceed by isolating a question and testing hypotheses, one by one, she argued that in economics,

> . . . questions cannot be isolated because every aspect of human society interacts with every other; hypotheses can be put forward only in the form of a "model" of the whole economy. . . . The "high theory" of the thirties consisted of advancing alternative hypotheses to replace those, derived from the theory of supply and demand for labor, which had been too much discredited in the slump.

She spoke of the difficulty of establishing statistical "facts" and of applying an economic model to statistical evidence:

> It may be possible to find evidence of the relationships within the model over a certain period of time and then to predict what they will be, say over the following years; but when it is found that the relationships turned out to be different, there is no way of telling whether it is because there was a mistake in specifying the model in the first place or because circumstances have changed meanwhile. And when they turn out the same, it is possibly by accident. (For instance, it has been found that a "Cobb-Douglas production function" will fit any time-series of outputs, whatever the technology, provided that the share of wages in value added was fairly constant over the period.)

She drew on Norbert Wiener, who said, "the economic game is a game where the rules are subject to important revisions, say, every ten years, and bears an uncomfortable resemblance to the Queen's croquet game in *Alice in Wonderland*. . . ."[6]

Robinson criticized mainstream economic theory in the familiar way before going on to some of the other questions. One is her much repeated but unanswered question, "What is growth for?" She conceded that "under the shadow of the arms race and its diffusion into the Third World, perhaps no merely economic questions are really of great importance; but even if it is a secondary question, we ought to consider it."

She asked, "What is the object of production in a modern industrial nation, and if we could have more of it (through technical change and capital accumulation), what should we use it for?" She knew the question did not arise for the classical economists, but she held that, given the inequality of the distribution of purchasing power between individuals, we must ask ourselves, "Do we want renewed growth in order to maintain and enhance disparities in consumption?" Second, do we want the kinds of consumption that generate disutility for many? Third, do we want the continual introduction of new commodities and creation of new wants that accompany growth but do not guarantee "a growth of satisfaction?" Robinson concluded, "These questions involve the whole political and social system of the capitalist world; they cannot be decided by economic theory, but it would be decent, at least, if the economists admitted that they do not have an answer to them."[7]

These questions provide an important key to understanding Robinson. She was not so much disillusioned with the subject of economics as with the economists themselves. Some of her contribution to economic analysis was in the questions she put, questions which few economists of her professional standing were raising. She had said to colleagues and students alike that you have to know the question before you can provide the answer. Though Robinson never claimed to be a philosopher of science, her questions on methodology implied that techniques used by economists must be reexamined from the point of view of philosophy, for many of the questions raised, especially beginning with her *Economic Philosophy*, were, in fact, philosophical.

Her politics: optimism or naïveté?

Joan Robinson spent her adult life in Cambridge, where she is remembered for her strong and independent views. She was not one of Schumpeter's "laborites," though she undoubtedly voted Labour Party; she was not a Keynesian Liberal; she was a critic of English colonialism and of capitalist society, a left-wing Keynesian. As for Americans, as Lord Kahn puts it, she hated not Americans, but "American guns."

In spite of Harry Johnson's inferences, she was not a "Marxo-Keynesian" (whatever that is), but instead a Kalecki-Keynesian, with an intellectual debt to Sraffa. She didn't limit her friendships to leftists and certainly not to Marxists, but she clearly preferred persons with her own values, which included much of old-fashioned nineteenth-century liberalism. Paul Samuelson once commented to somebody in Cambridge, "I suppose that Joan is a good friend and admirer of Maurice Dobb." "Oh, no, she has contempt for Maurice Dobb." "Contempt?" "Well, she really regards him as a lackey of Stalin." As Samuelson said,

> Joan Robinson wears no man's collar and no woman's collar, and if she is in Poland and there is a worker's uprising, as there was in Poznan, and the top brass is toasting her and she is supposed to give a lecture on some subject, she would ask, "Why are we talking about this subject? We should be talking about that which nobody was mentioning." The Polish economists, par-

ticularly the young ones, really liked her . . . on the other hand she was subject to tremendous enthusiasms.

Yet, Samuelson added, "she retreated from her early view of the Soviet system, but it didn't change her view of socialism."[8] Robinson was open to ideas of socialist experiment, but the record is that she was critical of some aspects of every existing society. She welcomed Dobb's 1956 amendment of his "rigid pro-Soviet views."

Robinson was, of course, aware of her upper-class origins. Sita Narasimhan gives the best account of Robinson's class consciousness: "One heard from her happy stories of riding and walking, but one also sensed a consciousness of the reaches of power and of human fallibility. Most important of all, though, is something that she used to say in a voice of outraged dismissal, 'You know, there was an 'us' and a 'them'."[9]

Robinson did not think of herself as a snob. She admitted that Keynes had been one:

> Keynes *was* a snob. If you had not been to a good school he cut you. He used to say: "The fellow simply hasn't driven up," and until you drove up under your own locomotive power (if any) he would not begin to argue with you. . . . Professor Kahn is not a snob. He takes infinite pains to explain a point to you, whatever school you come from.[10]

She thought of herself as being like Kahn. But she was aware that in the United States there were many "hippopotami."

More than once she admitted to being a bourgeois economist. She was not known as an activist, though toward the end of her life she contributed to the initiation of the Cambridge protest against nuclear armament. Instead, she was an educator of students, workers, and colleagues alike.

She considered capitalism the second best kind of economy, and she openly admired the revolutionary societies of China, North Korea and, to a limited extent, Castro's Cuba; but not the Soviet Union, particularly in its policies of domination of other Eastern European countries.

I looked for some evidence of her "left-wingness," and found only ideas. She had a lifelong commitment to a better world for the majority of people and for a science of economics that might help to bring this about. This is evident from her time as an undergraduate to her dying day. Her major shortcoming may have been that she expected more of economics than it could possibly deliver. Very late in life, she lost this optimism about economics. She wrote to me that she thought predominant economics was rather like "the onion in Peer Gynt. . . . I feel that by the time you have peeled off all the errors in orthodox theory, there is nothing left."[11] In spite of this, she never became cynical. She was shocked over the revelations of the Cultural Revolution in China, but she still seemed to believe that a new society was possible.

Part of her effectiveness as a speaker and teacher came through enthusiasm born of optimism. For many years, Robinson believed that economists could and would "escape the mud of static equilibrium"; she also thought Marxists could disown the labor theory of value. She thought people could and wanted to build a better world. Perhaps this is unwarranted optimism, but it was also the inheritance of the enlightenment. Another part of her power was her mastery of controversy. It may have been "Cambridge rudeness," but it was purposefully used. Her adversaries, like Solow and Leijonhufvud, miss her.

As for individuals, she was eager to help them. Many academic women remember her support of them at crucial moments, for example Ruth Cohen, Sita Narisimhan, and Sylvia Hewlett. When a student was recommended to her by an American colleague, she took an interest in him or her. All the better if he were left, but she did not shun others. Paul Sweezy told the story of one case: Mrs. Anne Meeropol, who had adopted the sons of the condemned Rosenbergs, came to his office and asked if he would recommend one of her sons to Cambridge. At that time, the young man's identity was still a secret. Sweezy said, "I will write to Joan Robinson if I can tell her who he is. So I wrote to Joan and told her the story so that she would know who was applying. She took it to heart, saw him in Cambridge, and he did a Ph.D. there and was a protégé of Joan's."[12]

Her interest in individuals was a characteristic her friends cherished. There were the three Settlement School women whom Robinson got to know as a student at St. Paul's. She continued to see them, to look them up, throughout her life. She helped younger colleagues to get into print. "She did not ignore us younger ones," said Hewlett. Robinson wrote a letter supporting Hewlett's tenure case and "did everything in the limits of her power." She encouraged the founding of, or became a patron of, several journals which provide an outlet for competing ideas.[13] The income from her estate will be used to finance scholarships at Cambridge for young students from developing countries. Robinson was active in the Cambridge Worker's Education Program, with its long tradition of a lecturer's going wherever necessary to give educational talks to workers. One letter, prized by her family, attests to her reaching out:

> Dear Madam, Many thanks to you for tonight—Taking Stock. You were Grand. Our Chancellor of the Exchequer is a grand Character to defend. I'm no writer, but i can Appreciate people of your Calibre. It is a treat to us Coalliers. God bless you Madam. Carry on with the good work. I am your Humble Fan.[14]

Joan Robinson embraced no political party or program without reservation. Instead, she remained the critic of all. Kenneth Arrow wrote her:

> Separate from my comments on your JEL essay ["What Are the Questions?"], I would like to ask where, if at all, you have put yourself on record about your views on the economic system. You have frequently stressed the ideological component in the economic theory of capitalism and made various side remarks

on the injustices and malfunctioning of the capitalist system. I have heard you in public lecture give a very favorable impression of the Chinese economy. It might be inferred that you are in favor of socialism and perhaps more particularly of some form of communism as that term is currently used. But in fact you always give me the impression of offering a purportedly objective set of statements, and refraining from drawing any conclusions as to desirable changes in the United Kingdom or the United States. Possibly, you take your role as that of a destroyer of myths, a clearer of ground upon which someone else will build. Or perhaps you wish to emphasize that conflict is inevitable, that no amount of research and thinking, especially since it is inevitably colored by power and ideology, can lead to policy recommendations which will persuade others . . . in which case argument about the shape of society is dismissed with a *de gustibus non est disputandum.* [15]

We do not have her answer.

For what Harcourt calls her "balancing" views of new communist societies, many thought her naïve. Galbraith found her very enthusiastic about China and critical of India when she swung through India while he was ambassador there. Clower described her as "full of revolutionary fervor and very excited about these new blossoming societies," in the early 1960s. At one point Robinson told Samuelson that "the Cultural Revolution wasn't such a bad thing and that a lot of professors could benefit from physical exercise." Arrow thought that "Mrs. Robinson seems to have great confidence in the ability of government officials to learn by doing." [16] Frank Roosevelt termed her proposal for "the nation as rentier" (in *Economics: An Awkward Corner*) "somewhat naïve—especially with regard to the benevolent character of the state." [17]

Beyond both optimism and naïveté is the possibility that Robinson was like Roosevelt's interpretation of Marx: "Marx never offered a detailed blueprint for a post-capitalist society. In the *Communist Manifesto* he asserted that the history of all hitherto existing society is the history of class struggles, and he clearly believed that such struggles would also shape the society of the future." [18]

Even a casual reading of Robinson's *Aspects of Development and Under-development* shows that she clearly saw conflicts of interest arising in China. She was a realist, as Sol Adler pointed out. No matter what policy the government pursued, the peasant cooperatives with the better land would be better off than others. She cheered the uprising in Poznan as only the beginning of the proletarian rebellion against a repressive government.

Her optimism was a belief that society could do better by its people and that some people, at least, would seek to bring this about. Perhaps this fervent hope temporarily blinded her at times, but "naïve" is not a term I would use in connection with Joan Robinson.

Sita Narasimhan, a friend and colleague at Cambridge, knew Robinson as well as any living person. In her memorial statement Narasimhan wrote, "Joan's directness is meant to challenge, as Vinoba's was. Neither had any desire to tell you what to think, or how you are to go about it. People like these have won a right to charm which they will not use. It is of the essence of the style to be disconcerting.''[19]

This is the right word for Joan Robinson's politics—disconcerting.

Why not a Nobel laureate?

There is evidence (I learned this through interviews) that Joan Robinson was regularly nominated for the Nobel Prize and was on what is called the short list of contenders at least once. Presumably, then, hers was one of those Assar Lindbeck has called '''hot' names.''[20] Why was she never honored?

Alfred Nobel left his money for prizes in only five areas: physics; chemistry; physiology and medicine; literature; and peace.[21] Sixty-seven years after the first Nobel Prize was given, the Central Bank of Sweden at its tercentenary created a ''Prize in Economic Sciences in Memory of Alfred Nobel.'' The bank places an annual amount, equal to a Nobel Prize, at the disposal of the Nobel Foundation. The standard procedures for choice of a Nobel laureate are used, and the presentation is made on Nobel Day.

The original skepticism of some of the natural scientists in the Royal Swedish Academy of Science toward the proposal was overcome partly through the efforts of Gunnar Myrdal and other economists who were members of the Academy. This memorial prize was first awarded in 1969, so that there were fourteen awards made to twenty economists before Joan Robinson's death in 1983. There were twenty female laureates in Robinson's lifetime, though none in economics.[22] Each field has its own recommending committee. Every fall, invitations to nominate candidates are sent out to ''statutorily competent'' individuals.[23]

A person must be nominated to win, but this is no problem as the Nobel committee members themselves can nominate. About seventy-five departments of economics (not always the same ones) from many countries are invited to suggest candidates. This nomination process usually produces 150 to 200 proposals, yielding seventy-five to 125 nominees. ''Spontaneous suggestions from persons who have not been asked to submit proposals are not considered.'' Not all nominators are equal. In the case of economics, Lindbeck said that the important thing is ''not how many suggestions each candidate has received but rather *who* the proponents of the various candidates are. Thus very competent nominators, whose judgment the committee ranks highly, may have a strong influence on the committee, particularly if their supporting arguments are convincing.''

According to Lindbeck,

A typical feature of the proposals is that the suggestions tend to be concentrated on well-known and highly respected economists, in particular on scholars in the field of "central" economic theory as traditionally understood. Economists who have been involved in controversies over economic policy issues are often suggested.

Lindbeck felt that the nominators often do not appreciate the necessity of awarding for "specific contributions."[24]

Each year, two or more studies are made of each candidate whom the committee regards as particularly meriting attention—that is, between twenty and thirty persons, "though usually only a handful of these are regarded as 'hot' names each year." The recommendation of the committee is then presented to the Academy. "So far, the proposals of the prize committee to the Academy have been unanimous."[25]

At the awards ceremony, a member of the Nobel Committee for economics makes a presentation, giving primary reasons for the choice. Each year the full text of the ceremony is published in translation by the Nobel Foundation. On the basis of these published award presentations, I constructed a table (see p. 216) which gives the insight of an outsider into the awards in economics during Robinson's lifetime.

Of course, many of the recipients might have fallen into more than one column. However, as I read it, of the twenty recipients, seven made special contributions to mathematics or applied statistical models, ten to theory, and three were difficult to categorize but do not fall under either of the former. For example, in making the 1974 award to Myrdal and Hayek, Erik Lundberg said,

> Hitherto the prize in Economic Science . . . has been awarded to researchers who have made pioneering contributions in what may be called "pure" economics. . . . However there are prominent researchers in the field of the social sciences whose range of interests covers other and wider areas than those embraced by the term "pure economics."[26]

George Stigler was thought to have "opened new and important fields for economic research."[27]

The Nobel committee for choosing an economist is interesting in itself. Once on the committee, a person may serve many years. Lindbeck does not say how the committee is selected. Of the fourteen committees 1969–82, Ragnar Bentzel served on all of them; Assar Lindbeck and Herman Wold on thirteen; Erik Lundberg on twelve; Bertil Ohlin on the first six—he was off two years before being awarded the prize; Ingvar Svennilson on the first three; Sune Carlson on nine. Lundberg interrupted his service for two years but returned in 1982 to serve as secretary of the committee which selected George Stigler. The new blood on the committee consists of Karl-Göran Mäler, Ingemar Stahl, and Lars Werin. Lindbeck reports that "a consensus has in fact developed quite 'automatically' within the committee, as if by some kind of

Table of Reasons*
1969–82

Mathematical/ Statistical	Theory	Other
1969 Frisch, Ragnar		
Tinbergen, Jan		
1970	Samuelson, Paul	
1971 Kuznets, Simon		
1972	Hicks, John R.	
	Arrow, Kenneth J.	
1973 Leontief, Wassily		
1974		Myrdal, Gunnar
		von Hayek, Friedrich
1975 Kantorovich, Leonid		
Koopmans, Tjalling C.		
1976	Friedman, Milton	
1977	Ohlin, Bertil	
	Meade, James	
1978	Simon, Herbert A.	
1979	Schultz, Theodore W.	
	Lewis, Arthur	
1980 Klein, Lawrence R.		
1981	Tobin, James	
1982		Stigler, George

---

*Lindbeck's reading of the committee's work employs five categories: 1. General ("basic") Economic Theory: Samuelson, Arrow, and Hicks; 2. Theoretical Contributions Concerning Specific Aspects of the Economy: Meade, Ohlin, Tobin, Lewis, Schultz, Simon, and Stigler; 3. Powerful New Methods of Economic Analysis, Their Development and Application: Frisch, Tinbergen, Leontief, Koopmans, and Kantorovich; 4. More Nearly "Pure" Empirical Research: Kuznets, Klein, and Friedman; and 5. Nonformalized Innovative Thinking: Hayek and Myrdal [Lindbeck 1985:39–45].

invisible hand, after intensive discussions."[28]

The committee has long recognized the existence of a "backlog of 'worthy' candidates." Lindbeck notes that some, like Viner and Kalecki, "missed" awards "due to death not long after the prize was initiated." (Both died in 1970.) He added to this list Frank Knight (d. 1972) and Roy Harrod (d. 1978) but did not mention Joan Robinson. (This mention of Harrod is particularly interesting in that no Keynes-Keynesian has ever been honored and the committee had ten opportunities to name Harrod.) The committee had felt some pressure "to speed up the awarding of important contributions that are relatively far back—and perhaps also in some cases of some elderly candidates provided they are regarded as very 'hot names'."[29] Prize-sharing can be a way of taking care of the backlog of worthies. Samuelson suggested that they might have given Robinson and Kalecki a joint prize, or given her a prize with Kaldor. "They could have given, very fairly, a prize for Robinson, Kaldor, and Harrod, whose work is all in the same line but is all distinct."[30]

Lindbeck denied that the politics of candidates was ever an issue. Using the prize-sharing of Myrdal and Hayek as an illustration, Lindbeck argued that "since the prize is conceived as a purely scientific award," the fact that the recipients are "often regarded as political 'antipoles' did not bother the committee." He also denied that the committee "was positively *attracted* by the idea of combining political antipoles."[31] Samuelson told me, "Now, giving a prize to Myrdal and Hayek—that's a bad joke, destined to make two people desperately unhappy. That's cheese and chalk."[32]

We can make a distinction between the politics of economics and politics per se. For these purposes, political differences are taken to be ideological differences. The politics of economics is another matter, and refers to the definition of the science and the identification of the basic theory. As Lindbeck noted, his view, and presumably that of the committee, is that the "General ('basic') Economic Theory" is "general equilibrium theory and welfare theory."[33] All could agree that Robinson did not even intend to make a specific contribution to general equilibrium theory. Whether the politics of economics carries over into politics per se is debatable. However, to show how far Robinson's work was from the temper of the Nobel committee in 1982 (her last chance), the speech by Lars Werin presenting the Nobel Prize to George Stigler can be quoted: Werin cites Stigler for

> . . . reintegrating basic theory with the actual market processes, and for clarifying the role of economic legislation. . . . Stigler . . . has built bridges between theory and facts . . . resolving seeming contradictions between them. In most cases, contradictions disappear if households' and firms' costs of obtaining information on market opportunities and adjusting to them are integrated into the theory. . . . The basic properties of the traditional theory thereby remain intact.

In other words, Stigler's special contribution was to preserve the traditional theory. Also mentioned by Werin was a hypothesis "proposed" by Stigler,

> . . . which, to paraphrase bluntly his own wording, reads: what you cannot achieve yourself, let the state do for you. . . . The extent of validity of this hypothesis is still unknown. . . . But reading between the lines of his recent writings, perhaps the hope may be discerned that the research which he has begun so successfully will also stimulate those engaged in politics to become more immune to external pressures."[34]

Perhaps some one of the natural scientists raised an eyebrow over an hypothesis not yet validated but only hoped for. There is more, but the reader can see that here was a reward for a person defending laissez-faire. Robinson persistently opposed it.

The national origin of the Nobel Laureates in economics is also of some interest, even though Nobel's will designated that it was to be ignored.

Table of National Origin

Scandinavian	Other European	UK	USA
1969 Frisch	Tinbergen		
1970			Samuelson
1971	(Kuznets)		Kuznets
1972		Hicks	Arrow
1973	(Leontief)		Leontief
1974 Myrdal	(Hayek)	Hayek	(Hayek)
1975	Kantorovich		
	(Koopmans)		Koopmans
1976			Friedman
1977 Ohlin		Meade	
1978			Simon
1979		Lewis	Schultz
1980			Klein
1981			Tobin
1982			Stigler

Kantorovich, inventor of linear programming, was a citizen of the Soviet Union. Leontief and Kuznets, though born in Russia, had careers in the United States, and Kuznets was educated in the United States. Hayek, first an Austrian economist, taught in both the United States and England. Of the two Dutch economists, Tinbergen and Koopmans, one calls the United States his home (Koopmans). Even Sir Arthur Lewis, who was born a British subject on St. Lucia Island, spent time at Princeton University during his long and varied career. So that eight of the twenty were American-born and five of the others had spent some important part of their careers in the United States. If any fact can demonstrate the dominance of American economics, this record does. Harvard, MIT, Princeton, Stanford, Pennsylvania, Carnegie Mellon, the University of California at Berkeley, and Yale scored, but Chicago came in with three (four, if you count Hayek). (Lindbeck counts Arrow as a Harvard laureate and scores Harvard three.)

England, once dominant in western economics, had only two laureates between 1969 and 1982—Hicks at Oxford and Meade at Cambridge. Neither of these were Keynes-Keynesians, though Meade was a member of the original Circus. Samuelson suggests that the committee has long

> . . . shown a little animus against the English. I think for example that there was resistance to giving Hicks the prize. He doesn't have footnotes; he doesn't acknowledge the work of other people, not excluding H. Wold's work, Wold being on the committee. Wold thought Norbert Wiener was a terrible person because he didn't acknowledge the work of all the mathematicians working on integrals, and this kind of stuff. And so I suspect that somebody like Lindbeck thought that the reswitching controversy was a tiresome methodological, secondary digression.[35]

As for politics in the ideological sense, Lewis and Myrdal were the only "social democrats." Hayek and Friedman were both founding members of the Mont Pelerin Society. George Stigler has been a member of Mont Pelerin, as was committee member Erik Lundberg. The one communist (Kantorovich) is a Russian mathematical economist. Certainly there were no western left-wingers.

Some economists I interviewed centered their remarks on either Joan Robinson's sex or her politics to explain her failure to win the prize. Even given the large number of economists who might qualify for a Nobel nomination, each person had either nominated her at some time or thought that she should have received the prize. The only question any raised was her own attitude toward her *Imperfect Competition*, which had been her most influential book on mainstream economics. On the one hand, it was written thirty-six years before there was a Nobel prize in economics. On the other, in the second edition in 1969, the year the Nobel was first offered to an economist, she had been highly critical of her own method. Leijonhufvud had heard when he was in Sweden that this might be a problem. Samuelson thought that her early work was so far back "that they kind of dropped some kind of statute of limitations, and they didn't seek to give Haberler a prize for his 1936 book on business cycles." Davidson thought it would have been embarrassing to the committee if she had received the prize on her *Imperfect Competition* "and some reporter read the second edition and found that she had received a Nobel Prize for everything that she disclaimed."

I checked the record on whether early work had qualified anyone. Though no one was awarded a prize solely on early work, their achievements before World War II were often mentioned in awarding speeches. In the award to Tinbergen and Frisch, it was noted that since the late twenties and early thirties they had been "working along the same lines." Hicks' *Value and Capital* (1939) was noted as having "breathed fresh life into general equilibrium theory." However, Hicks' *Theory of Wages* (1932) was not mentioned, and this is noteworthy, since Hicks' preface to a later edition revealed his puzzlement about the popularity of that book in America.

Leontief's dates for his early input-output models are not mentioned, but his

Structure of American Economy was published in 1941. Myrdal and Hayek were also cited as having done some pure economic research in the 1920s and 1930s before branching out to "other and wider" areas. Kantorovich invented linear programming in the 1930s, and Ohlin contributed to the development of international trade theory in the 1930s. The rest were younger men. The curiosity is not that Robinson did not win on *Imperfect Competition* but that many Americans continue to think of that as her only "specific achievement."[36]

Robinson's use of the literary as compared to the mathematical form must certainly have handicapped her (and Haberler too). When Bentzel made the awarding speech for Hicks, he said,

> Hicks used traditional differential analysis as a mathematical tool. When later more modern mathematical methods began to be introduced into economics, Arrow [who shared the prize with Hicks] used them to study the properties of general equilibrium systems.[37]

The fact was that *Accumulation*, coming as it did in the 1950s, still did not employ the "more modern mathematical methods."

Another black mark was possibly Robinson's constant criticism of orthodox theory. Schor heard that the committee thought of Robinson's work in her later years as "destructive." Indeed, in a statement which may have referred to Robinson, Lindbeck wrote,

> It is also clear that the prize awarding authority has tried to favor "constructive" contributions rather than contributions that are "destructive" in the sense of mainly launching criticism that does not lead anywhere. To provide "shoulders" on which other scholars can stand, and thus climb higher, has been favored over attempts to show that "everybody else" is wrong, or that the world is so complex that simple and coherent analytical structures are useless. Skillful polemics that do not seem to push research forward have not been regarded as worthy of being honored.[38]

But Schor thinks Robinson was passed over because she was a woman.

> If she had been a man, she would have been awarded a Nobel Prize. . . . Not only because she was a woman, but she was a particular type of woman and she was—like a man; she played hardball with them and no nonsense. . . . She didn't put on the social graces; it was a great game to her in some sense, a great intellectual game. . . . I don't say that in a bad sense, and she believed in it very deeply. You know, it was a great battle out there on an intellectual battleground. She played hard and I think they had trouble with that.[39]

Which raises the question of whether Robinson ever expected to receive the prize. She told at least one person that she would not accept it.[40]

Davidson thought he was able to talk her into the idea of accepting the money and using the platform. (She was on the short list at the time she visited Rutgers, so that newspaper reporters were calling Davidson to learn her background.) Eichner said, "It would be my fervent hope that she would never accept it." Robinson told Sol Adler, "I would rather have a grievance."[41]

Reading the record, one can infer Robinson's sins before the committee: she disowned the method in her early contributory work, *Imperfect Competition*; she worked diligently to undermine the hegemony of the central core of general equilibrium theory in all of her later work; she proposed another path in *Accumulation* but this path led nowhere as far as *mainstream* research programs are concerned (because it did not employ general equilibrium models); she engaged in the capital controversy which was also destructive of the central core of general equilibrium analysis, its complacency, and its methodology; she failed to use the latest mathematical techniques. Being a leftist, or what members of the Mont Pelerin Society are fond of calling "a Marxo-Keynesian," did not help. Being an unconventional woman did not ingratiate her. Perhaps Schor was right in saying that most men were a little afraid of Joan Robinson and her sharp tongue. The Nobel committee for choosing an economist is all male.

Samuelson suggested that Robinson would have or should have won a Nobel in the 1930s, sharing it with Chamberlin, but of course, there was no prize then.[42]

Lindbeck stated that the selection committee had "relied entirely on *qualitative judgment.*" Quantitative judgments such as the frequency of citations had never been considered. Yet he seemed pleased that the prize-winners usually ranked high on citation indices. He conceded that several had not: Kantorovich, Stone, Meade, and Ohlin. Lindbeck referred to Richard Quandt's study of citations in eight leading journals (five American, two British, and one international journal—*Econometrica*).[43] In 1976, Quandt reported that, with the exception of Myrdal and Kantorovich, all the prize winners had appeared at least once on his lists of the twenty most frequently cited economists. Quandt added, "If frequency of appearance on the lists is any guide toward predicting Nobel prize winners, the top candidates for a prize in the near future are R. F. Harrod and J. Robinson (3) and then, with two appearances each and in alphabetical order, W. J. Baumol, M. Friedman, G. Haberler, H. G. Johnson, L. R. Klein, F. Machlup, R. Solow, and G. Stigler."[44]

That Joan Robinson never won the Nobel Prize is mainly a reflection of the kind of economics which has been dominant in the profession and within the selection committee since the prize was initiated in 1968. Leijonhufvud doubted whether there was anyone in Sweden to argue for a Cambridge Keynesian, and as the record shows, no Cambridge Keynesian has been awarded a Nobel Prize.[45]

Some American views of Robinson's influence[46]

From 1933, the year *The Economics of Imperfect Competition* was published, until her death, Joan Robinson's influence was worldwide. To this day, any well-trained North American economist will know of her *Imperfect Competition* along with Chamberlin's *Monopolistic Competition*. But what if neither book, as Lester Telser has argued, had any impact on mainstream economics? More likely Samuelson is correct, and imperfect competition for the economic theorist is like oxygen to the living, "ever present . . . absorbed in the screen of science that has a lasting value."

How say we of all her Keynesian articles and books? The *Journal of Post Keynesian Economics* and the *Cambridge Journal of Economics* signal that this part of her work goes on.

What of her *Essay on Marxian Economics?* Solow thinks that this essay "could only have had an impact on people who might otherwise have fallen for Marxian economics," but it remains a much discussed benchmark of responsible opposition among the Marxists. Robinson's writing on Marx telegraphed her realization that not all good economics was made at Cambridge. After the war, her interest in political economy and in the classical problem of economic growth became ever more evident. And, of course, it opened up to her contacts with American Marxists and associates of the *Monthly Review* and political economists everywhere. For example, Alex Erlich, one of the immigrants, used her texts at Columbia University. This nourished a group of younger faculty at Columbia who were very receptive to her. Hewlett said that in the 1960s,

> . . . there was a sort of rotating pool of assistant professors, none of whom had tenure because Columbia did not admire this kind of work. . . . Still, there was always this little community of disciples that turned up whenever she was in New York. They might not be dominant at senior levels of research universities, but they were there. And she was greatly admired by them as a kind of mentor and entirely courageous intellectual power. They liked her kind of fire and spirit and they also liked her kind of irreverence for established theory.

So Robinson's influence thereafter reached beyond the mainstream to economists who agreed with her or at least made common cause with her against the tenets of neoclassical economics.

Still, what she wanted was to redirect that mainstream toward the Cambridge view. In her effort to generalize the General Theory, following Harrod's lead, she painstakingly argued and discussed with her colleagues the meaning of economic growth, and produced her *Accumulation of Capital* and *Essays in the Theory of Growth*. These books clearly addressed those she and others at Cambridge thought were in the mainstream, since it was not yet obvious to her how American Keynesians differed from Cantabrigians.

At the time of its publication, *The Accumulation of Capital* (1956) was an important work. (Eichner thought it the most important work of the twentieth century.) Davidson was in Weintraub's class, which worked through the volume. H. Uzawa taught it at Chicago and later at Stanford. Leijonhufvud thought that it was read by everybody. Clower thought it was very popular and widely used at the time.

At the same time two patterns developed, both of which weakened Robinson's influence. One was that younger people, trained in Walrasian economics and econometrics, began to produce their own growth models which had very little relation to Robinson's. The other pattern was that American theoretical economists began to lose interest in economic development. Leijonhufvud said, "When growth theory went out of fashion, then Joan Robinson went out of fashion." Clower remarked, "The whole subject was dying when her book came out." In other words, when the mainstream rejected the classical problems of economic development, growth, and the distribution of income, working instead in purely mathematical aspects of these problems, there was no longer any reason for American economists to ponder Robinson's difficult book on the accumulation of capital.

Leijonhufvud remembers this period when the capital controversy was ongoing. He told me,

> It didn't look that serious. It was Cambridge U.K. which insisted that it was serious, that it was fundamental, and that it went all the way down into foundations, this cleavage. But for most of us who went to graduate school it did not as yet look that way. So you had Joan's *Accumulation*, and you had Kaldor's growth model in the same breath with Hicks', Goodwin's, Solow's and the rest of the models. I can see it in retrospect: I came to understand it much later. I think I understand why Joan Robinson in the late 1950s suddenly got outraged with the way Keynesianism was going in the United States. And she decided that Solow's growth model was the cardinal sin. And from her own standpoint she was right.
>
> It has to do with the interest rate. . . . She and Kahn, and maybe they taught it to Keynes, had this model in which the interest rate mechanism couldn't coordinate saving and investment. . . . Adjustment had to come in income. . . . Now up until Solow and company started to get into growth theory, I think that when you sat in Cambridge, England, and looked at the American scene from afar it looked great. . . . Cambridge economics had been taught to the heathens in faraway countries and they were all saved. And these people called themselves Keynesians and they advocated Keynesian policies . . . and it all looked as if it was all right.
>
> And then Solow produced; out of the heart of these American Keynesians comes this model where saving governs investment. From Joan's standpoint that was fundamentally wrong, and nobody who believed that could possibly be a Keynesian. There must be something completely wrong here.

This was when she began calling them the "bastard Keynesians." Leijonhufvud continued, "I don't think that Solow ever understood that. Cambridge, Mass. people always thought that the vehemence in the position of Joan Robinson was unreasonable and they couldn't see why this was important. But Joan didn't really put it in that way. She got off on aggregation,'' that is, the measurement of capital.

Thus *Accumulation* was, for the mainstream, lost in the shuffle of the capital controversy and the burgeoning influence of mathematical models on the one hand, and the loss of interest in the problem of economic development on the other. The reason Eichner thought *Accumulation* so important was because it synthesized Harrod's growth dynamics, Keynes' theories of effective demand, and Kalecki's theories of income distribution, as well as Kalecki's version of the General Theory which includes imperfect competition. In other words, it incorporates all of the Cambridge tradition.

Since *Accumulation* is a difficult book, and the *Essays in the Theory of Economic Growth* not much easier, and since there is a lack of serious and continuing interest in growth, American economists have neglected these books in recent years. Economic growth and development are still important concerns elsewhere. Sylvia Hewlett, who does work in development, said,

> You know, if you go to a campus in Brazil, you will find people who have heard about Joan Robinson, ordinary undergraduates who know her name. At MIT, I'm not sure that people know the name. In other words, in different third world universities, Robinson's work is taught as an important theoretical influence and part of this whole endeavor to understand the whole colonial world. She is part of the international heritage that undergraduates would have been taught. That isn't true in the United States.[47]

Thus wherever economic growth is a subject, Joan Robinson's influence is felt.

Economic Philosophy was taken more seriously by Americans than Robinson meant it to be, and it remains one of her most influential works. Clower felt that it had a ''very strong impact. She has a line in there where there is no agreed procedure for knocking out doctrine so it has a very long life, and it's quoted again and again. A lot of people read that book. There are all kinds of nuggets of truth in it, deep insights into how we do economics.''

Though Robinson's and Eatwell's textbook presents an expert introduction to the Cambridge tradition, it cannot be said to have had much influence in North America, in part because there was no American edition. However, it was used on a few campuses in both the United States and Canada. Robinson's *Collected Economic Papers* also include several of her major theoretical articles, but are not widely studied.

Joan Robinson's traceable influence on *mainstream* economics after World War II thus may be slight, while her influence on other economists is very great. Solow elaborated:

> Here is someone who spent her whole life at the center of the oral tradition. I think she was a vast influence on generations of economists at Cambridge and

would have been if she had never written a word, just lectured and taught. But what I do think it is fair to say is that she has been far more influential in India and Italy than in the United States or the United Kingdom. Even the U.K., except as icon. There are lots of people who will tell you that Joan was absolutely right in everything she said, but you will not find a trace of her work in their work.

The important point is that Joan Robinson is influential wherever economists are interested in the kind of science she practiced. If one insists on an assumption of perfect competition, then *Imperfect Competition* is not important. If you exclude policy or politics from consideration, if you think of economic development as outside scientific economics, then none of her work on growth and development is important. If you are comfortable with the problem-limiting methodology required to build a mathematical model, then her questions about methodology are unimportant. Arjo Klamer, who had studied in Holland, was amazed to find his teachers in the United States enamored of abstract theory which employed the assumption of rational behavior. "When I suggested that the assumption is absurd, as I had been taught before, I was told that I did not understand economics. 'Did you ever read Friedman's essay on Positive Economics'? they would ask. 'Well, if you do, then you will understand that the realism of an assumption does not matter'."[48]

Joan Robinson must have troubled some of the true ideologues among American economists. They could not say she did not understand economics; they could not say that she did not know the boundaries of the science. They could only say that she did not know mathematics. And Stigler said she was a "logician." Yet if one read her works, it was impossible to allege that she lacked rigor in thinking. How can we account for her work having been slighted on many American university campuses, and for the monetarists' having arranged a competing address, presumably in order to avoid her Ely lecture, in New Orleans? Perhaps the silent treatment is one version of killing the messenger. In Robinson's case, in the long run, this will not work.

The problems of underdevelopment, growth, and income distribution are with us, and the Cambridge tradition, as was true in the case of Keynes' General Theory, offers an alternative not only to neoclassical formulations but also to those of Marx. As such, Robinson's work marks a true advance which cannot be totally lost except in some holocaust of history. Samuelson summarized some of her contributions:

First, she brought together, summarized, and synthesized in *Imperfect Competition* the discussion of the cost controversy that went on from 1922 on in England and America until 1933. She was a contributor to and an expositor of the early Keynesian system, particularly the international trade aspects of the early Keynesian system. She recognized the stagflation problem early: she already adverts to it in the book which came out about 1937 (the two books); she made an absolutely novel point (it had to be novel at that date) that when exchange rates depreciate, it doesn't necessarily worsen the terms of trade of the depreciating country, because if you look at it as export goods and import goods, there are four prices to look at . . . and then how do you know the ratio moves in any systematic way. . . . It was a minor point but a major insight. That was the kind of thing she did very well.

For all her popularity with students, Robinson was an economists' economist, theorist par excellence whose influence is difficult to trace because it occurred on the level of high theory where she dwelled. However, her early work was more influential in America than her generalization of the General Theory. And a part of the explanation is that American mainstream economics took a different path from Cambridge economics after World War II, preparing the ground for what Hewlett called "the sparring between schools of thought rather than a personal vendetta."

What is a useful image of Robinson's role in the development of economic thought? Earlier, I pictured her in an English garden, inventing tools to root out unwanted growths. Not a bad image for one who began as a "toolmaker" and in her last residency in the United States at Williams College, "planted a few seeds" which she hoped Juliet Schor would water. Using this image, one could conclude that Robinson's desire to influence American mainstream economics was frustrated because the world of economics after World War II was no longer an English garden. Furthermore, the tools themselves had changed so that mathematics was more important.

Others might have us believe that she was a Don Quixote, tilting with the sturdy windmill of neoclassical thought. She did struggle; but her efforts, though adversarial, were seriously intellectual. We must look to the philosophy of science to help us to understand her role.

Putnam's image of the boat under construction while at sea is helpful.* We can visualize Joan Robinson, shoving off from the mud of static equilibrium, attempting to sign on new crew from among numerous Americans, hailing the neoclassical boat and passing tools and insults back and forth, setting her own course on the uncharted waters with determination. Her boat is floating, sailing on, even without Robinson at the helm, scheduled to make port wherever political economics is welcome.

---

*See Introduction.

JR

APPENDIX

The notes in the Appendix provide background material on some of the subjects touched upon in the course of this book.

[For complete citations, refer by author and year to References. Abbreviations used are *CEP*: Joan Robinson's *Collected Economic Papers* and *JMK: The Collected Writings of John Maynard Keynes.*]

Chapter 1.1 **English economists and women's rights**

Women's rights had been an issue among some educated people, including notable economists, both in the nineteenth and twentieth centuries. In 1851, John Stuart Mill signed a famous document renouncing the rights which the law conferred on him over the "person, property and freedom of action" of Harriet Taylor, his new wife. But not all economists were as sympathetic to women's aspirations as Mill had been. In 1896 Alfred Marshall voted against full admission of women to Cambridge, an act that disappointed many in his circle, according to Keynes, for Marshall had otherwise been active in women's causes [*JMK* 10:220]. In 1921, the issue of the full admission of women's colleges to Cambridge University was again debated. The economists A. C. Pigou (otherwise known as a misogynist) and J. M. Keynes were among those 2,329 men supporting the right of full admission for women. But there were 3,213 votes against, and full rights for women at Cambridge had to wait until 1948.

Chapter 1.2 **Cambridge department of economics in 1921**

When Joan Maurice entered Cambridge, the department of economics included Gerald Shove (thirty-one years old), Alfred Marshall's nephew Claude Guillebaud (thirty-one), Maynard Keynes (thirty-eight)—so-called in Cambridge circles partly to distinguish him from his father J. N. Keynes, who was still Bursar of Pembroke—and Walter Layton, who was given a lectureship the same year as Keynes. Demobilization after World War I had brought back to the department not only Keynes from the Treasury and from his adventures in Versailles, but A. C. Pigou (forty-four) from ambulance driving, D. H. Robertson (thirty-one), who had been decorated in the Middle East fighting, and Austin Robinson, who had been an aviator. There were others in political science, but these were the economists remembered by Austin Robinson as central to the department of those days [Patinkin and Leith 1978:25–33].

Chapter 1.3 **Cambridge courses for students reading economics**

The Cambridge University *Reporter* for 1921 listed the "Lectures Intended for Candidates for the Economics Tripos Part I" as Mr. Robertson, Trinity, General Economics; Mr. Florence, Caius, Industry and Labour; Dr. Clapham, King's, English Economic History; Mr. Guillebaud, St. John's, Trade and Finance; Mr. Benians, St. John's, Recent Economic and General History of the USA; Mr. Lavington, Emmanuel, Structure and Problems in India; Mr. Shove, King's, Distribution and Labour; Mr. Henderson, Arts School, Money Credit and Prices; Mr. J. M. Keynes, Arts School, Realistic Monetary Problems; Mr. Butler, Trinity, Political Science; Mr. Passant, Sidney Sussex, Political Theory; Mr. Simpson, Trinity, Political Science; Mr. P. J. Baker, Effect of League of Nations; Mr. Yule, St. John's, Theory of Statistics. Certain "fee courses" were also offered, one being Professor Pigou's lectures in "Principles of Economics" and in "Public Finance." There would be no record of which of these lectures Joan Maurice attended, but we do know that of this list, the persons most helpful and influential in her early career were Pigou, Shove, Guillebaud, and Keynes.

Chapter 2.1 **Becoming a professional**

While Joan Robinson was developing her system of imperfect competition, she was also participating in the Circus and bearing children. As she lightheartedly remarked to a friend, "It is so much easier for a woman to be creative. All she has to do is bear a child."

The three articles published in this early period were: "Imperfect Competition and Falling Supply Price" [1932b]; "A Parable of Saving and Investment" [1933b]; and "The Theory of Money and the Analysis of Output" [1933c]; These articles are discussed in Chapter 4. Before she began lecturing in the fall of 1934, her fourth article, "What is Perfect Competition?" had been accepted by Harvard's *Quarterly Journal of Economics* [1934b]. Most important, her *Economics of Imperfect Competition* was published in 1933, a year before she was made an Assistant Lecturer. Austin Robinson expressed some regret that he had not really appreciated Joan Robinson as an economist in those early years. He thought that perhaps his being on the staff as lecturer actually delayed her being given that status [Interview].

Chapter 2.2 **Dedication of *Economics is a Serious Subject***

[JRP, KCA. The parenthetical references are mine.] The dedication was as follows:

"ACP—The first serious economist—with the gratitude of all [Pigou].

JMK—To the optimist who showed that optimism can be justified [Keynes].

GFS—To the English pessimist who beat them at their own game [Shove].

HM—To the pessimist who likes facts, with the apologies of an optimist.

CA—To the economist who knew it all, but never said so.

PS—To the pessimist who knew he could not trust us and asked the technique [Sraffa].

Mo T-H—To the economist who thinks that the shield is white [Tappan-Hollond].

RFK, EAGR—To the co-optimists and the optimistic pessimists and all serious economists [Kahn and AR].

MHAN—And to the pure mathematicians whose sympathy and well-deserved contempt had had a beneficial effect on the serious economist."

Chapter 3.1 **Reviews of *The Economics of Imperfect Competition***

Imperfect Competition was reviewed promptly in December 1933 in the *Economic Journal* by Shove, and in the *American Economic Review* by Corwin D. Edwards of New York University. However, Edwards' was a double review of Robinson's *Imperfect Competition* and Chamberlin's *Monopolistic Competition*. In the United States the two books were thereafter grouped together.

Shove [1933:660–661] praised the book "written by one of the younger generation of economists, who has worked in close contact with others." But he found it "surprisingly . . . disappointingly—conservative," by which he meant that the general approach and method of treatment were on established lines. He termed it "almost . . . an essay in geometrical political economy," even though the time had arrived "when we must leave our diagrams behind." Shove noted that "it is significant that Mrs. Robinson has been obliged to 'call in the assistance of a mathematician to provide certain proofs' based on the calculus of variations." (An American reviewer, A. J. Nichol [1934], also objected that Robinson had made difficult by using geometry what would have been easy with calculus.) Shove complained of her being "too prone to attribute fallacies to other writers on insufficient grounds."

Edwards' joint review [1934:688–690] recognized both books as representing a "new approach to value theory." He found them to be complementary rather than competitive. Robinson's book culminated in "a theory of the exploitation of labor by virtue of the imperfection of the market." Chamberlin omitted the analysis of distribution but "includes studies of differentiation of products and the significance of selling costs, both of which were skipped by Mrs. Robinson." As an institutionalist, Edwards was pleased with the prospect that "the general acceptance of imperfect market theories by the neo-classicists must change the issues in controversy between them and their critics." He found "little food in these books for the mild complacency of the theorists of perfect competition."

Nicholas Kaldor [1934:335–341], then at the London School of Economics but later a Cambridge colleague, wrote a review which, while not wholly laudatory, was to become Joan Robinson's own view regarding her work. The cogent points that Kaldor made were those that she later conceded to Chamberlin and to the profession. Kaldor wrote: (1) that *Imperfect Competition* was "ultra-Marshallian" in method: "In a sense, it represents the ultimate logical outcome of the Marshallian method"; (2) that she had neglected some of the more interesting problems, especially duopoly; (3) that her concept of "industry" was faulty; (4) that her book was really a treatise on monopoly rather than one on "imperfect competition"; and (5) that her demand curve concept relied on an assumption of perfect knowledge.

On the other hand, Kaldor praised her major thrust, saying, "the unrealistic assumptions in regard to the nature of competition form one of the main deficiencies of the traditional theory of value." He felt that her most valuable results were those which showed that the marginal productivity theory of the distribution of income relied on an assumption of perfect competition. Neither Kaldor nor Robinson ever changed their positions on this fundamental issue.

For the Chicago *Journal of Political Economy*, Joseph Schumpeter [1934:249–257] began by noting that the case of perfect competition was of fundamental importance, and even with its faults he saw it as an "almost indispensable background with which to compare . . . any other situation." He took a swing at the institutionalists: "In view of the fact that some of our institutionalist friends are still known to harbor a belief that a typical theorist believes in free competition as a fact, or still worse, that he 'advocates' it, it may even not be superfluous to point out that the theory of free competition is the only avenue to a rational theory of planning and of centralistic socialism." He was cognizant of the implications of imperfect competition and added, "we owe substantial progress to the works of all the theorists of imperfect competition, among whom Mrs. Robinson in this book establishes a claim, certainly to a leading, and perhaps to the first, place." This was generous, particularly when it is recognized that Chamberlin was Schumpeter's colleague at Harvard.

Later, in his *History of Economic Analysis*, Schumpeter [1954:1150–1151] said that Chamberlin's achievement sprang "without any warning, fully armed from Professor E. H. Chamberlin's head in 1933." Schumpeter called Chamberlin's *Monopolistic Competition* "one of the most successful books in theoretical economics that the period since 1918 has produced,'' and made a case for Chamberlin's having pulled off "a striking instance of subjective and objective originality.'' Frederick Jennings reminded me that Schumpeter must have known that Chamberlin was working on his theory earlier. This passage was probably part of the notes incorporated by his editors in his history after Schumpeter's death.

Schumpeter argued that *Imperfect Competition* lived up to the "standard of rigor set by the author in a pamphlet entitled *Economics is a Serious Subject.*" In his review, Schumpeter said, "As in the case of E. H. Chamberlin's book, the delay in publication has deprived it of some of the formal claims to priority which it would otherwise have had. . . ." But he thought that "Mrs. Robinson's genuine originality stands out from the whole perhaps better than it would if her book stood alone.''

Chapter 4.1 **Chamberlin's** *Monopolistic Competition*

When Edward Hastings Chamberlin wrote in a just-off-the-press copy of *The Theory of Monopolistic Competition*, "At last! With love to Mother from Edward, February 18, 1933,'' he must have been a singularly happy man. He had proposed the subject for a Ph.D. thesis as early as 1921, when he was a student at the University of Michigan.*

The young Chamberlin had sounded out his "beloved *maître,*" Professor Fred M. Taylor, but Taylor discouraged him about the topic, advising him to look for something else. However, at Harvard, Chamberlin received more encouragement from Allyn Young. There, under Young's direction, Chamberlin began in 1924—after taking the "generals,'' which are comprehensive examinations leading to, or in many cases, blocking the way to a doctorate. This became his thesis in 1927 and his book in 1933.

For his thesis, Chamberlin took great pains to study real markets and market processes, consulting what he called "the literature of business,'' including studies of advertising which he considered "a *necessary* part of the hybrid theory I was trying to write.'' One of the major differences in the writing of his *Monopolistic Competition* in comparison with Robinson's *Imperfect Competition* can be seen in the bibliography of this thesis.

Chamberlin's bibliography was divided into four sections: I. General Works and Journal Articles on Principles and Theory, including mainly English, French, Austrian, and American writers. II. The Theory of Duopoly (including Cournot). III. Books and Articles on Business Economics (including many articles from industry journals such as *Printer's Ink* and certain bulletins from

---

*His mother's copy is among his personal files. For the development of his thesis, see Schumpeter [1954:1150n] and Chamberlin's "The Early Development of Monopolistic Competition Theory,'' which is included in later editions of *Monopolistic Competition*.

business and government research). IV. The economic and legal literature of patents and trade marks.

Schumpeter [1954:1150–1151n] called the book "a striking instance of subjective and objective originality—and of originality of the purely theoretical type that owed nothing to 'the collection of direct empirical evidence'." This admiring comment can be taken as a jibe at any institutionalist yearning for an inductive rather than a deductive method, but I am not certain that it properly describes Chamberlin's method. Apparently, Schumpeter thought the preferred procedure was to achieve a theoretical breakthrough without the collection of data. Yet Chamberlin's account of the early development of his theory, and the very bibliography of Chamberlin's thesis and first edition, suggest that he made strenuous efforts to collect evidence for his theory. Schumpeter seems to have given credit for originality, but not for the tremendous scholarship which went into Chamberlin's thesis.

When Chamberlin wrote that happy note to his mother, what he did not know was that Keynes had recommended a similar book to Macmillan for publication, and that Joan Robinson's *Economics of Imperfect Competition* would appear within a few months to share his claim to fame.

Chapter 4.2 **Successive editions of Chamberlin's** *Monopolistic Competition*

Chamberlin continued to provide new materials, his own and bibliographical references, in successive editions. The evolving characteristics in each new edition reflect changes which occurred in economics and society over the period of their appearance, 1933 to 1962. The flyleaf reviews of the first edition were taken from *Journal of Business, American Federationist* (publication of the American Federation of Labor), and the *Journal of the Royal Economics Society.* By 1958, the flyleaf was closer to home, with comments by colleagues J. A. Schumpeter and J. K. Galbraith of Harvard and Jane Aubert-Krier of France, whom Chamberlin knew personally.

The second edition in 1936 added the subtitle, "A Reorientation of the Theory of Value," which remained through the subsequent editions. The bibliography, already vast, continued to grow with new sections on the controversies surrounding the theory. The first edition sold for $2.50 and the eighth sold in 1985 for $27.50. The book was translated into four languages: French; two editions in Spanish; Italian; and one edition in Japanese. The sales of English editions from 1933 to 1963 were, by five-year periods: 1938—3161 copies; 1943—4275 copies; 1948—8368 copies; 1953—9294 copies; 1958—6609 copies; and 1963—11,155 copies, plus 505 free copies and more than 6000 copies in the French and Spanish translations. The 1953 French translator was Guy Trancart, with a preface and introduction by François Perroux. The 1946 Spanish translators were Christobal Lara Beautell and Victor L. Urquidi. A second edition was produced in both Mexico and Buenos Aires in 1956. The Italian translation was of the seventh edition published in 1961, and the Japanese was the eighth edition. Although undated (at least in numerals readable by me), it must have been published after 1962, when the eighth English edition was produced.

Thus in Chamberlin's lifetime, he saw the sales of his book grow year by year. There was certainly no reason why he should not have continued to try to improve on this basic work. In the fifth edition, he added as Chapter IX a revision of his article, "The Difference between Monopolistic and 'Imperfect' Competition." In the preface (p. vii) he deplored the state of the argument as of December 1945: "It has been unfortunate that two theories as divergent in their interpretation of economic phenomena as Mrs. Robinson's and my own should have become identified in the minds of so many, even to the point of regarding them as differing only in terminology." He admitted to having at first "followed this line of least resistance." But "gradually it dawned that the explanation lay in a difference, not merely of words, but of fundamental conception as to how the phenomena in question were to be explained. The evidence that Mrs. Robinson's theory was *not* a blend of monopoly and competition revealed itself bit by bit. . ."(p. viii). He never changed his opinion that this was the nub of the question. In the eighth and last edition, he added the "Origin and Early Development of Monopolistic Competition Theory" as Appendix H. (This had appeared in the *Quarterly Journal of Economics*, November 1961.)

Chapter 5.1 **Other reviews of *Introduction* and *Essays in the Theory of Employment***

American reviewers tended to pick one essay from Robinson's collection and review that. For example, E. M. Bernstein [1937:254] particularly liked Robinson's "An Economist's Sermon," where it is "proven" that "economics is the dope of the religious people."

Americans also fell in with Keynes' definition of the "classics" as including Marshall and Pigou. For example, in the *American Economic Review,* Charles O. Hardy [1937:531] of the Brookings Institution limited himself to analyzing the fifth essay, "The Long Period Theory of Employment," commenting that the "chief difference between the classical doctrine and the Keynes doctrine as interpreted by Mrs. Robinson, is not in the logic of either system; it is in divergent initial assumptions as to the real nature of saving."

Hardy [1938:528–529] also reviewed her *Introduction.* He repeated his opinion that "whereas the classical doctrine rests on assumptions that are appropriate to a boom, the 'general theory of employment' assumes as normal the conditions which exist in a depression."

Selig Perlman [1937:1191], reviewing the *Essays* for political scientists, identified the author as "Miss Joan Robinson, . . the most outstanding disciple of Professor J. Maynard Keynes, whose questioning of the very basis of the classical theory has made him in the past six years the center of all discussion in Anglo-American economics.''

Finally, someone who knew both Joan Robinson and Keynesian economics reviewed the two works together for the *Canadian Journal of Economics and Political Science*. Lorie Tarshis [1938:585–587], still at Tufts, thought her *Introduction* was successful in presenting the General Theory clearly and accurately. His only regret was that she had not given much attention to the relationship between Keynes' theory and the classical theory. The *Essays* were addressed principally to the expert economist. He found two of these particularly important: "Disguised Unemployment" and "The Long Period Theory of Employment." (The latter was the same essay selected by Hardy in his review.)

P. T. Ellsworth [1938:730], then at the University of Cincinnati but later at the University of Wisconsin, welcomed the *Introduction* "as a prolegomena and companion piece to the *General Theory*."

The *Introduction* occasioned widespread interest among laymen as well as economists. Reviews were published in *The Nation* magazine and the *Annals of the American Academy*. For *The Nation*, Keith Hutchison [1938:652] reviewed *Introduction to the Theory of Employment* jointly with a book by "an engineer turned economist." Hutchison said, "Today we still find it difficult to grasp the fact that savings are no longer the controlling factor in promoting investment (meaning additions to new capital)." It was in this idea that he found the "heart of the General Theory."

E. Wight Bakke [1938:230] of Yale reviewed *Introduction* for the *Annals of the American Academy*. Since the book did not deal with factual events, Bakke found it "of limited usefulness for the student of theory" and of little if any value to the layman unaccustomed to following the intricacies of monetary theory. He concluded: "It is very definitely a student's handbook, and not a primer in the interpretation of employment fluctuations and not for those uninitiated into the vocabulary and habits of thought of the professional economist."

The *Economic Journal* review of *Introduction* was by Henry Smith [1938:74–76] of Oxford who refused "to attack a vulnerable position voluntarily adopted." Smith saw the parent work of Keynes as "an attempt to reduce to manageable dimensions the complex phenomena of general equilibrium." He recommended Robinson's book "without qualification to students, lay or professional, and most especially to those contemplating letters to *The Times* on the subject of public works!"

Chapter 6.1 Immigrants bring continental economics to the United States

Fortunately for the interested reader, Earlene Craver [1986 and 1987] and Axel Leijonhufvud have begun publishing from their study of the post-1930s continental influence on economics in America. They claim that the influence of the immigrants touched every field in economics and, I would add, methodological orientation as well. In selecting those few of the immigrants who came in direct contact with Joan Robinson, I do not wish to suggest that there was any uniformity of views among even this group. For example, Abba Lerner and Paul Baran, who wrote reviews of her work, were very different from each other in their economics.

Two points can be made. First, the immigrants were powerful in pushing American economists toward a narrower definition of economics, that is, away from the political economy with which Cambridge was comfortable. For example, Schumpeter thought political economy too vague a boundary. Second, there was a shove toward mathematical theory by at least some of the Europeans, Leontief for one. What was perhaps most important for economics in general was where the immigrants settled to do their work and whether their adopted university was an established center of influence.

The immigrants included Joseph Schumpeter (b. Hungary 1883–1950, Harvard 1932–50); Wassily Leontief (b. Russia 1906, Harvard 1936–1975, Nobel Prize 1973, New York University 1975-); Abba Lerner (b. Russia 1903–1982, University of Kansas City 1940–42, Roosevelt University, Chicago 1947–59, University of California at Berkeley 1965–71, Distinguished Professor of Economics Queens College, City University of New York 1971–78, Florida State University 1978–82); Friedrich A. von Hayek (b. Austria 1899, London School of Economics 1931–1950, University of Chicago 1950–1962, University of Freiburg in West Germany 1962–68, University of Salzburg 1968–1977, Nobel Prize 1974); Oskar Lange (b. Poland 1904–1965, University of Michigan 1936–43, University of Chicago 1943–45, Warsaw University 1955–65). Each of these touched Joan Robinson's life in some way.

Which of these immigrants influenced American economics? One was surely Schumpeter. In his position at Harvard, he became a teacher of the future leaders of the profession. His *History of Economic Analysis,* published posthumously (1954), is a compendium of his ideas. His course in advanced economic theory at Harvard stressed economic analysis, including Walrasian equilibrium theory. He also taught courses dealing with business cycles and money. Schumpeter, according to Samuelson, "had planned a great work on money, a full German tome, and Keynes uncharacteristically wrote such a thing." (This was Keynes' *Treatise on Money.*) Schumpeter's work was not published until 1970, twenty years after his death, and only now is being translated. He was believed by his students to be jealous of Keynes, probably because of this [Patinkin and Leith 1978:88–89].

In the summers of the 1930s, Schumpeter would go to Europe and visit Cambridge on the way, going or coming. There he would seek out Richard Kahn and the Robinsons and catch up on what theoretical developments had taken place during the previous year.

Another important immigrant was Wassily Leontief, who began teaching at Harvard in 1936. Like Schumpeter, Leontief influenced several generations of Harvard students, at least two of whom—Paul Samuelson and Robert Solow—are Nobel laureates. James Tobin had Schumpeter as his thesis adviser; Samuelson

[1972:xv] cited both Schumpeter and Leontief as responsible for "prolonged stimulation over many years." Leontief was, for Robert Solow [Klamer 1984:128], "the most important teacher I had." As late as 1947, Leontief was, according to Solow, "the only mathematical or rigorous economist at Harvard."

Also at Harvard was Gottfried Haberler, born in Austria and teaching at Harvard from 1937–71. His work on business cycles was at odds with Keynes', so that Haberler was considered an opponent of Keynesian economics [Klamer 1984:256].

Jacob Marschak (1898–1977) was, like Leontief, born in Russia. Initially he taught at the New School of Social Research in New York City, which was a popular and welcoming place for intellectual refugees in the late thirties and early forties. There Marschak, again like Leontief, emphasized the importance of mathematics and econometrics—"something that was quite unusual at that time" [Franco Modigliani in Klamer 1984:115]. Other distinguished immigrants trained as mathematical economists were John von Neumann, Oskar Morgenstern, Nicholas Georgescu-Roegen, and Leonid Hurwicz.

The one of these immigrants who was a personal friend to Joan Robinson was Oskar Lange, who had spent some time in Cambridge. Melvin Reder [1982:4] said Lange's appointment at the University of Chicago met several departmental needs.

> Lange was an up-to-the-minute young theorist in the vanguard of the Keynesian Revolution who had acquired a considerable reputation as a mathematical economist as the result of studies in the theory of capital and in utility theory. His work on the use of the price system to allocate resources in a socialist economy was widely considered to be a definitive answer to the Mises-Hayek attack on the economic efficiency of socialism and gave the Chicago department a leading participant in this debate.

Reder added that Lange "had a fully developed perspective of economics which constituted a distinct alternative to the 'Chicago View'." However, Lange resigned from Chicago in 1945 to become Ambassador from Poland to the United States.

New York City was a great attraction to immigrants. Modigliani, who immigrated from Italy in 1939, was present at a very distinguished seminar attended by Oskar Lange, Tjalling Koopmans, Abraham Wald, and Abba Lerner, all of whom had immigrated from Europe. Tjalling Koopmans (b. 1910, Holland), taught at the University of Chicago (1947–55) and then at Yale after 1961 until he retired. An econometrician, Koopmans won a Nobel Prize in 1975. Abraham Wald (b. 1902, Romania), who was a mathematical statistician, taught at Columbia University 1938–50. Abba Lerner was first a Trotskyite, then Hayekian, and later Keynesian. Of the immigrants who touched Joan Robinson's life in one way or another, then, three—Leontief, Marschak, and Lange—were mathematical theorists or econometricians. Three others—Schumpeter, Haberler, and Lerner—were not. According to Harcourt [1985:412], "Schumpeter, who had no mathematics, said that if Richard Goodwin would give a math course, he would attend [at Harvard]; so Goodwin gave a course on math and cycle theory to which Schumpeter, Haberler, and three or four others came."

Since 1948, when Schumpeter was elected president of the American Economic Association, ten of the presidents have been of European birth, eight being established scholars before coming to the United States. Inevitably, the importation of continental economists of such distinction had an impact, first on the Ivy League schools, then on Chicago, and eventually on all of American economics. Axel Leijonhufvud, himself an immigrant, thinks that in the late 1930s, "of the top of the American economic profession, more than half were immigrants." In spite of the great influence of immigrants, Leijonhufvud [Interview] was not willing to speculate on how much this migration affected American economic analysis. He said that Samuelson's and Friedman's generation was about to come up, "and they would have done pretty much the same thing they did in any case." Paul Samuelson had conceived and written most of his *Foundations* in 1937. However, Samuelson [Interview] does acknowledge a debt to Schumpeter, Haberler, and Leontief, as well as to to E. B. Wilson and Abram Bergson (A. Burk). In part because of the strong influence of these immigrants, American economics could not develop the way Cambridge economics did, even though Cambridge had its own immigrants, namely Sraffa, Kalecki briefly, and Kaldor.

Chapter 6.2 **Mathematical theory at Cambridge before World War II**

At Cambridge, reliance on mathematics in economic theorizing was considered guileful, somehow a substitute for thinking; hence Joan Robinson's remark that not knowing mathematics, she had to think. Samuelson [Patinkin and Leith 1978:73] relates a story that Keynes had warned Sidney Alexander "against the insidious disease of mathematics, that there was absolutely nothing in that sort of nonsense, and that he should not waste his time with it."

Lorie Tarshis [Ibid.] recorded the same warning in his notes taken from Keynes' lectures:

> He [Keynes] spent half a lecture once on it. He felt that the stuff of economics was not sharp or precise, and it was too easy to distort it and create for it the impression of an exactitude that it really lacked, and by subjecting it to mathematical manipulation also to wind up with a seriously distorted picture of the economy. . . . He had little patience with the use—or shall I say abuse?—of mathematics in economics.

Everyone at Cambridge knew that Marshall, himself a mathematician, had written that mathematics exercises "a powerful attraction on clever beginners."

Marshall thought "all of us use [mathematics] as an inspirer of, and check on, our intuitions and as a shorthand record of our results, but [mathematics]. . .generally falls into the background as we penetrate further into the recesses of the subject" [*JMK* 10:190].

For the Cantabrigian, the choice was one of a suitable language. That is to say, it was not believed that anything was sacrificed by using English rather than mathematics to explain what one meant. Austin Robinson [Patinkin and Leith 1978:31], speaking "feelingly as one brought up in the classical tradition," felt that Robertson passed on the traditions of Eton and Trinity by becoming "not only a master of the precise and exact use of words but also of the cautious, critical, analytical scholarship that belonged to Eton and Trinity and has now alas become defunct in economics, in a world that believes that only mathematics can be exact." At Cambridge this Trinity-Eton tradition persisted at least until Keynes' death in 1946. Joan Robinson was not a "failed mathematician" or one who refused to learn mathematics, but a person who was encouraged to embrace a language which was different from mathematics.

Chapter 6.3 **Samuelson on mathematics in economics**

The Cambridge skepticism of mathematics is not shared by Samuelson [1972:viii-x], who said in *Foundations of Economic Analysis* that he thought of "mathematics as recreation and tool." He argued there that by the time of Newton, the mathematical language of science had begun to replace the classics, Greek and Latin, and was on its way to becoming "a mandatory part of a proper education." He thought that in the last century this split between the need to know history and the classics and the need to know the language of science "has reached crisis proportions." In regard to Sir Charles Snow's recognition of the need for uniting "two cultures," Samuelson believed that "the learned man who is innocent of mathematics has for decades now been experiencing all the frustrations habitually associated with minority groups subject to waning prestige and remorseless pressure."

Samuelson's interest was in language and methodology. When he looked for the "core properties of diverse parts of economic theory," he concentrated on "certain general features of economic analysis: on the nature of an equilibrium system; on the general structure of a maximum problem; on the relationship between comparative statics and dynamics; and so forth." Thus, for Samuelson, economic analysis was taken "as given," in the received form of an equilibrium system and as an "intermediately hard" science with some affinity for the methodological problems in physics.

Chapter 6.4 **American visitors to Cambridge and Marshall lecturers**

After World War II, the Cambridge University department of economics instituted what they called the Marshall Lectureships to honor the memory of

Alfred Marshall. These provided an honor greater than mere financial reward. Lord Kahn [Interview 1984] said, "in choosing Marshall lecturers we took some account of topics, but the main object was to give us all, especially undergraduates, some knowledge of what distinguished economists were like. We covered a wide field. We tried to avoid having the same subject two years running."

These visitors were important in that they participated in the oral tradition of seminars and senior common rooms. A visitor's contribution to the development of Joan Robinson's ideas would vary. For example, Gunnar Myrdal's visit in 1950, when he lectured on the idea of political elements in economic theory, was important to Robinson's evaluation of the role of ideology in economics.

The first lecturer was T. H. Marshall, an insider, in 1948. After Myrdal's visit, more and more foreigners were invited. The first American to be a Marshall lecturer was Talcott Parsons of Harvard, a sociologist. Lord Kahn [Interview] said, "The people who wanted to bring sociology to Cambridge thought we should start by an experimental program. When Parsons' name came before the Faculty Board, I read out a passage which I had literally chosen at random from his most recent book lent to me by Noel Annan. The passage was actually meaningless. I said 'if this man comes to Cambridge, he will destroy the subject in three weeks.' But that was the person that Annan and Marshall wanted and so we must accept it. But I was wrong. He destroyed the subject in two weeks." Since no student is required to attend lectures at Cambridge, Dr. Parsons may have been disappointed in his audience.

The next American visitor came in 1957. William Fellner lectured on "Say's Law and Innovations in the Theory of Employment and Growth." Lord Kahn thought that Joan Robinson did not know Fellner very well. Commonwealth countries were also represented. Trevor Swan visited from Australia, and Lord Kahn thought that "Joan liked him very much. He was a very good friend of hers." Swan participated in the capital controversy, perhaps drawn in by what he heard while at Cambridge.

Robert M. Solow was a Marshall lecturer in the midst of the capital controversy (1963), undoubtedly enlivening the senior commons discussions. At the same time, Kenneth Arrow was in residence at Churchill College. Some of the faculty seminars bordered on the tumultuous. Once, in my hearing, Arrow pleaded with Robinson to allow him to finish putting his assumptions forward before she challenged them. Arrow returned later to deliver a Marshall lecture on "Economic Theory and Racial Discrimination" (1969–70).

Clark Kerr, fired from his Chancellorship of the University of California by then Governor Ronald Reagan in 1967, was the Marshall lecturer of 1967–68. He spoke on "Marshall, Marx and the Working Class." Lord Kahn does not remember whether Kerr was a friend of Robinson's.

In 1971–72, Paul M. Sweezy was the appointed Marshall lecturer. He spoke "On the Theory of Monopoly Capitalism." Lord Kahn believed Sweezy was "a very great friend of Joan's, not only because he was in Cambridge but she corresponded with him and met him when she went to America.''

Alex Leijonhufvud, who had written *On Keynesian Economics and the Economics of Keynes*, was the 1974–75 Marshall lecturer. Robinson blew hot and cold on Leijonhufvud. In 1976–77, John G. Gurley of Stanford addressed Cambridge on ''The Dialectics of Development: USSR against China.'' Kahn did not remember how friendly Gurley and Joan Robinson were.

Franco Modigliani was Marshall lecturer in 1982–83, the last year of Robinson's life. Lord Kahn thought Robinson had tried to read Modigliani. ''I don't think she succeeded.''

In addition to the visits of foreign scholars which became common after the war, Robinson herself took to the road. Kahn said, ''She was such an enormous traveler. I just couldn't keep a log of all her travels; she really loved it. Every year she would travel to some part of the world or another; sometimes she would go from one country to another.''

In addition to the Marshall lecturers, many other American visitors came, for example Milton Friedman, John Dunlop, and John Kenneth Galbraith. Of Galbraith's first visit in 1937, Kahn said, ''Yes, he was here, but somehow, he didn't attract our attention then; it was before the war.''

Chapter 7.1 **A variety of critics**

Acquaintances, such as Abba Lerner, responded to Robinson's *Essay on Marxian Economics* much as Shove had done. Lerner wrote to her (October 14, 1942, KCA) that he found her criticism of orthodox economics ''almost . . . bitter.'' He thought the difference between them lay in the fact that he ''would relate modern economic theory less to the description of the mechanisms of capitalism or to the laws of the development of capitalism, but would rather consider it as useful in developing the economic theory of a Socialist or quasi Socialist society.''

As early as 1949, the attack on ''left-wing'' Keynesianism began in the American economic journals. The Chicago *Journal of Political Economy* published Schumpeter's review article, ''English Economists and the State-Managed Economy'' [1949:372 and 376]. Schumpeter distinguished between ''laborite economists'' who promoted ''laborism'' in England and ''Marxo-Keynesians,'' all of whom accepted the ''assumption of the 'downward rigidity of wages'.'' Johnson, who was at Harvard in 1949, picked up the term ''Marxo-Keynesian'' and later applied it to Robinson, probably because Schumpeter had done so in lectures or in conversation.

Schumpeter did not see the program of the English Labour Party as ''socialism,'' but as ''laborism.'' Laborism was the state of things ''in which labor is the ruling class.'' On the other hand, Schumpeter foresaw a ''long-run tendency toward a genuinely socialist organization of English society in the sense of an organization that vests the control ('ownership') of means of production—the production program—and the claim to the imputed returns from means of production other than labor with a central agency of society, an agency that may, but need not, consist of government and parliament.'' Schumpeter would have been correct in calling Robinson a Kalecki-Keynesian, and it was certainly true that she accepted the downward rigidity of wages, but Robinson was never a ''laborite economist'' in the sense of unflagging support for positions taken by the Labour Party. Harcourt suggested that this explains why she was never honored by the Labour Party, though both Kahn and Kaldor were.

The onslaughts from the left were also worldwide and sustained. A critique of her essay was written after the war in German. Roman Rosdolsky [1977:xiv], who had survived both Auschwitz and Birkenau concentration camps, had come across one of the ''very rare copies'' of Marx's *Rough Draft* in 1953. He claimed he was neither a philosopher nor an economist and only wrote a commentary on the rough draft because so many Marxist theoreticians had fallen victim to the Hitler and Stalin regimes. Rosdolsky had several of Robinson's early publications in his hands as he wrote Chapter 33 which he entitled ''Joan Robinson's Critique of Marx.'' He compared her works to Marx's rough draft, claiming that Robinson was wrong about the labor theory of value, about Marx's method, the essence of capitalist exploitation, Marx's concept of capital, and the theory of the falling rate of profit. He thought, therefore, there was little to be learned from her criticisms of Marx [1977:530-550].

As for Robinson's socialism, Rosdolsky found it too reliant on Prudhon. Seen in this light, he felt the alleged ''socialist'' tendencies in Joan Robinson's writing which had so disturbed Schumpeter were easily explained.

However, Robinson was not totally without influence with Marxists. According to Harcourt [1982:200], some of the 1970s Marxists like Ian Steedman (a follower of Sraffa) took her advice to heart and attempted to ''rid the modern revival of Marxism of its Billy Graham aspects.'' But other Marxists, including Frank Roosevelt of the United States, ''have run a sustained attack on the post Keynesian school.''

Roosevelt [Schwartz 1977:412-413; 438-439; 450-452] has argued that radicals were at first attracted to the Cambridge school through its ''fame by attacking some of the central concepts of neoclassical economics.'' He thought these Cambridge people ''mystify the defining characteristics of capitalism and fail to grasp what the struggle for socialism is all about.'' Roosevelt accused Cambridge of ''commodity fetishism,'' where the Cambridge paradigm is no better than mainstream economics, because it insists on separating the physical from the social aspects of production. The great strength of Marx, according to Roosevelt, was his pointing out that the sale of labor power, that is, wage labor, was a peculiar form of commodity fetishism. He held that Robinson never understood Marx: ''Her total lack of understanding of Marx' concept of value was displayed in her *Essay on Marxian Economics* wherein she stated that under socialism the law of *value* will come into its own. . . .''

Roosevelt also dismissed what he called Robinson's remedies for the contemporary crisis of capitalism: to "eliminate 'functionless wealth', and provide the state with more revenue for improving health and educational services." He thought this proposal "naive—especially with regard to the benevolent character of the state." He asked whether, if the state were to assume the functions that had been previously performed by private capitalists, it would not just be "state capitalism" with the surplus value then appropriated by the state and the people still performing "alienated labor under the direction of an autocratic elite." This is the reasoning by which he supported his conclusion that Robinson didn't understand what was wrong with capitalism.

By the 1980s, Marxists began to call Robinson names. Arun Bose [1980:xii-xiv and xiiin], in referring to her as one of the "modern post-Keynesian ideological sheep in make-believe Marxist ideological wolves' clothing," accused post Keynesians of continuing to use Keynes' theory of exploitation, which "was definitely *not* a theory of 'exploitation of labor by capital'." Also, "The post-Keynesians seem to object to others using the axiomatic method in order to reserve the use of the method solely for themselves, for constructing 'time-less' post Keynesian models of the capitalist economy." The best Bose could say of post Keynesians was that they shared certain symptoms of schizophrenia with some orthodox Marxists. Bose objected not so much to Robinson's seeing Marxism as a "popular religion" as for her rejecting Marxism as a science on the "simplistic pronunciamento that 'Ideology demands acceptance. Science demands doubt'."

Bruce McFarlane in *Radical Economics* [1982:143 and footnotes 48 and 50] classified Robinson neither as a Marxist nor even a proper radical. Rather, he pointed out that the Marxists are frustrated with "neo-Ricardians," including Robinson who failed to do more than attack the "rentier-capitalists." In other words, she failed to attack the capitalist system as a whole. McFarlane argued, "A careful perusal of Joan Robinson's voluminous writings . . . likewise contributes little of substance to the famous question of capitalism versus socialism."

The Marxist taint that some neoclassical economists saw on Robinson was apparently invisible to many of the Marxists themselves. The icing on the cake of these varied responses was when the American magazine *Business Week* called Robinson "a socialist who sounds like a conservative" [October 20, 1975:80].

Chapter 8.1 **An account of growth theory**

Some of the differences between postwar economics at Cambridge and in the United States are related to the development of growth theory. The best succinct account of this is Phyllis Deane's [1978:190–204], from which this note is drawn. Beginning with Adam Smith's *Wealth of Nations*, English classical economists considered problems of wealth accumulation a central concern. After the marginal revolution (1870s), which broke with the old classical problem of the wealth of nations, economists became more concerned with the allocation of resources. (Robbins' *Essay on the Nature and Significance of Economic Science* in 1932 was simply a recognition of this change in the central problem.) The new marginal analysis, though seemingly more ''scientific,'' had little to offer in generating theories of economic growth. Thus for sixty years interest in growth was dormant. Yet one important person, Schumpeter, did publish his *Theory of Economic Development* in Germany in 1911. (Schumpeter's book was not translated into English until 1934.)

Continental economists, confronted in the East by the Soviet Union, continued to study Marx and economic growth, but English and American theorists were more interested in problems of trade cycles. The depression, Keynes' *General Theory*, World War II and its political and social aftermath, and the interest in econometrics, introduced a new era. Growth theory came into vogue when it was realized that there were problems of low-income countries struggling to sustain growth, some for the first time, while the industrialized countries were trying to expand investment to reach full employment.

Almost immediately, modern growth theory split into two separate lines of development which have become two different branches of economic theory. The first has been directed mainly to the problems of developing countries and is typified by W. Arthur Lewis' *Theory of Economic Growth*. The second became the mainstream of the theory of economic growth. Harrod in England and Domar in the United States were early contributors to growth models which set the pattern of the mainstream. The difficulty of the Harrod-Domar model was that it revealed ''explosive instability'' in growth patterns. At this point, there developed a ''deep rift'' between the directions taken by *two* mainstream varieties of growth theory. One was the neoclassical route of the production function. Using this path, theorists have applied marginalist techniques to a Keynesian-type aggregate and have made non-Keynesian assumptions about the way savings decisions govern the rate of capital formation. The other path was the modern Cambridge school, which has a predilection for assumptions which are either Keynesian or Ricardian in their inspiration. (This explains in part why so much of the capital controversy centered on choice of assumptions.)

Deane argues that one of the main attractions of the neoclassical type of model is that it seems to lend itself readily to empirical tests and predictions. Its disadvantages are that it is designed for full-employment conditions and that it has nothing to say about the distribution of income. The Cambridge-type models are often directed toward a discovery of what changes in income distribution accompany capitalist economic development. Basically the neoclassical models have the savings dog wagging the investment tail, while the Cambridge models have the investment dog wagging the savings tail. This is Meade's metaphor. Deane thinks that the ''protagonists are clearly seen to be fighting on different battle grounds.''

The split in the mainstream, described by Deane in much greater depth than I have given, profoundly influenced the reception of Robinson's *Accumulation* in America. But even Deane's explanation does not answer the question of why mainstream growth theory of both types lost status in North America after the 1960s.

Chapter 8.2 **Sraffa harks back to Ricardo**

The least talkative, yet one of the most influential, participants in the oral tradition at Cambridge was Piero Sraffa, whom Galbraith [1981:74] called "one of the most leisured men who ever lived." The saga of Sraffa's influence on the Cambridge tradition is a subject in itself. Kahn [1984:26] insisted that "mention of [Sraffa's] published works completely understates the enormously influential part which he has played in the development of Cambridge economics." Sraffa's influence on Robinson early and late was apparent from her testimonials.

When, after many years of work Sraffa published his introduction to and edition of Ricardo's works [1953], Robinson became especially interested in Sraffa's account of Ricardo's corn economy. Later, with the publication of his book, *Production of Commodities by Means of Commodities* (1960), she [*CEP* 3:iii] saw ways to make her critique of neoclassical capital theory "more cogent." In fact, Robinson said that the "noticeable difference" between her collected papers in Volume 3 and those in Volume 2 was attributable to Sraffa's publication.

Robinson agreed that Sraffa had provided a "Prelude to a Critique of Economic Theory," which phrase was the subtitle of his book. She cited Sraffa as the source of the idea of using a "blueprint" for each separate economy having given techniques [*CEP* 3:x-xi]. She used this image in her capital theory arguments. And Robinson [*CEP* 5:287] thought he had knocked out "once and for all the marginal productivity theory of distribution." She was also impressed that he had shown Marxists how to solve the transformation problem. She considered this quite an achievement in such a thin volume.

Very late in her life, Robinson raised some serious questions about the direction that followers of Sraffa were taking, but during the 1960s and early 1970s she thought that the "Anglo-Italian" branch of theory was emerging as a unified force, a Cambridge alternative to mainstream American economics.

Chapter 8.3 **The new Cambridge tradition and the Anglo-Italian School, 1949–1975**

Kahn [1977:386] has referred to "the effect which the study of orthodox economic theory can have upon a powerful mind." The same can be said of any graduate program in economics. Training of the mind screens out what is irrelevant to the program at hand, even in the case of the not-so-powerful mind. In this spirit, the Cambridge tradition will impress itself on the person who: begins with Marshall;

reads Keynes' *The End of Laissez Faire*; then Sraffa's 1926 article which challenged Marshallian economics; then *The General Theory* and the Moggridge [*JMK* 13:338] account of the Circus; next, Kalecki's essays or Robinson's accounts of his contribution; Harrod's *Towards a Dynamic Analysis* comes next, but is to be skimmed; Sraffa's Introduction to his edition of Ricardo's works; Robinson's *Accumulation* and Kaldor's article, "Alternative Theories of Distribution," or perhaps Robinson's *Essays in the Theory of Growth* along with Kaldor; then Sraffa's *Production of Commodities by Means of Commodities.*

This is essentially the intellectual route taken to arrive at the Cambridge view, a view different from that of American mainstream economics. Of course, if one is already powerfully attached to orthodox theory, then the deprogramming will not work. However, the person will at least understand that another view is possible, and that it is a positive program, not one relying only on criticisms of the mainstream. What about Ricardo and Marx? Their influence is felt mainly through the Sraffa and Kalecki contributions.

The reason the Cambridge tradition was for a time called the Anglo-*Italian* tradition was because of the contributions of Sraffa, later Pasinetti, and still more recently Garegnani; and also for want of another, agreed-upon name. The name, like the ideas, went through a serial development. Harcourt [1982:200 and 280] has used several handles for different sectors of the group: neo-Ricardian, neo-Keynesian, neo-Marxian, and more recently, Post-Keynesian. In the late 1970s, he began to call it the Post-Keynesian school of three major strands: Joan Robinson and her followers; Nicholas Kaldor; Sraffa himself "and the Italian wing of the Anglo-Italian school. . . . All three overlap and interrelate." In 1977 Harcourt [1982:237, 239] also named the leaders of the Post-Keynesian school as Robinson, Kahn, and Kaldor and, as "guiding spirit," Sraffa.

Harcourt saw Robinson, Kaldor, and Sraffa as united against a common enemy, but still "they are often as cross with, and in as much disagreement amongst themselves." He pictured them as "under attack from both ends of the ideological and analytical spectrum," meaning that they were fighting off both the Marxists of the left and the "orthodox neo-neoclassicals" of MIT. All these exchanges and "fights" are, of course, in the Cambridge tradition of advancing economic theory through controversy.

In Harcourt's view, the Cambridge and neoclassical schools differ "over the 'vision' of the economy that will go into the model to be used" [1975:21].

Chapter 9.1 How marginalism came to America

Eric Roll [1942:467–468] wrote, "it is a thankless task to review the American version of the marginal-utility doctrine." The "spontaneous appearance" of marginalism on the American continent, Roll thought, was "almost entirely the work of one writer, John Bates Clark," who had spent two years in Germany where he had probably acquired "his antagonism to some of the tenets of classical

political economy.'' Roll meant English economics when he said classical political economy. On the other hand, Schumpeter said Clark had already developed
his ideas before studying on the continent. Clark's most significant work was the
exposition of the marginal productivity theory of distribution, which Joan Robinson first attacked in her *Economics of Imperfect Competition* (without mentioning
Clark).

Chapter 9.2 **American response to Clark's defense of the status quo**

Many American economists (for example, Frank Fetter) objected to Clark's
efforts to make his theory of the marginal productivity distribution of income into
a defense of the status quo. Veblen—as Robinson learned in the 1970s [Hunt and
Schwartz 1972:59]—had seen the ''fallacy'' of Clark's use of ''capital.'' Frank
Taussig, a leading neoclassical economist at Harvard, also took the position that
''the statement that wages equaled the marginal net product of labor had to be
regarded as only one of the elements in a theory of wages'' [Roll:1942:475]. This
ambivalent view was eventually dropped from pure theory, probably in the process of mathematization of economic theory.

Roll [1942:479] provided some other support for Joan Robinson's belief that
the American Clark, as well as Böhm-Bawerk, had been anxious to defend the
status quo of income streams. However, the Clark/Böhm-Bawerk theories differed in many important details, one of the most important being that Clark
insisted there were two distinct kinds of capital. Roll also held that there was a
''smoldering disagreement between the American exponents of the doctrines of
the Austrian school and the Austrians themselves.'' Is this another example of
American economists borrowing ideas but doing with them as they please? Were
these then bastard marginalists?

Robinson's point that some neoclassical capital theory was conceived as a
reaction against Marx is thus substantiated. However, she overstated her case that
economics ''consisted mainly of dodging the question of distribution and concen-
trating on the analysis of the relative prices of commodities'' [*CEP* 5:37].
Perhaps Cambridge economists had to wait for Piero Sraffa's interpretation of
Ricardo to reformulate their theory, but Ricardo never really disappeared from
the American traditional teaching. Furthermore, the interest in distribution of
income and thus in capital theory had always been as prominent in America as it
had been on the continent.

I wondered if these facts of American economic teaching might explain the
sharp reaction which American economists had to Robinson's provocative essay,
''The Production Function and the Theory of Capital.'' For while the English
student was struggling with liquidity preference versus loanable funds, the
American student was over his head in the Knight-Hayek controversy over
capital. But Robert Solow said that although he had indeed gone through the

Knight-Hayek controversy, it had never made much sense to him. He was interested in Robinson's article because of his 1950s interest in growth theory.

Chapter 9.3 **Robinson's recognition of inflationary aspects of Keynesian policy**

Robinson included in Volume 4 of her *Collected Economic Papers* some of the essays she had written "while Keynes' *General Theory* was going through the press." In introducing them she noted [*CEP* 4:184], "it is certainly absurd to suppose that he [Keynes] was not aware of the prospect of inflation setting in when near-full employment is maintained for a run of years." In her essay, "Full Employment," she wrote, "the general upshot of our argument is that the point of full employment, so far from being an equilibrium resting place, appears to be a precipice over which, once it has reached the edge, the value of money must plunge into a bottomless abyss." She noted that through rises in the rate of interest, a complete collapse could be avoided. She suggested, however, that "obstacles, perhaps insuperable, to the control of employment and prices are presented by the fact that a regime of private enterprise is subject to violent oscillations of sentiment, which must be counteracted by public policy if the system is to run smoothly." Robinson was aware that "a policy of maintaining stable prices (supposing that such a policy can be formulated in a practicable manner) is by no means equivalent to a policy of maintaining stable employment." She concluded that perhaps a moderate level of employment is the best objective [*CEP* 4:189, 192, 195].

In 1943, Robinson wrote to the London *Times* on the subject of "Planning Full Employment." She warned, "If full employment is sought, the balance of trade must be maintained, on the one hand, by a controlled direction and stimulation of exports, and, on the other hand, by a system of priorities for imports which will give precedence to the more over the less necessary." She also suggested that "government investment must be confined to spheres which in no way compete with profit-seeking capital." Robinson did not mince words: "Unemployment in a private-enterprise economy has not only the function of preserving discipline in industry, but also indirectly the function of preserving the value of money." Only two solutions had been offered in the modern world—one under fascism, where trade unions were broken; the second where socialism removed the long and bitter antagonism between capital and labor by making capital the property of the community as a whole.

Robinson asked, would Sir William Beveridge's proposed "British revolution" represent a third course? She admitted that the "foregoing discussion had brought to the surface a disagreeable dilemma, which must be squarely met if intellectual confusion and economic and social disaster are not to ensue." She came out for a regulated economy [*CEP* 1:81–88].

In her *Accumulation of Capital,* Robinson employed the concept of the "inflation barrier," wherein the pressure for rising wages "checks an acceleration of accumulation that threatens to depress the real-wage rate intolerably" [1956a:48, 91, 238, 356 and *CEP* 3:51].

In 1958, she announced squarely that in formulating the theory of employment, Keynes had uncovered the fact "that unemployment is not just an accidental blemish in a private-enterprise system—it has a function. The function of unemployment in the *laisser-faire* system is to preserve the value of money." But by 1958, another problem had arisen—the Cold War. She concluded then, "It seems to me that the question of whether it is possible to have full employment without a falling value of money cannot be answered until we know whether it is possible to have full employment without the cold war" [*CEP* 2:271 and 279].

Robinson never understood how the bastard Keynesians could have repressed these points in their analysis.

Chapter 10.1 Robinson's view of switching and reswitching

According to Robinson [1981a:133], it was Sraffa's *Production of Commodities by Means of Commodities* which first introduced this language. His object was to engage in long-period analysis where alternative methods of production are known. Where this is the case, there "may be switch points at particular levels of the rate of profits at which two different methods of production of a particular output have the same cost." If so, any difference in the rate of profit may cause one technique to be preferred to another. Therefore, there may be decisions to change physical systems, which decisions are induced by differences in the rate of profits.

Robinson argued that this possibility changes the exposition from a logical (i.e., mathematical, non-temporal, non-spatial) problem to a problem which inevitably involves space and time. This is so because "two physically different systems could not coexist both in space and time." For Robinson, this required her to "abandon Sraffa and descend from purely logical comparisons into historical time." She added, "Switch points, at which two different physical systems operate at the same costs, must be thrown out along with the 'marginal productivity of capital' as an illegitimate concept."

Why did she argue that the marginal productivity of capital had to go? Because if there were no meaning to the "quantity of capital" apart from the rate of profit, then "the contention that the 'marginal product of capital' determines the rate of profit is meaningless." This finding was the product of the early stages of the capital controversy. Robinson also relied on the "significant 'Ruth Cohen case', which she had once seen as a 'curiosum'." The "Ruth Cohen case" was "that it is perfectly normal (within the accepted assumptions) for the same technique to be eligible at several discrete rates of profit." Robinson tells us that "it was from this that the soubriquet 'reswitching of techniques' was derived'' [1978a:103–104].

However, Harcourt points out that Robinson is mistaken in saying that the Ruth Cohen curiosum was the origin of reswitching. The curiosum is capital reversing, not reswitching, says Harcourt [Harcourt to author]. He refers us to Robinson's own statement in *The Accumulation of Capital*. There Robinson says that usually, "the degree of mechanization of the technique brought over the frontier by a higher wage rate is higher than that corresponding to a lower wage rate but it is possible that within certain ranges there may be a perverse relationship" [1956a:109–110].

Joan Robinson did not just criticize the existing switching models but proposed an alternative model engaging historical time [1981a:133–134]. Her criticisms of traditional models were mainly philosophical, drawing on what she understood to be the methodology of science. The questions she raised remain unanswered and her alternative models mainly unexplored. As was customary, professional response was limited to discussion of her criticisms of existing theory. The exchanges finally degenerated into an intellectual impasse.

Chapter 14.1 **Robinson's passports**

Those in her archival papers (dated 1946–1955 and 1960–1965) indicate the following travel:

- 1946: Denmark, Sweden, Norway
- 1947: France, Switzerland
- 1948: France
- 1949: Switzerland, Sweden
- 1950: Netherlands, France, Switzerland, Italy
- 1951: France, Switzerland, Austria, Czechoslovakia, Scandinavia
- 1952: Belgium, Czechoslovakia, USSR, Poland, Switzerland, West Germany, Austria, Norway, France
- 1953: Burma, Thailand, Geneva Airport, Egypt, Lebanon, Syria, Iraq, China, Vietnam, Hong Kong, Singapore
- 1954: France, West Germany, Netherlands
- 1955: Switzerland, Italy, India
- 1956–1959: (Missing)
- 1960: USSR
- 1961: USA, Canada, Cuba, Aeropuerto Barajas
- 1962: Aeropuerto Barajas, Poland, Czechoslovakia, Greece, Turkey
- 1963: Nepal, Delhi, Kathmandu, China, Moscow, Calcutta
- 1964: China, Moscow, North Korea
- 1965: Mexico, Cuba, USA, Canada

Chapter 14.2 **American Economic Association (AEA) debate**

In the late 1960s, the federal government (through the National Science Foundation and the National Institutes of Health) and the Russell Sage Foundation financed a three-year study, *The Behavioral and Social Sciences: Outlook and Needs*. Carl Kaysen and Robert Solow acted as co-chairmen for economics. Reports were written by various economists, James Tobin being one of them. The AEA then reviewed the reviewers. Nancy Ruggles edited a number of the reports and wrote the introductory chapter, "The Goals and Achievements of Economics." There she concluded, "Although the past achievements of economics have been substantial, they may well be dwarfed by the unsolved problems that face complex modern societies." Charles L. Schultze of The Brookings Institution commented in his review article, "However valid [Ruggles'] conclusion, one would scarcely reach it by reading the individual chapters" [1971:45].

John G. Gurley of Stanford was more pointed [1971:53, 59]. He felt that the authors of the survey had disregarded all of the literature of dissent and the many challenges to the basic tenets of present-day economics. Gurley feared that a reader of the report would think that "all is well with economics; that there is almost unanimous agreement on the fundamentals of the discipline; that economists are superbly prepared to solve what these authors call—incredible as it may seem—'newly-emerging problems' like poverty and 'hot subjects' like urban decay. The dominant tone of the survey is one of great self-satisfaction and self-confidence." Gurley grouped Joan Robinson with those he called "radical economists" who reject conventional economics.

In discussion, Robert Solow said he had decided to meet Gurley's "radical blasts" with more than an "embarrassed silence." Radical economics had been neglected "because it is negligible," said Solow. He argued that radical economists "have corrupted Thomas Kuhn's notion of a scientific paradigm, which they treat as a mere license for loose thinking." Solow thought that in the Kuhnian sense, "neoclassical economics is pretty clearly a scientific paradigm. It may be a bad one, or a worn-out one, or it may have served to advance the interests of the capitalist class, but it is the sort of thing Kuhn means. As far as I can see, radical political economics is no such thing. It is more a matter of posture and rhetoric than of scientific framework at all."

For the AEA this is where the argument stood when Robinson gave her Ely address the next year.

JR

ENDNOTES

These endnotes are cited by author, date, and page number. They are intended to be used in conjunction with the References. If an author has more than one publication during a year, these are referenced, for example, as 1980a, 1980b, and so on. If an author's publication is included in an edited work, it is referenced in brackets by the editor's name. The following abbreviations have been used:

AR: Austin Robinson

CEP: Collected Economic Papers by Joan Robinson, 5 vols. These are cited by volume number rather than year.

DNB: The Dictionary of National Biography, where the reference will be under the name of the deceased in a volume containing the years of his/her death.

JMK: The Collected Writings of John Maynard Keynes, 23 vols. These are cited by volume number rather than year.

JR: Joan Robinson

JRP: Joan Robinson Papers

KCA: King's College Archives, Cambridge University

Introduction

1. Robbins, Lord Lionel 1981a.
2. Ibid., 112. Keynes' thesis was *A Treatise on Probability*.
3. Ibid., 113–114. A commentator outside of economics sagely remarked, "The eighteenth century is littered with the wreckage of comprehensive generalizations with which the protagonists of the phlogiston doctrine, preformationism, vulcanism and a host of minor exploits in elegant deduction from self-evident principles obstructed the steady and piecemeal advance toward the solution of problems clearly conceived by the founders of British empiricism in their relation to vital social needs" [Hogben 1938:808].
4. The Cambridge University "Circus" refers to a group of young economists—Richard Kahn, James Meade, Piero Sraffa, Joan and Austin Robinson, who met informally to discuss John Maynard Keynes' *A Treatise on Money* (1930). Through their discussions, reported to Keynes by Kahn, they contributed to Keynes' development of his General Theory. (See Chapter 5.)
5. Putnam [Heath: 1981:118].
6. Her address, "The Second Crisis in Economic Theory," was delivered to the American Economic Association in 1971 when she was Ely Lecturer. In 1980, Lionel Robbins was also an Ely Lecturer. He then joined her views on the definition of economic science to some degree, saying that in the case of policy, an economist must introduce

"assumptions of value essentially incapable of scientific proof." He even called for parallel courses in politics and history [Robbins 1981b:9].

Chapter 1

1. The first earl of Egmont was the first president of the trustees of the colony which became the state of Georgia and which he founded with James E. Oglethorpe. His journal of their transactions has been published. See *DNB*. For Apostles, see Lowe 1985:115.

2. *New York Times* January 13, 1912. Sir Edward's papers are in the United States. See "Sir Edward Howard Marsh (1872–1953)" *DNB*.

3. "Sir Frederick Barton Maurice (1871–1951)" *DNB*.

4. Phyllis Maurice to author, postmarked January 14, 1988.

5. *DNB* 1951–1960:720.

6. Ibid., 721.

7. This incident ended General Maurice's military career. Austin Robinson thinks one consequence was that Nancy Maurice, an elder sister, was not able to attend a university. AR Interview, Sidney Sussex College, Cambridge University 1984.

8. Cf. Harcourt 1979:663.

9. "Frederick Denison Maurice (1805–1872)" *DNB*.

10. Phyllis Maurice, who was seven years younger than Joan, was forever going off to sleep with Joan's study light still burning. This sharing of a bedroom created a bond. Phyllis said, "We enjoyed a friendship and warm regard for each other which remained constant throughout Joan's long life." [Interviews, Bury St. Edmond 1984 and 1986 and letter postmarked January 14, 1988.] The Gilchrist Scholarship had a value of one hundred pounds "for a course of preparation for the profession of medicine or teaching." (A charge of 50 pounds per term covered the whole of the College charges for board, lodging, tuition, and Inter-Collegiate and Tripos Examinations. "All necessary furniture, bed and table linen are provided.")

11. See Appendix Note 1.1 English economists and women's rights. AR was married to Joan Maurice in 1926.

12. Mary Marshall to JR June 11, 1933, JRP, KCA.

13. Grant 1966:158–159.

14. Bradbrook 1969:x.

15. Alfred Waterhouse was the original designer. Grant 1966:158–159.

16. Bradbrook 1969:68 and Margaret Gaskell, Librarian of Girton College, to author January 31, 1985.

17. Two of the most famous Mistresses of Girton were in charge when Joan Maurice was there—Katherine Jex Blake, teacher of classics, and Jex Blake's cousin Bertha Phillpotts (1922–25).

18. Russell-Smith of Newnham 1922 [Bradbrook 1969:66].

19. AR [Patinkin and Leith 1978:30].

20. Howarth 1978:24. The Union Society at Cambridge meets for University-wide debates. *Granta* is a Cambridge, England magazine.

21. Ibid., 43–44.

22. Keith-Walters, Newnham 1925 [Phillips 1979:162].

23. Hewlett Interview, New York City 1985. Hewlett was at Cambridge on a University Research Fellowship.

24. AR [Patinkin and Leith 1978:27–28]. Marjorie Tappan was educated at Bryn Mawr College, Pennsylvania 1911–15, and received her Ph.D. at Columbia University in 1917. She became Director of Studies and Lecturer in Economics at Girton College in 1923 and was also in the same position at Newnham College 1923–1933. She was

made a Fellow of Girton in 1924. She married Hollond in 1929.

25. Cohen Interview, Cambridge 1984.

26. Skidelsky 1983:166.

27. Ibid., 184–185.

28. This was Keynes' opinion in "Alfred Marshall (1842–1924)" *DNB* (1922–1930), 563.

29. AR, "Arthur Cecil Pigou (1877–1959)" *DNB* (1951–1960), 815.

30. AR [Patinkin and Leith 1978:29–30].

31. AR Interview 1984.

32. AR 1947:26.

33. AR [Patinkin and Leith 1978:28].

34. Actually JR first went to Cambridge in October 1921. JR 1978a:ix.

35. Examiners for Tripos Part I were A. W. Flux, Leonard Alston, and T. H. Marshall, of Cambridge, and Douglas Knoop of Manchester. Examiners Part II were Lavington and Shove of Cambridge, W. R. Scott of Dublin and T. E. Gregory of London. At least one outside examiner is always used.

36. Harcourt 1979:663.

37. AR Interview, 1984.

Chapter 2

1. Shackle 1967:6 argued that the new developments were "the work of a mere handful of great theoreticians," among whom JR and Keynes were outstanding.

2. Kahn 1984:23–24.

3. AR explained: "What I do not think you have fully understood is that the dividing line between being a member of the Faculty here in Cambridge and not being a member of the Faculty was entirely invisible. If you were living in Cambridge and were prepared to supervise undergraduate students, there was nothing on earth to stop a colleague sending you pupils to look after. Joan, after we came back from India, did acquire small numbers of students in that way. But I doubt whether at that time she was ever teaching more than four hours a week. When she had written 'Imperfect Competition' and had something to say in lectures, the Faculty was prepared to put her name on the lecture list and she gave a small number of lectures. But there was no distinction between being a member of the Faculty and not being a member of the Faculty" [AR to author January 6, 1988].

4. I asked Margaret Gaskell of Girton whether JR supervised pupils from Girton. She answered, "No, almost certainly she did not supervise Girtonians" (Gaskell to author January 31, 1985). During the 1930s Joan Robinson tried to persuade Ruth Cohen, who had been a student at Newnham and later studied at Stanford but was then at Oxford, to take on the job at Newnham. Cohen did finally return to Cambridge [Cohen Interview, Cambridge 1984].

5. Cambridge University *Reporter*, 1934. See also Appendix Note 2.1 Becoming a professional.

6. AR Interview, 1984.

7. Keynes to JR October 21, 1932 JRP, KCA.

8. See Appendix Note 2.2 Dedication of *Economics is a Serious Subject*.

9. Schumpeter to JR March 20, 1933 JRP, KCA.

10. Schumpeter to JR May 15, 1933 JRP, KCA.

11. Samuelson Interview, Cambridge, Massachusetts 1985.

12. *CEP* 5:110. Robinson spelled it "laisser-faire" instead of the usual "laissez-faire." This was true in most of her publications until her Ely lecture, 1971, which was first published in the *American Economic Review*.

13. Tappan-Hollond to JR "16th CV," 1932 JRP, KCA.
14. Tappan-Hollond to JR October 23, 1932 JRP, KCA.
15. Ibid., KCA.

Chapter 3

1. AR [Patinkin and Leith 1978:27]. AR said he "retailed" this theoretical development to JR and Kahn.
2. JR 1978a:ix. S. J. Latsis [1976:26] holds that the cost controversy really began with J. H. Clapham's 1922 article in the *Economic Journal*, "Empty Economic Boxes."
3. JR 1969a:xiii–xv. She also mentioned AR's *Structure of Competitive Industry,* and Sraffa's and Shove's articles in the *Economic Journal* in June 1928 and March 1930. She admitted learning about the marginal revenue curve from Austin Robinson and his student C. H. P. Gifford of Magdalene College, "who was then reading for the Economics Tripos" (the luncheon origin); "shortly afterwards Mr. P. A. Sloan, of Clare College, showed me an unpublished essay in which it occurred. Next it was published by Mr. R. F. Harrod in the *Economic Journal* of June 1930"; and "meanwhile a number of explorers," including Professor T. O. Yntema, "had, unknown to me, arrived there long before," including "Dr. E. Schneider, Dr. H. v. Stackelberg, and Professor Mehta," all of whom seemed to have discovered marginal revenue "independently" (xv).
4. Ibid., xv.
5. JR 1978a:ix.
6. Quoted in Kahn 1984:61.
7. Keynes to JR March 29, 1934 *JMK* 13:422.
8. JR 1978a:x.
9. Samuelson Interview 1985.
10. Schumpeter 1954:1152.
11. Shove to JR October 24, 1931 JRP, KCA. All Shove letters are in JRP, KCA.
12. Shove to JR October 27, 1931 JRP, KCA. JR lectured on the "Pure Theory of Monopoly," Michaelmas Term [Cambridge University *Reporter* October 1931].
13. Ibid.
14. JR lectured on the "Economics of Imperfect Competition," Michaelmas and Lent terms [Cambridge University *Reporter* October 1933].
15. Pigou to JR undated JRP, KCA.
16. Pigou to JR February 28, 1935 JRP, KCA. This letter must have referred to proofs of his own work.
17. Pigou to JR undated JRP, KCA.
18. Shackle 1967:1
19. Ibid., 11. Shackle was referring to Augustin Cournot's *Mathematical Principles of the Theory of Wealth*, first published in 1838.
20. As JR mentioned, Cournot was accorded a footnote in Marshall's *Principles* but was not allowed to affect the theory. Nor was Cournot's use of calculus in his analysis influential at Cambridge at that time.
21. JR 1969a:xii.
22. Gram and Walsh 1983:518.
23. Shackle 1967:11.
24. Schumpeter 1954:61n, 650 and 884–885 respectively.
25. JR 1969a:301.
26. There were 288 Labor M.P.s as against 261 Conservatives and 57 Liberals. Pelling 1963:190.
27. Irving Bernstein 1971:1.

28. Edwards 1933:683. See Appendix Note 3.1 for full discussion of the other reviews of JR's *Imperfect Competition.*

29. Schumpeter 1934:253.

30. JR 1978:ix.

31. Schumpeter 1934:256.

32. Ibid., 249. but see Appendix Note 3.1. Schumpeter wasn't ready to give up "the theory of free competition" since it remained "the only avenue to a rational theory of planning and of centralistic socialism." Schumpeter's ideas are also discussed in Chapter 17.

33. Schumpeter to Kahn December 24, 1933 JRP, KCA.

34. Douglas to JR January 30, 1935 JRP, KCA.

35. Machlup 1934–35:202.

36. JR 1936d:148.

37. Machlup to JR April 14, 1938 JRP, KCA.

38. AR [Patinkin and Leith 1978:27].

39. JR 1969a:1.

40. Schumpeter 1954:474.

41. *CEP* 5:114.

42. Hutchison 1977: 165 and 76–77.

43. *CEP* 5:114.

44. Shackle 1967:47.

45. According to Marx, workers were exploited, receiving less than the value they added to the value of the product which they made. Marx was relying on the labor theory of value, which denies that capital adds to value, since capital is itself "embodied labor." But JR had not read Marx at this point, and was probably not familiar with the nineteenth-century controversy.

46. JR 1978a:x.

47. Shackle 1967:11.

48. JR 1978a:x.

49. *CEP* 5:112.

50. JR 1969a:x-xi.

51. Edwards 1933:683.

52. Guillebaud to JR June 1, 1934 JRP, KCA. JR lectured on the "Economics of Imperfect Competition" in Michaelmas Term and "Applications of Imperfect Competition" in Lent Term [Cambridge University *Reporter* October, 1934].

Chapter 4

1. Chamberlin to JR. JRP, KCA.

2. Typed manuscript, "The Early Development of Monopolistic Competition Theory," Chamberlin Personal Papers, p. 1.

3. Signatures of record before publication date of JR's book are John A. Chandler, L. C. Lockley, V. Orval Watts, W. S. Lake, G. Trepp, R. C. Weaver, Warren A. Roberts, Herbert Ashton, V. E. Carlson, W. S. Lake, Peter Guiran, S. B. Ferrias, and in 1933, F. W. Burton and N. W. Deacon. The thesis was dated April 1, 1927, deposited June 22, 1927, signed by Allyn Young, T. N. Carver, F. W. Taussig and first consulted April 11, 1930.

4. Blitch 1983a:3. Young died during the influenza epidemic in London, 1929.

5. Sources of documentation: Patinkin and Leith 1978:27; *JMK* 13:337–338 for the Circus; and 13:269 for the letter to Keynes about her "nightmare." Chamberlin's dating is in the copy of his book he gave his mother, now a part of Chamberlin Personal Papers.

6. Patinkin 1982:4.

7. Ibid., 91.

8. Obituary in Harvard University *Gazette* 1968:197. Signed by Abram Bergson, Paul Buck, Alexander Gerschenkron, Gottfried Haberler, Edward S. Mason, Chairman.

9. Cambridge has more than once been accused of "unnecessary originality," but the most famous example is when Gunnar Myrdal chided Keynes. Myrdal had published an analysis very similar to Keynes' but predating *The General Theory* by three years. Cf. Oser 1970:408–40. The doctrine is sometimes applied to other Englishmen as well, such as John Hicks, who allegedly did not cite the sources of his ideas. Actually, it comes from the English style of scholarship, which emphasizes individual thinking rather than "looking things up."

10. Lord Kahn Interview at King's College, Cambridge, November 1984.

11. Harvard University *Gazette* 1968:197–198. Chamberlin played the piano well and lectured at the University of Paris in French. Married to a Frenchwoman, Lucienne Foubert, he spent many summers happily among her kinfolk in Brittany or Normandy. Their one daughter, Monique, born in 1936, also became an accomplished pianist, and taught piano theory for ten years at Lesley College. They lived in a rambling house with extensive gardens at 4 Channing Street off Mount Auburn Street west of Harvard Square.

12. Chamberlin to Alvin Johnson November 24, 1936, Chamberlin Papers, Harvard Archives.

13. Chamberlin Personal Papers, undated. Thirty to forty economists participated in the round table, but Robinson was not among them. Her absence is not surprising. Travel was difficult and expensive in 1936.

14. Chamberlin to AR October 28, 1952, Chamberlin Papers, Harvard Archives. The letter indicates AR had wanted simply "Monopoly and Its Regulation." Chamberlin was to edit the volume from the Talloires, France conference, i.e., Chamberlin 1954.

15. Chamberlin 1937:557–580.

16. Kaldor 1938:525.

17. Lord Kahn Interview, 1984.

18. *CEP* 2:222n. JR (1953c) answered Chamberlin (1951).

19. JR 1969a:ix-x.

20. Newman 1960:587–600.

21. Chamberlin, Typescript of "The Early Development of Monopolistic Competition Theory," Chamberlin Personal Papers, 2–3. Chamberlin quotes JR 1966d:73. Chamberlin denied that there were "historical causes" of his achievement.

22. Chamberlin's typescript, "Some Differences between Monopolistic and Imperfect Competition," gives no reference for Hutt's alleged statement.

23. JR to Chamberlin September 10 but without a year indicated. Sent from 62a Grange Road, which means it could not be earlier than 1946. Chamberlin Personal Papers.

24. Mont Pelerin Society 1961, "Statement of the Aims." (My emphasis.)

25. JR 1969a:ix-x.

26. Chamberlin 1959:46.

27. Mont Pelerin Society 1961:1.

28. *CEP* 2:241.

29. *CEP* 5:114.

30. *CEP* 5:155–156.

31. Chamberlin Personal Papers.

32. Cf. Chamberlin, *The Theory of Monopolistic Competition*, 8th edition, 188–190.

33. AR to author, January 14, 1986.

34. AR says he hasn't the faintest recollection of what JR wore, "but very frequently after we came back from India, Joan would wear Indian type clothes and I suspect that that is what she must have been doing on that occasion." AR to author, January 6, 1988.

35. *CEP* 1:21.

36. Chamberlin Typescript, "Some Differences Between Monopolistic and Imperfect

Competition," p. 3, Chamberlin Personal Papers.

37. *CEP* 1:29n.

38. *CEP* 2:2.

39. JR to Chamberlin March 4, with Chamberlin's pencil note "1952," Chamberlin Personal Papers.

40. Attributed to Joan Robinson in "Summary Record of the Debate" [Chamberlin 1954:504].

41. Ibid., 245.

42. Ibid., 507.

43. Ibid., 255. Chamberlin was referring to a statement by Robert Triffin in *Monopolistic Competition and General Equilibrium Theory*, 128.

44. Ibid., 259.

45. JR was still a Lecturer. The next rank up would have been Reader. Participants from the United States included J. S. Bain, E. H. Chamberlin, J. M. Clark, C. D. Edwards, R. B. Heflebower, F. H. Knight, and F. Machlup. United Kingdom participants were G. C. Allen, W. A. Lewis, and Joan and Austin Robinson.

46. Harvard University *Gazette*, 1968:198.

47. JR to Chamberlin November 13, 1957 Chamberlin Personal Papers.

48. *CEP* 5:114.

49. I asked Edward S. Mason about this allegation in a letter. He replied, "I never knew that Chamberlin rewarded students who criticized her and I doubt whether this is true." Mason thought her *Imperfect Competition* "inferior to his work but she was later disrespectful of it herself." As to whether Chamberlin's attitudes toward her were considered fair among his friends, Mason replied, "I don't know whether his friends thought he was altogether fair, but he was not thought appreciably unfair." Mason to author November 22, 1985.

50. AR [Patinkin and Leith 1978:79].

51. JR 1962a:79.

52. JR 1969f:xi.

53. Kaldor [Worswick and Trevithick 1983:47].

54. Keynes 1936:5–13.

55. *CEP* 2:145.

56. Kaldor [Worswick and Trevithick 1983:47].

57. Telser 1968:315.

58. Reder 1982:11.

59. Ibid., p 17. This would occur whenever product demand curves slope downward or input supply curves slope upward.

60. Friedman 1953:15.

61. Ibid., 38–39.

62. Samuelson [Worswick and Trevithick 1983:217]. In the 1985 interview, Samuelson agreed that he had meant to include Robinson also in the Keynes-cum statement.

63. Reder 1982:17.

64. Latsis 1976:16 and 30.

Chapter 5

1. Keynes 1930.

2. AR [Patinkin and Leith 1978:33–34].

3. *JMK* 13:338–339.

4. Keynes' exposition was quoted in JR 1933b:75. In this parable, green peas were perishable consumption goods; but gold was standing in for capital goods, money, investment, and savings, a confused and confusing hybrid, as the Circus

groped its way toward the General Theory.

5. JR to Keynes April 9, 1932 *JMK* 13:268–269.

6. Keynes to JR April 14, 1932 *JMK* 13:269–270.

7. JR 1933c and *CEP* 1:viii for JR's statement.

8. *CEP* 1:58.

9. Ibid., 52.

10. Samuelson 1946:200n.

11. *CEP* 1:ix. Donald E. Moggridge says of the parable that it is the "classic case" of the problems of reconstructing the development of the General Theory. "Joan Robinson's 1933 *Economica* article [the parable] . . . is a good example of the position reached in Cambridge eighteen months earlier, soon after the end of the 'Circus' but a bad example of where things stood in late 1932 or early 1933" [when it was published]. Moggridge [Patinkin and Leith 1978:65].

12. Whether this is so or not has been discussed by, for example, Bertil Ohlin, who referred to "Samuelson's observation . . . that [this article] anticipated the essential parts of the *General Theory*." Ohlin [Patinkin and Leith 1978:164].

13. Samuelson [Patinkin and Leith 1978:118].

14. JR 1978a:xiv.

15. Tarshis [Patinkin and Leith 1978:51].

16. JR 1978a:58.

17. *JMK* 14:148.

18. Lerner to JR August 23, 1933 JRP, KCA.

19. Lerner to JR November 16, 1933 JRP, KCA.

20. *JMK* 14:148. Perhaps equally influential were Lerner's discussions with Tarshis.

21. JR 1978a:xv.

22. *JMK* 14:148. Heffers is a famous Cambridge bookstore. JR continued to refer to students as "our young men." Harcourt [1963:493] asked, "Why should Mrs. Robinson, of all people, be so imbued with the Oxbridge spirit as to think that undergraduates consist of young men only?"

23. Walsh 1970:128–129.

24. Samuelson is referring to Thomas S. Kuhn's *The Structure of Scientific Revolutions* [Patinkin and Leith 1978:118–119].

25. Straight 1983:57.

26. Straight to author November 25, 1985.

27. Ibid.

28. Straight 1983:57–58.

29. Ibid., 12. Straight noted that "strictly speaking, the student Marxists did not join the Communist Party of Great Britain." Straight to author March 26, 1988.

30. Galbraith 1971:48.

31. Bryce [Patinkin and Leith 1978:39–40].

32. Galbraith 1971:47.

33. Salant and Samuelson [Patinkin and Leith 1978:45].

34. Bryce [Patinkin and Leith 1978:40–41].

35. Tarshis [Harcourt 1982:375n].

36. Hansen 1939:1–15.

37. Galbraith 1971:50–51.

38. Hansen 1936:667n. He wrote: "Keynes's new work is especially inspired by Malthus. In connection with his current appreciation of the work of John A. Hobson (only slightly in evidence in the *Treatise* of six years ago) it is not without interest to turn back to a review of Hobson's *Gold, Prices and Wages* . . . written twenty-three years ago. In this review Mr. Keynes says: 'One comes to a new book by Mr. Hobson with mixed feelings, in hope of stimulating ideas and of some fruitful criticisms of orthodoxy from an independent

and individual standpoint, but expectant also of much sophistry, misunderstanding, and perverse thought. . . . The book is . . . made much worse than a really stupid book could be, by exactly those characteristics of cleverness and intermittent reasonableness which have borne good fruit in the past'. This characterization by Mr. Keynes himself is not altogether inapplicable, some will perhaps say, to his own book.''

39. Galbraith 1971:50–51.

40. Barber 1987:191.

41. Galbraith [1971:49–51] said Keynes wrote admiringly of this group of young Washington disciples, who included Richard Gilbert, Richard Musgrave, Alan Sweezy, George Jaszi, G. Griffith Johnson, and Walter Salant.

42. Arrow 1975:5. This was the John R. Commons Lecture for 1973.

43. Samuelson [Patinkin and Leith 1978:87].

44. Salant [Patinkin and Leith 1978:46–47].

45. Friedman 1972:936–937.

46. Warren S. Gramm [Samuels 1976:172–173] quoting from J. Ronnie Davis, *The New Economics and the Old Economists* (Ames: Iowa State University Press, 1971).

47. Friedman 1972:937.

48. JR 1962a:74–76. By classics JR meant Adam Smith and Ricardo, and not Marshall and Pigou as Keynes had.

49. JR 1937a.

50. *JMK* 14:147–148. There are some twenty-two letters between JR and Keynes in *JMK* 14:134–150.

51. AR [Patinkin and Leith 1978:33].

52. *JMK* 14:148–150. Keynes added: '' What my first reaction really boils down to is, I think this. I am gradually getting myself into an outside position towards the book, and am feeling my way to new lines of exposition. Perhaps you will see what I have in mind in my forthcoming lectures. But all this is still extremely half-baked, and what I really do not want to see expounded to the world at this stage are these half-baked changes. But obviously this is really subjective to my own state of mind. It has no bearing worth mentioning on your draft.''

53. JR 1937b.

54. Harrod 1937:326.

55. Hawtrey 1937:460. That Hawtrey should have reviewed her book is of interest, since while she had been writing it, Keynes had turned to her for advice on how to deal with Hawtrey [*JMK* 14:34]. She had replied to Keynes, ''I read these letters with great tho' painful interest. If it were I, I should have left all Hawtrey's other points and gone for him on p. 9 of April 3 . . . where he says 'If so, where is the money to come from?' It's no good talking to him until he has taken in the multiplier. . . .''

56. Smith 1938:75.

57. Straight 1938:52–53.

Chapter 6

1. JR 1978a:56.

2. AR Interview 1984.

3. Correspondence between JR and Sraffa [JRP, KCA] indicate their efforts to gain a position for Kalecki.

4. AR [Patinkin and Leith 1978:88]. AR reminds us that Marxism ''was not *au courant* among the economics faculty apart from Maurice Dobb.'' AR to author January 6, 1988.

5. JR 1936a.

6. Keynes wrote this letter on the back of a note from Lydia (Mrs. Keynes). There is

no record of what JR had said to him. *JMK* 13:651. Presumably Keynes was agreeing with the point that Ricardo was a forerunner of Marx.

7. JR 1936a:299–302. JR quoted Strachey in her review.

8. Lord Kahn Interview 1984. As noted on page 67, JR also said she read Marx as a distraction from the news. Kahn thought the Strachey exchange was the real reason. Curiously, Bruce McFarlane [1982:65] offered the rather baffling explanation that JR, "after studying Marx during a stay in France," produced her *Essay on Marxian Economics.*

9. Cf. Earlene Craver [1986], a study based on interviews conducted by Axel Leijonhufvud.

10. Shackle 1967:291–292.

11. Samuelson 1976:847.

12. Leijonhufvud Interview at the University of California, Los Angeles 1985. Craver and Leijonhufvud [1987] venture two hypotheses: "First it appears that the Europeans may have been more ready than the Americans to take the physical sciences as the epistemological model for a 'scientific' economics. Second, some of them at least saw the combination of mathematical specification and statistical confirmation as a bulwark against the intrusion of political ideologies into the social sciences. For the immigrants that had lived through the interwar period in Europe . . . this hope of building a 'wertfrei' social science, immune to propaganda of every kind, gave motivating force to the econometric movement."

13. Queen Mary's College was to remain in Cambridge during wartime. JR's father and mother lived "in a little house next to the university library." Once the United States entered the war, the American army occupied, among other buildings in Cambridge, 62 Grange Road, the house which JR's father purchased after the war and which became the Robinson residence until her death. "62 Grange Road" was the house at which she did much of her work and wrote many of her letters. For many years she slept always in a garden house, which was demolished after her death. AR says, "The hut in the garden was Joan's bedroom. She slept there right round the year. She never used it as a working place. She wrote on a table in the window inside the house." AR to author January 6, 1988.

14. AR Interview 1984.

15. Cambridge University *Reporter* 1939.

16. AR Interview 1984.

17. JR 1973i:x.

18. JR 1966d:vi.

19. JR 1941a, 1941b, 1944, and several book reviews.

20. JR 1981a:143.

21. AR Interview 1984.

22. Ibid.

23. Veazey [Hayman 1977:120–121].

24. *JMK* 13:469, Keynes in an early fragment of "what must have been a preface."

25. *JMK* 13:470. However, Keynes was not referring to quibbles. He recognized that the "appropriate quasi-formal style" of economists left room for a "thousand futile, yet verbally legitimate, objections"; and that much criticism could therefore be "altogether futile and maddeningly irritating."

26. Johnson 1975:107–108. "The Canadian Army had excited a series of riots by its troops in Aldershot, due to its inability to claim the shipping to send them home immediately as expected, and then decided to cool them off by sending the longest-service of them home on ships . . . and as many as possible of the remainder who possessed adequate educational qualifications back to school on the spot."

27. Silberston 1978:3.

28. Johnson 1978:91.

29. Johnson 1975.111.

30. Ibid., 107. There were nine other Canadian soldiers who prevented his feeling "either lonely or snubbed."

31. Ibid., 108. Cambridge undergraduates are not required to attend university lectures.

32. Ibid., 109–110.

33. Actually Johnson was working on his doctorate at Harvard. He interrupted his studies to return to Cambridge, and did not complete it until 1958, two years after leaving Cambridge. He need never have bothered with it had he stayed there. He did apply for his M.A. at Cambridge in 1951.

34. Ibid., 113.

35. Johnson to JR July 2, 1951 JRP, KCA.

36. Cambridge University *Reporter* 1949–56.

37 Kahn Interview 1984.

38. Johnson 1975:116.

39. Blaug 1985:101.

40. Silberston 1978:9–11.

41. Johnson 1975:120.

42. Silberston 1978:11.

43. Johnson 1978:161.

44. Johnson 1975:124.

45. Silberston 1978:12.

46. Blaug 1985:102–3. Blaug attributes this zeal to Johnson and JR certainly had it. Blaug's reference was to Johnson 1971b.

47. Nevertheless, her comment on T. W. Swan [1960] was included. Of the alternative theories of distribution, Kaldor [1956] was required. JR [1953e] was recommended but not required. Thus graduate students at the University of Chicago might be acquainted mainly with Robinson's earliest work.

48. Silberston 1978:11.

49. Johnson 1961.

50. *CEP* 3:100.

51. Samuelson 1972.

52. Leontief 1941.

53. Shackle 1967:292.

54. Samuelson 1972:vii.

55. Boulding 1948:199.

56. Samuelson 1972:xi-xiii.

57. Leontief 1982:104–105. An additional large but declining proportion (21.2 percent from March 1972 to December 1976, compared with 11.6 percent from March 1977 to December 1981) had been taken up with "analysis without mathematical formulation and data." Leontief thought economists ought to be concerned about the state of "splendid isolation in which academic economics now finds itself."

58. The quantity theory of money has many variants. The traditional one is that $MV = PT$, where M = Money, V = Velocity of Circulation, P = Price Level and T = Volume of Trade. While taken to be a theory in the 1920s, it is now recognized to be a tautology.

59. *CEP* 1:viii.

60. *CEP* 1:53–54.

61. *CEP* 1:61.

62. *CEP* 1:75.

63. *CEP* 4:99. This is the argument against the bastard Keynesians as well. In

this way, JR laid the blame for the rebirth of the quantity theory of money at the feet of the American Keynesians.

64. *CEP* 5:168ff and 174.
65. This is the only reference to Friedman in *CEP Index* and refers to *CEP* 5:16n.
66. JR 1971a:75–76.
67. Ibid., 87. JR is agreeing with Patinkin's analysis, which she cites.
68. Lord Kahn Interview 1984.
69. Deane 1978:213–214.

Chapter 7

1. JR 1942a. Because of the war, the book was not reviewed before 1944.
2. Schumpeter 1954:884–885.
3. JR 1966d:1–5.
4. Ibid., 17.
5. Ibid., 34
6. Ibid., 42.
7. Ibid., 51.
8. Ibid., 22.
9. Lord Kahn Interview 1984.
10. Johnson 1978:246.
11. Ibid., 215.
12. JR 1951b.
13. *CEP* 2:73.
14. JR 1956a:371.
15. JR 1966d:vi.
16. Ibid., 41.
17. Ibid., 90–91.
18. Mager 1942:472–473.
19. Shove 1944:47.
20. Ibid., 50.
21. Ibid., 60.
22. Ibid., 47–48.
23. Rogin 1944:134.
24. Ibid., 126–131.
25. According to Harcourt [1982:373], William F. Buckley, Jr. "took up the attack later, devoting a chapter in *God and Man at Yale* to Lorie's book, quoting vigorously out of context."
26. Samuelson Interview 1985.
27. *CEP* 4:265.
28. Ibid., 247–251.
29. *CEP* 2:6–7.
30. *CEP* 4:122–123. Samuelson [1962], in his presidential address to the American Economic Association, had called Marx a minor post-Ricardian.
31. *CEP* 4:26.
32. Ibid., 32.
33. *CEP* 5:290.
34. Harcourt 1982:200.
35. The *Monthly Review* was founded in 1949 as "an independent magazine devoted to analyzing, from a socialist point of view, the most significant trends in domestic and foreign affairs" (May issue). According to Paul Sweezy, Kalecki was affable and willing

to be used as a source of information on the world at large. Sweezy and Kalecki had known each other since before World War II. They enjoyed sharing ideas, particularly during this McCarthy period when people of their political persuasion felt repressed. Sweezy said Kalecki kept no books and didn't write anything down, which seemed a shame, since Kalecki was a great economist. Huberman and Sweezy were very sorry when Kalecki chose to leave New York and return to Poland. Telephone interview 1986 and Sweezy to author February 1988.

36. Sweezy telephone interview 1986. JR did not come to the United States until 1961.
37. JR 1951c:194.
38. Adler telephone interview March 4 and 5, 1988, and letter March 26, 1988.
39. JR 1951c:194–195.
40. JR 1952f:161–172.
41. Hutchison 1981:94. Hutchison does not say where in the pamphlet he found this expression of hope.
42. Ibid., 6.
43. Ibid., 94. Hutchison does not cite where JR did this.
44. JR 1953b:305–306 (November).
45. JR 1953b:389–401 (December).
46. JR 1953b:536–543 (February).
47. JR 1970b and 1972a.
48. Harcourt 1979:663.
49. JR 1961d:265–271.
50. JR 1962c:423–435 (December).
51. JR 1965b:547–549 (January).
52. JR 1966b:11–14 (February).
53. JR 1967g:45–50 (November).
54. JR 1971g:29–37 (January).
55. JR 1976b:50–51 (October).
56. JR referred to one of the essays she wrote in 1953 after reading Sraffa's introduction to Ricardo's *Principles*. Cf. *CEP* 5:247.
57. JR 1977j:50–59 (December).
58. JR 1977a:60–62 (October).
59. JR 1979l:52–53 (January).
60. JR 1979m:48–49, 56 (May).
61. JR 1983b:17 (October). Hal Kursk took notes and later discussed and corrected the work with JR.
62. Few economists read these essays in the *Monthly Review*. Several are now available in *CEP* 3, 4, and 5.
63. Schumpeter 1949:372.
64. Rosdolsky 1977. Rosdolsky (1898–1967) was a Ukrainian Marxist who was arrested by the Gestapo in Cracow in 1942 for aiding Jews, and was taken to Auschwitz in May 1943. He was one of the founders and leading theoreticians of the Communist Party of Western Ukraine, but he left the party in opposition to Stalinism in the late 1920s. He remained "true to the principles of revolutionary Marxism" and devoted himself to scholarship. (John-Paul Himka, *Monthly Review* January 1988, p. 33. See also Appendix Note 7.1 A variety of critics.)
65. JR 1954:141–167 and 1959d:104–106.
66. JR 1959d:106.
67. JR 1956b:269–273.
68. Becker 1977:6–7. The difference between a Marxist and a friendly enemy is that

"the latter criticizes, often *ex cathedra*, and shies away from reconstructive return. . . . The friend returns to first principles. . . ." JR thought that this was what she did: Cf. *CEP* 4:266. There she wanted to correct errors of statement as, for example, Marx's alleged failure to distinguish between capital stock and flows.

69. Bose 1980 and Roosevelt [Schwartz 1977:412–457].

Chapter 8

1. Even so, the environment at Cambridge was very different from the days of the Circus. The department was split between Keynesians and Robertsonians. However, attacks on Keynesians were not a new phenomenon. Keynes had written Harrod even before the appearance of the General Theory, "experience seems to show that people are divided between the old ones whom nothing will shift and are merely amazed by my attempts to underline the points of transition so vital in my own progress, and the young ones who have not been properly brought up and believe nothing in particular. . . . I have no companions it seems, in my own generation, either of earliest teachers or of earliest pupils." Deane 1978:207.

2. JR 1979f:ix.

3. Ibid., vi. In later years JR decided this statement was unfair to Marshall, since Marshall had also wanted dynamic theorizing at Cambridge.

4. Kahn 1984:4.

5. JR 1956a:vi.

6. JR 1979f:10n.

7. Harrod 1937:328.

8. JR 1952a:164.

9. Rothbarth [1946:383–390] was a young colleague who, though an alien, volunteered for service in World War II and was killed.

10. Lord Kaldor Interview 1984. Kaldor [1937] provides "sort of a review of the capital theory controversy starting with Frank Knight."

11. *CEP* 1:155.

12. Goodwin 1952:930.

13. Smithies 1953:636 and 641.

14. Lord Kaldor Interview 1984. Harry Johnson was a member and mentioned that P. T. Bauer, though prominent, was not invited. Silberston [1978] said other nonmembers included Dennis Robertson, Michael Farrell, Ronald Henderson, Alan Prest, Malcolm Fisher, and Maurice Dobb. Other members were Sraffa, "regarded with great respect, but he never came"; Dick Stone "though he didn't often come"; and also Robin Marris, Robin Matthews, Jan Graff, Brian Reddaway, Dick Goodwin, Ken Berrill, and Ruth Cohen.

15. Silberston 1978:10.

16. Samuelson Interview 1985.

17. Solow Interview at MIT, Cambridge, Massachusetts 1985.

18. Johnson 1978:161.

19. JR 1963a:v.

20. Barna 1957:490. In 1966 *Accumulation* was published in French with a translation by Benjamin Stora.

21. Klein 1958:623–624.

22. A production function is the technical relationship between factors of production (capital and labor), assuming a given state of knowledge.

23. JR 1959f:490.

24. Keirstead 1957:559.

25. Lerner 1957:694.

26. Solow 1956a:201.
27. Lerner 1957:693–694.
28. Ibid., 698–699.
29. Ibid., 693–694.
30. JR 1963a:v and 76.
31. Worswick 1963:296–297.
32. Green 1963:386–392. Green compared J. E. Meade's *A Neo-classical Theory of Economic Growth*; F. A. Lutz and D. C. Hague, eds. *The Theory of Capital*, and the "Symposium" in the *Review of Economic Studies*.
33. Hamberg 1963:1109. Hamberg argued that in the past people had the "wisdom of waiting until one's words or models stood the test of time. But the game must be waxing too hot to justify such restraint. In Mrs. Robinson's latest collection, we have three out of four essays that must have gone to press before the ink was hardly dry on the original journal articles." See also 1113–1114.
34. Solow [Klamer 1984:145].
35. Cf. Deane 1978.

Chapter 9

1. There was also the Knight-Hayek controversy before World War II, but this had less in common with the Cambridge controversies than did the nineteenth-century controversy, because although about the nature of capital, it was not about issues in the distribution of income.
2. *CEP* 1:155.
3. *CEP* 1:173.
4. *CEP* 2:75.
5. Harcourt 1972:1.
6. *CEP* 2:114, 131.
7. Cf. JR correspondence and exchanges with Samuelson and Solow in Chapter 10 and *CEP* 2:120.
8. JR 1981a:107.
9. Harcourt 1972:12 and his Bibliography. These did not include Böhm-Bawerk, Marx, or Frank Knight of earlier controversies. The list contained eighteen articles by JR, written between 1953 and 1970; eight articles by Paul Samuelson, written between 1961 and 1966; and thirteen articles by Robert Solow, written between 1956 and 1970.
10. Ibid. Actually Solow viewed his article as an attempt to "diffuse polemics." Solow to author 1988.
11. Harcourt 1972:13.
12. JR 1978a:113.
13. Keynes had introduced confusion by including Pigou and Marshall among the classical economists. In using the term neoclassical, JR was referring to some of the same people, indeed, to anyone after 1870 who, in her view, accepted Say's Law. JR was rather extravagant in accusing anyone who used Walrasian models as "believing in Say's Law."
14. JR 1974e:54. Solow considers Debreu's view rather extreme. JR thought many economists knew Debreu was correct and yet continued teaching as though it were not so. This was part of what she meant by "abdicating."
15. Solow, for example, argues that capital receives a return because it is productive, and that " 'waiting' is a scarce, productive activity, so capitalists have to be paid for it, not 'ought' to be paid." Solow to author February 2, 1988.
16. JR 1974e:55.
17. Ibid., 59.
18. This was due in part to Keynes' ignoring JR's *Imperfect Competition*.

19. Cf. *CEP* 1:182.
20. JR 1969a:vi.
21. *CEP* 2:120.
22. JR 1963a:6.
23. *CEP* 2:120.
24. *CEP* 4:254–263.
25. JR 1978a:126–136.
26. *CEP* 3:50.
27. *CEP* 5:69. Elsewhere in the article (60), JR associated mainstream teaching with the United States.
28. *CEP* 5:88. Samuelson feels that JR refused to understand what he was arguing. Samuelson Interview 1985 and see Chapter 10.
29. *CEP* 5:210–211.
30. Chakravarty 1983.
31. *CEP* 3:100–101.
32. *CEP* 5:80.
33. *CEP* 5:122. This is her major argument and not actually an accusation that the bastard Keynesians "believed" in Say's Law.
34. Ibid., 122.
35. Ibid., 217.
36. *CEP* 4:176–198; *CEP* 1:81–88; and *CEP* 2:271–279.
37. JR 1956a: 48, 91, 238, and 356.
38. *CEP* 5:217. This fundamental point is used by Davidson to differentiate post Keynesians from each other.
39. *CEP* 5:173.
40. Ibid., 199.
41. JR named page 348.
42. JR referred to Samuelson 1976:373.
43. *CEP* 5:217.

Chapter 10

1. Solow Interview 1985.
2. Klamer 1984:128–130.
3. *CEP* 2:114–131.
4. Solow to JR November 26, 1956. All letters and typescripts referred to in this section are part of Solow Personal Papers. There are some 200 pages of this part of his papers. He kindly lent copies to me. I have attempted to capture the spirit of the exchanges.
5. JR 1956d:102.
6. Solow to JR November 26, 1956.
7. JR to Solow December 4, 1956. This response did not seem to Solow an answer to his question.
8. Both JR and Solow continued in the 1950s to write articles relevant to the capital controversy. JR: 1957e, 1958c, 1959a. Solow: 1956b, 1957.
9. Solow 1962:207–218; JR 1962b:258–266.
10. Solow Interview 1985.
11. JR 1971f:167–173.
12. Fisher 1960.
13. Fisher 1970:405.
14. JR quoting Fisher 1971.

15. *CEP* 4 171–173.

16. Solow's notes make it a little difficult to determine exactly what he said in this paragraph.

17. Solow 1970 is the printed edition of the Radcliffe Lectures delivered at the University of Warwick. JR's review: JR 1971d.

18. JR 1981a:136.

19. Samuelson Interview 1985.

20. *Foundations of Economic Analysis* was not published until 1947, mainly because of World War II. In the Preface, Samuelson acknowledged the influence of Professors Abram Bergson, Joseph A. Schumpeter, Wassily Leontief, and E. B. Wilson. The impact of European intellectual immigrants on American economists is documented by the reference to "the middle two," said Samuelson. He added that Gottfried Haberler also influenced him. Samuelson to author, March 4, 1988.

21. Samuelson Interview 1985. JR was then forty-five years old, twelve years Samuelson's senior. Samuelson was born in 1915 in Gary, Indiana.

22. *CEP* 4:258.

23. Samuelson thinks he may have been at that meeting of the secret seminar when "she got started on the theory of capital. It was 1952 in the spring, just after she had come back from Russia. This was maybe in Richard Kahn's rooms. Piero Sraffa and Joan were talking about just what you meant by deepening capital." Samuelson Interview 1985.

24. Samuelson 1972:276ff.

25. Ibid., 118.

26. Ibid., 122 and 146 respectively.

27. On the other hand, Samuelson says he gave Lawrence Klein the title for Klein's dissertation, "The Keynesian Revolution," in his [Samuelson's] obituary of Keynes: Samuelson 1946:200. Samuelson to author March 4, 1988.

28. Samuelson to author March 4, 1988: See Samuelson's *Economics,* third to eighth editions, for his "neoclassical synthesis" that embodies Keynes' *General Theory.*

29. *CEP* 3:56n and 57–58.

30. Ibid., 58n.

31. Minhas 1963 and *CEP* 3:30.

32. *CEP* 4:147. JR (in 1969) explained, "The real mistake was to suppose that a pseudo-production function, which relates the rate of profit to the value of capital at the prices corresponding to that rate of profit, provides the 'neoclassical parable'. Neoclassical 'capital' is a physical quantity which is independent of prices."

33. *CEP* 4:169.

34. Ibid., 18–19, an address given between 1965 and 1972.

35. Ibid., 53, an address given 1968.

36. Ibid., 63, written c. 1968.

37. *CEP* 5:88.

38. Ibid., 83–84n. Most of Samuelson's reply (1975) is reprinted here.

39. Ibid., 86n.

40. Ibid., 87n.

41. Ibid., 89.

42. Samuelson Interview 1985.

43. Ibid., and communication March 4, 1988.

44. Ibid. See also Samuelson's chapter, "Remembering Joan," in forthcoming book on JR by George R. Feiwel.

45. Cf. *CEP* 2:191n. Referring to Samuelson 1958.

46. Cf. *CEP* 2:27–48.

47. Samuelson to JR April 13, 1971 JRP, KCA. Letter includes a numerical example.

Samuelson says he sent JR a number of numerical examples. Samuelson to author March 4, 1988.

48. JR to Samuelson October 14, 1971 written from Canada, JRP, KCA.
49. Samuelson to JR January 28, 1972 JRP, KCA.
50. JR to Samuelson February 1, 1972 JRP, KCA.
51. This was one of JR's favorite Samuelsonisms. She also quoted it *CEP* 3:35.
52. JR to Samuelson February 15, 1972 JRP, KCA.
53. Samuelson to JR February 28, 1972 JRP, KCA.
54. JR to Samuelson March 15, 1972 JRP, KCA.
55. Samuelson to JR undated. Eichner Personal Papers. (Robinson sent a copy of this letter to Eichner with some comments on it.)
56. Samuelson to JR April 14, 1972 JRP, KCA.
57. JR to Samuelson June 15, 1973 JRP, KCA.
58. Samuelson to JR June 23, 1973 JRP, KCA.
59. JR 1975b and Samuelson 1975. JR had already written on this subject in a review article which I introduce here as well: JR 1970e.
60. Ruth Cohen, retired Principal of Newnham College, finds it amusing that visiting American scholars always ask her about this. Cohen Interview 1984.
61. JR 1970e:145.
62. Ibid., 146.
63. *CEP* 5:81. JR explained her point: "The machines required for different techniques on his 'surrogate production function' are different with respect to engineering specifications, but with each technique, the ratio of labor to machines required to produce the machines is the same as that required to produce the homogeneous consumption goods. That is to say, the cost of capital is determined solely by labor embodied in the machines required for each technique and the time pattern of all techniques is the same."
64. Ibid., 81–83. Actually, JR first set out in *Accumulation* "what came to be called a pseudo-production function, purporting to list the techniques specified in a supposed 'book of blueprints' representing the state of technical knowledge." Cf. *CEP* 2:viii (second edition). JR said Solow was the first to call it a "pseudo production function" in 1963 [Solow 1963]. Also see *CEP* 5:82–83 where she says, "the pseudo-production function [meaning hers in *Accumulation*] was constructed in order to show that the concept of the marginal productivity of capital has no meaning." However, Solow thinks he invented the pseudo-production function rather than simply naming someone else's concept. Solow to author March 1988.
65. *CEP* 5:77–80.
66. Ibid., 81–82.
67. Samuelson [*CEP* 5:83 and 85 respectively].
68. Ibid., 86–87. Here Samuelson was referring to the Japanese film widely considered a masterpiece. The director, Akira Kurosawa, took his script from two stories by Ryunosuke Akutagawa. The first story takes place at the ruined Rashomon, the largest gate in Kyoto, the ancient capital of Japan, and mainly gives the film its name. In the second story, "In a Grove," the "reader is presented with seven testimonies and given no indication of how he should think about them. Akutagawa's point was the simple one that all truth is relative, with the corollary that there is thus no truth at all" [Richie 1965]. The film examines four conflicting yet equally credible accounts of the same crime in "a brilliant cinematic questioning of the nature of truth" [Bowden 1976].
69. Samuelson Interview 1985.

Chapter 11

1. JR [Kahn 1984:203].
2. Clower Interview 1985. The interview was conducted at Professor Clower's office at the University of California, Los Angeles. Unless otherwise indicated the quotations in this chapter are taken from that interview.
3. JR to Clower September 27, 1976 JRP, KCA.
4. Clower [Hahn and Brechling 1966:103–125].
5. Ibid., 103, 111, 124.
6. JR [Kahn 1984:203].
7. Leijonhufvud earned a master's degree at the University of Pittsburgh in 1961 and the Ph.D. from Northwestern in 1967.
8. Leijonhufvud 1968:8.
9. JR 1969d:581–583.
10. Leijonhufvud Interview 1985. Unless otherwise indicated, the quotations in this section are taken from an interview with Professor Leijonhufvud in his office at the University of California, Los Angeles.
11. JR to Leijonhufvud. Leijonhufvud Personal Papers.
12. JR [Kahn 1984:203].
13. JR 1982:295–296. Review of Leijonhufvud 1981.
14. Ibid.
15. Leijonhufvud [Worswick and Trevithick 1983:179]. Having written on "Keynes and the Classics," he rather liked the subject but not the title, which he has now changed for speeches he makes to, "Whatever happened to Keynesian Economics?" (Interview).
16. Johnson 1975:121–122.
17. Ibid., 345 note 3.
18. Ibid., 86–87.
19. Weintraub: 1977:392.
20. Bronfenbrenner [Weintraub 1977:414].
21. Ibid., 419.
22. *CEP* 4:19 referring to Solow 1970. JR referred to this in their private correspondence as his "butter economy." *CEP* 5:38 refers to Samuelson.
23. Deane 1978:201n.
24. *CEP* 4:144.
25. Ibid., 152.
26. AR to author January 14, 1986.
27. *CEP* 4:167–173.
28. Samuelson Interview 1985.
29. Solow Interview 1985.
30. Leijonhufvud and Clower Interviews 1985.
31. Leijonhufvud [Latsis 1976:107].
32. Ibid.

Chapter 12

1. Harcourt does not think this means that "the English in general liked or understood her. There was considerable hostility from those who did not know her and even (intellectually anyway) from those who did." Harcourt to author August 30, 1987.
2. Shackle 1953:73
3. Ibid., 74.

4. Arrow 1953:621.
5. Ibid., 622.
6. *CEP* 1:92.
7. Arrow 1953:622–623.
8. Klein 1958:622.
9. *CEP* 3:v.
10. Bronfenbrenner 1961:413–414.
11. Bronfenbrenner [Weintraub 1977:414].
12. Minsky 1961:497–498.
13. Clower 1961:701–702.
14. Worswick 1962:174–175. S.A. Ozga [1962:174–175] also reviewed *Exercises,* as did Harcourt [1961]. Harcourt thought the method of getting students to draw diagrams might answer critics of *Accumulation* who complained that there were "very few 'pictures'."
15. JR 1962a:21 and 24–25.
16. Hunter 1968:495.
17. JR 1962a:46–47.
18. Ibid., 98–100.
19. Ibid., 124.
20. Ibid., 147.
21. Klappholz 1963:321–322.
22. Baran 1963: 455–458.
23. Harcourt to author August 30, 1987.
24. Stigler 1963:192–193.
25. Harcourt 1963:493.
26. Boulding 1963:657–658.
27. Jaffe 1963:164–165.
28. JR 1981a: 105 and 112.
29. *Economic Philosophy* (JR 1962a) was also popular in Australia, where it was reviewed by Harcourt 1963.
30. *CEP* 3:xv (Second edition)
31. Ibid., iii.
32. Sraffa 1960.
33. Uzawa 1968:204–206.
34. Eschag 1967:351.
35. JR 1966a:7, 14, 11, 67–70.
36. Sharpe 1969:99–100.
37. Eschag 1967:608.
38. JR 1970b and 1972a. For a review, see Copper 1970.
39. JR 1970b:foreword
40. JR 1971a:xv.
41. Ibid., 142, 144.
42. Moszer 1972:69–70; Breimyer 1973:130–131.
43. Asimakopulos 1972:316.
44. Marglin 1973:535–536.
45. Hahn 1972b:206.
46. Tobin 1973 102–103.
47. I am grateful to Graydon Anderson for insisting that I emphasize that American university departments of economics did take account of these factors in their applied texts.
48. Tobin 1973: 105–109, including 106n.
49. In 1931 the Department of Economics had nine lecturers and only one professor of

economics. Marjorie Tappan-Hollond was the only other woman. In JR's last year of teaching, thirty-nine years later, there were nine professors, two readers, twenty lecturers, and ten assistant lecturers, not to mention the twenty-seven lecturers in the Department of Applied Economics and the ten junior research officers. Cambridge University *Reporter*.

50. Meaning Skidelsky's?

51. JR 1973b.

52. JR to Eichner November 7, 1973. All correspondence between JR and Eichner is from Eichner Personal Papers. There are letters which JR wrote to McGraw-Hill among her archival papers KCA, but these are not open to scholars.

53. JR to Eichner October 31, 1973. Eichner Personal Papers.

54. Eichner Personal Papers. A quote from a report dated November 7, 1973.

55. Eichner to JR December 18, 1973.

56. Eichner to JR July 2, 1974.

57. JR to Eichner July 20, 1974.

58. de Schweinitz 1976: 176, 179.

59. Houston 1975:114–116.

60. Gurley 1974:449–450.

61. Needham [Schwartz 1977:305–306, 324].

62. Roosevelt [Schwartz 1977:420].

63. Ibid., 412–413.

64. Ibid., 457 note 157. Roosevelt quoted a Robinson/Eatwell statement about the USSR: "The main obstacle to reforms . . . comes from the objections of the bureaucracy in giving up the power that it enjoys over industry and allocating more independence and initiative to managers, technicians, and engineers."

65. Ibid., 451–452.

66. JR 1979a:ix. JR acknowledged help from several development economists.

67. Ibid., 143.

68. Jameson 1981:266–267.

69. Chakravarty Interview at Cambridge University, 1984. He visited Cambridge from the Delhi School of Economics.

70. JR 1978a, which offers a selection of fifty years of papers "found most useful to students" along with "Reminiscences." JR said 1981d is "mainly concentrated on the dismal 1970s." *CEP* 4 and 5 are a potpourri of subjects.

71. Vandoorne 1980:929.

72. *CEP* 5:43–47.

73. Ibid., 44 and 47.

74. JR 1981d:128–129.

Chapter 13

1. Galbraith 1981:63.

2. Ibid., 35.

3. Galbraith 1971:348–349.

4. Ibid., 351–352.

5. Galbraith 1984:10.

6. Galbraith 1981:88.

7. Galbraith Interview at his home in Cambridge, Massachusetts 1985.

8. Galbraith 1981:74–75.

9. Ibid.

10. Ibid., 199. The object of the study was to evaluate the success of the air attacks by the Allies. Galbraith's subordinates included Nicholas Kaldor and others "about to become famous"—among them Paul A. Baran, E. F. Schumacher, and Edward Denison.

11. Galbraith Interview 1985.

12. Galbraith 1981:63.

13. Ibid., 526.

14. Ibid., 31. Galbraith learned that his nomination (which is equivalent to election) was opposed by Milton Friedman, who argued in part that Galbraith should not be honored by an organization that had denied a similar honor to Veblen. Galbraith thinks this argument may, instead, have aided his case.

15. Galbraith to McGraw-Hill, JRP, KCA.

16. Veazey [Skidelsky 1977:16].

17. Galbraith Interview 1985.

18. Robbins 1981a:114–116. Robbins was defending the deductive method against interlopers such as "a Veblen, or a Hamilton," who were attempting to use historical analysis and induction. Robbins complained that such methods produced no "concrete laws." Thus institutionalists were seen by Robbins as opponents of the traditional English methodology. Galbraith never accepted the mantle of institutionalism. There is a tale, perhaps apocryphal, that Rosemary Summerfield, fresh from Texas and a graduate student of Galbraith's, asked him why he didn't just come out and admit to being an institutionalist. His rumored reply was that it would be worth his job. When asked about this supposed incident, Galbraith replied with a chuckle that he doubted he was ever so worried about his job.

19. Galbraith 1981:29.

20. Immediately after World War II, Galbraith had written *A Theory of Price Control* (1952a). He considers it [1981:174–175] "one of my more important books. No other combines such technical competence as I possess in economics with such experience in the subject [as head of domestic price control during World War II]. It was so regarded by its reviewers. But there were few of these and, initially, few readers of any kind. The experience persuaded me that one could spend one's life producing professionally well-regarded books that would go extensively unread. And one could be even less fortunate. In the natural course of events, one's books come to those reviewers, the established specialists in the field, who are the strongest defenders of the established view. It is a system that selects an adverse jury for all inclined to innovation. I decided that henceforth I would submit myself to a wider audience, a decision that, in contrast with some others, I have not regretted."

21. Galbraith 1952b reviewed by JR 1952g:925–926.

22. JR 1952g:928. David Reisman [1980:112] concluded that "Galbraith in his pursuit of a balanced society became progressively more interventionist" over the next quarter century. But Galbraith [Interview] countered with, "I always took for granted that a successful economy required a large role of the state and that as a practical matter I had reached the peak of my practical interventionist commitment in World War II when I was nominally, at least, in charge of all the prices in the United States. You could hardly be more interventionist than that."

23. JR 1962a:140

24. *CEP* 2:8. I asked Galbraith if he remembered Schumpeter's ever discussing JR with him. "No, I don't. I'd be surprised if he didn't, because it was almost all that he did discuss, mostly unfavorably."

25. *CEP* 2:242–245.

26. JR 1962a:132–134.

27. *CEP* 3:112 and 4:35.

28. *CEP* 3:171.

29. *CEP* 5:14.

30. Ibid., 94.

31. Ibid., 182.

32. Gambs 1975:348 and 112–113. Gambs was annoyed, for example, that Galbraith, in his *China Passage*, made no mention of JR's *Cultural Revolution in China*.

33. Reisman 1980:166. Reisman [173] explained Galbraith's alleged neglect of credit to others in this way: "Galbraith for two decades regarded himself as virtually isolated within the economics profession; . . . he believed himself forced in consequence to aim at a much wider readership than that of specialists alone; . . . he fully appreciated how essential simplification and verbal brilliance are likely to prove if one seeks to reach a generalist audience."

34. Galbraith 1981:3.

35. Hession 1972:17.

36. Galbraith 1981:63

37. Hession 1972:210 and Ellis 1948.

38. Galbraith [Ellis 1948:103].

39. Galbraith 1981:391.

40. Galbraith 1971:34.

41. Galbraith [1981:264] reports a luncheon remark that Henry Luce made to John F. Kennedy which was relayed to him by Kennedy. Said Luce, "I taught Kenneth Galbraith to write. And I tell you I've certainly regretted it." What Luce had taught him was "to drain out excess verbiage."

42. Galbraith 1971:30.

43. Gruchy 1972:168 quoting from Galbraith 1967:215.

44. Galbraith 1981:537 from a political speech made in 1980.

45. *CEP* 3:172.

46. Galbraith Interview 1985.

47. Ibid.

Chapter 14

1. Among JRP, KCA are only those passports covering 1946 to 1955 and 1960 to 1965. See Appendix Note 14.1 Robinson's passports.

2. Clarissa Kaldor to JR January 2, 1960 JRP, KCA.

3. Clower and Davidson Interviews 1985. AR reminded me that there was a period when a foreigner could not visit the USA if she had a visa from mainland China in her passport, and that JR was more interested in visiting China than the USA.

4. JR to Solow January 17, 1961. At Harvard, JR proposed to speak on "Time in Economic Theory." Solow Personal Papers. All correspondence between them is from Solow Personal Papers, copies of which Solow kindly lent me.

5. Solow to JR February 13, 1961. He asked her, "Can I make a case that this is a matter of the utmost national importance and the Council of Economic Advisers can hardly survive if I am not here?" Solow wasn't able to leave Washington for the occasion.

6. JR 1978a:xviii.

7. Clower Interview 1985. After her visit, Clower went to Liberia to finish his study. In the fall of 1962, he visited Cambridge at JR's invitation. At this time he decided "development was a rubbish subject." He then went on to other things. By 1976, JR had relegated Clower to the classification of a "distinguished neoclassical." But in the meantime, they got on well.

8. Clower Interview 1985. Unless otherwise indicated, all subsequent quotations from Clower in this chapter were taken from this interview.

9. Johnson 1975:110. I am assuming that this occurred on the 1961 visit. Johnson gives no date.

10. Grubbs telephone interview 1985.

11. C.A. Watts & Co., Ltd. to Ayres September 18, 1961, Ayres Papers, University of Texas Archives.

12. Ayres to JR September 25, 1961, Ayres Papers, University of Texas Archives.

13. Breit [1979:33–35] styles Ayres "American institutional economist and social philosopher." Born in Lowell, Massachusetts, May 6, 1891, Ayres studied philosophy at Brown University and later at the University of Chicago. He taught philosophy at Amherst and Reed Colleges, and was associate editor of *The New Republic* in the 1920s. Ayres was appointed professor of economics at the University of Texas (Austin) in 1930.

14. Ayres to Robinson, October 16, 1961 JRP, KCA.

15. JR 1962a:109.

16. Rostow to JR May 29, 1951 JRP, KCA. Rostow was working on *The Process of Economic Growth* (1952).

17. Rostow to JR June 7, 1951 JRP, KCA.

18. Cf. Rostow 1960.

19. JR 1962a:110–111. "Thus the airplane is a combination of a kite and an internal combustion engine. . . ." from Ayres 1944:112.

20. Ayres 1961.

21. JR 1962a:13.

22. Ayres to JR November 1, 1962 JRP, KCA.

23. Cf. Gordon 1980:87.

24. JR had not read Ayres' new manuscript on values which contained his more recent thinking, and there is no suggestion in the correspondence that she ever did.

25. Ayres to JR November 1, 1962 JRP, KCA.

26. JR 1962a:10–11.

27. Ayres to JR November 12, 1962 JRP, KCA. Harry Johnson [Patinkin and Leith 1978:107], writing of Cambridge, said, "The automobile was virtually unknown to the academic, even in the early 1950s. (The only car owners I recall were Ruth Cohen, who had been corrupted by a travelling fellowship in the United States prewar, and Nicholas Kaldor, who was independently very wealthy.)"

28. Ayres to JR November 28, 1962 JRP, KCA.

29. Ayres to JR October 17, 1963 JRP, KCA.

30. Moore had influenced Keynes. Thus it is fair to say that Moore's teaching that one could and should influence the outcome of events was a belief which separated Keynes and then JR from the Marshallian tradition, and certainly from the utilitarianism of Bentham. We do not know whether JR replied to Ayres' questions about the early influence of Moore.

31. JR 1962a:3. However, JR [1962a:23] rejected Popper's idea "that the natural sciences were no better than the social sciences."

32. Ayres, trying as he was to understand the evolutionary development of society and its values, including its knowledge (technology) and its institutions, never felt any pressure to talk in terms of testable hypotheses.

33. JR 1962a:11.

34. JR 1966a; Ayres to JR February 7, 1969 Ayres Papers, University of Texas Archives.

35. Cf. Harcourt 1979. However, Lord Kahn, who is most likely to know, denied that JR thought of all Americans as fitting a stereotype. Sol Adler agreed with Kahn that JR liked many Americans (Interviews). Her correspondence with Ayres, which was in progress during the summer of 1962 when President John F. Kennedy stood down Nikita Khrushchev over the existence of Soviet ballistic missiles in Cuba, substantiates a good-humored antagonism.

36. Ayres to JR November 1, 12, and 28, 1962 JRP, KCA. Her letters are missing. But in the *Monthly Review* [JR 1961d:271] she referred to the USA as the "wrong mother in the

judgement of Solomon.'' See Chapter 7.

37. Ayres to JR February 7, 1969. Unless otherwise indicated, all quotations from letters between Ayres and JR are in the Ayres Papers, University of Texas Archives.

38. JR 1966a:72.

39. JR to Ayres January 20, 1968.

40. Ayres to JR January 28, 1969.

41. JR to Ayres February 4, 1969.

42. Ayres to JR January 28, 1969.

43. Fishman to author November 26, 1985.

44. E. F. Patterson of Davidson College and the author invited JR to their campuses. Patterson said, ''She was really huffy over the phone.'' In a letter to him in the 1970s she said, ''I wonder what made you think of asking me.'' JR to Patterson April 24, 1973 Patterson Personal Papers.

45. Economics 124:''Political Economy of Advanced Capitalist Countries''; 124a ''Marxian Economics''; 124b ''Chinese and Indian Development''; and 124C ''Advanced Topics in Economics.''

46. Paul Baran, who had long been at Stanford, was no longer living.

47. Weinstein telephone interview 1986.

48. Weintraub to JR February 1, 1972 JRP, KCA.

49. Andrew Postlewaite to author December 12, 1985.

50. Weintraub to JR November 29, 1973 JRP, KCA.

51. ''Commemorative,'' American Economics Association Convention Program, 1985.

52. More than one person interviewed echoed, ''If you know Joan, she can't even carry her own pocketbook, and there has to be somebody around to usher her, pick up the bills, and do things of that sort.''

53. Davidson Interview 1985.

54. Tobin 1973:102.

55. JR 1978a:1–13.

56. Tobin 1973:102.

57. JR 1978a:10–13.

58. Tobin [1973:102–103 and 105] found nothing new in the arguments. He thought the thesis was essentially the same as her *Economic Heresies* (1971) and that it was a replay of the capital controversy and her ''running battle with Paul Samuelson, Robert Solow, *et al*—the 'neo-neoclassicals'.'' Tobin argued, ''the growing numbers of radical economists have been saying the same things. But the profession, 'straight' as well as radical, has been responsive to new challenges, even if slow to anticipate them.''

59. JR 1981a:1–32.

Chapter 15

1. Davidson 1967a.

2. JR to Davidson June 21, 1967. All correspondence referred to between JR and Davidson comes from Davidson Personal Papers, copies of which he kindly lent to me.

3. Davidson was an instructor in physiological chemistry at the University of Pennsylvania before his army service. After the Korean war, he took an MBA at City University of New York and returned to the University of Pennsylvania for a doctorate in economics. Davidson is now Professor of Economics at the University of Tennessee, Knoxville, and editor of the *Journal of Post Keynesian Economics*.

4. Davidson [1980:155] classified himself with Harrod and Shackle as a Keynes Keynesian; JR as neo-Keynesian; Solow, Samuelson, Tobin, Clower, and Leijonhufvud as neoclassical synthesis Keynesians.

5. JR to Davidson July 13, 1967.
6. Davidson to JR August 30, 1967.
7. Davidson 1967b.
8. Davidson to JR January 29, 1968.
9. Davidson to JR April 29, 1968.
10. Eichner received his Ph.D. from Columbia University. He was Professor of Economics at Rutgers University when he died in 1988 of a heart attack at the age of fifty.
11. All correspondence between JR and Eichner is from Eichner Personal Papers, copies of which he kindly lent me. Eichner also put the many undated letters in chronological order.
12. In an undated letter to JR after her visit to Columbia, Eichner outlined his vision: "This alternative would have as one leg, the emphasis on macrodynamic models; as another leg, the emphasis on the development and utilization of human resources; as still another leg a realistic theory of the representative firm, that is the large bureaucratic corporation; and finally, as a fourth leg, a neo-Marxian theory of income distribution purged of all elements of marginal productivity theory." Eichner had not completed this work at the time of his premature death.
13. Eichner to JR, undated answer to her April 1969 comments handwritten on his manuscript.
14. Kurihara 1954.
15. Kregel 1973.
16. Eichner Interview 1985.
17. Davidson to JR February 17, 1970.
18. Davidson Interview 1985. Unless otherwise indicated, subsequent quotations attributed to Davidson are from this interview.
19. Eichner Interview 1985. Unless otherwise indicated, subsequent quotations attributed to Eichner are from this interview.
20. Eichner, Howard Wachtel, Janos Horvath, Tom Asimakopulos, Hyman P. Minsky, M. Ghandou, Donald Harris, Paul Davidson, John Gurley, Howard Sherman, Victoria Chick, J. A. Kregel, A. C. Samli, Martin Pfaff, Robert Lekachman, Kenneth Boulding, and Edward Nell. Stephen Marglin had planned to attend "but was thwarted by imperfect communications."
21. A letter was sent by the post Keynesians to Galbraith who in turn wrote to George Borts, editor of the *American Economic Review*. Galbraith suggested that he was in substantial agreement with the complaint. Borts then told Eichner that the problem was one of maintaining the quality of the journal. Borts noted that the econometricians had been forced to establish their own journal because they were denied access to the *American Economic Review*. Eichner insisted that at the very least referees should not be allowed to remain anonymous. This was brought up at the next meeting of the American Economic Association in Toronto, when Kenneth Arrow was president. The post Keynesians then corresponded with the next two presidents, Walter Heller and Robert A. Gordon, asking the latter for a session on post Keynesian issues. Gordon replied that the topics were already selected and that the closest was a session, "A Critical Look at Keynesian Models." When an official AEA committee met to consider the orientation of the two journals (*AER and JEL*), they ended by recommending the reappointment of the two current editors. Again, the post Keynesians tried for a Keynesian session under Franco Modigliani in 1975, but they were told that all sessions were already set up. Eichner Personal Papers contain relevant letters and replies.
22. Shaikh 1974. Shaikh is now at the New School for Social Research, New York City.
23. JR 1979i:179–180 and Garegnani 1979:181–187.
24. JR to Davidson May 9, 1979.

Chapter 16

1. May 21, 1975 according to the University of Maine records. However, *CEP* 5:43 has this address as having been given in May 1977.

2. Thomas D. Duchesneau to author November 27, 1985.

3. Vandoorne 1980:929-930. See Chapter 12 for fuller discussion.

4. *CEP* 5:43-47.

5. Sylvia Ann Hewlett was born in England and studied economics both in England and America. She won an exhibition to attend Cambridge University at the age of seventeen, and graduated in 1967 with First Class Honors. She was a Kennedy Scholar at Harvard University in 1967-68, took an M.A. degree at Cambridge University, and a Ph.D. in Economics from London University in 1973. She is now Vice President for Economic Studies, United Nations Association of the United States. While a research fellow at Girton College, she came to know JR personally. Hewlett's interests and publications are mainly in the field of developing countries. She had fellowships both in Brazil and Ghana.

6. "Nomination Papers for Gildersleeve Professorship," October 28, 1974, Barnard College.

7. Hewlett Interview in New York City 1985. All quotations attributed to Hewlett are from this interview.

8. JR 1983b:15-17.

9. Members of the honorary degree selection committee were Andrew Heiskell, Chairman, Herbert P. Wilkins, Glen W. Bowersock, Edward O. Wilson, Patricia Graham, Steven Weinberg, and Paul M. Bator, according to the Office of the Governing Boards of Harvard University.

10. Harvard University *Gazette* Commencement Issue, June 1980.

11. JRP, KCA.

12. Tanner Lectures were established in 1978 at Cambridge University to be administered by the University of Utah. Their aim is to "seek to advance and reflect upon the scholarly and scientific learning relating to human values and valuation."

13. Juliet B. Schor graduated magna cum laude from Wesleyan University in 1975 and earned her Ph.D. at the University of Massachusetts in 1982. JR encouraged Schor to submit an article from her dissertation to the *Economic Journal* [Schor 1985]. Schor was at Williams College when JR visited there, but was appointed Assistant Professor of Economics at Harvard University in 1984.

14. These and subsequent quotations are taken from an interview with Schor at Harvard University, 1985.

15. JR to Schor December 29, 1982. All correspondence between JR and Schor is from Schor Personal Papers. Schor kindly lent me copies of these letters.

16. JR to Schor November 25, 1982.

17. JR to Schor December 29, 1982 from New Hamburg, Canada.

18. JR to Schor January 6, 1983.

19. Lewis to author November 15, 1985. JR must have considered herself as visiting the students at Stanford rather than the institution, for she taught courses there as well.

Chapter 17

1. JR 1977c.

2. *CEP* 5:90-98.

3. JR 1981a:1.

4. Schumpeter 1934:256-257.

5. JR 1981a:1-2.

6. Ibid., 3–4. Her quotation is taken from Wiener 1964:90–91.

7. Ibid., 31–32.

8. Samuelson Interview 1985.

9. Narasimhan 1983:215–216.

10. *CEP* 4:252–253.

11. JR to author June 6, 1981.

12. Sweezy telephone interview 1986.

13. *Review of Economic Studies, Journal of Post Keynesian Economics*, and *Cambridge Journal of Economics*, to name only three.

14. Evan Williams in South Wales to JR April 20, 1950. Copy lent to author by Stephen Marglin.

15. Arrow to JR July 25, 1977 JRP, KCA.

16. Arrow 1953:622–623.

17. Roosevelt [Schwartz 1977:450–451]. When JR visited Vassar in 1976, Roosevelt said in discussion that he had written his article to show the Nobel Prize judges that JR was not "dangerous." JRP, KCA.

18. Ibid., 436.

19. Narasimhan [1983:214] said Vinoba Bhave "walked from village to village proclaiming that 'land is free like air and water'."

20. Lindbeck 1985:52.

21. When Nobel wrote his will in 1895 in Paris, Sweden and Norway were still one country. (This union was dissolved in 1905.) There was to be "no consideration whatever" given to the nationality of the candidates. The first prizes were awarded in 1901. According to Lindbeck [1985:38], "the basic idea of the original Nobel prizes was to award *specific achievements* rather than 'outstanding persons'."

22. Two in physics, three in chemistry (and another the year of JR's death), seven in peace, six in literature, and two in physiology and medicine. Ten of these were shared prizes. Between 1901 and 1977 only four percent of laureates were women [Opfell:1980:xiii].

23. These include previous Nobel laureates; members of the prize-awarding bodies; the Nobel Committees; professors in various prize fields at specifically mentioned universities; presidents of representative authors' organizations; members of certain international parliamentary or legal organizations; and members of parliaments and governments.

24. Lindbeck 1985:46–47. The petition signed by 500 women on behalf of JR was probably not considered at all, given these procedures. Samuelson thought it might even have "got their back up." [Interview 1985]

25. Lindbeck 1985:47. The committee begins work in February. Secret votes are cast in October or November and the awards are announced. Prizes are awarded in December.

26. Nobel 1974:240.

27. Nobel 1982:247.

28. Lindbeck 1985:47.

29. Ibid., 52.

30. Samuelson Interview 1985. Prizes can be shared by halves; by thirds; or by one-half, one-fourth, one-fourth.

31. Lindbeck 1985:53–54.

32. Samuelson Interview 1985.

33. Lindbeck 1985:39.

34. Nobel 1982:245–246.

35. Samuelson Interview 1985. Lindbeck [Nobel 1970:255–256] made the awarding speech for Samuelson, noting that the fourth area of Samuelson's specific achievement was that "Samuelson has made outstanding contributions . . . in the field of *capital theory*. . . . Samuelson . . . showed, partly in cooperation with Robert Solow, that it is

possible to develop a logical capital theory—and to speak about a welldefined price of capital—even without adopting such an aggregate concept of capital." Lindbeck also mentions the turnpike theorem, but not the reswitching controversy.

36. Davidson tells a story where he suggested to an economist who wanted to nominate JR that he should name *Accumulation* as the specific achievement. The answer was, "That garbage? Never!" [Davidson Interview]

37. Nobel 1972:202–203.

38. Lindbeck 1985:50.

39. Schor Interview 1985.

40. Before 1983, three people had refused Nobel Prizes, but none were economists. In discussion on a visit to Vassar in 1976, JR is reported by Stephen Rousseas as saying that since she had opposed the institution of the Nobel Prize in the social sciences, she would not know quite what to do if it were offered to her. JRP, KCA.

41. Interviews already referred to.

42. Samuelson [1981:150n] wrote in a footnote that Ohlin would have received a Nobel Prize in 1940 either by himself or with either or both Jacob Viner and Gottfried Haberler, or with Eli Heckscher. Samuelson added, "One cannot forebear playing the game of might-have-been. Here is the most likely scenario of awards from 1901 on: Böhm-Bawerk, Marshall, J. B. Clark, Walras, and Wicksell; Carl Menger, Pareto, Wicksteed, Irving Fisher, and Edgeworth; Sombart, Mitchell, Pigou, Adolph Wagner, Allyn Young, and Cannan; Davenport, Taussig, Schumpeter, Veblen, and Bortkiewicz; Cassel, J. M. Keynes, Heckscher, J.R. Commons, and J. M. Clark; Hawtrey, von Mises, Robertson, H. L. Moore and F. H. Knight." He broke off speculation in his note as of 1930. His list is interesting in two respects: it indicates the dominance of English and European economics over American before 1930; and it gives prominence to institutionalists among the Americans mentioned.

43. Lindbeck 1985:51.

44. Quandt 1976:752. Friedman won a prize that year, and Klein, Stigler, and Solow later.

45. Nicholas Kaldor died in 1986, so, as of 1988, there is only Richard Kahn who might represent the early Cambridge Keynesians.

46. Unless otherwise indicated, all quotations in this section are from interviews previously referred to.

47. Hewlett noted that the New School of Social Research in New York City is an exception, in that two tracks are offered to the Ph.D.—one the orthodox track and the other the alternative track. John Eatwell teaches there in alternate semesters, drawing on his studies at both Harvard and Cambridge.

48. Klamer 1984:ix.

JR

REFERENCES

Allen, Peter (1978) *The Cambridge Apostles*. Cambridge: Cambridge University Press.

Archibald, G. C. (1961) "Chamberlin versus Chicago," *Review of Economic Studies* 29:2–28 (October).

Arrow, Kenneth J. (1953) "Review of Joan Robinson's *Collected Economic Papers*, vol. 1," *Econometrica* 21:621–623 (October).

————— (1975) "Thorstein Veblen as an Economic Theorist," *American Economist* 19:5–9 (Spring).

Asimakopulos, A. (1972) "Review of Joan Robinson's *Economic Heresies*," in *Canadian Journal of Economics* 5:314–316 (May).

Ayres, Clarence E. (1944) *Theory of Economic Progress*. Chapel Hill: University of North Carolina Press.

————— (1961) *Toward a Reasonable Society: The Values of Industrial Civilization*. Austin: University of Texas Press.

Bakke, E. Wight (1938) "Review of Joan Robinson's *Introduction to the Theory of Employment*," in *Annals of the American Academy* 38:230–231 (July).

Baran, Paul A. (1963) "Review of Joan Robinson's *Economic Philosophy*," in *American Economic Review* 53:455–458 (June).

Baranzine, Mauro (1982) *Advances in Economic Theory*. New York: St. Martin's Press.

Barber, William J. (1987) "The Career of Alvin H. Hansen in the 1920's and 1930's," *History of Political Economy* 19:191–205 (Summer).

Barna, T. (1957) "Review of Joan Robinson's *Accumulation of Capital*," in *Economic Journal* 67:490–493 (September).

Becker, James F. (1977) *Marxian Political Economy*. Cambridge: Cambridge University Press.

Bernstein, E. M. (1937) "Review of Joan Robinson's *Essays in the Theory of Employment*," in *Southern Economic Journal*, 27:253–254 (October).

Bernstein, Irving (1971) *The Turbulent Years*. Boston: Houghton Mifflin.

Blackburn, R., ed. (1972) *Ideology in the Social Sciences*. Huntington, New York: Fontana.

Blaug, Mark (1985) *Great Economists Since Keynes*. London: Harvester.

Blitch, Charles P. (1983a) "Allyn A. Young: A Curious Case of Professional Neglect," *History of Political Economy* 15:1–24 (Spring).

————— (1983b) "Allyn Young on Increasing Returns," *Journal of Post Keynesian Economics* 5:359–372 (Spring).

Böhm-Bawerk, Eugen (1949), ed. by Paul Sweezy (and others) *Karl Marx and the Close of His System*. New York: Augustus M. Kelley.

Bose, Arun (1980) *Marx on Exploitation and Inequality.* New Delhi: Oxford University Press.

Boulding, Kenneth (1948) "Samuelson's Foundations: the role of mathematics in Economics," a review of Paul Samuelson's *Foundations of Economic Analysis* in *Journal of Political Economy* 56:187–199 (June).

————— (1963) "Review of Joan Robinson's *Economic Philosophy*," in *American Sociological Review* 28:657–658 (August).

Bowden, Liz-Anne (1976) *Oxford Companion to Film.* Oxford: Oxford University Press.

Bradbrook, M.C. (1969) *That Infidel Place: A Short History of Girton College 1869–1969.* London: Chatto and Windus.

Breimyer, Harold F. (1973) "Review of Joan Robinson's *Economic Heresies*" in *American Journal of Agricultural Economics* 55:130–131 (February). Reviewed with A. G. Papandreou's *Paternalistic Capitalism.*

Bronfenbrenner, Martin (1961) "Review of Joan Robinson's *Collected Economic Papers*, vol. 2," in *American Economic Review* 51:413–414 (June).

————— (1971) *Income Distribution Theory.* Chicago: Aldine.

————— (1979) "Review of Joan Robinson's *Contributions to Modern Economics*," in *Economic Journal* 89:446–447 (December).

Breit, William (1979) "Clarence Ayres," *Biographical Supplement, International Encyclopedia of the Social Sciences.* New York: Free Press, 33–35.

Brun, Ellen and Hersh, Jacques (1977) *Socialist Korea: A Case Study in the Strategy of Economic Development.* New York: Monthly Review Press.

Buck, Paul, ed. (1965) *Social Sciences at Harvard, 1860–1920.* Cambridge: Harvard University Press.

Business Week (1975) "A Socialist who sounds like a conservative," p. 8 (October 20).

Cambridge University *Reporter* (numerous years).

Chakravarty, Sukhamoy (1983) "Joan Robinson: An Appreciation," *Economic and Political Weekly* (Bombay) October 1, 1983.

Chamberlin, Edward H. (1929) "Duopoly: Value Where Sellers are Few," *Quarterly Journal of Economics* 44:63–100 (November).

————— (1933) *The Theory of Monopolistic Competition.* Cambridge: Harvard University Press. First of eight editions.

————— (1934) [and others] "Imperfect Competition," [discussion] in *American Economic Review*, Papers and Proceedings, 24:21–32 (March).

————— (1937) "Monopolistic or Imperfect Competition," *Quarterly Journal of Economics* 51:557–580 (August), and "Erratum" 52:185 (November).

————— (1938) "Reply" [to Nicholas Kaldor], *Quarterly Journal of Economics* 52:530–538 (May).

————— (1951) "Monopolistic Competition Revisited," *Economica*, N.S. 18:343–362 (November).

————— (1952) "'Full Cost' and Monopolistic Competition," *Economic Journal* 62:318–325 (June).

————— (1954), ed. *Monopoly, Competition and Its Regulation*, International Economic Association. London: Macmillan.

————— (1959) "Can Union Power be Curbed?" *Atlantic Monthly* 203:46–50 (June).

Clower, Robert (1961) "Review of Joan Robinson's *Exercises in Economic Analysis*," in *American Economic Review* 51:701-2 (September).

Copper, John D. (1970) "Review of Joan Robinson's *Cultural Revolution in China*," in *Pacific Affairs* 43:438–439 (Fall).

Crane, David, ed.(1981) *Beyond the Monetarists.* Toronto: James Lorimer.

Craver, Earlene (1986) "The Emigration of Austrian Economists," *History of Political Economy* 18:1–32 (Spring).

———— (1987) with Axel Leijonhufvud, "Economics in America: The Continental Influence," *History of Political Economy* 19:173–182 (Summer).

Davidson, Paul (1967a) "The Importance of Demand for Finance," *Oxford Economic Papers* N.S. 19:245–253 (July).

———— (1967b) "A Keynesian View of Patinkin's Theory of Employment," *Economic Journal* 77: 559–578 (September).

———— (1980) "Post Keynesian Economics," and "A Table of Political Economy," *The Public Interest* Special Ed., *The Crisis of Economic Theory* 151–173.

Deane, Phyllis (1978) *The Evolution of Economic Ideas*. Cambridge: Cambridge University Press.

Dictionary of National Biography: John Perceval (1711–1770); Spencer Perceval (1762–1812); Sir John Frederick Maurice (1841–1912); Frederick Denison Maurice (1805–1872); Sir Frederick Barton Maurice (1871–1951); Sir Edward Howard Marsh (1872–1953). Vols. 13, 25, and by year of death. Oxford: Oxford University Press.

Dorfman, Joseph (1949) *Economic Mind in American Civilization*, vol. 3. New York: Viking Press.

Edwards, Corwin D. (1933) "Review of Joan Robinson's *The Economics of Imperfect Competition*," in *American Economic Review* 23:683–685 (December).

Eichner, Alfred S. (1975) with Kregel, J. A. "An Essay on Post-Keynesian Theory: A New Paradigm in Economics," *Journal of Economic Literature* 13:1293–1315 (December).

———— (1978), ed. *A Guide to Post-Keynesian Economics*. Foreword by Joan Robinson. Armonk, New York: M. E. Sharpe.

Eatwell, John and Milgate, Murray, eds. (1983) *Keynes's Economics and the Theory of Value and Distribution*. London: Gerald Duckworth.

Ellis, Howard S. (1948) *A Survey of Contemporary Economics*. Philadelphia: Blakiston.

Ellsworth, P.T. (1938) "Review of Joan Robinson's *Introduction to the Theory of Employment*," in *Journal of Political Economy* 46:730 (October).

Eschag, Eprime (1967a) "Review of Joan Robinson's *Collected Economic Papers*, vol. 3," *Economic Journal* 77:351–354 (June).

———— (1967b) "Review of Joan Robinson's *Economics: An Awkward Corner*," in *Economic Journal* 77:607–609 (September).

Ferguson, C.E. (1970) *Neoclassical Theory of Production and Distribution*. Cambridge: Cambridge University Press.

Findlay, Ronald (1963) "The Robinson Model of Accumulation," in *Economica* N.S. 30:1–12 (February).

———— (1963) "Reply," *Economica* N.S. 30:411–412 (November).

Fisher, Franklin (1969) "The Existence of Aggregate Production Functions," *Econometrica* 37: 553–577 (October).

———— (1970) "Tests of Equality between Sets of Coefficients in Two Linear Regressions," *Econometrica* 38: 361–366 (March).

———— (1971a) "Aggregate Production Functions and the Explanation of Wages," *Review of Economics and Statistics* 53: 305–325 (November).

———— (1971b) "The Existence of Aggregate Production Functions: Reply," *Econometrica* 39:405 (March).

Foster, John (1981) "Joint review of Joan Robinson's *Contributions to Modern Economics* and *The Generalization of the General Theory*," in *Economic Journal* 91:1041–1043 (December).

Frain, H. LaRue (1934) "Review of Joan Robinson's *Economics of Imperfect Competition*," in *Annals of the American Academy* 176:224–5 (November).

Friedman, Milton (1953) *The Methodology of Positive Economics*. Chicago: The University of Chicago Press.

————— (1970) "Counter-Revolution in Monetary Theory." First Wincott Memorial Lecture, University of London, published by The Institute of Economic Affairs.

————— (1972) "Comments of the Critics," *Journal of Political Economy* 80:906–950 (September/October).

Galbraith, John Kenneth (1952a) *A Theory of Price*. Cambridge: Harvard University Press.

————— (1952b) *American Capitalism: The Concept of Countervailing Power.* Boston: Houghton Mifflin.

————— (1958) *The Affluent Society*. Boston: Houghton Mifflin.

————— (1967) *The New Industrial State*. Boston: Houghton Mifflin.

————— (1971) *Economics of Peace and Laughter*. Boston: Houghton Mifflin.

————— (1981) *A Life In Our Times*. Boston: Houghton Mifflin.

————— (1984) "General Keynes," *New York Review of Books* November 22, 10–14.

Gambs, John S. (1975) *John Kenneth Galbraith*. Boston: Twayne Publishers.

Gapinski, James H. and Rockwood, Charles E., eds. (1979) *Essays in Post-Keynesian Inflation*. Cambridge: Ballinger.

Garegnani, Pierangelo (1979) "Notes on Consumption, Investment, and Effective Demand: A Reply to Joan Robinson," *Cambridge Journal of Economics* 3:181–187 (June).

Gillman, Joseph M. (1954) "The Labor Theory of Value: a Discussion," *Science & Society* 18:141–167 (Spring).

Goodwin, Richard M. (1952) "Review of Joan Robinson's *The Rate of Interest and Other Essays*," in *Economic Journal* 62:930–935 (December).

Gordon, Wendell (1980) *Institutional Economics*. Austin: University of Texas Press.

Gram, Harvey and Walsh, Vivian (1983) "Joan Robinson's Economics in Retrospect," *Journal of Economic Literature* 21:518–550 (June).

Grant, Michael (1966) *Cambridge*. London: William Morrow.

Green, H. A. John (1963) "Recent Contributions to the Theory of Economic Growth," *Canadian Journal of Economics and Political Science* 29:386–92 (August).

Gruchy, Allan G. (1972) *Contemporary Economic Thought*. New York: Augustus M. Kelley.

Gurley, John G. (1971) "The State of Political Economics," *American Economic Review*, 61:53–62. "Discussion" 61:63–68 (May).

————— (1974) "Review of Joan Robinson's and John Eatwell's *Introduction to Modern Economics*," in *Economic Journal*, 84:447–450 (June).

Hahn, F. H. with Brechling, F. P. R., eds. (1966) *Theories of Interest Rates*. New York: St. Martin's Press.

————— (1972a) *Share of Wages in National Income*. London School of Economics and Political Science: Weidenfeld and Nicolson.

————— (1972b) "Review of Joan Robinson's *Economic Heresies*," in *Economica* N.S. 39:205–206 (May).

————— (1979) with Hollis, Martin, eds. *Philosophy and Economic Theory*. Oxford: Oxford University Press.

————— (1983) *Money and Inflation*. Cambridge: MIT Press.

Hamberg, D. (1963) "Review of Joan Robinson's *Essays in the Theory of Growth*," in *American Economic Review* 63:1109–1114 (June-December).

Hansen, Alvin (1936) "Mr. Keynes on Underemployment Equilibrium," *Journal of Political Economy*, 44:667–686 (October).

————— (1939) "Economic Progress and Declining Population," *American Economic Review* 29:1–15 (March).

Harcourt, Geoffrey C. (1961) "Review of Joan Robinson's *Exercises in Economic Analysis*," in *Economic Record* 37:393–395 (September).

————— (1963) "Review of Joan Robinson's *Economic Philosophy*," in *Economic Record* 39:492–493 (December).

————— (1967) with Karmel, P. H. and Wallace, R. H. *Economic Activity*. Cambridge: Cambridge University Press.

————— (1969) "Some Cambridge Controversies in the Theory of Capital," *Journal of Economic Literature*, 7:369–405 (June).

————— (1972) *Some Cambridge Controversies in the Theory of Capital*. Cambridge: Cambridge University Press.

————— (1975) "Theoretical Controversy and Social Significance: An Evaluation of the Cambridge Controversies," Edward Shann Memorial Lecture, University of Western Australia Press.

————— (1977), ed. *The Microeconomic Foundations of Macroeconomics*. International Economic Association, New York: Westview Press.

————— (1979) "Joan Robinson," *Biographical Supplement, International Encyclopedia of Social Science*, 663–671. New York: Free Press.

————— (1982), ed. by Kerr, Prue *Social Science Imperialists*. London: Routledge & Kegan Paul.

————— (1985) "A Twentieth Century Eclectic: Richard Goodwin," *Journal of Post Keynesian Economics* 7:410–421 (Spring).

—————(1986), ed. by Hamouda, O. F. *Controversies in Political Economy*. New York: New York University Press.

—————(1987), ed. *Keynes and his Contemporaries* London: Macmillan. Reprinted.

Hardy, Charles O. (1937) "Review of Joan Robinson's *Essays in the Theory of Employment*," in *American Economic Review* 27:529–532 (September).

————— (1938) "Review of Joan Robinson's *Introduction to the Theory of Employment*," in *American Economic Review* 28:528–529 (September).

Harris, Seymour E. (1955) *John Maynard Keynes*. New York: Charles Scribner.

Harrod, R. F. (1937) "Review of Joan Robinson's *Essays in the Theory of Employment*," in *Economic Journal* 47:326–330 (June).

————— (1948) *Towards a Dynamic Economics*. London: Macmillan.

————— (1969) *Life of John Maynard Keynes*. New York: Augustus M. Kelley.

Hart, H. L. A. (1985) "Oxford and Mrs. Thatcher," *New York Review of Books* 32:7–9 (March 28).

Harvard University *Gazette* (1968) "Obituary: E. H. Chamberlin," 43: 197–198 (March 23).

————— (1980) Commencement Issue 55 (June).

Hausman, Daniel M., ed. (1984) *The Philosophy of Economics*. Cambridge: Cambridge University Press.

Hawtrey, R. G. (1937) "Review of Joan Robinson's *Essays in the Theory of Employment*," in *Economica* N.S., 4:455–460 (November).

Hayman, Ronald, ed. (1977) *My Cambridge*. London: Robson Books.

Heath, A. F., ed. (1981) *Scientific Explanation*. Oxford: Clarendon Press.

Heertje, Arnold, ed. (1981) *Schumpeter's Vision: Capitalism, Socialism and Democracy after 40 Years*. New York: Praeger.

Hession, Charles H. (1972) *John Kenneth Galbraith and his Critics*. New York: New American Library.

————— (1984) *John Maynard Keynes*. New York: Macmillan.

Hicks, J. R. (1965) *Capital and Growth*. Oxford: Clarendon Press.

————— (1983) *Classics and Moderns: Collected Essays on Economic Theory*, vol. 3. Oxford: Basil Blackwell.

Hogben, Lancelot (1938) *Science for the Citizen*. London: George Allen & Unwin.

Houston, David (1975) "Review of Joan Robinson's and John Eatwell's *Introduction to*

Modern Economics,'' in *Sloan Management Review* 16:114–116 (Spring).

Howarth, T. E. B. (1978) *Cambridge Between Two Wars.* London: Collins.

Hunt, E. K. and Schwartz, Jesse G. (1973) *A Critique of Economic Theory.* New York: Penguin Education.

Hunter, William D. G. (1968) "Review of Joan Robinson's *Economic Philosophy,*" in *Canadian Journal of Economics,* 1:495–496 (May).

Hutchison, Keith (1938) "Review of Joan Robinson's *Introduction to the Theory of Employment,*" in *The Nation,* June 4, 652–653. Reviewed with Arthur Dahlberg's *When Capital Goes on Strike.*

Hutchison, T. W. (1977) *Knowledge and Ignorance in Economics.* Oxford: Basil Blackwell.

———— (1978) *On Revolutions and Progress in Economic Knowledge.* Cambridge: Cambridge University Press.

———— (1981) *Politics and Philosophy of Economics.* New York: New York University Press.

International Economics Association (1954) *University Teaching of Social Sciences: Economics.* UNESCO.

Jaffe, William (1963) "Review of Joan Robinson's *Economic Philosophy,*" in *Annals of the American Academy,* 348:164–165 (July).

Jameson, Kenneth P. (1981) "Review of Joan Robinson's *Aspects of Development and Underdevelopment,*" in *Journal of Economic Issues* 15:264–267 (March).

Johnson, Harry G. (1961) "The General Theory After Twenty-five Years," *American Economic Review* 51: 1–17 (May).

———— (1962) *Money Trade and Economic Growth: Essays in Monetary Economics.* Cambridge: Harvard University Press.

———— (1971a), ed. *Income Distribution Theory.* Chicago: Aldine.

———— (1971b) "The Keynesian Revolution and the Monetarist Counter-Revolution," *American Economic Review,* 61:1–14 (May).

———— (1975) *On Economics and Society.* Chicago: University of Chicago Press.

———— (1978) with Johnson, Elizabeth *The Shadow of Keynes.* Chicago: University of Chicago Press.

Kahn, Richard F. (1977) "Malinvaud on Keynes," *Cambridge Journal of Economics* 1:375–388 (December).

———— (1984) *The Making of Keynes' General Theory.* Cambridge: Cambridge University Press.

Kaldor, Nicholas (1934) "Mrs. Robinson's Economics of Imperfect Competition," *Economica* N. S. 1:335–341 (August).

———— (1937) "Annual Survey of Economic Theory; The Recent Survey On the Theory of Capital," *Econometrica* 5:201–233 (July).

———— (1938) "Professor Chamberlin on Monopolistic and Imperfect Competition," *Quarterly Journal of Economics* 52:513–529 (May).

———— (1956) "Alternative Theories of Distribution," *Review of Economic Studies* 23:83–100.

———— (1972) "The Irrelevance of Equilibrium Economics," and "Appendix," *Economic Journal* 82:1237–1255 (December).

Keirstead, B. S. (1957) "The Structure and Accumulation of Capital," including a review of Joan Robinson's *Accumulation of Capital* and L. M. Lachmann's *Capital and its Structure,* in *Canadian Journal of Economics and Political Science* 23:555–559 (November).

Keynes, John Maynard (1930) *A Treatise on Money.* 2 vol. London: Macmillan.

———— (1936) *The General Theory of Employment Interest and Money.* New York: Harcourt Brace.

————— (various years), ed. by Moggridge, Donald. *The Collected Writings of John Maynard Keynes*. London: Macmillan and Cambridge University Press. Referred to as *JMK*.

Klamer, Arjo (1984) *Conversations with Economists*. Totowa, New Jersey: Rowman & Allanheld.

Klappholz, Kurt (1963) "Review of Joan Robinson's *Economic Philosophy*," in *Economica* N. S. 30:321–322 (August).

Klein, Lawrence R. (1958) "Review of Joan Robinson's *Accumulation of Capital*," in *Econometrica* 26:622–624 (October).

————— (1966) *The Keynesian Revolution*. New York: Macmillan.

Knox, A. D. (1953) "Review of Joan Robinson's *The Rate of Interest and other Essays*," in *Economica* N. S. 20:170–171 (May).

Kregel, J. A. (1973) *The Reconstruction of Political Economy*. Foreword by Joan Robinson. New York: John Wiley.

Kuenne, Robert E. (1967) *Monopolistic Competition Theory: Essays in Honor of E. H. Chamberlin*. New York: John Wiley.

Kuhne, Karl (1979) *Economics and Marxism*, vol. 2. Translated by Robert Shaw. New York: St. Martin's Press.

Kurihara, Kenneth K. (1954) *Post Keynesian Economics*. New Brunswick, New Jersey: Rutgers University Press.

Latsis, Spiro J. (1976) *Method and Appraisal in Economics*. Cambridge: Cambridge University Press.

Lawson, Tony and Pesaran, Hashem (1985) *Keynes Economics: Methodological Issues*. London and Sydney: Croom Helm.

Leijonhufvud, Axel (1968) *On Keynesian Economics and the Economics of Keynes*. Oxford: Oxford University Press.

————— (1981) *Information and Coordination*. Oxford: Oxford University Press.

Leontief, Wassily (1941) *The Structure of American Economy 1919–1929*. Oxford: Oxford University Press. Second edition, enlarged, *1919–1939*, published in 1951.

————— (1982) "Letter," *Science* 217:104–105 (July).

Lerner, Abba P. (1936) "Mr. Keynes' General Theory of Employment Interest and Money," *International Labor Review*. 34:435–454 (October).

————— (1957) "Review of Joan Robinson's *Accumulation of Capital*," in *American Economic Review* 47:693–699 (September).

Lindbeck, Assar (1985) "The Prize in Economic Science in Memory of Alfred Nobel," *Journal of Economic Literature* 23:37–56 (March).

Loasby, Brian J. (1976) *Choice, Complexity and Ignorance*. Cambridge: Cambridge University Press.

Lowe, Victor (1985) *Alfred North Whitehead*, vol. 1:1861–1910. Baltimore: Johns Hopkins University Press.

Machlup, Fritz (1934–1935) "The Commonsense of the Elasticity of the Theory of Substitution," in *Review of Economic Studies* 2:202–213.

————— (1976) *Essays on Hayek*. Foreword by Milton Friedman. New York: New York University Press.

McFarlane, Bruce (1982) *Radical Economics*. New York: St. Martin's Press.

Mager, Harold (1942) "Review of Joan Robinson's *Essay on Marxian Economics*," in *The New Republic* 107: 472–473 (October 12).

Marglin, Stephen A. (1973) "Review of Joan Robinson's *Economic Heresies*," in *Economic Journal* 83:535–538 (June).

Minhas, B. S. (1963) *An International Comparison of Factor Costs and Factor Use*. Amsterdam: North Holland Publishers.

Minsky, Hyman P. (1961) "Review of Joan Robinson's *Collected Economic Papers*, vol. 2," *Journal of Political Economy* 69:497–498 (October). (Mislabeled Volume 1.)

————— (1975) *John Maynard Keynes*. New York: Columbia University Press.

Mont Pelerin Society (1961) *Statement of Aims* (January 1).

Moggridge, Donald, ed., vols. 1–29 *The Collected Writings of John Maynard Keynes*. London & Cambridge: Macmillan and Cambridge University Press. Referred to as *JMK*.

Morison, Samuel Eliot (1937) *Three Centuries of Harvard*. Cambridge: Harvard University Press.

Moszer, Max (1972) "Review of Joan Robinson's *Economic Heresies*," in *Monthly Labor Review* 23:69–70 (March).

Narasimhan, Sita (1983) "Joan Robinson In the Radical Vein: a Laywoman's Homage," *Cambridge Journal of Economics*. 7:213–219 (September/December).

Nevile, J. W. (1963) "Review of Joan Robinson's *Essays in the Theory of Economic Growth*," in *Economic Record* 39:385–386 (September).

Newman, Peter (1960) "The Erosion of Marshall's Theory of Value," *Quarterly Journal of Economics* 74:587–600 (November).

Nichol, A. J. (1934) "Review of Joan Robinson's *Theory of Imperfect Competition*," in *Journal of Political Economy* 42:257–259.

Nobel Foundation (numerous years) *The Prize for Economic Science in Memory of Alfred Nobel*. Official Translation.

Opfell, Olga (1978) *The Lady Laureats*. London: The Scarecrow Press.

Oser, Jacob (1970) *The Evolution of Economic Thought*, second ed. New York: Harcourt Brace.

Ozga, S. A. (1962) "Review of Joan Robinson's *Exercises in Economic Analysis*," in *Economica* N.S. 29:301–302 (August).

Pajestka, Jozef and Feinstein, C. H., eds. (1980) *The Relevance of Economic Theories*. International Economics Association. New York: St. Martin's Press.

Patinkin, Don (1976) *Keynes' Monetary Thought*. Durham, North Carolina: Duke University Press.

————— (1978) with Leith, J. Clark, eds. *Keynes, Cambridge and the General Theory*. Toronto: University of Toronto Press.

————— (1981) *Essays on and in the Chicago Tradition*. Durham, North Carolina: Duke University Press.

————— (1982) *Anticipations of the General Theory*. Chicago: University of Chicago Press.

Pelling, Henry (1963) *A History of British Trade Unionism*. London: Pelican Original.

Penrose, Edith (1980) "Review of Joan Robinson's *Aspects of Development and Underdevelopment*," in *Economic Journal*, 90:623–625 (September).

Perlman, Selig (1937) "Review of Joan Robinson's *Essays in the Theory of Employment*," in *American Political Science Review* 31:1191–1192 (December).

Phillips, Ann, ed. (1979) *A Newnham Anthology*. Cambridge: Cambridge University Press.

Putnam, Hilary (1981) "Philosophers and Human Understanding," in Heath (1981).

Quandt, Richard E. (1976) "Some Quantitative Aspects of the Economics Journal Literature," in *Journal of Political Economy* 84:741–755 (August).

Reder, Melvin W. (1982) "Chicago Economics: Permanence and Change," *Journal of Economic Literature* 20:1–38 (March).

Reisman, David (1980) *Galbraith and Market Capitalism*. New York: New York University Press.

Richie, Donald (1965) *The Films of Akira Kurosawa*. Chapel Hill, North Carolina: University of North Carolina Press.

Robbins, Lionel (1963) *Politics and Economics*. New York: St. Martin's Press.
———— (1971) *Autobiography of an Economist*. London: Macmillan.
———— (1981a) *An Essay on the Nature and Significance of Economic Science*. New York: Macmillan. 3rd ed. (1st ed. 1932)
———— (1981b) "Economics and Political Economy," Richard T. Ely Lecture in *American Economic Review*, Papers and Proceedings 71:1–10 (May).
Robinson, Austin (1947) "John Maynard Keynes," *Economic Journal* 57:1–68 (March).
———— (1978) "Keynes and his Cambridge Colleagues," in Patinkin and Leith (1978).
Robinson, Joan (1920s) with Dorothea Morison (afterwards Mrs. R. B. Braithwaite) "Beauty and the Beast," an undergraduate paper presented to the Marshall Society. *CEP* 1:225–233 and *Contributions to Modern Economics* 267–274.
———— (1932a) *Economics is a Serious Subject*. Cambridge: Students' Bookstore.
———— (1932b) "Imperfect Competition and the Falling Supply Price," *Economic Journal* 42:544–554 (December).
———— (1933a) *The Economics of Imperfect Competition*. London: Macmillan. Second ed. 1969.
———— (1933b) "A Parable of Saving and Investment," *Economica* 39:75–84 (February). (First written in the summer of 1931 according to *JMK* 13:268.)
———— (1933c) "The Theory of Money and the Analysis of Output," *Review of Economic Studies* 1:22–26 (October). *CEP* 1:52–58 and *Contributions to Modern Economics* 14–19.
———— (1934a) "Euler's Theorem and the Problem of Distribution," *Economic Journal* 44:398–414 (September). *CEP* 1:1–20.
———— (1934b) "What is Perfect Competition?" *Quarterly Journal of Economics* 49:104–120 (November). *CEP* 1:20–35.
———— (1934c) "Mr. Fraser on Taxation and Returns," *Review of Economic Studies* 1:137–140 (February).
———— (1935a) When reprinted the following were entitled "Essays 1935": "Introduction"; "Full Employment"; "Disguised Unemployment"; "The Foreign Exchanges"; "Beggar-My-Neighbor Remedies for the Unemployment"; "An Economist's Sermon"; all reprinted from *Essays in the Theory of Employment* in *CEP* 4:174–241. "Beggar-My-Neighbor Remedies for Unemployment" also in *Contributions to Modern Economics*, 190–200.
———— (1935b) "A Fundamental Objection to Laissez-Faire," *Economic Journal* 45:580–582 (September). Reprinted in as "An Inherent Defect in Laissez-Faire," *CEP* 1:49–51.
———— (1936a) "Review of John Strachey's *The Nature of Capitalist Crisis*," in *Economic Journal* 46:298–302 (June). [Referred to in *JMK* 13:651 note]
———— (1936b) "Review of R.F. Harrod's *The Trade Cycle*," in *Economic Journal* 46:690–693 (December). *CEP* 1:59–61.
———— (1936c) "Disguised Unemployment," *Economic Journal* 46:225–237 (June) and "Rejoinder" to Harold Berger, *Economic Journal* 46:759–760 and in *Essays in the Theory of Employment* (1937a); then see above (1935a).
———— (1936d) "Comment: Reply to F. Machlup," *Review of Economic Studies* 3:148 (February).
———— (1937a) *Essays in the Theory of Employment*. London: Macmillan. 1947 second ed. Oxford: Basil Blackwell.
———— (1937b) *Introduction to the Theory of Employment*. London: Macmillan.
———— (1938a) "The Concept of Hoarding," *Economic Journal* 48:231–236 (June). *CEP* 1:62–68 and *Contributions to Modern Economics* 29–34.

————— (1938b) "The Economics of Hyper-Inflation," a review of Bresciani-Turroni's *The Economics of Inflation* in *Economic Journal* 48:507–513 (September). *CEP* 1:69–77.

————— (1939) "Review of Gunnar Myrdal's *Monetary Equilibrium*," in *Economic Journal* 49:493–495 (September). *CEP* 1:78–80.

————— (1941a) "Marx on Unemployment," *Economic Journal* 51:234–248 (June/September).

————— (1941b) "Rising Supply Price," in *Economica* 8:1–8 (February). *CEP* 1:35–44.

————— (1941c) "Marx and Keynes." This paper appeared in Italian in *Critica Economica* in November 1948. "The first two paragraphs are taken from an article which appeared in *Economic Journal* in June-September 1941." *CEP* 1:133–145.

————— (1942a) *An Essay on Marxian Economics*. London: Macmillan. 1966 second ed. New York: St. Martin's Press.

————— (1942b) "Review of Neil H. Borden's *The Economic Effects of Advertising,*" in *Economica* N.S. 9:294–96 (August). *CEP* 1:46–48.

————— (1942c) "Economic Consequences of a Decline in the Population of Great Britain," a paper written during the war and not published until *CEP* 1:115–132.

————— (1943a) "Planning Full Employment," London *Times* January 22 and 23. *CEP* 1:81–88.

————— (1943b) "Review of J.A. Schumpeter's *Capitalism, Socialism and Democracy*," in *Economic Journal* 53:381–383 (December). *CEP* 1:152–154 and *What Are the Questions?* 141–143.

————— (1943c) "Review of Ruby Turner Norris' *The Theory of Consumer's Demand*," in *Economic Journal* 53:115–117 (April). *CEP* 1:44–46.

————— (1944) "An analysis of the Department of Commerce Report: 'Official Paper: The United States in the World Economy'," *Economic Journal* 54:430–437 (December). *CEP* 1:206–213.

————— (1945a) "War-Time Inflation," a paper which is the basis of a lecture delivered in Paris in January 1945. *CEP* 1:89–98.

————— (1945b) "Review of 'The Economics of Full Employment: Six Studies in Applied Economics Prepared at the Oxford Institute of Statistics'," *Economic Journal* 55:77–82 (April). *CEP* 1:99–104.

————— (1946a) "Obstacles to Full Employment," *Nationaløkonomisk Tidsskrift*, based on a lecture given to the Nationaløkonomisk Forening at Copenhagen on December 6, 1946. *CEP* 1:105–114.

————— (1946b) "The Pure Theory of International Trade," *Review of Economic Studies* 14:98–112. *CEP* 1:182–205.

————— (1949a) "The Theory of Planning," a review of Maurice Dobb's *Soviet Economic Development Since 1917*, in *Soviet Studies* (October). *CEP*: 175–181.

————— (1949b) "Mr. Harrod's Dynamics," a review of R.F. Harrod's *Towards a Dynamic Economics*, in *Economic Journal* 59:68–85 (March). *CEP* 1:155–174.

————— (1950a) "The Labor Theory of Value," a review of Eugen von Böhm-Bawerk's *Karl Marx and the Close of his System*; Rudolf Hilferding's *Böhm-Bawerk's Criticism of Marx;* and Ladislaus von Bortkiewicz' *On the Correction of Marx's Fundamental Theoretical Construction in the Third Volume of Capital*, ed. by Paul Sweezy, in *Economic Journal* 60:358–363 (June). *CEP* 1:146–151.

————— (1950b) "Exchange Equilibrium," in *Economia Internazionale* (May). *CEP* 1:214–224.

————— (1951a) *Collected Economic Papers* vol. 1, Oxford: Basil Blackwell. Reprinted by Cambridge: MIT Press.

————— (1951b) "Introduction," to translation of Rosa Luxemburg's *Accumulation of*

Capital. London: Routledge & Kegan Paul. Reissued 1968, New York and London: Modern Reader Paperback. *CEP* 2:59–73.

———— (1951c) "Preparation for War," *Cambridge Today*; reprinted in *Monthly Review* 2:194–195 (October).

———— (1951d) "The Rate of Interest," *Econometrica* 19:92–111 (April). Reprinted in *The Rate of Interest and Other Essays*, Macmillan in 1952 and with the same collection retitled *Generalization of the General Theory and Other Essays*, Macmillan in 1979. *CEP* 2:246–265 and *Contributions to Modern Economics* 35–52.

———— (1952a) *The Rate of Interest and Other Essays.* London: Macmillan. See (1979f) for second edition, issued as *The Generalization of the General Theory.* New York: St. Martin's Press.

———— (1952b) "A Note on Bank Rate," part of a symposium on monetary policy, in *Bulletin* of Oxford University Institute of Statistics (August). *CEP* 2:266–270.

———— (1952c) "The Model of an Expanding Economy," *Economic Journal* 62:42–53 (March). *CEP* 2:74–87.

———— (1952d) "Notes on Marx and Marshall," which formed "Part of the 'Acknowledgments and Disclaimers'" in *The Rate of Interest and Other Essays. CEP* 2:18–26.

———— (1952e) "A Comment," on E. H. Chamberlin's "'Full Cost' and Monopolistic Competition," *Economic Journal* 62:325 (June).

———— (1952f) "Moscow, 1952. Notes on a Journey Made in September 1952," *Monthly Review* 3:157–172 (October).

———— (1952g) "Review of John Kenneth Galbraith's *American Capitalism: the Concept of Contervailing Power*," in *Economic Journal* 62:925–928 (December).

———— (1953a) "On re-reading Marx." Cambridge: Students' Bookshops.

———— (1953b) "Letters From a Visitor to China, July, 1953," *Monthly Review* Part 1, 4:302–310 (November); Part 2, 4:397–407 (December); Part 3, 4:477–480 (January 1954); Part 4, 4:536–543 (February 1954).

———— (1953c) "'Imperfect Competition' Revisited," *Economic Journal* 63:579–593 (September). *CEP* 2:222–238, and *Contributions to Modern Economics* 166–181.

———— (1953d) "Introduction" to "Essays 1953" (Original title "On re-reading Marx," a pamphlet published by Students' Bookshops in 1953.) Other "Essays 1953" are "Would you believe it?" "A Lecture Delivered at Oxford by a Cambridge Economist," and "An Open letter from a Keynesian to a Marxist." *CEP* 4:247–268. " A Lecture . . ." was again republished in *Contributions to Modern Economics* 137–145. "An Open letter . . ." was republished in *What Are the Questions?* 165–169.

———— (1953e) "The Production Function and the Theory of Capital," *Review of Economic Studies* 21:81–106. Partly reprinted in *CEP* 2:114–131 and *Contributions to Modern Economics*, 76–90.

———— (1954) "The Labor Theory of Value: A Discussion," *Science & Society* 18:141–151 (Spring). *CEP*, 2:49–58.

———— (1955) "Marx, Marshall and Keynes," Lectures delivered at the Delhi School of Economics and published by the school as Occasional Paper #9. *CEP* 2:1–17. Also in *Contributions to Modern Economics* 61–75.

———— (1956a) *The Accumulation of Capital.* London: Macmillan.

———— (1956b) "Mr. Wiles' Rationality: A Comment," *Soviet Studies* 7:269–273 (January).

———— (1956c) "India 1955: Unemployment and Planning," *Capital* (Calcutta), Annual Supplement (December). *CEP* 3:182–191.

———— (1956d) "The Production Function and the Theory of Capital—a reply," *Review of Economic Studies* 23:247.

————— (1956e) "A Comment: the Industry and the Market," *Economic Journal* 66:360–361 (June).

————— (1957a) "The Theory of Distribution," an amended version of a paper published in French in *Économie Appliquée* (October-December). *CEP* 2:145–158.

————— (1957b) "Population and Development," a paper read at an economic seminar in Moscow University in July. *CEP* 2:107–113.

————— (1957c) "Notes on the Theory of Economic Development," Published in French in *Annales de la Faculté de Droit de Liège 1957. CEP* 2:88–106.

————— (1957d) "What Remains of Marxism?" a contribution to a symposium in 1957. *CEP* 3:158–166.

————— (1957e) "Economic Growth and Capital Accumulation—A Comment," *Economic Record* 33:103–108 (April).

————— (1958a) "The Philosophy of Prices," said to cover the same ground as "Some Reflections on the Philosophy of Prices," given at Manchester School, May 1958. The introduction indicates that it was to be published in Polish in *Ekonomista* but this did not happen. "Survey: 50's" in *What Are the Questions?* says that it was rejected by the Soviet journal, *Voprosi Ekonomiki*. First published: *CEP* 2:27–48. Also in *Contributions to Modern Economics* 146–165.

————— (1958b) "Imperfect Competition Today." An Italian version of this paper appeared in *Il Mercurio* (December) *CEP* 2:239–245.

————— (1958c) "Saving Without Investment" was not published until *CEP* 2:191–196 but was written earlier and suggested by Paul Samuelson's "An Exact Consumption-Loan Model of Interest," *Journal of Political Economy* 66:467–482 (December).

————— (1958d) "Full Employment and Inflation," the basis of a lecture delivered at the University of Rennes in March 1958. *CEP* 2:271–279.

————— (1958e) "The real Wicksell effect," *Economic Journal* 68:600–605 (September). *CEP* 2:185–190.

————— (1959a) "Accumulation and the Production Function," *Economic Journal* 69:433–442 (September). *CEP* 2:132–144.

————— (1959b) "A Comment," on G.D.N. Worswick's review of her *Accumulation of Capital* in *Oxford Economic Papers* 11:141–142 (June).

————— (1959c) "Some Problems of Definition and Measurement of Capital," *Oxford Economic Papers* 11:157–166 (June) and in French *Cahiers de l'Institut de Science Économique Appliquée* (July). *CEP* 2:197–208.

————— (1959d) "The Falling Rate of Profit: A Comment," *Science & Society* 23:104–106 (Spring).

————— (1959e) "Depreciation," in Italian in *Rivista di Politica Economica* (November). *CEP* 2:209–221.

————— (1959f) "Letter to the Editor," *Econometrica* 27: 490 (July).

————— (1960a) *Collected Economic Papers* vol. 2. Oxford: Basil Blackwell. Second ed. 1978. Reprinted 1979 Cambridge: MIT Press.

————— (1960b) "Capital, Technique and Relative Shares," not previously published. *CEP* 2:159–184.

————— (1960c) "Review of B. S. Keirstead's *Capital, Interest and Profits,*" in *Canadian Journal of Economics and Political Science* 26:488–490 (August).

————— (1960d) "General Liquidity," *The Banker* (London) (December). *CEP* 3:125–131.

————— (1960e) "A Review of T. J. Hughes' and D. E. T. Luard's *The Economic Development of Communist China,*" in *Economic Journal* 70:409–410 (June).

————— (1960f) "Teaching Economics," *Economic Weekly* (Bombay) (January). *CEP* 3:1–6.

————— (1961a) *Exercises in Economic Analysis*. London: Macmillan.

————— (1961b) "Own Rates of Interest," *Economic Journal* 71:596–600 (September). *CEP* 3:132–138.

————— (1961c) "Piero Sraffa: *Production of Commodities by Means of Commodities*," in *Oxford Economic Papers* 13:53–58. Also in *What Are the Questions*? 144–150.

————— (1961d) "Has Capitalism Changed?" *Monthly Review* 12: 265–271 (October), *CEP* 3: 167–172 and *Contributions to Modern Economics* 223–228.

————— (1961e) "Beyond Full Employment," *Annals of Collective Economy* (Liège) (April-June). *CEP* 3:103–112.

————— (1961f) "Prelude to a Critique of Economic Theory," *Oxford Economic Papers* N.S. 13:53–58 (February). *CEP* 3:7–14.

————— (1961g) "Equilibrium Growth Models, a Review Article," *American Economic Review* 51:360–369 (June). *CEP* 3:15–29.

————— (1962a) *Economic Philosophy*. London: C. A. Watts and Chicago: Aldine in 1964; reprinted New York: Doubleday for Anchor Books.

————— (1962b) "Comment On Solow et al.," *Review of Economic Studies* 29:258–266.

————— (1962c) "Marxism: Religion and Science," *Monthly Review* 13: 423–435 (December). *CEP* 3: 148–157. Also in *What Are the Questions*? 155–164.

————— (1962d) "Review of H. G. Johnson's *The General Theory after Twenty-Five Years*," in *Economic Journal* 72:690–692 (September).

————— (1962e) "Latter Day Capitalism," *New Left Review* (London) (July-August). *CEP* 3:113–124.

————— (1962f) "Review of E. S. Kirby's *Contemporary China*," in *Economic Journal* 72:734 (September).

————— (1962g) "A Neo-Classical Theorem," *Review of Economic Studies* 29:219–226 (June).

————— (1963a) *Essays in the Theory of Economic Growth*. New York: St. Martin's Press.

————— (1963b) "Learning by Doing: A Further Note," *Review of Economic Studies* 30:167–168 (October).

————— (1963c) "Findlay's Robinsonian Model of Accumulation: A Comment," *Economica* N.S. 30: 408–410 (November). "Robinson on Findlay on Robinson," CEP 3:48–51.

————— (1964a) "Factor Prices Not Equalized," *Quarterly Journal of Economics* 78:202–207 (May). *CEP* 3:30–38.

————— (1964b) "Solow on the Rate of Return," *Economic Journal* 74:410–417 (June). *CEP* 3:36–47

————— (1964c) "China, 1963: The Communes," *The Political Quarterly* (London) (July). *CEP* 3:192–206.

————— (1964d) "The Final End of Laissez-Faire," *New Left Review* (London) (Summer). *CEP* 3:139–147.

————— (1964e) "Kalecki and Keynes," from *Essays in Honor of Michal Kalecki*, 1964. *CEP* 3:92–102 and *Contributions to Modern Economics* 53–60.

————— (1964f) "Consumer's Sovereignty in a Planned Economy," *Essays in Honor of Oskar Lange* 1964. *CEP* 3:70–81.

————— (1965a) *Collected Economic Papers* vol. 3. Oxford: Basil Blackwell 1975. Second ed., same. Reprinted in 1980, Cambridge: MIT Press.

————— (1965b) "Korea, 1964: Economic Miracle," *Monthly Review* 15: 541–549 (January). (In *Monthly Review* entitled "Korean Miracle.") *CEP* 3:207–215.

————— (1965c) "Harrod's Knife-Edge," *CEP* 3:52–55.

————— (1965d) "Pre-Keynesian Theory After Keynes," *Australian Economic Papers* 3:25–35 (June-December). *CEP* 3:56–69 and *Contributions to Modern Economics* 91–102.

————— (1965e) "A Reconsideration of the Theory of Value," *New Left Review* (London) (June). *CEP* 3:173–181.

————— (1965f) "The Political Economy of Communism," *Indian Economic Review* I, No.1 (New Series). *CEP* 3:82–91.

————— (1965g) "The New Mercantilism," an Inaugural Lecture, delivered at the University of Cambridge in 1965, Cambridge University Press 1966. *CEP* 4:1–13, and *Contributions to Modern Economics*, 201–212.

————— (1966a) *Economics: An Awkward Corner*. London: George Allen & Unwin. First American ed. 1967. New York: Pantheon.

————— (1966b) "Cuba—1965," *Monthly Review* 17: 10–18 (February).

————— (1966c) "Comment on Samuelson and Modigliani," *Review of Economic Studies* 33:307–8 (October).

————— (1966d) *An Essay on Marxian Economics*. Second ed. New York: St. Martin's Press.

————— (1967a) with K.A. Naqvi, "The Badly Behaved Production Function," *Quarterly Journal of Economics* 81:579–591 (November). *CEP* 4:74–86.

————— (1967b) "Socialist Affluence," from *Socialism, Capitalism, and Economic Growth, Essays in Honor of Maurice Dobb. CEP* 4:33–47 and *Contributions to Modern Economics* 240–253.

————— (1967c) "Smoothing Out Keynes," Review of Robert Lekachman's *The Age of Keynes* in *New York Review of Books* (January 26). *CEP* 5:178–183.

————— (1967d) "Growth and the Theory of Distribution," *Annals of Public and Cooperative Economy* 38:3–7 (January-March). *CEP* 5:71–75.

————— (1967e) "Communications," and "The Soviet Collective Farm as a Producer Cooperative: Comment," *American Economic Review* 57:222–223 (March).

————— (1967f) "Marginal Productivity," *Indian Economic Review* N.S. 2:75–84 (April). *CEP* 4:129–138.

————— (1967g) "The Economic Reforms," *Monthly Review* 18:45–50 (November).

————— (1968a) "The Poverty of Nations," Review of Gunnar Myrdal's *Asian Drama* in *Cambridge Quarterly* (Autumn). *CEP* 4:106–113.

————— (1968b) "Economics Versus Political Economy," Review of Fred M. Gottheil's *Marx's Economic Predictions* and Wassily Leontief's *Input-Output Economics* in *Indian Economic Review* (April). *CEP* 4:25–32.

————— (1968c) "A Defense of Adam Smith's Deer and Beaver Model," *Journal of Economic Studies* (University of Aberdeen, Scotland) 29–33 (July).

————— (1968d) "Value and Price," presented as a background paper for the symposium on the influence of Karl Marx on contemporary scientific thought. Paris, May 8–10, 1968. *CEP* 4:48–58.

————— (1969a) *The Economics of Imperfect Competition*. Second ed. London: Macmillan.

————— (1969b) "A Model for Accumulation Proposed by J.E. Stiglitz," *Economic Journal* 79:412–413 (June).

————— (1969c) "Macroeconomics of Unbalanced Growth: A Belated Comment," *American Economic Review* 59:632 (September).

————— (1969d) "Review of Alex Leijonhufvud's *On Keynesian Economics and the Economics of Keynes*" in *Economic Journal* 79:581–583 (September).

————— (1969e) "The Theory of Value Reconsidered," a lecture delivered at

University College, London, November 1968. Published in *Australian Economic Papers* in June. *CEP* 4:59–66 and *Contributions to Modern Economics*, 182–189.

——— (1969f) *Introduction to the Theory of Employment*. Second ed. London: Macmillan.

——— (1969g) "A Further Note," *Review of Economic Studies* 36:260–262 (April).

——— (1970a) *Freedom and Necessity: An Introduction to the Study of Society*. London: George Allen & Unwin. First American ed.: New York: Pantheon.

——— (1970b) *The Cultural Revolution in China*. Baltimore, Maryland: Penguin Books.

——— (1970c) "Harrod after Twenty-One Years," *Economic Journal* 80:731–36. "Reply" 80:741 (September). *CEP* 4:67–73.

——— (1970d) "Foreword" to E. L. Wheelwright's and Bruce McFarlane's *Chinese Road to Socialism*. New York: Monthly Review Press.

——— (1970e) "Capital Theory Up-to-Date," Review of C. E. Ferguson's *Neoclassical Theory of Production and Distribution* in *Canadian Journal of Economics* 3:309–317 (May). *CEP* 4:144–54 and *Contributions to Modern Economics* 103–113. "Reply," *Canadian Journal of Economics* 4:254–56 (May 1971). *CEP* 4:155–62 includes Ferguson's "Comment on Mrs. Robinson's Article," as well as her reply and two postscripts.

——— (1970f) "The Need for a Reconsideration of the Theory of International Trade," written in 1970. Published in *International Trade and Money* (ed. M. B. Connolly 1973 London: George Allen & Unwin). *CEP* 4:14–24 and *Contributions to Modern Economics* 213–22.

——— (1970g) "Economics Today," a lecture delivered at the University of Basel, December 1969. *CEP* 4:122–28.

——— (1971a) *Economic Heresies: Some Old-Fashioned Questions in Economic Theory*. New York: Basic Books (1973). Harper Torchbooks (1973) with new introduction.

——— (1971b) "Continuity and the 'Rate of Return'," *Economic Journal* 81:120–121 (March). *CEP* 4:164–66.

——— (1971c) "Michal Kalecki," *Cambridge Review* (October). *CEP* 4:87–91.

——— (1971d) "Solow Once More," Review of R. M. Solow's *Growth Theory, an Exposition*. The Radcliffe lectures delivered at the University of Warwick in 1969, and published by Oxford University Press in 1970. *Kyklos* 24:189–192 (December). *CEP* 4:139–43.

——— (1971e) "The Second Crisis of Economic Theory," Richard T. Ely lecture at the American Economic Association meeting in New Orleans, December 27, 1971, *American Economic Review* 62:1–10 *Proceedings* May 1972. *CEP* 4:92–105 and *Contributions to Modern Economics* 1–13.

——— (1971f) "The Measure of Capital: The End of Controversy," given at the World Congress of the Econometric Society in Cambridge, England and published in *Economic Journal* 81:597–602 (September). *CEP* 4:167–73.

——— (1971g) "The Relevance of Economic Theory," *Monthly Review* (January). *CEP* 4:114–21.

——— (1971h) "The Existence of Aggregate Production Functions: Comment," *Econometrica* 39:405 (March).

——— (1972a) *Economic Management in China*. London: Anglo Chinese Educational Institute 1975. Reprint with new postscript.

——— (1972b) "What Has Become of the Keynesian Revolution?" Presidential Address, Section F, British Association for the Advancement of Science (Economic Studies), 1972. Reprinted in *After Keynes*. Oxford: Basil Blackwell 1973. *CEP* 5:168–77.

———— (1973a), ed. *After Keynes.* Papers presented to Section F (Economics Section) at the 1972 annual meeting of the British Association for the Advancement of Science. Oxford: Basil Blackwell.

———— (1973b) with John Eatwell. *An Introduction to Modern Economics.* Maldenhead: McGraw-Hill.

———— (1973c) *Collected Economic Papers* vol. 4. Oxford: Basil Blackwell. 1980 Reprinted by MIT Press.

———— (1973d) "Ideology and Analysis." A contribution to the Festschrift for Eduard Marz, Europaverlags AG Wien 1973. *CEP* 5:254–61.

———— (1973e) "Review of Gunnar Myrdal's *Against the Stream.*" Not previously published. *CEP* 5:106–9 and *What Are the Questions?* 151–4.

———— (1973f) "Formalistic Marxism and Ecology Without Classes," Review of Arghiri Emmanuel's *Unequal Exchange, a Study of the Imperialism of Trade* and Richard Wilkinson's *Poverty and Progress* in *Journal of Contemporary Asia. CEP* 5:241–7.

———— (1973g) "Chinese Agricultural Communes," in Charles K. Wilber, ed. *Political Economy of Development and Underdevelopment.* New York: Random House.

———— (1973h) "Communication: Samuelson and Marx," *Journal of Economic Literature* 11:1367 (December).

———— (1973i) "Foreword," to J. A. Kregel's *Reconstruction of Political Economy: An Introduction to Post-Keynesian Economics.* New York: John Wiley.

———— (1974a) "Inflation West and East," *Frontier* (Calcutta) October 19, 1974. *CEP* 5:217–21.

———— (1974b) "Reflections on the Theory of International Trade," Lectures given at the University of Manchester, University of Manchester Press 1974. *CEP* 5:130–45.

———— (1974c) "History Versus Equilibrium," *Thames Papers in Political Economy* 1974, Thames Polytechnic London. *CEP* 5:48–58 and *Contributions to Modern Economics* 126–36.

———— (1974d) "Markets." A shorter version of this paper appeared in *Encyclopedia Britannica* 15th ed. 1974. *CEP* 5:146–67.

———— (1974e) "The Abdication of Neo-Classical Economics," from *Economic Theory and Planning: Essays in Honor of A. K. Das Gupta,* Ashok Mitra. Calcutta: Oxford University Press. *CEP* 5:32–42.

———— (1975a) "Value Before Capitalism," *Kyklos* 28:143–8. *CEP* 5:99–105.

———— (1975b) "The Unimportance of Reswitching," *Quarterly Journal of Economics* 89:32–9 and "Reply," 89:53–5 (February). *CEP* 5:76–89. Part of Samuelson's reply is also included in *CEP.*

———— (1976a) "The Age of Growth," Gildersleeve lecture at Barnard College March 2, 1976. *CEP* 5:120–9 and *What Are the Questions?* 33–42.

———— (1976b) "An Eyewitness Account of the Cultural Revolution," Review of John and Elsie Collier's *China's Socialist Revolution* in *Monthly Review* 28:50–51 (October).

———— (1977a) "Socialist Korea," Review of Ellen Brun's and Jacques Hersh's *Socialist Korea: A Case Study in the Strategy of Economic Development,* in *Monthly Review* 29:60–62 (October).

———— (1977b) "The Meaning of Capital." Draft of the article which appeared in French in *Revue d'Économie Politique* (March). *CEP* 5:59–70 and *Contributions to Modern Economics* 114–25.

———— (1977c) "What are the Questions?" *Journal of Economic Literature* 15:1318–39 (December). *CEP* 5:1–31 and *What Are the Questions?* 1–32.

———— (1977d) "Morality and Economics." Commencement address in May at the University of Maine. *CEP* 5: 43–7. (University of Maine said it was 1975.)

————— (1977e) with Frank Wilkinson, "What Has Become of Employment Policy?" *Cambridge Journal of Economics* 1:5–14 (March). *CEP* 5:197–209 and *Contributions to Modern Economics* 254–66.

————— (1977f) "Michal Kalecki," Michal Kalecki Memorial Lecture reprinted from *Oxford Bulletin of Economics and Statistics* 39:7–17 (February). *CEP* 5:184–196.

————— (1977g) "The Guidelines of Orthodox Economics," *Journal of Contemporary Asia* vol. 7, no. 1. *CEP* 5:222–227.

————— (1977h) "Employment and the Choice of Technique," *Society and Change: Essays in Honor of Sachim Chaudhuri*. Calcutta: Oxford University Press. CEP 5:228–240.

————— (1977i) "The Labor Theory of Value as an Analytical System," a contribution to the Conference of the Economic Section of the Academy of Sciences of Montenegro (October). *CEP* 5:289–297.

————— (1977j) "The Labor Theory of Value," Review of Ronald L. Meek's Studies in *The Labor Theory of Value*, second ed. 1976, *Monthly Review* 29:50–59 (December). *CEP* 5:280–288 and *What Are the Questions?* 183–191.

————— (1977k) "The Relevance of Economic Theory," in Jesse Schwartz, ed. *Subtle Anatomy of Capitalism*. Santa Monica: Goodyear.

————— (1978a) *Contributions to Modern Economics*. New York: Academic Press.

————— (1978b) "The Organic Composition of Capital," *Kyklos* 31:5–20. *CEP* 5:262–274 and *What Are the Questions?* 170–182.

————— (1978c) "Keynes and Ricardo," *Journal of Post Keynesian Economics* 1:12–18 (Fall). *CEP* 5:210–216.

————— (1978d) "Formalism Versus Dogma," Review of Ian Steedman's *Marx After Sraffa*, in *Journal of Contemporary Asia* (November). *CEP* 5:275–279.

————— (1979a) *Aspects of Development and Underdevelopment*. Cambridge: Cambridge University Press.

————— (1979b) "Spring Cleaning," chapter in G. R. Feiwel, ed. *Issues in Contemporary Macroeconomics and Distribution*. London: Macmillan. 175–182.

————— (1979c) "Stagflation," The David Kinley Lecture, University of Illinois at Urbana, published in *Challenge* November-December 1979 (called "Solving the Stagflation Problem") and in *Quarterly Review of Economics and Business* (Autumn) (called "Employment and Inflation") and *What Are the Questions?* 43–53.

————— (1979d) "Marxism and Modern Economics," a contribution to the Encounter at Brazilia, 1979. Published in *What Are the Questions?* 192–202.

————— (1979e) "Misunderstanding in the Theory of Production," *Greek Economic Review* vol. 1, no. 1 (August). Also in *What Are the Questions?* 135–140.

————— (1979f) *The Generalization of the General Theory*. New York: St. Martin's Press. Reissue of 1952 *A Rate of Interest & Other Essays*. New Introduction 1978.

————— (1979g) *Collected Economic Papers* vol. 5. Oxford: Basil Blackwell 1980. Reprinted by MIT Press.

————— (1979h) "Has Keynes Failed?" *Annals of Public and Cooperative Economy* 27–29 (March).

————— (1979i) "Garegnani on Effective Demand," *Cambridge Journal of Economics* 3:179–180 (March).

————— (1979j) "Thinking About Thinking," published for the first time in *CEP* 5:110–119. Also in *What Are the Questions?* 54–63.

————— (1979k) "The Disintegration of Economics," a lecture never before published. *CEP* 5:90–98 and *What Are the Questions?* 96–104.

————— (1979l) "Mao Tse Tung on Soviet Economics," Review of Mao Tse Tung's *A Critique of Soviet Economics* in translation, *Monthly Review* 30:52–53 (January).

————— (1979m) "Comments on China Since Mao," *China Now* (September-

October 1978). *Monthly Review* 30:48–56 (May).

——— (1980a) "Review of John Maynard Keynes' *Collected Writings*, vol. 29," *Economic Journal* 90:391–393 (June).

——— (1980b) with A. Bhaduri, "Accumulation and Exploitation: an Analysis in the Tradition of Marx, Sraffa, and Kalecki," *Cambridge Journal of Economics* 4:103–116 (June). Also in *What Are the Questions?* 64–77.

——— (1980c) "Who is a Marxist?" not previously published. *CEP* 5:248–253.

——— (1980d) "Time in Economic Theory," *Kyklos* 33:219–229 and *What Are the Questions?* 86–95.

——— (1980e) *Further Contributions to Modern Economics*. Oxford: Basil Blackwell, and in the United States as *What Are the Questions?*

——— (1981a) *What Are the Questions?* Armonk, New York: M.E. Sharpe. Published in 1980 as *Further Contributions to Modern Economics*. Oxford: Basil Blackwell.

——— (1981b) "Survey: 1950's," *What Are the Questions?* 105–111. Amended version of the "Introduction" to *CEP* vol. 2, second ed., 1975.

——— (1981c) "Survey: 1960's," *What Are the Questions?* 112–122. Amended version of "Introduction" to *CEP* 3.

——— (1981d) "Debate: 1970's," *What Are the Questions?* 123–130.

——— (1981e) "Retrospect: 1980," *What Are the Questions?* 131–134.

——— (1982) "Shedding Darkness," Review of Axel Leijonhufvud's *Information and Coordination* in *Cambridge Journal of Economics* 6:295–296 (September).

——— (1983a) with Frank Wilkinson, "Ideology and Logic." Paper given to an international congress on Keynes in Milan in May. Forthcoming, Cambridge University Press.

——— (1983b) "The Economics of Destruction," based on notes taken by Hal Kursk at an address in Toronto May 9, 1980, and later discussed with Professor Robinson. *Monthly Review* 15–17 (October).

Rogin, Leo (1944) "Review of Joan Robinson's *Essay on Marxian Economics*," in *American Economic Review* 34:124–134 (March).

Roll, Eric (1942) *History of Economic Thought*. New York: Prentice Hall.

Rosdolsky, Roman (1977) *The Making of Marx's Capital*. Translated by Pete Burgess. London: Pluto Press.

Rostow, Walt W. (1952) *The Process of Economic Growth*. New York: W.W. Norton.

——— (1960) *The Stages of Economic Growth: a Non Communist Manifesto*. Cambridge: Cambridge University Press.

——— (1963) *Economics of Take-Off into Sustained Growth*. New York: St Martin's Press.

Rothbarth, Erwin (1946) "Causes of the Superior Efficiency of USA Industry compared with British Industry," *Economic Journal* 56:383–390 (September).

Samuels, Warren, ed. (1976) *The Chicago School of Political Economy*. Association for Evolutionary Economics and Lansing: Michigan State University.

Samuelson, Paul (1946) "Lord Keynes and The General Theory," *Econometrica*, 14:187–200 (July).

——— (1958) "An Exact Consumption Loan Model of Interest," *Journal of Political Economy* 66:467–482 (December).

——— (1962) "Economists and the History of Ideas," *American Economic Review* 52:1–18 (March).

——— (1966a) "Reply to Pasinetti and Robinson," *Review of Economic Studies* 33:321–330 (October).

——— (1966b) "A Summing Up," *Quarterly Journal of Economics* 80:568–583 (No. 4).

——— (1972) *Foundations of Economic Analysis*. New York: Atheneum.

———— (1975) "Steady State and Transient Relations, a reply on reswitching," *Quarterly Journal of Economics* 89:40–47 (No. 1).

———— (1976) *Economics*. New York: McGraw-Hill. (And other editions.)

———— (1981) "Bertil Ohlin 1899–1979," *Journal of International Economics* 11:147–163 (No. 2).

Schor, Juliet (1985) "Changes in the Cyclical Pattern of Real Wages: Evidence from Nine Countries 1955–80," *Economic Journal* (June).

Schultze, Charles L. (1971) "The Reviewers Reviewed," *American Economic Review*, Papers and Proceedings 61:45–52 (May).

Schumpeter, Joseph A. (1934) "Review of Joan Robinson's *Economics of Imperfect Competition*," in *Journal of Political Economy* 42:249–257 (November).

———— (1942) *Capitalism, Socialism and Democracy*. New York: Harper and Brothers.

———— (1949) "English Economists and the State Managed Economy," *Journal of Political Economy* 57:372–376 (October).

———— (1954) *History of Economic Analysis*. Oxford: Oxford University Press.

Schwartz, J. G., ed. (1977) *The Subtle Anatomy of Capitalism*. Santa Monica: Goodyear.

de Schweinitz, Karl (1976) "Review of Joan Robinson's and John Eatwell's *Introduction to Modern Economics*," in *Journal of Economic Issues* 10:176-(March).

Seckler, David Wm. (1975) *Thorstein Veblen and the Institutionalists*. London School of Economics and Political Science, and Boulder, Colorado: Associated University Press.

Shackle, G. L. S. (1953) "Review of Joan Robinson's *Collected Economic Papers*, vol. 1," *Economica* 20:73–74 (February).

———— (1967) *The Years of High Theory*. Cambridge: Cambridge University Press.

Shaikh, Anwar (1974) "Laws of Production and Laws of Algebra: The Humbug Production Function," *Review of Economic Statistics* 56:115–20 (February).

Sharpe, M. E. (1969) "Review of Joan Robinson's *Economics: an Awkward Corner*," in *Science & Society* 33:99–100 (Winter).

———— (1973) *John Kenneth Galbraith and the Lower Economics*. White Plains, New York: International Arts and Sciences Press.

Shove, Gerald F. (1928) "Varying Costs and Marginal Net Products," *Economic Journal* 38:258–266 (June).

———— (1930) "Increasing Returns and the Representative Firm: A Symposium"; "The Representative Firm and Increasing Returns," *Economic Journal* 40:94–116 (March). Other participants were Piero Sraffa and Dennis H. Robertson. 40:79–93.

———— (1933) "Review of Joan Robinson's *Economics of Imperfect Competition*," in *Economic Journal* 43:657–661 (December).

———— (1944) "Mrs. Robinson on Marxian Economics," Review of Joan Robinson's *Essay on Marxian Economics* in *Economic Journal* 54:47–61 (April).

Silberston, Aubrey (1978) "Harry Johnson as a Young Man," Imperial College of Science and Technology, London (February). Also printed in *Economic Analysis and Policy*, University of Queensland, Australia, September 1977 and "errata," March 1978.

Skidelsky, Robert (1977) *The End of the Keynesian Era*. London: Macmillan.

———— (1983) ed. *John Maynard Keynes* vol. 1. London: Macmillan.

Smith, Henry (1938) "Review of Joan Robinson's *Introduction to the Theory of Employment*," in *Economic Journal* 48:74–76 (March).

Smithies, Arthur (1953) "Review of Joan Robinson's *Rate of Interest and other Essays*," in *American Economic Review* 43:636–641 (September).

Solow, Robert M. (1956a) "The Production Function and the Theory of Capital," *Review of Economic Studies* 23:101–108.

———— (1956b) "A Contribution to the Theory of Economic Growth," *Quarterly Journal of Economics* 70:65–94 (February).

———— (1957) "Technical Change and the Aggregate Production Function," *Review of*

Economics and Statistics 39:312–320 (August).
————— (1962) "Substitution and Fixed Proportions in the Theory of Capital," *Review of Economic Studies* 29:207–218 (June).
————— (1963) "Heterogeneous Capital and Smooth Production Functions," *Econometrica* 31:623–645 (October).
————— (1970) *Growth Theory*. Oxford: Oxford University Press.
————— (1971) "Discussion," *American Economic Review* 61:64–65 (May).
————— (1975) "Brief Comments," *Quarterly Journal of Economics* 89:48–52 (February).
Sraffa, Piero (1953) *Works and Correspondence of David Ricardo*. Cambridge: Cambridge University Press.
————— (1960) *Production of Commodities by Means of Commodities: Prelude to a Critique of Economic Theory*. Cambridge: Cambridge University Press.
Stigler, George (1963) "Review of Joan Robinson's *Economic Philosophy*," in *Journal of Political Economy* 71:192–193 (April).
Storr, Richard J. (1966) *Harper's University*. Chicago: Chicago University Press.
Straight, Michael (1938) "Review of Joan Robinson's *Introduction to the Theory of Employment*," in *The New Republic* 53–54 (May 18).
————— (1963) *After Long Silence*, New York & London: W. W. Norton.
Swan, T. (1956) "Economic Growth and Capital Accumulation," *Economic Record* 32:334–361 (November).
Tarshis, Lorie (1938) "Review of Joan Robinson's *Introduction to the Theory of Employment*," in *Canadian Journal of Economics and Political Science* 4:585–87.
Telser, Lester (1968) "Review of *Monopolistic Competition Theory: Studies in Impact of Monopolistic Competition, Essays in Honor of E. H. Chamberlin*," in *Journal of Political Economy* 76:311–315 (March/April).
Tobin, James (1973) "Review of Joan Robinson's *Economic Heresies,*" in *The Public Interest* 102–9 (Spring).
UNESCO (1954) *The University Teaching of Social Sciences: Economics* (International Economic Association).
Uzawa, H. (1968) "Review of Joan Robinson's *Collected Economic Papers* vol. 3," *American Economic Review* 58:204–206 (March).
Vandoorne, Marc (1980) "Review of Joan Robinson's *Collected Economic Papers* vol. 5," *Economic Journal* 90:929–930 (December).
Walsh, Vivian (1970) *Introduction to Contemporary Microeconomics*. New York: McGraw-Hill.
Weintraub, Sidney, ed. (1977) *Modern Economic Thought*. Philadelphia: University of Pennsylvania Press.
Wiener, Norbert (1964) *God and Golem*. Cambridge: MIT Press.
Wiles, P. (1955) "Are Adjusted Rubles Rational?" *Soviet Studies* 7:143–160 (January).
————— (1956) "Rejoinder to All and Sundry," *Soviet Studies* 8:134–143 (October).
Worswick, G. D. N. (1962) "Review of Joan Robinson's *Exercises in Economic Analysis*" in *Economic Journal* 72:172–5 (March) (reviewed with J. S. Duesenberry's and L. E. Preston's *Cases and Problems in Economics*. London: George Allen & Unwin 1960).
————— (1963) "Review of Joan Robinson's *Essay in the Theory of Growth*," in *Economic Journal* 73:295–297 (June).
————— (1983) with Trevithick, James, eds. *Keynes and the Modern World*. Cambridge: Cambridge University Press.

JR

NAMES INDEX

JR

SUBJECT INDEX

JR

ABOUT THE AUTHOR

Marjorie Shepherd Turner, b. December 12, 1921, studied economics at The University of Texas (Austin) where she was elected to Phi Beta Kappa in 1943 and received her Ph.D. in economics with a minor in philosophy in 1954.

She taught at the University of Arizona, Tucson and San Diego State University, where she took her turn as Department Chairman and Director of the Institute of Labor Economics.

In 1963, Turner and her husband (Merle B., who was a professor of psychology) took sabbaticals at Cambridge University, England. She attended lectures of Joan Robinson and others, including the visiting Americans Robert M. Solow and Kenneth J. Arrow. This was the beginning of her interest in the subject of this book. Two of her scholarly articles resulted from this experience: "Wages in the Cambridge Theory of Distribution" in *Industrial and Labor Relations Review,* April 1966; and "A Comparison of Some Aspects of the Cambridge Theory of Wages and Marginal Productivity Theory" in *Journal of Economic Issues*, September 1967.

After a retirement voyage to New Zealand on their yacht, the Turners took up residence in the Oregon Cascades. There, between sailing trips, she began her study of Joan Robinson by reading Robinson's complete works.

Marjorie Turner has one son, one stepson, and two grandsons.